**The Linguistic Integration of Adult Migrants /
L'intégration linguistique des migrants adultes**

# The Linguistic Integration of Adult Migrants
# L'intégration linguistique des migrants adultes

—

Some Lessons from Research /
Les enseignements de la recherche

Edited by / édité par
Jean-Claude Beacco, Hans-Jürgen Krumm, David Little,
Philia Thalgott

on behalf of / pour le compte du
Council of Europe / Conseil de l'Europe

**DE GRUYTER**

COUNCIL OF EUROPE

CONSEIL DE L'EUROPE

ISBN 978-3-11-047747-4
e-ISBN (PDF) 978-3-11-047749-8
e-ISBN (EPUB) 978-3-11-047758-0

This work is licensed under the Creative Commons Attribution-NonCommercial-NoDerivs 3.0 License. For details go to http://creativecommons.org/licenses/by-nc-nd/3.0/.

**Library of Congress Cataloging-in-Publication Data**
A CIP catalog record for this book has been applied for at the Library of Congress.

**Bibliographic information published by the Deutsche Nationalbibliothek**
The Deutsche Nationalbibliothek lists this publication in the Deutsche Nationalbibliografie; detailed bibliographic data are available on the Internet at http://dnb.dnb.de.

© 2017 Jean-Claude Beacco, Hans-Jürgen Krumm, David Little, Philia Thalgott, Council of Europe, published by Walter de Gruyter GmbH, Berlin/Boston
The book is published with open access at www.degruyter.com.

Printing and binding: CPI books GmbH, Leck
♾ Printed on acid-free paper
Printed in Germany

www.degruyter.com

Philia Thalgott
# Foreword

The Council of Europe (47 member States, based in Strasbourg) has been working on migration-related issues for over four decades, and has affirmed the importance of education for migrants in nearly 30 recommendations and resolutions from its Committee of Ministers and its Parliamentary Assembly, including Conventions.

The Council of Europe's new project on the Linguistic Integration of Adult Migrants (LIAM) aims to support member States in the development of policy and practice based on a clear recognition of adult migrants' human rights. This is especially important at a time when surveys conducted in the course of the project show a growing tendency for member States to attach language requirements to the granting of citizenship, the right to residence, and sometimes the right to enter the country in the first place.

As affirmed by official texts of the Council of Europe as well as of the European Union, access to education is particularly important for migrants. Furthermore, language is central to many of the issues raised by migration, particularly integration and social cohesion. Therefore, providing adult migrants with opportunities to learn the language of the host country and assessing their developing proficiency can aid their integration in the host society.

However, while language competences are an important component of integration, they cannot be a pre-condition for integration, since acquiring a language is potentially a lifelong process.

For some years, the Council of Europe has offered its member States not only clear and agreed principles and guidelines but also targeted practical support to help them respond to the challenges of linguistic integration.

As a first step towards compiling an inter-disciplinary inventory of relevant research findings, in order to better understand how research can support the development of policy and practice in this field, the Council of Europe organised a symposium on "The linguistic integration of adult migrants: lessons from research" in Strasbourg on 30 March – 1 April 2016. This publication offers documented results of research presented during the symposium by researchers and practitioners from a wide range of contexts and disciplines.

It is anticipated that relevant Ministries in Council of Europe member States will be able to use these findings to inform their decisions concerning the linguistic integration of adult migrants.

Language Policy Programme
Education Policy Division / Education Department
Directorate of Democratic Citizenship and Participation
Directorate General Democracy
**Council of Europe, Strasbourg**
www.coe.int/lang-migrants

Philia Thalgott
# Avant-propos

Le Conseil de l'Europe (47 Etats membres, basé à Strasbourg) traite de la question des migrations depuis plus de quarante ans. Une trentaine de recommandations et résolutions de son Comité des ministres et de son Assemblée parlementaire, y compris des conventions, soulignent l'importance de l'éducation pour les migrants.

Le nouveau projet du Conseil de l'Europe pour l'intégration linguistique des migrants adultes (ILMA) vise à aider les Etats membres à développer des politiques fondées sur une reconnaissance sans équivoque des droits de l'homme des migrants adultes. Ceci est particulièrement important à la lumière des enquêtes menées dans le cadre du projet ILMA qui montrent une tendance croissante des Etats membres à conditionner à des compétences en langues le droit à la nationalité et à la résidence, voire l'entrée dans le pays.

Comme le soulignent les textes officiels du Conseil de l'Europe mais aussi de l'Union européenne, l'importance de l'accès à l'éducation pour les migrants est primordiale. La langue a en en outre un rôle clé pour de nombreuses questions liées à la migration, en particulier, l'intégration et la cohésion sociale. En conséquence, offrir aux migrants adultes des opportunités d'apprendre la langue du pays d'accueil et d'évaluer l'évolution de leurs compétences peut favoriser leur intégration dans le pays d'accueil.

Néanmoins, si les compétences en langue sont une composante importante de l'intégration, elles ne sauraient en être un préalable, puisque l'acquisition de compétences langagières constitue un processus qui se développe au long de la vie.

Depuis quelques années, le Conseil de l'Europe propose à ses Etats membres non seulement des principes et orientations consensuels et clairement formulés, mais aussi des dispositifs pratiques et ciblés pour les aider à faire face au défi de l'intégration.

Afin d'examiner dans quelle mesure les enseignements de la recherche peuvent étayer le développement des politiques et leur mise en œuvre et comme première étape vers un inventaire interdisciplinaire des résultats de la recherche, le Conseil de l'Europe a organisé un symposium sur « L'intégration linguistique des migrants adultes : les enseignements de la recherche » (Strasbourg, 30 mars – 1$^{er}$ avril 2016). La présente publication propose des résultats analytiques de recherches présentés lors du symposium par des chercheurs et des praticiens issus d'un large éventail de contextes et de disciplines.

On espère que les Etats membres du Conseil de l'Europe seront en mesure de s'appuyer sur ces résultats pour étayer leurs décisions relatives à l'intégration linguistique des migrants.

Programme Politiques linguistiques
Division des Politiques éducatives / Service de l'éducation
Direction de la citoyenneté démocratique et de la participation
Direction générale de la Démocratie
**Conseil de l'Europe, Strasbourg**
www.coe.int/lang-migrants/fr

# Table of Contents / Sommaire

Philia Thalgott
**Foreword —— V**

Philia Thalgott
**Avant-propos —— VII**

Jean-Claude Beacco, Hans-Jürgen Krumm and David Little
**Introduction (*English version*) —— 1**

Jean-Claude Beacco, Hans-Jürgen Krumm et David Little
**Introduction (*version française*) —— 5**

## 1 Language and integration: some key issues /
Langue et intégration : questions clés

Ofelia García
**Problematizing linguistic integration of migrants: the role of translanguaging and language teachers —— 11**

Claude Springer
**Migrants connectés, intégration sociale et apprentissage/certification en langues : prendre en compte la nouvelle donne numérique —— 27**

Rosemarie Tracy
**Language testing in the context of migration —— 45**

## 2 Policies for language and integration /
Politiques pour les langues et l'intégration

Reinhilde Pulinx, Piet Van Avermaet
**The impact of language and integration policies on the social participation of adult migrants —— 59**

François Grin, Guillaume Fürst
**Quels sont les facteurs qui renforcent l'exigence d'apprentissage par les migrants de la langue du pays d'accueil ?**
    Analyse multivariée des attitudes envers l'altérité linguistique de 40 000 jeunes hommes suisses —— 67

Furio Bednarz
**Professional and social integration of migrants and language learning: convergences and challenges at the European level** —— 75

Brian North, Enrica Piccardo
**Mediation and the social and linguistic integration of migrants: updating the CEFR descriptors** —— 83

Kate Hammer
**Sociocultural integration and second language proficiency following migration** —— 91

Monika Jezak, Encarnacion Carrasco
**Integration trajectories of adult (im)migrants in minority and minoritized contexts: Ottawa and Barcelona** —— 97

Jamel Sarraj
**L'intégration linguistique des migrants adultes : la mise en œuvre des politiques publiques dans la région suisse alémanique de Zurich** —— 105

## 3 Linguistic repertoires and integration /
Répertoires linguistiques et intégration

Thomas Laimer, Martin Wurzenrainer
**Multilingualism as a resource for basic education with young migrants** —— 117

Büşra Hamurcu Süverdem
**La place de la L1 dans les familles bilingues franco-turques en Alsace** —— 123

Salih Akin
**La loyauté linguistique au sein des membres de la communauté kurde en France** —— 131

Isabelle Bambust
**Le résident européen percevant sa propre aptitude linguistique dans un contexte judiciaire – une première recherche empirique sans prétention —— 139**

Antonella Benucci
**Répertoires linguistiques des détenus étrangers en Italie et en Europe : premiers résultats des projets RiUscire et DEPORT. —— 147**

## 4 Language teaching for integration: content, methods and materials / Formations en langue pour l'intégration : contenu, méthodes et matériels

Émilie Lebreton
**Les besoins langagiers des adultes migrants : une notion complexe à appréhender —— 155**

Thomas Fritz, Dilek Donat
**What migrant learners need —— 163**

Myriam Schleiss, Margrit Hagenow-Caprez
*fide* **– On the way to a coherent framework —— 169**

Enrica Piccardo, Danielle Hunter
**Settlement, integration and language learning: possible synergies. A task-based, community-focused program from the Region of Durham (Ontario, Canada) —— 175**

George Androulakis, Anastasia Gkaintartzi, Roula Kitsiou and Sofia Tsioli
**Research-driven task-based L2 learning for adult immigrants in times of humanitarian crisis: results from two nationwide projects in Greece —— 181**

Michel Gout
**Quatre approches didactiques pour la formation linguistique des nouveaux arrivants —— 187**

Peter Lenz, Malgorzata Barras
**Does teaching chunks and fluency make a difference in migrants' language learning?**
    Results of an intervention study in intensive German courses for adult migrants —— 195

Christa Nieuwboer, Rogier van't Rood
**Progress in proficiency and participation: an adult learning approach to support social integration of migrants in Western societies —— 201**

Katherine Swinney
**Networks and super connectors —— 207**

Sabrina Machetti, Lorenzo Rocca
**Integration of migrants, from language proficiency to knowledge of society: the Italian case —— 213**

Agnes Kukulska-Hulme, Mark Gaved, Ann Jones, Lucy Norris and Alice Peasgood
**Mobile language learning experiences for migrants beyond the classroom —— 219**

Mariet Schiepers, Annelies Houben, Annelies Nordin, Helga Van Loo, Helena Van Nuffel, Leen Verrote and Kris Van den Branden
**Creating a dynamic and learner-driven online environment for practising second language skills: guiding principles from second language acquisition and online education —— 225**

# 5 Language testing and assessment for integration / Evaluation des compétences en langues pour l'intégration

Jane Lloyd, Michaela Perlmann-Balme
**Language tests for access, integration and citizenship: an outline for policymakers from the ALTE perspective —— 235**

Boris Printschitz
**All a question of the "right" capital? Subjectification – the hidden mechanism behind language tests for residence permit in Austria —— 241**

Coraline Pradeau
**Les évaluations « Français langue d'intégration » (France, *FLI*) et « Français en Suisse – apprendre, enseigner, évaluer » (*fide*) : une alternative aux tests de langue certifiés pour la naturalisation française et suisse —— 249**

Paola Masillo
**Linguistic integration and residence policies in Italy: issues and perspectives —— 257**

Jitka Cvejnová, Kamila Sladkovská
**Examens en vue de l'obtention du titre de séjour permanent en République tchèque**
    Un bilan des expériences, 2009 – 2014 —— **265**

Sari Ohranen, Heidi Vaarala and Taina Tammelin-Laine
**Developing placement assessment in integration training for adult migrants in Finland —— 273**

# 6 Language and the workplace /
Les langues sur le lieu de travail

Anke Settelmeyer
**What management assistants of retail services and medical assistants need to read, write, speak and listen to in the workplace —— 283**

Aurélie Bruneau
**Langues et insertions : pluralité des parcours et des perceptions**
    Appropriations langagières, sociales et professionnelles de femmes migrantes —— **289**

Michele Gazzola
**Language skills and employment status of adult migrants in Europe —— 297**

Matilde Grünhage-Monetti, Alexander Braddell
**"Integration ... needs language, the language of the workplace":**
**The contribution of work-related second language learning to the integration of adult migrants —— 303**

Alexander Braddell, Linda Miller
**Supporting migrants in low-paid, low-skilled employment in London to improve their English —— 309**

Matilde Grünhage-Monetti, Anna Svet
**"The fight against exclusion from the labour market begins ... in the workplace": Work-related second language development towards inclusion and participation —— 315**

Kerstin Sjösvärd, Alexander Braddell
**Using workplace learning to support the linguistic integration of adult migrants – lessons from a decade of work in Sweden —— 321**

Sonya Sahradyan
**Learning and maintaining languages in the workplace: migrant NGO practitioners in Finland —— 329**

# 7 Towards linguistic integration: specific learner groups / Les groupes d'apprenants spécifiques : vers une intégration linguistique

Samira Moukrim
**Barrières linguistiques et problèmes de communication dans les milieux de la santé —— 337**

Marcello Amoruso, Mari D'Agostino
**Teenage and adult migrants with low to very low education levels: learner profiles and proficiency assessment tools —— 345**

Stefano Kluzer, Rocco De Paolis
**Using tablets for L2 learning with illiterate adult migrants: results from experiments in Piedmont and Emilia Romagna —— 351**

Fernanda Minuz, Alessandro Borri
**Literacy and language teaching: tools, implementation and impact —— 357**

Marie Hélène Lachaud
**La « raison orale », un levier pour la formation linguistique des migrants et l'intégration dans le pays d'accueil —— 365**

Antonella Benucci, Marilisa Birello
**Immigrants and prison: good practices in Europe —— 371**

## 8 Linguistic integration: teachers and researchers / Intégration linguistique : enseignants et chercheurs

Massimiliano Spotti
**"Crawlers, footers and runners": language ideological attributions to adult language learners in a Dutch as L2 classroom —— 379**

Maude Vadot
**Qu'est-ce que l'intégration ?**
Analyse de discours de formateurs et formatrices linguistiques intervenant auprès de migrants adultes en France —— **387**

Eric Mercier
**Langues et insertions : pluralité des parcours et des perceptions**
Quelle pertinence à l'obligation de formation et d'examen linguistique ? —— **395**

Marie-Cécile Guernier, Marie-Hélène Lachaud et Jean-Pierre Sautot
**Conceptions linguistiques et méthodes pédagogiques : quelle efficience pour l'intégration des adultes migrants ? —— 403**

Carla Bagna, Luana Cosenza and Luisa Salvati
**New challenges for learning, teaching and assessment with low-educated and illiterate immigrants: the case of L2 Italian —— 411**

Rola Naeb, Martha Young-Scholten
**International training of teachers of low-educated adult migrants —— 419**

Véronique Castellotti, Emmanuelle Huver et Fabienne Leconte
**Demande institutionnelle et responsabilité des chercheurs : langues, insertions, pluralité des parcours et des perceptions —— 425**

Jean-Claude Beacco, Hans-Jürgen Krumm and David Little
# Introduction (*English version*)

The Council of Europe's primary aim is to promote respect for human rights, democracy and the rule of law and to establish a common democratic and legal area across the continent. All of its actions are shaped by these values and by an enduring concern with social inclusion, social cohesion and respect for diversity; hence its interest in the linguistic integration of adult migrants.

The Council of Europe has been a pioneer in the field of language teaching and learning for the past five decades, and the project on the Linguistic Integration of Adult Migrants (LIAM) is part of its continuing work in this domain. The project's purpose is to support member states in the development of coherent and effective policies and to encourage them to review existing policies in the light of shared Council of Europe values and principles. It also seeks to identify and share good practice, and where language tests are obligatory, to promote transparency and equity according to internationally accepted codes of practice. The project's website (www.coe.int/lang-migrants) brings together a large body of documents, materials and practical tools.

In January 2014 the Parliamentary Assembly of the Council of Europe (PACE) adopted a recommendation to the Committee of Ministers entitled "Integration tests: helping or hindering integration?" (Recommendation 2034 [2014]). The report that accompanied the recommendation (Document 13361 [2014]; rapporteur Tineke Strik) raised a number of questions about language and knowledge-of-society tests, some of which can be answered only with reference to research findings related not only to tests but to the whole range of issues that surround the linguistic integration of adult migrants. This helps to explain the LIAM project's decision to organise an academic symposium entitled "The Linguistic Integration of Adult Migrants: Lessons from Research", which was held in Strasbourg from 30 March to 1 April 2016 and provided the content of this book.

A further consideration was the more general concern that integration policies can easily violate human rights and the dignity of migrants by imposing language requirements without due regard to what is known about, for example, human motivation and the relation between language and identity. If severe sanctions are attached to failure in a language test, that is more likely to hinder than promote successful learning; and our mother tongue is so central to our self-concept that any attempt to downgrade or suppress it is likely to have damaging psychological results. Better informed integration policy would seek to exploit what we know from research and pedagogical practice about the prerequisites for successful language learning by migrants.

The contributions to this volume reflect the wide range of issues that need to be addressed in an equally wide range of contexts. They also reflect an awareness of the epistemological and ethical challenges that confront research that has powerful social implications. The keynote articles by Ofelia García, Claude Springer and Rosemarie Tracy discuss language and integration from socio- and psycholinguistic perspectives. The fifty-one contributions which follow are grouped according to seven broad themes: policy; linguistic repertoires; language courses (content, methods and materials); language testing and assessment; language in the workplace; the needs of specific learner groups and approaches appropriate to them; and the situation, beliefs and responsibilities of teachers and researchers.

Five issues emerge from the volume taken as a whole. First, it is clear that there is a substantial amount of empirical research and reflected pedagogical experience from which political decision-making could profit. At the same time, however, much more research is needed, especially on the impact that integration policies have on the people they are designed to help and on the effects and side effects of certain measures. For example, the surveys carried out among member states by the Council of Europe's LIAM project[1] reveal a widespread tendency to increase the language requirements that migrants must meet as a precondition for residence or citizenship. Research is needed to determine whether this has had a positive or a negative impact on integration. Research is also needed to answer the question posed by the Parliamentary Assembly's Recommendation 2034[2] of 2014: Do language tests help or hinder integration? To date, few governments investigate the impact of the policies they enact. Evaluation is essential, however, in order to avoid wasting public money on measures that fail to achieve their goals.

Secondly, in the course of the symposium the role played by adult migrants' linguistic repertoires and language biographies was often stressed. There is in principle no contradiction between welcoming new languages and supporting plurilingualism on the one hand and helping migrants to acquire the language of their host country on the other. On the contrary, as a number of contributions show, the one supports the other when teachers devise activities that give legitimacy to migrants' linguistic repertoires and exploit them in their classes. This prompts the question: What measures can be taken to promote the more wide-

---

[1] R. Pulinx, P. Van Avermaet & C. Extramiana. 2014. *Linguistic Integration of Adult Migrants: Policy and practice*. Final report on the 3rd Council of Europe survey. Strasbourg: Council of Europe. Available at www.coe.int/lang-migrants → Activities → Surveys.
[2] http://www.assembly.coe.int/nw/xml/XRef/Xref-DocDetails-en.asp?FileID=20482&lang=en

spread adoption of such approaches? Clearly, more co-operation and exchange are necessary.

Thirdly, the many contributions that focus on language in the workplace undermine the naïve assumption that if adult migrants first take a language course, linguistic integration will follow more or less automatically. On the contrary, there is no direct route from language learning to employment and integration. The reverse is also true, however: employment does not automatically create language competence. Approaches which separate language classes from the other dimensions of integration are far less likely to succeed than integrated approaches that embed language learning in the workplace or some other participatory context and thus ensure that from the beginning the language of the host society is part of the linguistic repertoire that the adult migrant deploys in daily life. In this connection, many contributions stress the importance of allowing migrants to express themselves personally, which results in authentic language use and opens the way to "identity work" in another language. These considerations imply that civil society, employers, associations of all kinds, and language teachers should share responsibility for the linguistic integration of adult migrants. Interdisciplinary research is needed to explore the close and complex relation between social participation and language learning and inform the development of effective pedagogical approaches. Successful models already exist in some countries, so again the question arises: How can such models be disseminated?

Fourthly, the contributions in this volume remind us that there is no such thing as a typical migrant. Socially, culturally and linguistically migrant populations are infinitely diverse; in terms of educational capital they range from the illiterate to the highly qualified; and they include vulnerable groups such as the elderly, the deaf, and people serving prison sentences. This means that it makes no sense to provide just one type of language course for adult migrants or to impose the same language requirement on everyone. It also means that the analysis of migrants' language needs should be an obligatory prerequisite for the development of language courses and learning activities; and if migrants are to take ownership of the learning objectives they are asked to achieve, they themselves should be actively involved in needs analysis. At the same time, it must be acknowledged that for some migrants, especially refugees, language learning is not a top priority and providing them with a language course is not necessarily the best way of helping them.

Finally, many contributors emphasized, directly or indirectly, the crucial role played by associations and volunteers who organize activities for adult migrants, especially refugees. The LIAM project is currently developing a toolkit to support such activities; in due course it will be made available on the Council of Europe's website.

The symposium reminded us repeatedly that linguistic tolerance and goodwill play an essential role in effective communication with migrants, and that concepts of integration and the findings of research studies can be used to create a balance between welcoming linguistic and cultural diversity and helping migrants to learn the language of their host country. We hope that this volume will encourage further research while helping member states to develop integration policies that are appropriately informed and accord with the Council of Europe's core values.

Jean-Claude Beacco, Hans-Jürgen Krumm et David Little
# Introduction (*version française*)

Le Conseil de l'Europe a pour mission principale de promouvoir le respect des droits de l'homme, de la démocratie et de l'Etat de droit et d'instaurer un espace démocratique et juridique commun sur l'ensemble du continent. Toutes ses activités sont guidées par ces valeurs et par le souci constant d'assurer l'inclusion et la cohésion sociales et le respect de la diversité – d'où l'intérêt de l'Organisation pour l'intégration linguistique des migrants adultes.

Depuis cinquante ans, le Conseil de l'Europe est un véritable chef de file en matière d'enseignement et d'apprentissage des langues. Le projet sur l'Intégration linguistique des migrants adultes (ILMA) s'inscrit dans les travaux que l'Organisation mène en permanence dans ce domaine. Il vise à soutenir les Etats membres dans l'élaboration de politiques cohérentes et efficaces et à les encourager à réexaminer leurs politiques existantes à la lumière des valeurs et principes partagés que défend le Conseil de l'Europe. Il a également pour objectif d'identifier et de mettre en commun de bonnes pratiques et de promouvoir la transparence et l'équité, conformément aux codes de pratiques reconnus au niveau international, dans les contextes où les tests de langue sont obligatoires. Le site Internet consacré à l'ILMA (www.coe.int/lang-migrants/fr) propose tout un ensemble de documents, de matériels et d'outils pratiques à cette fin.

En janvier 2014, l'Assemblée parlementaire du Conseil de l'Europe (APCE) a adopté une Recommandation adressée au Comité des Ministres intitulée « Les tests d'intégration : aide ou entrave à l'intégration ? » (Recommandation 2034 [2014]). Le rapport qui accompagne l'instrument (Document 13361 [2014] ; rapporteure : Tineke Strik) soulève un certain nombre de questions concernant les tests de langue et ceux de connaissance de la société, dont certaines ne peuvent trouver de réponse que dans les travaux de recherche consacrés non seulement à ces tests, mais aussi à l'ensemble des questions relatives à l'intégration linguistique des migrants adultes. C'est dans ce contexte que les responsables du projet sur l'ILMA ont décidé d'organiser un symposium intitulé « L'intégration linguistique des migrants adultes : les enseignements de la recherche » (Strasbourg, 30 mars – 1$^{er}$ avril 2016), dont est issu le présent ouvrage.

Les participants à cet événement se sont également penchés sur une préoccupation plus générale liée au fait que les politiques d'intégration peuvent facilement porter atteinte aux droits de l'homme et à la dignité des migrants en fixant des exigences linguistiques, sans tenir dûment compte des connaissances acquises sur les motivations des personnes et le lien entre la langue et l'identité, par exemple. Le fait de sanctionner sévèrement l'échec aux tests de langue risque davantage d'entraver la réussite de l'apprentissage des langues que de la favoriser. En outre, notre langue maternelle joue un rôle tout à fait essentiel dans la façon dont nous nous percevons nous-mêmes ; aussi, toute tentative de la faire passer au second plan ou de « l'effacer » peut-elle avoir des répercussions néfastes sur le plan psychologique. Pour mieux éclairer les politiques d'intégration, il conviendrait de mettre à profit les connaissances issues de la recherche et les pratiques pédagogiques relatives aux conditions préalables à la réussite de l'apprentissage des langues par les migrants.

Le présent ouvrage montre la grande diversité des questions à traiter, lesquelles se posent dans une diversité de contextes tout aussi grande. Il reflète également une prise de conscience des défis épistémologiques et éthiques auxquels sont confrontés les chercheurs, ce qui a d'importantes implications sociales. Dans leurs articles respectifs, les intervenants invités (Ofelia García, Claude Springer et Rosemarie Tracy) examinent la question de la langue et de l'intégration d'un point de vue social et psycholinguistique. Puis viennent les cinquante et une contributions présentées ci-après qui sont regroupées autour des sept grands thèmes : politique ; répertoires linguistiques ; formations en langue (contenu, méthodes et matériels) ; évaluation des compétences en langues ; la langue sur le lieu de travail ; les besoins de groupes d'apprenants spécifiques et les approches pertinentes pour eux ; la situation, les convictions et responsabilités des enseignants et des chercheurs.

La lecture de l'ouvrage fait clairement ressortir cinq grands points. Tout d'abord, s'il existe indéniablement une quantité considérable de travaux de recherche empirique et de rapports sur des expériences pédagogiques qui pourraient être mis à profit par les décideurs politiques, bien d'autres études sont nécessaires, en particulier sur l'impact des politiques d'intégration sur leur public cible, ainsi que sur les répercussions et effets secondaires de certaines mesures. Par exemple, les enquêtes menées dans les Etats membres du Conseil de l'Europe participant au projet relatif à l'ILMA[1] font apparaître une tendance générale au durcissement des critères linguistiques que doivent remplir les migrants pour pouvoir prétendre à un titre de séjour ou à la citoyenneté. Il faudrait mener des études pour déterminer si cette pratique a eu des effets positifs ou négatifs sur l'intégration. Des études sont également nécessaires pour pouvoir répondre à la question soulevée par la Recommandation 2034[2] adoptée par

---

[1] R. Pulinx, P. Van Avermaet & C. Extramiana. 2014. *Intégration linguistique des migrants adultes : politique et pratique*. Rapport final sur la 3ᵉ enquête du Conseil de l'Europe. Strasbourg : Conseil de l'Europe. Disponible en ligne à l'adresse suivante : www.coe.int/lang-migrants/fr → Activités → Enquêtes.

[2] http://www.assembly.coe.int/nw/xml/XRef/Xref-DocDetails-FR.asp?FileID=20482&lang=FR

l'Assemblée parlementaire en 2014 : les tests de langue favorisent-t-ils ou entravent-t-ils l'intégration ? Pour le moment, rares sont les gouvernements qui évaluent l'impact des politiques qu'ils mettent en œuvre. Or, une telle évaluation est primordiale pour éviter de dilapider l'argent public en l'investissant dans des mesures qui n'atteignent pas leurs objectifs.

En second lieu, les participants au symposium ont souligné à maintes reprises le rôle des répertoires plurilingues et des biographies langagières des migrants adultes. En principe, l'accueil de nouvelles langues et le soutien au plurilinguisme, d'une part, et l'apport d'une aide aux migrants pour l'acquisition de la langue de leur pays hôte, d'autre part, ne sont pas incompatibles. Au contraire, comme le montrent un certain nombre de contributions, ils se soutiennent mutuellement lorsque les enseignants conçoivent des activités qui reconnaissent les répertoires linguistiques des migrants et les mettent à profit dans leurs cours. Dès lors, on peut se demander quelles mesures pourraient être prises pour favoriser une adoption à plus grande échelle de telles approches. Il ne fait aucun doute qu'un renforcement de la coopération et des échanges est nécessaire.

Troisième point : les nombreuses contributions ayant trait à la langue sur le lieu de travail s'attachent à réfuter le postulat simpliste selon lequel, si les migrants adultes commencent par suivre une formation en langue, l'intégration linguistique suit à peu près automatiquement. En réalité, il n'existe pas de relations directes entre l'apprentissage de la langue, l'emploi et l'intégration. Cependant, l'inverse est également vrai : l'emploi n'engendre pas automatiquement des compétences en langues. Les approches de l'apprentissage linguistique qui reposent sur une distinction entre les cours de langue et les autres dimensions de l'intégration ont moins de chances de réussir que les approches intégrées, qui inscrivent cet apprentissage dans le contexte professionnel ou dans un autre contexte participatif et qui veillent donc à ce que, dès le départ, la langue de la société d'accueil fasse partie du répertoire linguistique utilisé par le migrant adulte dans la vie quotidienne. A cet égard, bon nombre de contributions soulignent l'importance de laisser les migrants s'exprimer personnellement, ce qui permet une utilisation authentique de la langue et ouvre la voie à un « travail identitaire » dans une autre langue. Il s'ensuit que la responsabilité de l'intégration linguistique des migrants adultes devrait être assumée conjointement par la société civile, les employeurs, les associations de toutes sortes et les enseignants de langue. Des travaux de recherche interdisciplinaire sont nécessaires pour étudier la relation étroite et complexe entre la participation sociale et l'apprentissage des langues et pour éclairer la mise au point d'approches pédagogiques efficaces. Il existe déjà des modèles couronnés de succès dans certains pays. Là encore se pose la question de savoir comment diffuser ces dernières à plus grande échelle.

Quatrièmement, les contributions reproduites dans le présent ouvrage nous rappellent que le « migrant typique » n'existe pas. Les populations de migrants sont extrêmement diverses sur les plans social, culturel, linguistique et éducatif, certains étant illettrés, et d'autres, hautement qualifiés ; en outre, ces populations englobent des groupes de personnes vulnérables, telles que les personnes âgées, les malentendants et les personnes incarcérées. Par conséquent, il serait absurde de ne proposer qu'un seul type de formation en langue pour migrants adultes ou d'imposer les mêmes critères linguistiques à tous. De plus, la mise au point de formations en langue et d'activités d'apprentissage de la langue devrait obligatoirement être précédée d'une analyse des besoins des migrants. Et, si l'on veut permettre à ces derniers de s'identifier aux objectifs d'apprentissage qui leur sont fixés, il convient de les associer étroitement à cette analyse. Parallèlement, il faut reconnaître que pour certains migrants (en particulier les réfugiés), l'apprentissage de la langue n'est pas la première des priorités. Par conséquent, le fait de proposer une formation en langue à ces personnes n'est pas forcément la meilleure manière de les aider.

Enfin, bon nombre de contributeurs ont souligné, directement ou indirectement, le rôle essentiel des associations et bénévoles qui organisent des activités à l'intention des migrants adultes, et en particulier des réfugiés. Un ensemble d'outils visant à soutenir ces activités est actuellement conçu dans le cadre du projet relatif à l'ILMA ; il sera mis à disposition sur le site Internet du Conseil de l'Europe en temps utile.

Le symposium a été l'occasion de rappeler à plusieurs reprises que la tolérance linguistique et la bonne volonté sont essentielles pour communiquer de façon efficace avec les migrants. Il a également permis de souligner que l'on pouvait s'appuyer sur les concepts liés à l'intégration et les sur conclusions de la recherche pour trouver le juste équilibre entre l'accueil de la diversité linguistique et culturelle, d'une part, et l'apport d'une aide aux migrants pour acquérir la langue de leur pays hôte, d'autre part. Nous espérons que le présent ouvrage encouragera la poursuite des travaux de recherche dans ces domaines, tout en aidant les Etats membres à mettre au point des politiques d'intégration qui soient suffisamment éclairées et qui respectent les valeurs fondamentales du Conseil de l'Europe.

1 **Language and integration: some key issues**
  Langue et intégration : questions clés

Ofelia García
# Problematizing linguistic integration of migrants: the role of translanguaging and language teachers

**Abstract:** This paper problematizes the concept of linguistic integration of migrants, by proposing an alternative way of posing the question. It reviews the transformations of sociolinguistics in the 21st century, and offers a critical perspective on the ontology of language, native speakers and bilingualism. After introducing the concept of translanguaging, the paper poses principles of language education for adult migrants, which take into account this different conceptualization of language, bilingualism and education. It ends by proposing a renewed vision of language education for migrants, and calls for language teachers to take up different roles from those in the past.

**Résumé :** L'article problématise le concept d'intégration linguistique des migrants en proposant une autre approche de la question. Il examine les transformations de la sociolinguistique au XXI$^e$ siècle et pose un regard critique sur l'ontologie du langage, du locuteur natif et du bilinguisme. Après une présentation du concept d'apprentissage translinguistique, l'article pose des principes de l'éducation linguistique des migrants adultes en prenant en compte cette conceptualisation différente du langage, du bilinguisme et de l'éducation. En conclusion, il propose une vision nouvelle de l'éducation linguistique des migrants et invite les enseignants à changer de rôles par rapport à ceux qui étaient les leurs par le passé.

# 1 Introduction

Displacements and movements of people into different spaces characterize the world today. Sometimes people flee war, other times economic poverty, yet other times religious and ethnic discrimination or oppressive political systems. As a result of this movement, national languages have become deterritorialized (Canagarajah 2005): languages considered "national", are increasingly spoken in diasporic communities all over the world. In this increasingly interconnected

**Ofelia García,** The Graduate Center, City University of New York, USA,
E-mail: ogarcia@gc.cuny.edu

world developed nations still wield significant power and authority and may use what is considered the "standard" national language as a tool of differentiation between migrants who are welcomed and integrated, and those who are not.

This paper starts out by problematizing the concept of linguistic integration of migrants, and posing a different question that takes into account conceptual advances in our understandings of language and language education. It briefly reviews the transformations of sociolinguistics in the 21st century and proposes principles of language education for adult migrants which take account of these different conceptualizations. It also calls for a renewed vision of language education and for language teachers to take up different roles from those in the past.

## 2 Reframing language

Linguistic integration often means no more than ensuring that migrants speak the language of the political state into which they come. The rationale for this position is that adult migrants cannot participate in the national society and its economy unless they speak the national language. But what is the "national language", and why is it used as the basis for deciding who is welcomed and who is not?

Since the mid-20th century, sociolinguists have insisted that language and speakers form an assemblage; language cannot exist without speakers, and speakers cannot speak without language. The founders of sociolinguistics – Joshua A. Fishman, John Gumperz, Dell Hymes, William Labov – certainly understood that language is a deeply personal and social affair, tied to an individual's lived experience. Poststructuralist and post-colonial sociolinguists have gone one step further, focusing on language as appropriated by speakers and questioning the concept of a *"named" national language* (Makoni and Pennycook 2007; Mignolo 2000; Pennycook 2010). Arguing from a linguistics position, Otheguy, García, and Reid (2015: 286) emphasize that named languages have been invented, even as linguistic objects:

> A named language *cannot* be defined linguistically, cannot be defined, that is, in grammatical (lexical or structural) terms. And because a named language cannot be defined linguistically it is not, strictly speaking, a linguistic object; it is not something that a person speaks.

Many sociolinguists today propose that "languaging" might be a sufficient term to capture the plural linguistic practices of speakers as they move across different contexts, "a social process constantly reconstructed in sensitivity to environmental factors" (Canagarajah 2007: 94).

By advancing the view that language belongs to the speaker rather than to the nation state, critical poststructuralist sociolinguists aim to break out of static conceptions of language that keep power in the hands of the few (Flores 2013; Flores and García 2014). The constructed national language matches the linguistic features of those who wield power, guaranteeing their authority. The different linguistic features of others, especially migrants, and by necessity their fluid language practices – the product of being forced to interact in a new communicative context – are then stigmatized (García and Li Wei 2014).

# 3 Reframing speakers

If language is constructed and inhabited by people, it cannot be limited to the descriptions and conventions adopted by nation states (or national groups) and their academies and educational institutions. The language of a particular geographic space is increasingly inhabited today by people of many provenances and with very different language practices, and the categorization of speakers as native/non-native has been increasingly questioned (see, for example, Canagarajah 1999; Cook 1999; Doerr 2009; Leung, Harris, and Rampton 1997; Martin-Rojo 2010; Piller 2002).

Who then is a native speaker? Is Luis, born to a migrant family from Andalucia in Catalonia, a native speaker of what we call Spanish, Catalan, or both? And how about Zineb, born in Catalonia to a migrant family from Morocco, who is growing up speaking what are called Berber, Moroccan Arabic or Darija, Catalan and Spanish? What is it that Luis and Zineb speak natively? From a societal perspective, they are called bilingual or multilingual. They are said to speak different named languages and are considered to be simultaneous bilinguals/multilinguals. In the schools that they attend in Barcelona, they are not considered "native speakers" of Catalan, although they have spoken it fluently since they started speaking as babies, for they attended a *llar d'infants* ('nursery') from the age of four months. Luis and Zineb speak, they have language, their own, which they use efficiently to communicate with the very different communities with which they come into contact. They know how to activate different features of their unitary language system (and suppress others) to communicate successfully with various speakers in the Barcelona context. The question of whether they are native speakers of Catalan or not, or of Spanish, Berber, Darija, is a question that doesn't pertain to Luis and Zineb's lives or to a world that is increasingly inter-connected. The category of native speaker is just another way to keep power in the hands of the few and exclude those who are different. It reifies the linguistic practices of the powerful class within the state as the only legitimate practices, and thus ensures that only the powerful have access to the material goods that it distributes. As Canagarajah has said: "We are all translinguals, not native speakers of a single language in homogeneous environments" (Canagarajah 2013: 8).

# 4 Reframing the linguistic integration of migrants

If we do not conceive of languages as real linguistic entities spoken in a political state, and do not accept the notion of native speakers, then we must ask whether the linguistic integration of migrants should be the focus of our attention as language scholars. We know that migrants need to participate meaningfully in society. But linguistic integration of migrants who are minoritized, given the narrow definition of national language and native speaker considered above, cannot be the goal for that participation. History all over the world has confirmed that a shift to dominant language practices has not led to the structural incorporation of minoritized groups in the dominant society's economic, political, and social life. Perhaps the most important example of this is the history of enslaved people who were brought from the African continent to the Americas. Although the US African American population has shifted completely to English, they have continued to be subjected to discrimination. Their complete relinguification has not led to their structural incorporation; they remain victims of racism and what Flores and Rosa call the "eyes of whiteness", and its "mouth" and "ears". Flores and Rosa's *raciolinguistic perspective* focuses on how listening subjects hear and interpret "the linguistic practices of language-minoritized populations as deviant based on their racial positioning in society as opposed to any objective characteristics of their language use" (Flores and Rosa 2015: 151). What Flores and Rosa propose is that scholars and teachers must go beyond the national constructions of appropriate language in order to pay attention to what is being said and why it is being said, that is, in order to give voice to migrants.

As critical poststructuralist sociolinguists and language teachers embroiled in the dynamic movements and unequal treatment of migrant families in the 21st century, we need to pose and attempt to answer the following questions: Have language teachers a role to play in reversing the effects of "the coloniality of power and knowledge" (Quijano 2000) that has been installed within understandings of language and language education? And if they have, what might that role be?

In the rest of this article, we attempt to answer these questions. We start by reviewing traditional understandings of languages and bilingualism that need to be disrupted in order to move forward.

# 5 Traditional tools of the trade: languages and bilingualism

Language teachers are often at the forefront of issues dealing with migrants. They are called upon to alleviate what is seen as the "language problem" caused by population displacement and movement. But they are given tools that were developed before the dynamic migrations that reflect today's "superdiversity" (Vertovec 2007). Among the most obsolete of these tools is the framing of languages as L1/L2 and of bilingualism.

Despite the sociopolitical and sociolinguistic transformations of the world in the 21st century discussed above, conceptions of language education remain unchanged. Language teachers continue to speak about "second" language education and "second" language acquisition, even though many scholars have problematized the concepts of language and native speaker and have unmasked the reasons for their appeal at the level of the political state and its institutions. We continue to speak about "additive" and "subtractive" bilingualism, as if languages were whole units that can be added or subtracted. And we rely on "second" language pedagogies that build on diglossic separation models, without recognizing the more dynamic language practices characteristic of the world today. A monolingual model of language and bilingualism is promoted, even though the world is highly multilingual and language practices are heteroglossic.

Because languages continue to be posited as autonomous structures or boxes that are L1s, L2s, L3s, etc., bilingualism/multilingualism is seen as the addition (or subtraction) of those boxes. The distinction between "additive" and "subtractive" bilingualism was first made by Wallace Lambert in 1974. Whereas additive bilingualism was the goal of Canadian French immersion programs for anglophone children in Quebec, French being added to English, programs to teach Spanish-speaking children in transitional bilingual education in the US aimed at subtractive bilingualism, replacing their "native" language by English. This was before the changes in immigration policy which started to take effect in the 1970s and brought speakers with very different language practices to Canada and the US. Whether bilingualism was seen as additive or subtractive, it was conceptualized from a monolingual national perspective. Students had to become either two monolingual persons in one (Grosjean 1982) or had to shift to the dominant language (Fishman 1966).

Ways to teach what were seen as "second" languages relied on pedagogies that maintained the separation between "languages", and the languages taught were handed down in grammar books and according to the conventions determined by the authoritative bodies of nation states, without too much regard to how people actually spoke them.

When language teachers are asked to participate in the linguistic integration of migrants, they come equipped with these traditional concepts of language, bilingualism and pedagogy. They often respond to the nation state's demands for linguistic integration without thinking of the sociopolitical and sociolinguistic changes that are fueling the demand for their expertise. The next section offers a view of language education focused not on the traditional notions supported by nation states, but taking into account the migrants themselves as bilingual/multilingual speakers with legitimate practices and voices.

# 6 Beyond languages and with speakers: translanguaging as tool

The term *translanguaging* was coined in 1994 in Welsh (*trawsieithu*) by Cen Williams and translated into English by Colin Baker (2011). Originally, it referred to a pedagogical practice where students in bilingual Welsh/English classrooms alternated languages for the purposes of receptive or productive use. Since then, the term has been used to refer to the complex and fluid language practices of bilinguals and the pedagogical approaches that leverage those practices.

It is interesting to note that translanguaging was coined and developed "in the border", by minoritized bilingual communities and with a bilingual lens. The purpose was not for a monolingual anglophone community to acquire a "second language", as in French immersion programs in Quebec: nor was it for a monolingual language-minoritized community like the Spanish-speaking one in the United States to acquire English, also as a "second" language. The purpose of translanguaging was to augment the pupil's activity in *both* languages (Lewis, Jones, and Baker 2012a, 2012b). García has described translanguaging as "an approach to bilingualism that is centered not on languages [...] but on the practices of bilinguals that are readily observable" (García 2009: 44). These practices, in which bilinguals "intermingle linguistic features that have hereto been administratively or linguistically assigned to a particular language or language variety"

(García 2009: 51), are "the normal mode of communication that, with some exceptions in some monolingual enclaves, characterizes communities throughout the world (García 2009: 44). In education, translanguaging goes beyond code-switching and translation because it refers to the *process* by which bilingual students perform bilingually in the myriad multimodal ways of classrooms.

Going beyond named languages as autonomous linguistic structures, "Translanguaging is the deployment of a speaker's full linguistic repertoire without regard for watchful adherence to the socially and politically defined boundaries of named (and usually national and state languages)" (Otheguy, García, and Reid 2015: 281). It is constructed and inhabited by people who see themselves as speaking *their* own language, and not simply the languages of one or another national group. By posing a going *beyond* named languages (Li Wei 2011) translanguaging dwells with, and around, the bilingual speaker in the entanglement of worlds and words created by the coloniality of power.

Again, translanguaging does not refer to bilingual speakers' ability to go across named languages (what is often called code-switching), which gives legitimacy to the construct of named languages. Seen from the speaker's internal perspective, translanguaging gives agency and legitimacy to the bilingual speaker. The bilingual/multilingual speaker's repertoire is not simply made up of two or more languages; instead it consists of a unitary language system. In posing a unitary language system from which bilinguals select different features according to the communicative situation at hand, translanguaging acknowledges the dialogic nature of the features, with none of them in a hierarchical position. Thus, translanguaging works against the power differential of languages as controlled by dominant nation states. All speakers control the features they use, and the work of language teachers then consists not in adding a whole language system separate from that which the speaker already holds, but in making new linguistic features available which the speaker then integrates and appropriates into their own language repertoire. This builds a multilingual identity that does not necessarily correspond to two or more national identities. Because it gives the agency to speakers, translanguaging is a most promising theory for the language education of adult migrants.

# 7 Translanguaging in the language education of adult migrants: Why? What? How?

Language teachers who take up translanguaging start by enabling migrants to recognize their full language repertoire and helping them incorporate new features into their own language system. This is an important shift because migrants are not simply acquiring a "second" language. To illustrate this point, let's compare Christine and Carlos. Born in France to educated middle-class parents, Christine has spoken French since birth. In school she learned English, and then Spanish. Now 36, she considers French her L1, English her L2, and Spanish her L3. She is secure in her identity as a francophone and uses French personally and professionally in her daily life. She seldom uses English, although she often reads reports in English for work; she says that she likes Spanish better than English, but uses it only to sing songs she loves. Christine considers only French as her own language. The others are simply "gifts" which she borrows.

In contrast, Carlos was born and grew up in Peru and is now 43. In the home where he was raised, he spoke Spanish and Quechua. However, at school only Spanish was taught, although Quechua was frequently used. Carlos is a talented musician, and in Peru he was part of a bilingual musical group that sang songs in Quechua and Spanish. He considered himself a bilingual Peruvian, with neither language identified as L1 or L2. At the age of 38, because of economic hardship, Carlos migrated to Germany. When he first arrived, he took a German language "integration" course. Two years ago, he married a German-speaking woman. He is required to use German as his everyday lived language, both at home and at the Peruvian restaurant where he works and sings in Spanish and Quechua. German is not his L2 or L3; it has become his own (although not his sole) *everyday lived language.*

The difference between Christine, a "second" language learner, and Carlos, a migrant who must live every day by using new language features, is telling. Second language learners like Christine are learning the language of "the other". Migrant learners like Carlos, however, must gain new features to integrate into their *own* language repertoire and appropriate for everyday lived use. They must become bilingual/multilingual German-speakers, not just speakers of German as a "second" language.

In taking up a translanguaging lens to teach Carlos German, his teacher, Hildegard, understands the difference between teaching a "second" language and teaching an everyday lived language. She knows she must focus not on teaching the German language, but on giving Carlos "voice". And she understands that in teaching Carlos, she must redress the power differentials that are installed in German, Spanish, and Quechua. To do so, Hildegard focuses not on Carlos' limited proficiency in German or his learner status, but on his strengths, on what he already knows, on his ways of making meaning and engaging with the world. In Hildegard's classroom, students are grouped according to home languages or languages that they understand, to ensure they understand the German language class. On his first day, Carlos joins the Spanish-speaking group and Hildegard asks them to talk to him and find out who he is, what he knows, and what he is engaged in doing. Hildegard needs the group's help because she speaks neither Spanish nor Quechua, and members of the group can already use some features of German to make themselves understood.

Carlos tells the group that he plays the *quena*, the traditional flute of the Andes, in a Peruvian restaurant. Many of the Latin American students in the group do not know what a quena is; Carlos tells them it's a word in Quechua. Some of them do not know what Quechua is, and wonder how it is that Carlos also speaks Spanish. Carlos explains that Quechua literally means "people's language" and is used to refer to the ways of speaking of some people in the Andes. He explains that in Peru it is an official language, along with Spanish, and was spoken in the Inca Empire. The students communicate all this to Hildegard, who asks Carlos to bring his quena to class. The group translates this request for Carlos.

Hildegard goes home and looks up quena in Wikipedia. The next day she brings the handout shown in Figure 1 and Carlos brings his quena. Hildegard begins by doing a shared reading exercise with the whole class. She first shows the quena that Carlos has brought in and points to the notches as she reads the first sentence; she counts the holes it has as she reads the second sentence; and she points to plastic and wood in the room as she reads the third sentence. She then asks the students to read along with her, and repeats this three times.

| |  |
|---|---|
| Die Quena ist eine Kerbflöte. | |
| Ursprünglich wurde die Quena mit 3 oder 5 Löchern in Dur-Tonleitern gespielt; heute hat sie meistens 7 Löcher. | |
| In Peru und Bolivien kostet sie zwischen 50 Cent (aus Bambus oder Plastik) und 80 Euro (hochentwickelte Modelle aus hartem Holz, teilweise mit einem Mundstück aus Knochen).[1] | |

**Figure 1:** Hildegard's handout

[1] The quena is a notched flute. Originally the quena was played with 3 or 5 holes in major scales; today it usually has 7 holes. In Peru and Bolivia it costs between 50 cents (bamboo or plastic) and 80 euros (sophisticated models made of hard wood, some with a mouthpiece made of bone)

Hildegard then tells the students to get into their home language groups. She asks them to look up the electronic translation of the German text using the iPad that each group has, to edit the translation if need be, and to copy it next to the German text in the handout. Carlos' group comes up with the following electronic translation:

> La quena es una flauta dentada. Originalmente la quena se juega con 3 o 5 agujeros en las escalas mayores; hoy cuenta con la mayoría 7 agujeros. En Perú y Bolivia que cuesta entre 50 centavos (de bambú o de plástico) y 80 euros (modelos sofisticados de madera dura, algunos con una boquilla de hueso).

Because Carlos is a newcomer in the Spanish-speaking group, Hildegard sits with that group and observes Carlos carefully. Of the translation, Carlos says: "Uno no juega la quena, uno la toca" ('You don't "play" the quena, you play it'), and a discussion ensues in Spanish about the difference between *jugar* (used to play games) and *tocar* (used to play instruments). Carlos participates fully. This tells Hildegard that he is a competent speaker of Spanish and knows how to be persuasive.

The group struggles to match the translation to the German text. They annotate the German text with Spanish words. They frequently use Google Translate to find the meaning of individual words and improve their understanding, which they share with each other (for example, Carlos learns that nouns in German are capitalized). The students work assiduously together. They make a vocabulary list, and those who speak more German ask Hildegard many questions about German language structures, sharing her answers with the rest of the group.

The group is then asked to copy the Spanish text they have agreed on next to the German in the handout, and then to answer some questions in whichever language they can. Hildegard watches Carlos write the text with ease, which tells her he is practiced in writing Spanish.

When all home language groups are secure in their understanding of the German text and how it works, Hildegard asks them to pose questions in German about the quena. They come up with:
- Was ist ein Quena? ('What is a quena?')
- Wieviele Löcher hat die Quena? ('How many holes does the quena have?')
- Wieviel kostet sie? ('How much does it cost?')

Hildegard then tells all the groups to devise some interview questions for Carlos and his group about the quena. With much help from each other, electronic translations, and the teacher, the groups come up with the following questions, which Hildegard puts on the electronic whiteboard:
- Wo hast du auf einer Quena spielen gelernt? ('Where did you learn to play the quena?')
- Wie alt warst du? ('How old were you?')

- Wo spielst Du die Quena zur Zeit? ('Where do you play the quena now?')
- Ist es schwierig oder leicht auf der Quena zu spielen? ('Is it difficult or easy to play the quena?')

Carlos answers each question in Spanish, and some of his group members translate as best they can for the class. Hildegard helps them.

Hildegard then asks Carlos to play the quena. She tells the students that the quena makes her feel sad, and asks them how the melody they have heard makes them feel. Student after student offers words of emotion, some in German, but others in Arabic, Turkish, Kurdish, Armenian, Spanish, and other languages. Overall, the students feel that the sound of the quena makes them *traurig* ('sad'). Carlos learns the word *traurig*, and Hildegard and others in the class learn the word *triste*. All of them learn the Turkish word *üzgün*, and the Arabic *hazin*. For homework, Hildegard asks the students to find people in their communities who play an instrument and ask them at least one question.

Carlos' first lessons in this German language class bring much more than he expected. Instead of being given structures of a new and isolated language to acquire, he is allowed to interpret new linguistic features as part of his own expanding language repertoire, and not simply as an add-on. In so doing, Carlos begins to transform his engagement with the German-speaking world that surrounds him. German is no longer just the language of Germans and books; "German" language features start to be internalized into his linguistic repertoire and appropriated and used as his own linguistic features.

The principles of this translanguaging pedagogy for adult migrants are easy to identify:
- Give migrants "voice" and help them to develop it.
- Build on their strengths and interests.
- Make sure that students are "doing" language, performing genuine and authentic tasks, not just that they "have" language structures.
- Recognize the entanglements of migrants' worlds and words and use them in the process of finalizing the product that you intend.
- Ensure that they appropriate new features into an expanded repertoire that is their own, and not just that of a nation state or specific national group.

Although it is Carlos, as an engaged and interested speaker, who guarantees that there has been learning, Hildegard as the teacher has an important role, and it is to the teacher's role that we now turn.

# 8 Translanguaging and the role of language teachers

To teach adult migrants, language teachers must take up a translanguaging stance, shed their authoritative position, and adopt different roles. We summarize these four teacher roles as *the detective, the co-learner, the builder,* and *the transformer.*

*The detective.* Four questions frame this role:
- What does this adult person know?
- Why does this adult person want to "invest" (Norton 2000) in using new features?
- What are this adult person's preferred ways of making meaning?
- How does this adult person use language?

Language teachers need to know their adult students: what motivates them, and how they use language and make meaning in life. There is a difference between being able to perform linguistically only with features of the national language being taught, and speakers' ability to perform linguistically. García, Johnson and Seltzer (2017) refer to these different performances as *language-specific performances* and *general language performances.* Teachers need to understand whether students are able to express complex thoughts, explain, persuade, argue, compare and contrast, give directions, recount events, and do other things with language, regardless of whether they could do this only with the features of the language being taught. They also need to know if students are able to make inferences, identify key ideas, and associate ideas from multiple texts when reading, and are able to produce written texts of opinion, information, explanation and narration, regardless of the language features used. Teachers' detective work needs to happen in collaboration with others – other speakers in the class, other teachers, outside agencies, the community of speakers; and with other resources – multilingual texts and electronic translators.

*The co-learner.* Teachers who take up a translanguaging stance must also become co-learners (Li Wei 2014). In that respect, they need to ask themselves two questions:
- What can I learn from this adult person? From his/her interests? From his/her funds of knowledge (Moll et al. 1992) and funds of languaging?
- How do I distribute agency equally in the classroom?

To carry out the role of co-learner, teachers must be interested in the different worlds and words of their students. They engage their students in collaborative research and linguistic ethnographies of the community. They are curious about students' worlds, their words, and their entanglements. And as teachers of migrants, they are also interested in social justice.

Teachers who consider themselves co-learners engage their adult students in representing and producing their worlds and words using all the features of their repertoire. Some of the ways in which this might be achieved are:
- interviewing each other and others in the community of speakers;
- asking students to share and write their life stories;
- producing video-documentaries with the students.

*The builder.* Teachers of adult migrants must be more than detectives and co-learners, they must also be builders. They must ask themselves:
- How do I build an affinity space (Gee 2004) that bridges differences in age, class, race, gender and educational level, and in which people can participate in various ways according to their interests and abilities?
- How do I build a space that reflects the entanglement of different worlds and words and their power differentials, and is flexible enough to accommodate differences?
- How do I provide language affordances that capture and express interests? Engagement?

To do so, teachers give adult learners freedom to work within affinity groups and participate freely in selecting the topics and features that they would want to share.

*The transformer.* This is the role that makes teachers who take up translanguaging effective in teaching migrants. Informed by translanguaging theory, they ask themselves:
- How can I make visible the rhetorical narrative of modernity/coloniality, and dwell in the border with adult migrants as they expand their repertoire with new features and practices?

To transform the social reality of migrants, teachers must be ready to build on the human ability to re-mix and recontextualize; that is, to inscribe language performances and identities into new contexts. Teachers who take up translanguaging must transform the vision of what it is to teach a "second" language to migrants. They must make visible how permitting only the dominant language in a "second" language classroom is an act of symbolic violence (Bourdieu 1991), that is, violence exercised in a group with their complicity. These teachers must transform this reality by making explicit how the construct of national language, and the rhetorical narrative of modernity/coloniality that has produced it, serves to oppress, rather than liberate, migrants. Teachers who aim to transform the migrants' social realities must teach them to become critical sociolinguists (Rymes and Leone 2014) so that they can analyze language and understand how it is lodged with power, and why and how some language practices are delegitimized and those of the mythical "native speakers" of an "L1" are held up as the sole exemplars.

# 9 Conclusion

Translanguging disrupts the modernist/colonial logic of national languages and focuses on the available features and practices of people and especially migrants to make meaning, free of the constraints and defined boundaries of named languages. It also acknowledges that national languages have had, and continue to have, real and material effects on people. Thus, migrants must also perform linguistically with features that many describe as the "other" language.

The advantage of educating adult migrants with translanguaging theory and pedagogy in mind is that in focusing on the practices of *people*, it gives agency to minoritized speakers, decolonizes linguistic knowledge, and engages all of us in the social transformations that the world so sorely needs today. Translanguaging offers a way of capturing the expanded complex practices of speakers who cannot avoid having had languages inscribed in their bodies, and yet live between different societal and semiotic contexts. Adult migrants are the best example of this living between and beyond borders – national, political, linguistic, social, ideological. Translanguaging theory offers language teachers a way to engage them.

# References

Baker, Colin. 2011. *Foundations of bilingual education and bilingualism*, 5th edn. Bristol, UK: Multilingual Matters.
Bourdieu, Pierre. 1991. *Language and symbolic power*. Cambridge, MA: Harvard University Press.
Canagarajah, Suresh. 1999. *Resisting English imperialism in English*. Oxford: Oxford University Press.
Canagarajah, Suresh. 2005. *Reclaiming the local in language policy and practice*. Mahwah, NJ: Lawrence Erlbaum.

Canagarajah, Suresh. 2007. The ecology of global English. *International Multilingual Research Journal* 1(2). 89–100.
Canagarajah, Suresh. 2013. *Translingual practice: Global Englishes and cosmopolitan relations*. London: Routledge.
Cook, Vivian. 1999. Going beyond the native speaker in language teaching. *TESOL Quarterly* 33(2). 185–209.
Doerr, Neriko Musha. 2009. *The native speaker concept: Ethnographic investigations of native speaker effects*. Berlin: de Gruyter.
Fishman, Joshua A. 1966. *Language loyalty in the United States: The maintenance and perpetuation of non-English mother tongues by American ethnic and religious groups*. The Hague: Mouton.
Flores, Nelson. 2013. The unexamined relationship between neoliberalism and plurilingualism: A cautionary tale. *TESOL Quarterly* 47(3). 500–520.
Flores, Nelson & Ofelia García. 2014. Linguistic third spaces in education: Teachers' translanguaging across the bilingual continuum. In David Little, Constant Leung and Piet Van Avermaet (eds.), *Managing diversity in education: Languages, policies, pedagogies*, 243–256. Bristol, UK: Multilingual Matters.
Flores, Nelson & Jonathan Rosa. 2015. Undoing appropriateness: Raciolinguistic ideologies and language diversity in education. *Harvard Educational Review* 85(2). 149–171.
García, Ofelia. 2009. *Bilingual education in the 21st Century: A global perspective*. Malden, MA & Oxford: Wiley/Blackwell.
García, Ofelia & Li Wei. 2014. *Translanguaging: Language, bilingualism and education*. London, UK: Palgrave Macmillan.
García, Ofelia, Susana Johnson & Kate Seltzer. 2017. *The translanguaging classroom: Leveraging student bilingualism for learning*. Philadelphia: Caslon.
Gee, James Paul. 2004. *Situated language and learning: A critique of traditional schooling*. New York & London: Routledge.
Grosjean, François. 1982. *Life with two languages*. Cambridge, MA: Harvard University Press.
Lambert, Wallace E. 1974. Culture and language as factors in learning and education. In Frances E. Aboud & Robert D. Meade (eds.), *Cultural factors in learning and education*, 91–122. Bellingham, Washington: 5th Western Washington Symposium on Learning.
Leung, Constance, Roxy Harris & Ben Rampton. 1997. The idealised native speaker, reified ethnicities, and classroom realities. *TESOL Quarterly* 31(3). 543–560. DOI:/10.2307/3587837/abstract.
Lewis, Glyn, Bryn Jones & Colin Baker. 2012a. Translanguaging: Origins and development from school to street and beyond. *Educational Research and Evaluation* 18(7). 641–654.
Lewis, Glyn, Bryn Jones & Colin Baker. 2012b. Translanguaging: Developing its conceptualisation and contextualisation. *Educational Research and Evaluation* 18(7). 655–670.
Li Wei. 2011. Moment analysis and translanguaging space: Discursive construction of identities by multilingual Chinese youth in Britain. *Journal of Pragmatics* 43. 1222–1235.
Li Wei. 2014. Who's teaching whom?: Co-learning in multilingual classrooms. In Stephen May (ed.), *The multilingual turn: Implications for SLA, TESOL and bilingual education*, 167–190. New York: Routledge.
Makoni, Sinfree & Alistair Pennycook. 2007. *Disinventing and reconstituting languages* Clevedon, UK: Multilingual Matters.

Martín-Rojo, Luisa. 2010. *Constructing inequality in multilingual classrooms*. Berlin: Mouton de Gruyter.

Mignolo, Walter. 2000. *Local histories/Global designs: Coloniality, subaltern knowledges, and border thinking*. Princeton: Princeton University Press.

Moll, Luis, Cathy Amanti, Deborah Neff & Norma Gonzalez. 1992. Funds of knowledge for teaching: Using a qualitativae approach to connect homes and classrooms. *Theory into Practice* 31(2). 132–141.

Norton, Bonnie. 2000. *Identity and language learning: Gender, ethnicity and educational change*. Harlow, UK: Longman.

Otheguy, Ricardo, Ofelia García & Wallis Reid. 2015. Clarifying translanguaging and deconstructing named languages: A perspective from linguistics. *Applied Linguistics Review* 6(3). 281–307.

Pennycook, Alistair. 2010. *Language as a local practice*. London & New York: Routledge.

Piller, Ingrid. 2002. Passing for a native speaker: Identity and success in second language learning. *Journal of Sociolinguistics* 6(2). 179–208.

Quijano, Aníbal. 2000. Coloniality of power, Eurocentrism, and Latin America. *Nepantla. Views from South* 1(3). 533–580. http://www.unc.edu/~aescobar/wan/wanquijano.pdf (accessed 2 June 2016).

Rymes, Betsy & Andrea Leone. 2014. Citizen sociolinguistics: A new media methodology for understanding language and social life. *Working Papers in Educational Linguistics* 29(2). 25–43. http://www.gse.upenn.edu/wpel/sites/gse.upenn.edu.wpel/files/29.2Rymesand-Leone.pdf (accessed 15 July 2016).

Vertovec, Stephen. 2007. Super-diversity and its implications. *Ethnic and Racial Studies* 30 (6). 1024–1054.

Williams, Cen. 1994. *Arfarniad o Ddulliau Dysgu ac Addysgu yng Nghyd-destun Addysg Uwchradd Ddwyieithog*, [An evaluation of teaching and learning methods in the context of bilingual secondary education]. Bangor: University of Wales, Bangor, doctoral thesis.

Claude Springer
# Migrants connectés, intégration sociale et apprentissage/certification en langues : prendre en compte la nouvelle donne numérique

**Résumé :** Ce début du XXI$^e$ siècle est marqué par l'explosion des réseaux sociaux. La dimension sociale, que l'on peut déduire de la prise en compte de l'approche actionnelle mais également des réseaux sociaux, doit être interprétée dans sa globalité, à la fois physique et virtuelle. L'acteur social est aujourd'hui connecté, confronté à des « textes » qui ne relèvent plus uniquement du mode écrit et de la littératie classique, ni même de la plurilittératie. La question de l'intégration linguistique des migrants doit ainsi prendre en compte la nouvelle donne numérique pour pouvoir passer du migrant connecté à l'apprenant migrant connecté.

**Abstract:** The early 21st century has seen a proliferation of social networks. The social dimension, which is implicit in the focus on an action-oriented approach and also in social networks, must be interpreted in its entirety, in both physical and virtual terms. Social agents nowadays go online and encounter "texts" which are no longer solely written and based on conventional literacy, nor on pluriliteracy for that matter. The linguistic integration of migrants must accordingly take into account the new digital environment so as to facilitate the transition from "online migrant" to online migrant learner.

## 1 Entrée en matière : le migrant des poètes alsaciens

L'Alsace, qui accueille plusieurs institutions européennes et ce symposium, offre un éclairage particulier à la question qui nous préoccupe, celle de l'intégration linguistique des migrants adultes. De manière très symbolique, *Les Serments de Strasbourg* de 842 instituent un certain bilinguisme avec le français et l'allemand, ou plus exactement le proto français, le gallo-roman, et le proto alle-

**Claude Springer,** professeur émérite, Université Aix-Marseille,
claude.springer@univ-amu.fr

mand, le francique rhénan. *Les Serments* sont pour moi emblématiques d'une Alsace multilingue avec l'alsacien comme langue identitaire et langue d'un tiers-espace entre la France et l'Allemagne. L'histoire tragique des guerres a marqué cette région qui, comme d'autres, s'est vue assimilée malgré elle aux pays qui la convoitaient.

Les artistes et poètes alsaciens ont exprimé à leur façon une autre approche de la langue et de l'identité.

## 1.1 Jean Hans Arp (1886–1966) : l'indicible et l'indétermination

Il a connu les deux guerres mondiales. Il est né, comme il aime le dire, de la nature, il est né de Strasbourg, il est né d'un nuage : « Ich bin in Strassburg geboren. Ich bin in einer Wolke geboren ». La détermination indéterminée de son origine alsacienne montre la difficulté à se définir par une nationalité, par une ville particulière. Son lieu de naissance, l'Alsace ne serait pour lui qu'une potentialité a-territoriale, un espace flottant difficile à situer. La sculpture et la poésie sont intimement liées à sa vie et à sa philosophie. Elles sont complémentaires comme les trois langues qu'il parle. Une des sculptures de Jean Hans Arp, *Nombril et deux idées*, représente, pour moi, un corps disloqué par la guerre. La guerre est un Wahnsinn, une folie, qu'il exprime à travers l'Unsinn, le non-sens que la poésie permet d'exprimer. Le nombril est une figure poétique qui représente l'origine, le centre de la vie, de l'intime mais aussi le centre du langage, l'origine du nom. Ce nom est vide et disparait dans le néant. Le nombril symbolise aussi les entrailles du poète, l'univers du rêve, de sa langue maternelle, l'alsacien, langue de l'enfance. Les deux idées qui sont posées maladroitement sur le corps peuvent représenter ses deux langues apprises scolairement. Il y a du Jean et du Hans à la fois.

Les poèmes de Jean Hans Arp ne sont pas très connus (Arp, 2014). *Die Grosse Firgelei*, s'intéresse à la langue, façon dada, dont il fut un des promoteurs. Il montre la part d'indicible et d'incompréhensible de toute langue. La part du rêve, du nuage, de l'intime. La langue ne saurait être réduite à son seul usage communicatif fonctionnel. Je me permets cette glose : Firgelei m'a dit textuellement ce qui suit, dit le poète. Une langue est belle si elle permet de s'attarder et de rêver, de penser et de fantasmer. Une langue est belle si elle chante des fleurs de rêve. Seule la langue de l'enfance rend possible ces rêveries, la langue fonctionnelle en est incapable. Dans le poème *Seither spaziere ich, Depuis lors je me promène,* Jean Hans Arp pose la question de l'identité : qui suis je ? d'où suis-je ? Il y a cette impossibilité de faire son unité. Cet autre que l'on cherche est parti loin, dans le pays des rêves. Il est devenu inaccessible. Il n'y a plus moyen de lui poser les questions qui taraudent. On ne peut plus savoir qui on est et d'où on vient.

Ces poèmes de fin de vie montrent l'autre aspect de la langue que les linguistes ignorent malheureusement. La langue n'est pas qu'un outil pour communiquer, pour se débrouiller dans les situations quotidiennes. Elle est aussi poésie, rêverie, imaginaire. Le poète nous parle des conséquences de l'assimilation et de notre modernité, qui ne nous permet plus réellement de nous définir par une origine nationale et culturelle. Le nouvel homme que nous devenons finit par être un étranger, un migrant. Il vit dans un nouvel espace, un tiers espace, et a du mal à renouer les fils de son origine. Les souvenirs lointains font désormais partie du Traumheitland, du pays des rêves.

## 1.2 André Weckmann (1924 – 2012) : violence de l'assimilation

André Weckmann, est né après la 1$^e$ guerre mondiale à Steinbourg. Il a écrit plusieurs recueils de poèmes en alsacien (Huck, 1989). Le premier poème *Sproch* définit la langue. La langue, pour le poète, est faite des choses simples de la vie. La langue c'est la vie, dans sa matérialité et sa banalité. C'est surtout les histoires d'une vie, histoires qui fondent notre généalogie, qui remonte à notre origine. La langue s'inscrit ainsi dans l'histoire d'un lieu, dans les histoires que partage une communauté. Langue et identité sont intimement liées et se nourrissent des liens que nous tissons avec les autres. Le regard du poète sur la banalité de la vie nous fait comprendre la dimension sociale de la langue. Le deuxième poème sur les Alsaciens, *Älsässer*, rappelle les douleurs d'une région déchirée par les guerres, le non-sens de la nationalité qui fait que l'on peut être selon les moments de l'histoire l'ennemi des uns et des autres et se faire tuer par les uns ou les autres. L'Alsacien est comme un apatride dans son propre pays, un étranger qui ne sait pour qui et pour quoi il va encore se faire pendre.

Ces deux poèmes questionnent de la même façon l'idée de nation, de nationalité, d'identité et d'intégration linguistique. L'intégration linguistique ressemble à une dépossession culturelle si on considère que la langue est bien celle de l'origine, celle des rêves et de la création, celle de l'intime fantasmé.

## 1.3 Premières impressions : Langue et intégration

La vision de la langue qui est exprimée par les poètes est loin de celle qui ressort de nos analyses linguistiques et didactiques. Nous avons la fâcheuse manie à ne prendre en compte que les simples mécanismes linguistiques et communicatifs. La langue est avant tout la vie, la vie simple de tous les jours, une façon de « se donner la main ». Mais c'est aussi, la poésie, l'imaginaire de nos histoires, des « fleurs de rêve », que l'on offre. Tout peut basculer, soudainement, nos repères et nos mots peuvent être désintégrés : « e hass » peut d'un coup devenir « un lapin », pour reprendre un autre poète alsacien Claude Vigée (2000), par le simple jeu de l'intégration/assimilation linguistique. Les migrants vivent cette violence et questionnent la langue, l'identité, l'assimilation. Les regards des poètes alsaciens nous permettent de mieux comprendre la violence de l'assimilation/intégration mais aussi les liens indestructibles qui lient langue et identité. Et, en fin de compte, ne faut-il pas admettre que l'image du migrant est celle de l'humanité ?

Amin Malouf résume bien cette première approche (1998) :

> « Sans doute mes propos sont-ils ceux d'un migrant, et d'un minoritaire. Mais il me semble qu'ils reflètent une sensibilité de plus en plus partagée par nos contemporains. N'est-ce pas le propre de notre époque que d'avoir fait de tous les hommes, en quelque sorte, des migrants et des minoritaires ?
>
> Nous sommes tous contraints de vivre dans un univers qui ne ressemble guère à notre terroir d'origine ; nous devons tous apprendre d'autres langues, d'autres langages, d'autres codes ; et nous avons tous l'impression que notre identité, telle que nous l'imaginions depuis l'enfance, est menacée.
>
> Beaucoup ont quitté leur terre natale, et beaucoup d'autres, sans l'avoir quittée, ne la reconnaissent plus. »

Les poètes, les artistes, les migrants ressentent avec force ces aspects universels de la condition humaine, de la modernité, de la migration.

# 2 Faire évoluer notre vision du migrant adulte : le migrant connecté

La migration au XXI$^e$ siècle ne peut se penser en dehors d'une société globalisée et interconnectée. Elle s'inscrit bien entendu dans cette histoire éternelle des guerres et des conquêtes qui débouchent inexorablement sur des déplacements de populations. Beaucoup d'études sur les migrants s'inscrivent logiquement dans cette vision classique et universelle de la migration. La plupart ignorent cependant l'évolution introduite par la société mondialisée du savoir numérique interconnecté et des réseaux sociaux. Il nous faut reconsidérer l'image que nous avons du migrant adulte déraciné au profit d'une image conforme à l'homme d'aujourd'hui qui est interconnecté et interagit sur les réseaux sociaux. Je propose d'explorer trois pistes. La première renvoie à la complexité qui inclut l'imaginaire et à la poésie ; la deuxième au paradoxe de la proximité et de la distance et la troisième à la société interconnectée.

## 2.1 Imaginaire et poésie de la langue et de la vie

Morin (2015: 30) propose de prendre en compte les deux polarités de l'homme. Pour lui, l'homme ne se réduit pas au prosaïque, au rationnel, au fonctionnel. On ne peut réduire les besoins vitaux aux seuls besoins de communication pour le quotidien. L'homme a également besoin de s'évader, besoin d'imaginaire, besoin de poésie.

La polarité prosaïque de la vie commande tout ce que nous faisons par contrainte, pour survivre, pour gagner notre vie. Et il y a la polarité poétique de la vie, c'est-à-dire celle où l'on s'épanouit personnellement, où l'on vit en communion, où l'on a des moments d'harmonie et de joie. Moments que donnent l'amour, l'amitié, la liesse. C'est cela qui est vivre, vivre poétiquement.

Cette part d'indicible fait partie du tout social, des interactions entre les individus, des histoires personnelles, des mondes symboliques qui constituent ce que l'on nomme la culture. L'homme peut se concevoir, certes, comme un être rationnel, mais il est aussi une personne émotionnelle qui s'inscrit dans une histoire de vie en mouvement. L'idée qu'il existerait une langue de survie, garantissant l'intégration sociale dans une société d'accueil, réduit le migrant à la seule polarité prosaïque de la vie. Cette optique a pour conséquence de focaliser la formation sur les situations quotidiennes de survie oubliant l'indispensable besoin d'imaginaire et de communion. Le descriptif du français langue d'intégration en France, par exemple, s'inscrit explicitement dans cette vision réductrice et présente les urgences du quotidien auxquelles on ajoute « des petits riens relationnels ». Or, justement, ces petits riens relationnels constituent le tout des langages sollicités et expriment le vivre poétiquement. La langue est aussi et surtout le lieu symbolique du social, le lieu de l'imaginaire poétique.

## 2.2 Le paradoxe de la distance et de la proximité

La figure de l'étranger de Simmel (1908) permet d'envisager le migrant différemment. L'étranger fonctionne comme un symbole des relations humaines, mais aussi comme un symbole de la distance et de la mobilité, dans son aspect relationnel ou imaginaire. Il y a ainsi un paradoxe dans la mesure où l'étranger est à la fois ici et ailleurs, mais aussi dans un tiers espace, un *iciailleurs*, qu'il construit en permanence. La mobilité de l'étranger s'oppose à la sédentarité, l'étrangeté à la familiarité. Et en fin de compte, l'étranger est en nous. Nous pouvons nous sentir étrangers chez nous, lorsque nous allons vers d'autres communautés, lorsque nous avançons en âge en observant nos enfants, etc., comme nous avons déjà pu le dire.

Raphaël (2008 : 11) résume cette figure de l'étranger de la manière suivante : « cette ambivalence dans les rapports à l'étranger ne rejoint-elle pas ce qui caractérise toute relation qu'une personne entretient avec son entourage, et qui porte toujours la marque de la distance et de la proximité ? Tout homme fait l'expérience contradictoire de l'unité de son être et, en même temps, d'une faille, d'une certaine étrangeté à lui-même. » Pour Raphaël, il s'agit bien de « la forme exacerbée de toute relation humaine ». Il reprend la formule de Simmel : « La distance à l'intérieur de la relation signifie que le proche est lointain, mais le fait même de l'altérité signifie que le lointain est proche ».

Le migrant possède ainsi un capital social riche d'expériences dans diverses communautés. On ne peut que constater que la plupart des réflexions et des propositions de formation pour les migrants font l'impasse sur cette réalité complexe en se concentrant uniquement sur l'ici du pays d'accueil et sur un système artificiel d'interactions fonctionnelles, prosaïques pour reprendre Morin.

## 2.3 Des réseaux de liens sociaux interconnectés

De nombreuses études s'intéressent aux réseaux de liens que tissent les migrants dans leur aventure. Le monde d'internet ne connait pas les frontières et les barbelés que l'on érige pour freiner les migrants dans leur quête d'un meilleur lieu de vie. Diminescu (2005 : 277) reprend la réflexion de Simmel et estime que « mobilité et connectivité forment désormais un ensemble de base dans la définition du migrant du XXI$^e$ siècle ». Elle résume cette nouvelle approche de la manière suivante : « Hier : immigrer et couper les racines ; aujourd'hui : circuler et garder le contact. Cette évolution semble marquer un nouvel âge dans l'histoire des migrations : l'âge du migrant connecté. » Il s'agit donc de « Considérer le migrant dans la totalité de ses mobilités (physiques, imaginaires, virtuelles) » (Diminescu 2005 : 278). L'intégration sociale n'est pas le fait de l'institution, c'est une forme d'intégration par le bas, nous dit Diminescu.

Bashi (2007) développe la même analyse au sujet des migrants de la Caraïbe, en référence aux liens forts et faibles de Granovetter (1973). Elle montre l'intérêt de l'étude des réseaux de liens qui caractérisent l'homme moderne et tout migrant. La sociologie transnationale montre que la migration n'est pas un simple déplacement spatial d'un lieu d'origine vers un lieu d'arrivée avec une obligation d'acculturation vers le lieu d'arrivée. Le processus migratoire doit être pris dans sa complexité et sa richesse. Le migrant est un acteur social qui vient avec un projet de vie. Il est en relation constante avec des personnes ressources, dans une toile aux liens multiples. Ces nœuds d'entraide constituent le tiers espace de la migration et permettent au migrant de trouver une place. La survie du migrant dépend de ces carrefours de liens sociaux qui se nouent et se dénouent entre lieu d'origine et lieu d'accueil. Notre vision sociologique du migrant comme personne déracinée, inculte, sans projet, doit impérativement être modifiée pour prendre en compte les points d'appui que les migrants utilisent.

## 2.4 Une société interconnectée

Siemens (2004) définit le nouveau courant du connectivisme et présente les principes de l'apprentissage avec le numérique de la manière suivante : l'apprentissage est chaotique, il est continu, il est complexe, il consiste à réaliser des connexions entre des informations en flux continu. L'apprentissage est une co-création qui se réalise dans des communautés de pratiques. Il émerge des multiples interactions, dans les liens que la toile tisse en permanence. L'intelligence ne peut plus être uniquement représentée dans un cerveau individuel. Elle se développe aussi dans un réseautage collaboratif. De nouvelles formes d'apprentissage et de socialisation se développent selon une approche collaborative, de réciprocité, comme c'est le cas du mouvement *Do it yourself* ou *Do it together*.

Par ailleurs, Granovetter (1973) montre que chaque individu dispose de différents réseaux de liens sociaux. Le réseau intime, celui des amis sur les réseaux sociaux, est caractérisé par le temps passé ensemble à échanger, par l'intime fondé sur la confiance mutuelle et la réciprocité, comme l'avait défini Simmel. Ce réseau de l'intime constitue la forme première de sociabilité : ce sont les liens forts. Cependant, un deuxième type de réseau doit être pris en considération. Il est constitué de liens dits faibles. Ces liens forment un pont vers d'autres communautés, d'autres réseaux. Ils sont indispensables dans la mesure où ils permettent de faire circuler de nouvelles informations ; c'est le cas par exemple du réseau professionnel, du réseau autour de centres d'intérêts. Granovetter montre qu'un individu a plus de chances de trouver du travail s'il dispose de liens hors de son réseau intime, l'information étant alors plus diversifiée.

## 2.5 Premier bilan : quelles conséquences ?

Il est urgent de questionner la vision institutionnelle de la politique migratoire et d'intégration, mais aussi notre vision sociologique du migrant comme personne déracinée et inculte. Le migrant adulte aujourd'hui doit être reconnu dans cette nouvelle dimension communautaire qui caractérise tout individu à l'ère du numérique.

Nous pouvons avancer la définition suivante. Le migrant est un individu mobile qui se déplace d'un endroit à un autre, porteur d'un projet. Il est donc ici et ailleurs à la fois, dans un espace hybride, un *iciailleurs*. Les artéfacts numériques accompagnent cette mobilité qui n'est plus uniquement spatiale et géographique mais aussi virtuelle et imaginaire. Il n'y a plus une démarcation nette entre l'ici et l'ailleurs, comme on le pensait en opposant réel et virtuel, ou société d'accueil et société d'origine. Le migrant connecté continue à développer des liens forts avec sa communauté d'origine et noue aussi d'autres liens vers de nouvelles communautés. En tant qu'acteur social, il produit des objets culturels qui illustrent une co-construction symbolique hybride caractérisant la richesse de la migration. La formation des migrants repose aujourd'hui malheureusement sur une approche sociologique qu'il nous faut dépasser.

## 3 Présentation du contexte : Marseille

Le contexte de Marseille va nous permettre d'illustrer cette nouvelle sociologie transnationale. La ville est en effet représentative de l'histoire des migrations et des difficultés d'intégration. La communauté comorienne de Marseille s'inscrit bien dans l'évolution que nous venons de décrire. Les associations marseillaises réalisent un travail indispensable pour permettre et faciliter la solidarité. Malheureusement, les nouvelles orientations législatives pour les migrants, qui intègrent les propositions européennes pour l'intégration linguistique, ont pour conséquence de renforcer une vision caricaturale et dépassée de la migration. Elles ignorent ces gisements indispensables de cohésion sociale.

## 3.1 Sociologie de Marseille

Peraldi, Duport et Samson (2015) décrivent la complexité sociologique de Marseille. Marseille est à la fois le port de la Méditerranée synonyme de voyage, de commerce, de transit et la porte de la Méditerranée synonyme d'accueil, de communautés, de métissages culturels. Marseille a connu de nombreux flux migratoires, venus de l'Europe, en particulier les Italiens qui ont constitué une communauté importante dans le quartier du Panier (celui de la série télévisée *Plus belle la vie*). On se souvient aussi des Arméniens qui ont fui le génocide dans les années 1910/20. Ils furent plus de 70 000 à venir à Marseille par la mer. Les Maghrébins constituent une communauté très importante. Ils sont venus à différentes périodes et en particulier après la décolonisation. Faut-il rappeler les 500 000 rapatriés d'Algérie ? Les Africains sont également très présents, comme d'autres communautés.

Marseille a une image ambivalente avec d'un côté celle du melting pot, forte du multiculturalisme et du vivre ensemble, et de, l'autre côté, celle de violence, de délinquance proche du Chicago des années 1960. La ville est constituée de quartiers plus ou moins mélangés, avec une mobilité entre les quartiers nord, qui accueillent les migrants, et les quartiers sud où se trouvent les plages. Marseille Espérance fut créée en 1990 pour réunir toutes les communautés religieuses : communauté arménienne, communauté bouddhiste, communauté catholique, communauté juive, etc. Cet exemple d'approche communautariste permet de comprendre la spécificité marseillaise qui se distingue de l'approche républicaine et laïque d'autres villes françaises.

Marseille est riche aussi des cultures qui se créent au fil du temps dans ce laboratoire social qu'est la ville, dans ce tiers espace qui rend possible la création artistique. La poésie du rap et la musique ethnique permettent aux migrants sédentarisés de faire entendre leurs voix. L'art est une forme importante de la socialisation des jeunes et le rap marseillais est très vivant. Il est largement installé dans les quartiers nord et parle du mal être de la jeunesse et des désillusions de vivre dans une société qui promet l'égalité mais les stigmatise à cause de la couleur de leur peau et de leur religion. On comprend que la maitrise linguistique n'est pas porteuse d'intégration, que les diplômes de l'école ne procurent pas du travail. Il y a donc bien un échec du système d'intégration linguistique des migrants comme l'exprime Soprano, chanteur comorien de Marseille. Le migrant, basané et musulman, pourtant né en France, reste un immigré, un outsider, un looser, un exclu, un paria, un voyou. Les objets culturels, dont la mode ethnique, la cuisine, le sport, sont les emblèmes de la créativité de ces communautés. Ils constituent la diversité et la richesse du patrimoine culturel français.

## 3.2 Un exemple parmi d'autres : la communauté comorienne de Marseille

L'exemple de la communauté comorienne de Marseille (il y a plus de Comoriens à Marseille qu'à Moroni) illustre l'opposition entre une sociologie de l'immigration, qui développe la vision de l'immigré déraciné, propre au courant républicain universaliste dominant en France, et une sociologie de la mobilité et du transnationalisme. L'approche de la mobilité s'intéresse aux nouvelles formes collectives d'appartenance sociale, dont les intérêts, les valeurs et les comportements dépassent les frontières. Le migrant, en tant qu'acteur, est porteur d'un projet migratoire. Il est citoyen du monde et s'intéresse à la politique de son pays qui lui permet de voter et de participer au destin de son pays, alors même que le pays d'accueil lui refuse cette participation citoyenne. La communauté comorienne est très active sur internet. Des associations se retrouvent sur *Facebook* et dévoilent la vie sociale au quotidien dans toute sa banalité. On y trouve tous les ingrédients de l'*iciailleurs*. Et pourtant, les principales propositions de formation linguistique ignorent cette richesse. Elles ne prennent en compte que la seule vision de l'insertion vers le pays d'accueil. Elles ignorent la réalité sociale du migrant connecté. Pourquoi taire la créativité que l'on trouve dans les nombreux objets culturels de la migration ? Pourquoi refuser de voir cette intelligence collective, ces lieux d'apprentissage formels et informels ?

## 3.3 Quelques exemples du tissu associatif : l'association *Mot à Mot* et *Femmes d'ici et d'ailleurs*

La Friche de la Belle de Mai à Marseille est un concentré d'associations. L'association *Mot à Mot* s'est installée dans des locaux associatifs partagés. Elle vise la formation linguistique des migrants (90 % de femmes). Elle est dirigée par trois femmes permanentes, salariées (titulaires d'un master français langue étrangère). Les salaires proviennent de divers financements qui ne relèvent pas des fonds pour les migrants.

L'association s'inscrit dans les valeurs de l'éducation populaire qui reconnait à chacun la volonté et la capacité de progresser et de se développer. C'est une vision citoyenne et humaniste de la formation qui débouche sur une gestion participative de l'association.

Le circuit officiel pour les migrants ne couvre pas toute la demande de formation. *Mot à mot* s'adresse ainsi aux migrants qui échappent au circuit officiel, que ce soit pour l'alphabétisation ou le français langue étrangère. L'association propose aussi des ateliers passerelles pour aider les migrants à passer le permis de conduire (comprendre le code de la route), à accompagner les mères pour comprendre l'école et mieux suivre les enfants, pour développer les capacités artistiques, etc. Il n'est pas difficile de comprendre que ces associations, même réduites dans leurs ambitions et possibilités financières, jouent un rôle indispensable dans l'accueil et l'accompagnement des migrants. Elles sont mises en danger par la rationalisation de la commande et de l'offre institutionnelles pour les migrants.

L'association *Femmes d'ici et d'ailleurs*, créée en 1994, a pour objectif d'accompagner les femmes qui vivent en marge de la société. Il s'agit d'entraide entre femmes intégrées et femmes qui viennent d'arriver. Les locaux sont vastes et adaptés aux objectifs de l'association. L'association vise l'autofinancement. Elle fait partie d'un réseau d'associations locales et internationales qui sont tournées vers l'économie solidaire. La formation linguistique fait partie de la demande des personnes, en particulier l'alphabétisation. Cependant, ce n'est qu'un élément d'une approche fondée sur la définition d'un projet personnel avec une mise en valeur des compétences et de l'expertise de chaque personne. Pour cette association, il est indispensable de partir des savoir-faire de la personne et de voir comment ils peuvent être développés pour s'adapter à la réalité du marché. Il s'agit de faire émerger des projets personnels et de montrer qu'ils sont réalisables. La cuisine est importante. On apprend à calculer le coût d'un repas familial, à acheter et cuisiner des produits bio (en relation avec les paniers bio marseillais), à préparer des buffets pour plusieurs dizaines de personnes et à faire le service, à participer à la cuisine associative, etc. Cette formation peut déboucher sur des projets de créations d'entreprises de restauration, d'insertion professionnelle dans des structures existantes. Il en va de même pour la couture et la retouche. On met en valeur la confection d'origine puisqu'il y a des débouchés réels avec les différentes communautés ethniques (vêtement pour le mariage, les fêtes familiales, etc.). Il y a aussi des débouchés économiques dans les différents marchés (marché aux puces de Noailles, marché du Soleil).

On le voit, l'insertion sociale et professionnelle est au cœur de ce type d'association. L'apprentissage de la langue est important mais n'a de sens que par rapport à un projet de vie personnel ou collectif. On est dans la formation solidaire à la fois formelle mais aussi informelle. L'offre institutionnelle est bien trop normative, avec pour conséquence d'exclure ce type de pédagogie de l'accompagnement et de la solidarité.

## 3.4 Deuxième bilan : prendre en compte le migrant acteur social

Ces exemples montrent que le circuit officiel pour les migrants ne couvre pas l'ensemble des besoins réels de la migration. L'État impose de plus en plus de contrôles, que l'on nomme pudiquement « qualité », de plus en plus de rationalisation par le biais de l'audit, avec pour conséquence d'exclure un nombre significatif d'offres solidaires qui sont pourtant au plus près des réalités quotidiennes que vivent les migrants. On traite et gère l'urgence qui se réduit aux cours de langues. On oublie que chaque migrant est un acteur social porteur d'un projet, disposant d'un capital social consistant, vivant dans un milieu aux mille facettes.

## 4 Migrants et société numérique : revisiter la didactique des langues

Peut-on ignorer que les services publics sont aujourd'hui dématérialisés ? Peut-on ignorer que le code écrit n'est plus la seule modalité de communication ? N'est-il pas devenu incontournable d'envisager la littératie de manière plus large en l'englobant dans une littératie numérique multimodale ? Cette nouvelle réalité demande de revisiter les fondements de la didactique.

### 4.1 La sémiotique symbolique sociale

Nous avons vu, avec Simmel et l'école de Chicago, l'importance de l'interactionnisme symbolique. Chaque personne construit un univers de sens, un univers symbolique. Le dialogisme est inhérent à ce processus de co-construction symbolique, comme l'a montré Volochinov (1977) en parlant de compréhension responsive.

Le linguiste Halliday (1975) proposait lui aussi une approche sociale de la langue et mettait en avant le « meaning potential » (le potentiel de signification) situant le langage dans le cadre plus large d'une sémiotique sociale. Le système linguistique n'est qu'un mode, parmi d'autres, d'actualisation des significations. Kress et van Leewen (2001) ont poursuivi les réflexions de Halliday pour définir la multimodalité, qui constitue aujourd'hui une caractéristique essentielle des messages que l'on produit ou lit sur la toile. Le répertoire de ressources n'est pas seulement plurilingue, il est avant tout sémiotique. La communication n'est possible que si l'ensemble des personnes partagent et co-construisent les éléments de cette sémiotique sociale. La question du sens multimodal est ainsi centrale, en particulier pour la toile, et ne peut plus être réduite au seul mode graphique écrit. Nous utilisons sur internet, de manière intentionnelle, différents modes pour signifier. Lebrun, Lacelle & Boutin (2012) proposent de prendre en compte cette nouvelle « littératie médiatique multimodale » à l'école. La formation des migrants devrait également en tenir compte.

## 4.2 De la compétence numérique à la société numérique inclusive

L'exclusion sociale et l'illettrisme, dans ce monde interconnecté, ne relèvent plus uniquement de la capacité à lire, comprendre, écrire et compter. Les prochains illettrés auront certes des difficultés avec la littératie fonctionnelle mais risquent également d'être des illettrés numériques. Les instances nationales et internationales proposent depuis le début des années 2000 différentes définitions autour de la notion de littératie numérique. Nous sommes ainsi passés d'une approche purement technologique de la compétence numérique (utiliser l'ordinateur et internet) à une approche plus critique centrée sur le traitement de l'information et des médias (Unesco 2003/08). La compétence numérique est devenue une compétence clé (Parlement européen 2006) et a été reprise dans la plupart des référentiels. La Commission européenne (2007) s'intéresse à la question de la société numérique inclusive. Il ne suffit plus uniquement de compétence informatique de base mais de la capacité à résoudre des problèmes avec le numérique dans le cadre de la vie quotidienne et professionnelle. Les futurs citoyens, dont les migrants adultes, ont besoin d'une formation adaptée. Pour cela les enseignants doivent eux aussi devenir compétents en littératie numérique afin qu'ils ne deviennent à leur tour des illettrés du numérique. Prenski (2001 : 2) parlait de « digital immigrant teachers ».

Centeno (2011), lors d'un atelier sur la compétence numérique et l'inclusion sociale pour l'horizon 2020, montre l'importance d'une approche par projet et résolution de problème, c'est-à-dire une approche qui prendrait mieux en compte les situations sociales complexes. Il s'agit de s'engager dans le tournant social (Springer 2009) et de préparer l'avenir avec une approche de la globalité et de la complexité. Cette ouverture vers une société inclusive se retrouve dans différents référentiels professionnels. C'est le cas du référentiel de l'association nationale de lutte contre l'illettrisme, en France, qui a conçu en 2009 un référentiel des compétences clés en situation professionnelle. Il est intéressant de noter que ce référentiel souligne que l'employabilité, pour les personnes fragiles, ne peut plus se résumer au seul savoir parler, lire, écrire et compter. Il est aujourd'hui essentiel de prendre en compte non seulement la compétence en littératie numérique mais aussi la compétence sociale et l'apprendre à apprendre.

## 4.3 Revisiter la didactique des langues

Il est donc temps de revisiter la didactique des langues, ainsi que les courants de l'apprentissage, pour tenir compte de la nouvelle donne numérique. En didactique des langues, malgré l'insistance sur la plurilittératie, la littératie fonctionnelle demeure majoritairement prise en compte par les manuels et les certifications (lire, comprendre et produire un texte simple dans une langue). On vise le socle de base du code écrit, comme c'est le cas pour l'alphabétisation et les niveaux élémentaires en français langue étrangère. Une nouvelle évolution est devenue nécessaire. La littératie numérique multimodale devrait, pour les raisons évoquées, être prise en compte. Elle ne se rajoute pas à la plurilittératie mais l'englobe dans la mesure où elle permet de prendre en compte les différents modes et modalités des littératies.

D'un point de vue pédagogique, une approche projet autour de tâches sociales complexes (Springer 2010) permet de situer les apprentissages dans la complexité et le symbolisme social. L'apprentissage pourrait se faire à partir de scénarios ouverts permettant la résolution de problèmes concrets (Huver et Springer 2011). Il s'agit de ne pas rester aux niveaux taxonomiques élémentaires de reproduction et de renverser en quelque sorte la taxonomie de Bloom pour donner toute son importance à l'action sociale (figure 1).

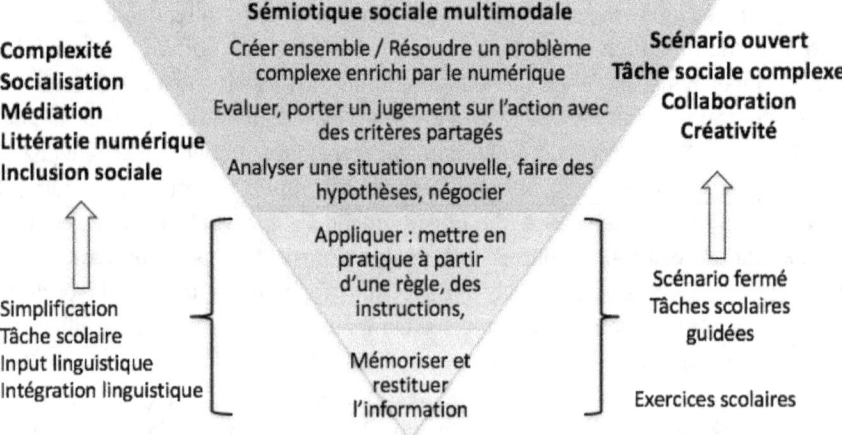

**Figure 1 :** Une approche alternative de la formation

Cette visée phénoménologique de la formation prend la globalité humaine en compte : les aspects utilitaristes du quotidien (la polarité prosaïque) mais aussi les aspects symbolique, imaginaire et poétique (la polarité poétique). L'évaluation pourrait alors rendre compte du processus expérientiel. C'est une évaluation qui rend justice aux valeurs et aux principes humanistes de l'apprentissage. Kress parle de « principles of learning » (2010 : 183) pour ce type d'évaluation de l'expérience. Il s'agit bien de rendre compte de la capacité à signifier dans différents modes et modalités. On le comprend, plurilittératie et interculturel (ce que l'OCDE nomme aujourd'hui compétence globale) sont intégrés dans cette approche du symbolisme social. Le schéma suivant (Figure 2) montre le passage d'une évaluation qui vise la conformité aux standards de la certification à une évaluation socialement partagée qui tient compte de la complexité sociale. Il s'agit dans ce cas de permettre aux participants de cartographier les compétences mises en œuvre dans les différents projets et de référentialiser de cette manière des compétences qui dépassent les compétences linguistiques du CECR.

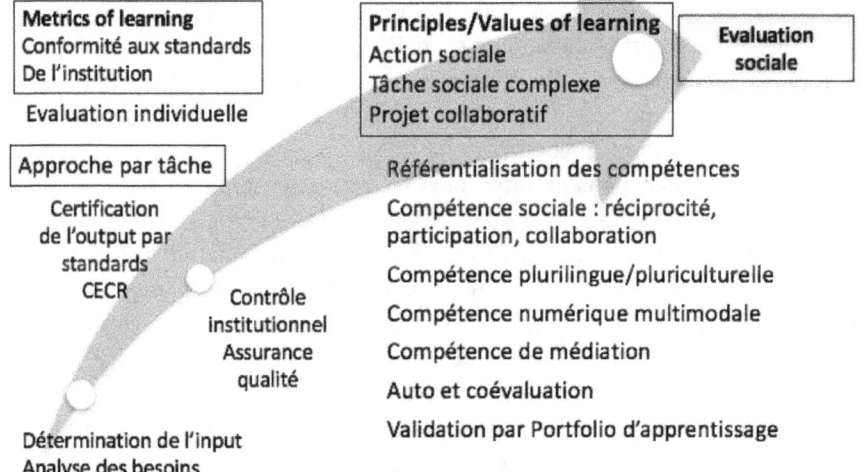

**Figure 2 :** D'une évaluation visant la conformité aux standards de la certification à une évaluation socialement partagée

En ce qui concerne la validation institutionnelle, il serait tout à fait possible d'imaginer des portfolios d'apprentissage et de validation des compétences présentant les réalisations concrètes des migrants, leurs projets, tout au long d'une période, comme c'est le cas dans la procédure de validation des acquis d'expérience. Ce type d'évaluation s'intéresse à la valorisation des identités sociales en développement, à l'engagement sémiotique dans le cadre d'expériences socialement partagées, à la création d'objets culturels et de ressources multimodales.

Si nous souhaitons rendre autonomes les migrants adultes, si nous souhaitons les accompagner dans la réalisation de leur projet personnel et social, il est alors nécessaire de favoriser créativité et estime de soi (Springer 2014). Il n'est pas raisonnable d'enfermer le migrant adulte dans une pédagogie de l'urgence qui se limite aux situations et tâches de la vie quotidienne supposées définir le minimum vital pour s'intégrer dans la société d'accueil.

## Conclusion

Et maintenant ? Il semble que le statu quo de type formation en urgence pour le court terme s'impose et soit même renforcé partout en Europe. C'est le schéma institutionnel que nous connaissons aujourd'hui. Beaucoup de réflexions se sont focalisées sur cette offre d'urgence dans le cadre de l'ILMA. Le développement de l'e-learning, avec des plateformes institutionnelles ou commerciales, pour la formation linguistique des migrants est déjà une réalité dans plusieurs pays en Europe. Malheureusement, l'e-learning s'inscrit dans l'optique prosaïque de la survie et de l'urgence. Le risque réel est d'aboutir à une consommation de ressources linguistiques prédéfinies et à une homogénéisation de la formation avec une évaluation pour mesurer, plus facilement encore, la conformité aux standards visés (le « metrics of learning » de Kress, op. cit.).

Peut-on passer du migrant connecté à l'apprenant migrant connecté ? Il faudrait pour cela dépasser le court terme et s'engager dans le moyen et long terme. Proposer des formations d'accompagnement à moyen et long terme pourrait permettre le développement de projets pour une insertion/inclusion sociale. Le curriculum, dans ce cas, ne peut être qu'un curriculum situé et non pas prescrit. Il est défini par les acteurs eux-mêmes, au fur et à mesure des développements. Les besoins qui émergent des projets ne sont pas que langagiers et n'ont pas à être dictés technocratiquement par une ingénierie externalisée. L'évaluation sociale et collaborative pourrait alors s'inscrire dans une valorisation des expériences et des compétences multiples, selon les principes et les valeurs de l'apprentissage. La certification externe n'a pas de sens dans ce contexte.

La formation des différents formateurs est un réel souci. Le référentiel de l'Unesco (2011) propose des pistes intéressantes pour la formation des enseignants afin d'intégrer le numérique et l'approche projet. Cependant, ces évolutions ne seront possibles que si les décideurs sont sensibilisés à ces problèmes et convaincus de l'intérêt de faire évoluer la vision de la formation des migrants ainsi que les pratiques formatives. Il est urgent de donner une plus grande marge de manœuvre aux acteurs de terrain et aux apprenants migrants pour que se réalise le souhait d'une société apprenante et inclusive qui figure pourtant dans tous les textes politiques.

## Références

Arp, Jean Hans. 2014. *La Grande Fête sans fin*. Editions Arfuyen.
Agence nationale de lutte contre l'illettrisme. 2009. *Référentiel des compétences clés en situation professionnelle (RCCSP)*. http://www.anlci.gouv.fr/Mediatheque/Entreprises/Entreprise/Referentiel-des-competences-cles-en-situation-professionnelle-RCCSP (consulté le 10 février 2016).
Bashi, Vilna Francine. 2007. *Survival of the knitted. Immigrant social networks in a stratified world*. Stanford : Stanford University Press.
Centeno, Clara. 2011. *Digital competencies and inclusion*. JRC European Commission. http://is.jrc.ec.europa.eu/pages/documents/2011_05_23_DigitalCompetenceeInclusion_v4.pdf (consulté le 12 février 2016).
Commission européenne. 2007. *Initiative européenne i2010 sur l'insertion numérique*. http://eur-lex.europa.eu/legal-content/FR/TXT/HTML/?uri=CELEX:52007DC0146&from=FR (consulté le 20 janvier 2016).
Diminescu, Dana. 2005. Le migrant connecté : pour un manifeste épistémologique. *Migrations société* 102. 275–292.
Granovetter, Mark. 1973. The Strength of Weak Ties. *American Journal of Sociology*. 78(6), 1360–1380. https://sociology.stanford.edu/sites/default/files/publications/the_strength_of_weak_ties_and_exch_w-gans.pdf (consulté le 15 janvier 2016).
Halliday, Michael Alexander. 1975. *Learning how to mean: explorations in the development of language*. London : Edward Arnold.
Huck, Dominique. 1989. *André Weckmann, écrivain de son temps*. Strasbourg : Centre régional de documentation pédagogique.
Huver, Emmanuelle & Claude Springer. 2011. *L'évaluation en langues*. Paris : Didier.
Kress, Gunther. 2010. *Multimodality: A Social Semiotic Approach to Contemporary Communication*. New York : Routledge.
Kress, Gunther & Theo van Leeuwen. 2001. *Multimodal Discourse: The Modes and Media of Contemporary Communication*. Oxford : Oxford University Press.
Lebrun, Monique, Nathalie Lacelle & Jean-François Boutin. 2012. *La littératie médiatique multimodale. De nouvelles approches en lecture-écrire à l'école et hors de l'école*. Québec : Presses de l'Université du Québec.
Maalouf, Amin. 1998. *Les identités meurtrières*. Le Livre de Poche.
Morin, Edgar. 2015. *Penser global. L'humain et son univers*. Paris : Robert Laffont.
Parlement Européen. 2006. Journal officiel de l'Union européenne. 2006. http://eur-lex.europa.eu/LexUriServ/LexUriServ.do?uri=OJ:L:2006:394:0010:0018:fr:PDF (consulté le 20 janvier 2016).

Peraldi, Michel, Claire Duport & Michel Samson. 2015. *Sociologie de Marseille*. Paris : La Découverte.

Prensky, Marc. 2001. Digital natives, digital immigrants. *On the horizon* 9.5, 1–6.

Raphaël, Freddy. 2008. Le juif comme paradigme de l'étranger dans l'œuvre de G. Simmel. *Sociétés* 3 (n° 101). 81–90. https://www.cairn.info/revue-societes-2008-3-page-81.htm (consulté le 25 mai 2016).

Simmel, Georg. 1979 [1908]. Digressions sur l'étranger. In Yves Grafmeyer & Joseph Isaac (eds.), *L'École de Chicago, naissance de l'écologie urbaine*, 53–77. Paris : Ed. Du Champ urbain.

Siemens, George. 2004. Connectivism: A learning theory for the digital age. *International Journal of Instructional Technology and Distance Learning*. http://www.itdl.org/Journal/Jan_05/article01.htm (consulté en octobre 2015).

Springer, Claude. 2009. La dimension sociale dans le CECR : pistes pour scénariser, évaluer et valoriser l'apprentissage collaboratif. In Evelyne Rosen. *La perspective actionnelle et l'approche par les tâches en classe de langue*. Le français dans le monde. Recherches et applications, n°45. 25–34.

Springer, Claude. 2010. Les projets collaboratifs (TIC) : quelles compétences pour quelle évaluation ? In *Actes du Congrès International : Communiquer avec les langues cultures*. Thessalonique : University Studio Press, 516–528.

Springer, Claude. 2014. *La question de l'évaluation en formation des enseignants de langues : de l'évaluation de la performance à l'évaluation de la collaboration créative*. Actes du colloque Créativité et apprentissage : un tandem à réinventer ? https://hal.archives-ouvertes.fr/hal-01300903/document (consulté le 20 février 2016).

Unesco. 2003. *Déclaration de Prague : Vers une société compétente dans l'usage de l'information*. http://www.enssib.fr/bibliotheque-numerique/documents/1900-declaration-de-prague-vers-une-societe-competente-dans-l-usage-de-l-information.pdf (consulté le 20 janvier 2016).

Unesco. 2008. *Programme Information pour tous (PIPT). Vers des indicateurs de la maîtrise de l'information*. http://www.uis.unesco.org/Library/Documents/wp08_infolit-fre.pdf (consulté le 20 janvier 2016).

Unesco. 2011. *Un référentiel de compétence pour les enseignants*. http://unesdoc.unesco.org/images/0021/002169/216910f.pdf (consulté en avril 2014).

Vigée, Claude. 2000. *Les Orties Noires. Schwarzi Sengessle*. Un requiem alsacien. Oberlin.

Volochinov, Valentin Nikolevitch. 1977. *Le marxisme et la philosophie du langage*. Paris : Éditions de Minuit.

Rosemarie Tracy
# Language testing in the context of migration

**Abstract:** Over the last decades, the development of instruments measuring linguistic abilities has become increasingly important. The tests developed on the basis of the *Common European Framework of Reference for Languages* (CEFR) are a good case in point. Originally backed by and promoting a positive European vision of multilingual, mobile citizens, and celebrating the linguistic and cultural diversity of Europe as unifying factors, more recently the CEFR has faced concerns that it is being turned into an immigration-control instrument, a role it was not intended for. This metamorphosis forms the backcloth and starting point of a more general discussion of the complexity of language testing, and areas in which the CEFR should be optimized are identified.

**Résumé :** Au cours des dernières décennies, l'élaboration d'instruments de mesure des compétences en langues a pris de plus en plus d'ampleur. Les tests calibrés par rapport au *Cadre européen commun de référence pour les langues* (CECR) illustrent bien cette tendance. A l'origine, ce dernier a été conçu comme un instrument qui repose sur une vision européenne positive promouvant la mobilité et le plurilinguisme des citoyens et valorisant la diversité linguistique et culturelle de l'Europe en tant que trait d'union entre les peuples. Cependant, plus récemment, certains acteurs se sont déclarés préoccupés par le fait que l'on est en train de faire du Cadre un instrument de contrôle de l'immigration, ce à quoi il n'a pas vocation. Cette question est l'occasion d'engager une discussion plus générale sur la complexité de l'évaluation des compétences en langues ; elle permettra également de définir des domaines dans lesquels le CECR devrait être amélioré.

## 1 Introduction

Regardless of the domain under investigation, developing and applying diagnostic tools and interpreting their results raises questions beyond validity, objectivity, reliability, and fairness concerning culture, age and gender. In view of the impact for the individuals assessed, be it with respect to medical, psychological or

**Rosemarie Tracy,** University of Mannheim, Germany, E-mail: rtracy@mail.uni-mannheim.de

pedagogical interventions, the burden of responsibility is considerable. While consequences may not be immediately life-threatening when it comes to language, they can easily lead to exclusion from social or therapeutic services, from educational opportunities, from the job market, and from citizenship. As for the *Common European Framework of Reference for Languages* (CEFR; Council of Europe 2001), awareness of its potential impact has been stressed for a long time, for example: "The ways in which the CEFR is used have implications for social cohesion, access to employment, citizenship, mobility and mutual understanding in Europe" (Goullier 2007: 18). While Coste about ten years ago welcomed this "wind of assessment" as "a good wind and a healthy one" (2007: 41), nowadays researchers and practitioners are increasingly concerned about unintended impacts (cf. Van Avermaet 2016), i.e. the "dual use" potential of testing, namely the (mis)use of research originally designed for different purposes.[1] Rather than report on research, as the overall title of this volume suggests, I wish to add to the growing concern that the CEFR, after all an influential benchmark of language proficiency, could be turned into a "migration management mechanism to limit the number of migrants" (Strik 2013: 3), and "hindering integration and leading to exclusion" (ibid.: 1; also ALTE 2016; McNamara 2011).

In what follows, I will first (section 2) underscore the non-triviality of investigating and measuring linguistic competence and identify some reasons for this. Section 3 turns to selected issues relating to the CEFR, such as the problematic status of descriptors and level distinctions. On the basis of examples taken from the German test for immigrants I will ask (somewhat provocatively) what we want immigrants to think communicating in their new language and "being integrated" is all about. Finally (section 4), I briefly suggest that it is time to reconcile the CEFR with current adult second-language research and to embrace linguistic theories which can provide a cross-linguistically useful *tertium comparationis* beyond the functional approach prevalent so far.

## 2 Linguistic competence: invisible, (largely) inaudible, and highly complex

While testing may be "a universal feature of social life" (McNamara 2000: 3), measurement of linguistic abilities is a particularly tough case in point. But testing by means of a standardized, reliable and objective procedure is only one way of going about assessing proficiency. Diagnostic tools include more or less con-

---

[1] See http://www.dfg.de/pm/2016_13a.

strained observation guidelines and questionnaires (to be filled out by parents, teachers or even learners themselves), corpus studies based on written texts and spontaneous speech, screenings and elicitation techniques targeting specific structures in production and/or comprehension tasks. Due to the complexity of linguistic knowledge systems and behavior, to heterogeneous learning scenarios and to inter- and intra-rater variability, none of these approaches are without problems. Nevertheless, despite theoretical and methodological complications, language assessment is important. Within educational settings, such as foreign language teaching, we want to determine whether specific criteria or standards can be met by learners or, put differently, how good we were at teaching. It is also important to find out whether someone trained as a nurse or mechanic in one language context, is capable of acting professionally in another. Knowing that Specific Language Impairment (SLI) is one of the most frequent developmental pathologies, affecting 6–8% of all children, we certainly wish to identify those at risk as early as possible. Also, faced with young immigrant second-language learners, educators increasingly recognize their need for diagnostic instruments yielding insight into the current state of a learner's system, and those financing intervention programs call for evaluation procedures informing them about the effectiveness of language-fostering programs. Beyond learning contexts, we also want to be able to differentiate between stroke patients afflicted by different kinds of aphasia in order to offer appropriate interventions.

Since learners of different ages and exposure differ in acquisition strategies and outcome, we need to distinguish at least first language learners (L1), simultaneous first language learners (2 L1/3 L1), successive child L2 and L3 learners – ignoring additional languages – , and older L2/L3 etc. learners (pre- and post-puberty). To complicate matters, in immigrant contexts we also encounter so-called *heritage* speakers, i.e. second-generation immigrants (and later generations) who are exposed to their parents' attriting or quantitatively reduced L1 resources and who therefore acquire their home language to varying degrees (Polinsky and Kagan 2007). At the same time, they may be highly proficient L2 speakers of their environment's majority language.

From a research point of view, in order to better understand similarities and differences across learner types, we would require some idea of the quality and the quantity of the input available to them, as well as information concerning age of onset and length of exposure. This means that we cannot follow the principle "one size fits all", and we certainly should not simply compare second-language learners with norms obtained from L1 learners or, even worse, with some idealized notion of what native speakers can do, without actually conducting controlled research. Note, too, that any acquisition type may be coupled with specific language impairment (SLI). In the case of young L2 learners the identification of children at risk for SLI is complicated by the fact that typically developing L2 learners may initially go through phases very similar to children with SLI. It comes as no surprise, then, that pediatricians and therapists experience problems differentiating typical and atypical L2 learners and struggle with misclassifications, i.e. under- and overdiagnosis (cf. Grimm and Schulz 2014). This mirrors concerns about the reliability of rater judgment which have been voiced by experts in adult language testing (cf. McNamara 2000; Wisniewski 2010).

When it comes to choice of adequate diagnostic instruments, conflicts of interest on the part of different stakeholders are unavoidable. Policy makers want the procedure and the training of personnel to be inexpensive; pediatricians, teachers and whoever else is directly involved in assessing large numbers of participants want the process to be fast and the interpretation straightforward. At the same time, at least therapists and teachers require more than *diagnostics lite* if they want to support and trigger the next step in the acquisition process.

Some problems faced by all approaches are due to the very complexity of natural languages. "Language", after all, is only a shorthand expression for many different knowledge systems, also called "levels of representation", such as the lexicon, phonological, morphosyntactic, semantic, pragmatic and, in the literate, orthographic levels. Crucially, none of these predominantly implicit knowledge systems are directly accessible. Unlike someone's ability to swim or to drive a car, what we say, write or how we react to what others say and write, is only an indirect and often poor reflection of what we know, i.e. of what we have internally represented. But while observation in a literal sense is never an option – with some exceptions concerning phonetic and prosodic properties –, the analysis and reconstruction of successive learner systems on the basis of substantial corpora is feasible. Given longitudinal data it is possible to reconstruct individual learner profiles, to identify intra- and inter-individual developmental patterns and to draw inferences concerning abstract levels of representation. Especially in the case of unknown languages or under-researched learner types and acquisition paths, this established fieldwork methodology is an indispensable first step. But since the collection of spontaneous speech, with subsequent transcription and annotation is theoretically and analytically highly demanding and time-consuming, it does not offer itself for cross-sectional attempts at judging the linguistic proficiency of large numbers of speakers. Another serious drawback of naturalistic data collection in unconstrained conversational settings is that structures we would like to catch may never be produced. Just waiting for passives, relative clauses, or long-distance wh-questions or other patterns to "happen" would be a highly inefficient approach. So if we want to find out whether specific structures are within the reach of individual learners or learner types, we have to create conditions favoring their production and/or elicit relevant comprehension responses. Again, this is no trivial enterprise (for excellent overviews see the collection of articles in Li Wei and Moyer 2008; McDaniel, McKee and Cairns 1998; Menn and Ratner 2000). Choosing to speak and choice of speech act or repertoire are voluntary activities, and a learner's ability is easily underestimated whenever he or she remains silent. On the other hand, we may also overestimate someone's competence because he or she happens to behave appropriately. Faced with utterances they cannot process, learners may mimic someone else's example, from putting on their shoes to laughing at jokes they did not really "get". At a pragmatic level, this mimicry is a clever strategy, demonstrating cooperativity and politeness. In order to elicit very specific verbal or non-verbal reactions as dependent variables, we have to design clever experiments, and what may start as a small-scale experiment may eventually turn into a standardized, norm-referenced, validated and psychometrically supported test. Hence, as pointed out by Grimm (1994: 17; my translation), "testing is a lot simpler than observing".

## 3 The CEFR: "an instrument of reference, not an object of reverence" (Coste 2007: 46)

The CEFR, launched in 2001, has been very successful both with respect to its educational impact and as a standard and common "currency" (cf. McNamara 2011) against which other assessment instruments can be calibrated and hence validated. The vision that gave rise to it welcomed and embraced Europe's linguistic and cultural diversity as an asset and encouraged mobility and multilingualism in an additive sense, i.e. without a threat to a speaker's first language(s). In order for the CEFR to fulfill its function as a generalized frame of reference, a "descriptive metasystem" (North 2007: 29), it (largely) abstracts away from language-specific grammars and focuses on tasks that are functionally and pragmatically equivalent across languages. In the attempt to guarantee comparability and transparency, an impressive technical and statistical machinery has been created (ALTE 2011, 2016).

Despite the remarkable career of the CEFR, there is room for improvement. Many "can do" statements contain among their descriptors quantifying ("large", "small", "short", "limited", etc.) or qualifying expressions ("relatively simple", "elementary", "complex"). Descriptors refer to vocabulary or other features the test-taker appears to be "more" or "less familiar" with, is "more" or "less likely to encounter", or to terms and tasks which are "more or less related to everyday experience". There is also reference to what interlocutors can "easily" or "partially" understand. As has been pointed out by many, the theoretical and empirical basis for these to some extent intentionally vague classifications is missing (cf. Hulstijn 2007; Quetz 2010; Vogt 2011). Similarly, because there is no appeal to psycholinguistic theories of text comprehension (cf. Quetz 2010: 188– 189), it is difficult, if not impossible, to appreciate what makes texts assigned to particular proficiency levels more or less complex than others. According to some critics, the current practice of text choice and assignment to specific levels is "completely erratic" (cf. Quetz 2010: 197).

To be sure, other diagnostic instruments on the market struggle with similar shortcomings. A prominent diagnostic questionnaire aiming at the verbal behavior of bilingual children acquiring German as a second language (SISMIK; Ulich and Mayr 2003) expects raters to decide whether specific constituents, for instance articles in noun phrases, are (a) "left out most of the time", (b) "mostly deviant", (c) "sometimes deviant", (d) "mostly correct" in children's spontaneous speech (ibid.: 8; my translation). Faced with these options, the rater finds her-/himself in a dilemma. If articles are *sometimes* deviant, they could also be *mostly* correct. Crucially, we would have to know how many obligatory contexts (i.e. noun phrases requiring an article) were produced altogether, i.e. how many opportunities to produce articles learners missed or used.

The CEFR's A–B–C levels and their subdivisions suggest a progressive scale of complexity among different, consecutive states of proficiency. "The CEFR is a concertina-like reference tool that provides categories, levels and descriptors that educational professionals can merge or sub-divide, elaborate or summarise, adopt or adapt according to the needs of their context – whilst still relating to the common hierarchical structure" (North 2007: 22). However, at times, descriptors and evaluation criteria are not formulated in a manner consistent with some developmental logic, as can be seen in the following examples from the German test for immigrants (*Deutsch-Test für Zuwanderer*; Perlmann-Balme, Plassmann and Zeidler 2009: 65; my translation). At level B1 learners can "reply spontaneously and relatively comprehensively" to follow-up questions (cf. the 2nd column of line 1b), while at A2 (column 3) they "reply briefly" (the original German "knapp" is a bit more negative; with a pragmatic focus it can also mean "curtly") and/or only "partially understandably". While it seems intuitively possible to contrast *briefly* with *relatively comprehensively*, this does not mean that the former, reduced response, is communicatively inadequate. The other A2 criterion, "partially understandably", is not matched with an explicit, more positive evaluation at B1 (for instance: "is easily understandable"/"can be understood easily", etc.). Note, too, that it is unclear what could be *spontaneous* – presumably intended as a positive indicator for level B1 – about an answer to a (follow-up) question. For A2, no more rudimentary alternative or precursor, such as "can respond after pausing/hesitating ..." is mentioned. Also, for A1 in the category "Speaking" (p.65; cf. line 2a, column 4), candidates "can allude to the main contents of a photo in very few words", for A2 (column 3), they can "label a photo's main contents briefly and very generally". This also raises the question of how to objectively tell "alluding in very few words" from "labeling something briefly and very generally". For B1 (column 2), test-takers "can mention main contents but also details". While the reason for these differences may be lack of vocabulary, we might also be dealing with poor test-taking strategies or lack of understanding of the task. The latter two, at least, could be remedied by encouraging test-takers to mention all objects they can make out/recognize in the pictures they are shown.

The authors of the German test explicitly concede that for some areas tasks are not linked via a theoretically motivated rating scale: "Since migrants have to be able to perform relatively complex activities early on, some complex achievements have been assigned to the lowest level, A1, at which these activities have to be implemented" (Perlmann-Balme et al. 2009: 27; my approximate translation). Hence the decision in favor of particular tasks is motivated by language-external criteria, not by any developmental (functional or pragmatic) progression or logic.

Even though the main focus of the CEFR is not on grammatical form and correctness, selected aspects are taken into account and are included among the descriptors. Reference to grammar crops up, for instance, when descriptors contain comments such as "generally good command over grammatical structures despite clearly noticeable L1 influence" (Perlmann-Balme et al. 2009: 65; my translation). What makes this statement interesting is the expectation that raters know enough about test takers' L1 to arrive at such a conclusion. In some cases, for instance where the rater knows that a specific L1 has no articles or no subject-verb agreement, transfer (i.e. zero articles, no overt agreement) seems reasonable. But in order to make such a statement raters need more than information about the first languages of test-takers. In addition, they need to be aware of the transitional curriculum of L2 learners, regardless of their L1. Again, from a linguistic point of view, these are complex issues, and raters should not be tempted to draw conclusions they simply cannot reach with any degree of confidence.

Since testing is all about comparisons (whether against a fixed criterion or a norm reference), interesting "dual perspective" problems are to some extent pre-programmed, with the rater's own attitude playing a crucial role. To take an example from child L2 acquisition: testers/raters may focus on the fact that a four-year-old girl with Russian or Turkish as L1 and German as an early L2 (first exposure at age 3), does not yet produce the range of word order patterns found in monolingual German speakers of the same age. But how reasonable is it to even expect her to come within the range of monolinguals, given her limited exposure to German? Once examiners take into account that, despite a shorter and less intense exposure time (one year vs. four years), this child actually performs astonishingly well in comparison to her reference group, namely other children first exposed to German at the age of 3, they should be able to focus more easily on what has already been achieved, very much in the spirit of the "can do" statements of the CEFR.

Finally, let us for one moment adopt a test-taker perspective. While the areas focused on throughout the immigrant test for German are based on extensive need analyses (Perlmann-Balme et al. 2009:7) and certainly make good topics for classroom discussions outside the test situation, the test items proposed for these domains yield a depressing impression of what kind of interaction we would most likely encounter and what scary challenges we might have to cope with early on. Quite a number of items could lead us to conclude that there is considerable need for immigrants to protest, in writing, against unjustified accusations (for instance after being issued a traffic ticket; p.35), or to withdraw from a previously signed contract (p.36). We are also supposed to demonstrate our ability to request (for our children) leave of absence from school due to illness or other family catastrophe, and to apologize to teachers for having missed our language classes. There is, in short, a considerable list of either some (imagined) wrongdoing experienced or some (imagined) *faux-pas* already committed by us or imminent. Even though it is recommended that cultural clichés and stereotypes be avoided (p.27), several tasks call for comments on potential stereotypes, cf. the four instances mentioning being on time (punctuality/*Pünktlichkeit*, p. 37). Also, linguists – to step out of the test-taker role – will hardly fail to be impressed by the fact that learners are expected to comment on similarities and differences between their first language and the current target language, as well as on the usefulness of previously learned languages for the acquisition of new languages. It would seem, then, that many test demands faced by immigrant test takers are challenging enough for native speakers and even researchers, let alone for the lay person and the novice language learner.

## 4 CEFR futures: catching up with theory

As pointed out by McNamara, "a language test is only as good as the theory of language upon which it is based" (2000: 86). This means that tests emerging on the basis of the CEFR may be in trouble since there is no explicit linguistic theory or theoretically motivated descriptive framework backing them. This does not just hold for grammatical form but also for functional, pragmatic aspects, and for theories of second/foreign language learning. North (2007: 27) cites 20-year-old L2 research, concluding that there is no evidence for learning orders and that linguistic theories fail to provide an uncontroversial theoretical framework for cross-linguistic comparison in the domain of grammar. Given that the search for invariant formal and functional principles and attempts at explaining cross-linguistic variation has been at the core of linguistic research for decades and within many differing theoretical approaches (e.g. Chomsky 1986; Goldberg 2006; Haegeman 1991, to mention only a few), North's conclusion appears to be unnecessarily pessimistic. While "uncontroversial" conclusions may be as unrealistic for language as for other diagnostic areas, the identification of relevant typological, formal and functional properties is possible, and could serve as a *tertium comparationis* needed for cross-linguistic comparisons.

Likewise, intensive research with respect to the acquisition types mentioned above has brought about a wealth of evidence concerning cross-linguistically comparable developmental paths and inter-individual differences. Some of the most interesting comparative data and insights were obtained in L2 research on immigrants in projects funded by the European Science Foundation in the last decades of the past century (cf. Klein and Perdue 1997; Watorek, Benazzo and Hickmann 2012). Independently of individual languages, there is strong evidence of very similar structure-building processes and correlations between the emergence of the syntactic architecture and functional categories (such as case, agreement, tense, negation; cf. Dimroth and Jordens 2009; Doughty and Long 2003; Hawkins 2001; Vainikka and Young-Scholten 2011; Watorek, Benazzo and Hickmann 2012, again to mention only a few). Regardless of theoretical persuasion, the corpora obtained within these projects and beyond, the methodological and experimental expertise, and the insight gained into learner types and developmental paths in many languages can certainly give additional impetus to attempts to place future tests based on the CEFR on a stronger theoretical and empirical footing.

# 5 Conclusion: chickens, eggs, and verbivores

Over the last decades, language testing, "not a topic likely to quicken the pulse or excite much immediate interest" (McNamara 2000: 3), has turned into an area of considerable relevance across all levels of the education system and across learner types and has led to intensive discussions among researchers, test designers, people in charge of language policies and allotment of resources, language teachers, therapists, and, in the case of children, parents and pediatricians. While different stakeholders are not very likely to agree as to the best diagnostic instrument to use, they may be willing to concede that we should make sure that there is something to test in the first place and that it is of foremost importance to invest in the quality and quantity of the learning experience available to learners of all ages.

After all, humans are excellent language learners, and, as very pointedly formulated by Pinker, we are "verbivores, a species that lives on words" (2007: 24). As the coinage "verbivore" – a blend of "verb(al)" and "herbivore" – highlights, we get a lot of enjoyment out of the non-utilitarian functioning of our linguistic abilities. I would like to encourage those interested in optimizing language tests and especially in language teaching to make sure we do not lose sight of this resourcefulness, which comes for free – an effortless, untaught side-effect of linguistic competence. This playful function appears to be missing from current assumptions of what the immigrant "needs".

Language plays an important and ubiquitous role in identity construction, for the negotiation of common ground, for political participation and integration. While our measurements of linguistic proficiency may correlate with a number of personal traits, such as motivation, a talent for role-play, risk taking, musicality and many others, linguistic competence cannot indicate who will, in the end, be a loyal citizen, observe traffic laws and pay taxes. This means that linguists and other professionals need to draw the line and withstand increasing political pressures and demands. As pointed out by Van Avermaet (2016: 6), "These language tests often decide whether you can enter a country; stay in a country; get a permanent residency, or citizenship. They decide whether you are in or out. [...] Within this highly ideologized and politicized context, [...] language testers must reflect carefully not just on the reliability, but more than ever on the validity of their instruments."

In a way, we are faced with a chicken-and-egg problem, namely with the question of which comes first: language proficiency or integration. It is time to articulate more clearly that integration into a community of speakers who are interested in what language learners think and feel, is a most powerful incentive for language acquisition and for realizing our *verbivore* potential by exploiting the linguistic and communicative resourcefulness of learners and their interlocutors alike.

# References

ALTE (Association of Language Testers in Europe). 2011. *Manual for language test development and examining.* Strasbourg: Council of Europe. http://www.coe.int/t/dg4/linguistic/ManualLanguageTest-Alte2011_EN.pdf (accessed 17 August 2016).

ALTE. 2016. *Language tests for access, integration and citizenship: An outline for policymakers.* http://www.alte.org/attachments/files/alte_lami_language_test_policy_booklet_web_en_0 m4wh.pdf (accessed 9 August 2016).

Chomsky, Noam. 1986. *Knowledge of language: Its nature, origin, and use.* New York: Praeger.

Coste, Daniel. 2007. Contextualising uses of the Common European Framework of Reference for Languages. In F. Goullier, *The Common European Framework of Reference for Languages (CEFR) and the development of language policies: Challenges and responsibilities*, 40–49. Strasbourg: Council of Europe. http://www.coe.int/t/dg4/linguistic/Forum07_webdocs_EN.asp#TopOfPage (accessed 18 August 2016).

Dimroth, Christine & Peter Jordens (eds.). 2009. *Functional categories in learner language.* Berlin: de Gruyter.

Doughty, Catherine J. & Michael H. Long (eds.). 2003. *The handbook of second language acquisition.* Malden, MA: Blackwell.

Goldberg, Adele E. 2006. *Constructions at work: The nature of generalization in language.* Oxford: Oxford University Press.

Goullier, Francis. 2007. *The Common European Framework of Reference for Languages (CEFR) and the development of language policies: Challenges and responsibilities.* Strasbourg: Council of Europe. http://www.coe.int/t/dg4/linguistic/Forum07_webdocs_EN.asp#TopOfPage (accessed 18 August 2016).

Grimm, Angela & Petra Schulz. 2014. Specific language impairment and early second language acquisition: The risk of over- and underdiagnosis. *Child Indicators Research* 7 (4). 821–841.

Grimm, Hannelore. 1994. Sprachentwicklungsstörung: Diagnose und Konsequenzen für die Therapie. In Hannelore Grimm & Sabine Weinert (eds.), *Intervention bei sprachgestörten Kindern: Voraussetzungen, Möglichkeiten und Grenzen*, 3–32. Stuttgart: Fischer.

Haegeman, Liliane. 1991. *Introduction to Government & Binding Theory.* Oxford: Blackwell.

Hawkins, Roger. 2001. *Second language syntax.* Oxford: Blackwell.

Hulstijn, Jan H. 2007. The shaky ground beneath the CEFR: Quantitative and qualitative dimensions of language proficiency. *The Modern Language Journal* 91(4). 663–667.

Klein, Wolfgang & Clive Perdue. 1997. The Basic Variety (or: Couldn't natural languages be much simpler?) *Second Language Research* 13(4). 301–347.

Li Wei & Melissa G. Moyer (eds.). 2008. *The Blackwell guide to research methods in bilingualism and multilingualism.* Malden, MA: Blackwell.

McDaniel, Dana, Cecile McKee & Helen S. Cairns (eds.). 1998. *Methods for assessing children's syntax.* Cambridge, MA: MIT Press.

McNamara, Tim. 2000. *Language testing.* Oxford: Oxford University Press.

McNamara, Tim. 2011. Managing learning: Authority and language assessment. In Radhika Jaidev, Maria Luisa C. Sadorra, Wong Jock Onn, Lee Ming Cherk & Beatriz Paredes Lorente (eds.), *Global perspectives, local initiatives: Reflections and practices in ELT*,

39–51. Singapore: National University of Singapore, Centre for English Language Communication.

Menn, Lise & Nan B. Ratner (eds.). 2000. *Methods for studying language production*. Mahwah, NJ: Lawrence Erlbaum.

North, Brian. 2007. The CEFR Common Reference Levels: Validated reference points and local strategies. In F. Goullier, *The Common European Framework of Reference for Languages (CEFR) and the development of language policies: Challenges and responsibilities*, 19–28. Strasbourg: Council of Europe. http://www.coe.int/t/dg4/linguistic/Forum07_webdocs_EN.asp#TopOfPage (accessed 18 August 2016).

Perlmann-Balme, Michaela, Sybille Plassmann & Beate Zeidler. 2009. *Deutsch-Test für Zuwanderer, A2–B1*. Berlin: Cornelsen.

Pinker, Steven. 2007. *The stuff of thought: Language as a window into human nature*. New York: Penguin.

Polinsky, Maria & Olga Kagan. 2007. Heritage languages: In the "wild" and in the classroom. *Language and Linguistics Compass* 1(5). 368–395,

Quetz, Jürgen. 2010. Der Gemeinsame europäische Referenzrahmen als Grundlage für Sprachprüfungen: Eine kritische Beschreibung des Status quo. *Deutsch als Fremdsprache* 04/2010. 195–202.

Strik, Tineke. 2013. Integration tests: Helping or hindering integration? Report of the Committee on Migration, Refugees, and Displaced Persons. Strasbourg: Council of Europe, Parliamentary Assembly, Doc. 13361.

Ulich, Michaela & Toni Mayr. 2003. *SISMIK: Sprachverhalten und Interesse an Sprache bei Migrantenkindern in Kindertageseinrichtungen*. Freiburg: Herder.

Vainikka, Anne & Martha Young-Scholten. 2011. *The acquisition of German: Introducing Organic Grammar*. Berlin: de Gruyter.

Van Avermaet, Piet. 2016. Foreword. In ALTE, *Language tests for access, integration and citizenship: An outline for policymakers*. http://www.alte.org/attachments/files/alte_lami_language_test_policy_booklet_web_en_0 m4wh.pdf (accessed 9 August 2016).

Vogt, Karin. 2011. *Fremdsprachliche Kompetenzprofile: Entwicklung und Abgleichung von GeR-Deskriptoren für Fremdsprachenlernen mit einer beruflichen Anwendungsorientierung*. Tübingen: Narr.

Watorek, Marzena, Sandra Benazzo & Maya Hickmann (eds.). 2012. *Comparative perspectives on language acquisition: A tribute to Clive Perdue*. Bristol: Multilingual Matters.

Wisniewski, Katrin. 2010. Bewertervariabilität im Umgang mit GER-Skalen: Ein- und Aussichten aus einem Sprachtestprojekt. *Deutsch als Fremdsprache* 03/2010. 143–149.

## 2 Policies for language and integration
Politiques pour les langues et l'intégration

Reinhilde Pulinx, Piet Van Avermaet
# The impact of language and integration policies on the social participation of adult migrants

**Abstract:** Knowledge of the language of the so-called host society is considered as one of the most crucial elements for successful integration and as the main lever to increase immigrants' level of self-reliance and to stimulate social interaction and participation. This small-scale qualitative study, situated in Flanders (Belgium), aims to gain more insight into the impact of integration programmes, with knowledge of the language of the host society as nucleus, on opportunities for social participation and building sustainable social networks.

**Résumé :** Comprendre et parler la langue du pays d'accueil est considéré comme l'un des facteurs clés d'une intégration réussie et comme le principal levier pour renforcer le niveau de confiance en soi des migrants et stimuler l'interaction et la participation sociale. Cette étude qualitative menée à petite échelle en Flandre (Belgique) se propose de mieux comprendre les effets des programmes d'intégration centrés sur la connaissance de la langue du pays d'accueil, ainsi que sur les possibilités de participation sociale et de construction de réseaux sociaux durables.

## 1 Introduction

Over the last three decades, most western European societies have become characterized by diverse and transitory migration processes, consisting of migrants frequently moving within the European space, refugees and asylum seekers, migration in the context of family reunification, marriage migration, exchange students and high-skilled workers. Traditional processes of acculturation or intergenerational assimilation no longer seem to occur automatically. The recent wave of migration, the so-called European refugee crisis, consisting of refugees originating from war zones in the Middle East and Africa, exerts great pressure

---

**Reinhilde Pulinx** (corresponding author), Centre for Diversity and Learning, Linguistics Department, Ghent University, E-mail: Reinhilde.pulinx@ugent.be
**Piet Van Avermaet**, Centre for Diversity and Learning, Linguistics Department, Ghent University, E-mail: Piet.vanavermaet@ugent.be

on western European societies when it comes to developing and implementing policies around concepts such as social cohesion, integration, citizenship, identity, and language (Van Avermaet 2009; Van Avermaet and Gysen 2009).

Questions about the meaning of national identity, maintaining social cohesion and preserving national, cultural and linguistic heritage are of growing concern for policy makers and society as a whole (Van Avermaet 2009; Van Avermaet and Gysen 2009). Proficiency in the national language and knowledge of society are considered essential and definable elements of citizenship and successful integration processes (Shohamy 2006).

In this contribution we report on the impact of the Flemish integration programmes, with knowledge of the language of the host society as nucleus, on creating opportunities for new migrants to engage in social participation and to build sustainable social networks.

## 2 Active citizenship: distinguishing "good" and "not so good" citizens

In western Europe, present-day integration policies often make use of the notion "active citizenship", aimed at encouraging migrants to participate socially, politically and economically in the host society. New members of society are not only expected to respect the law, but in addition to make an active contribution to civil society initiatives (Verhoeven and Ham 2010).

In the literature, multiple definitions of "active citizenship" can be found, all including some common characteristics (Odé and Walraven 2013): 1) social involvement and participation; 2) active participation in public debate, political and democratic institutions; 3) active citizenship has to include all members of society; 4) active citizenship presupposes certain cognitive and social skills; and 5) loyalty towards the society a person lives in.

Hence, expectations are being created – by the government and the wider society – about what it means to be a good citizen and a not so good citizen (Odé and Walraven 2013). As Odé and Walraven (2013) explain further, a good citizen does what civil society asks of him or her: participating in the voluntary and associative sector, contributing to neighbourhood initiatives, and integrating as fully as possible in the host society. The not so good citizen takes a more passive attitude towards life and society, looking primarily to the government and its institutions and not him/herself when action is required (Odé and Walraven 2013).

In several western European countries new immigrants have to take an integration course that consists of a language course and a course in societal knowledge referred to as the norms and values of the so-called host society. In Flanders, this course is called *inburgering*, literally meaning 'becoming a citizen'. This implies that immigrants are not seen as citizens before migration, or at least not citizens of the "right kind", living by moral standards reconcilable with the host society. However, not only first-generation migrants have to demonstrate unremittingly and continually how good their linguistic and societal knowledge is, as pivotal parts of becoming a "good citizen". The requirement to achieve and continuously demonstrate moral citizenship is passed on to the second and third (and now even fourth) generation of people with a migrant background. Members of the majority are exempted from this kind of scrutiny.

## 3 Social participation through social networks

Adult migrants often have to build completely new social networks in the host country – in unfamiliar surroundings, characterized by a different lingua franca, and different social agreements and conventions. At the same time, they try to maintain transnational social contacts with family and friends in their home country or elsewhere. These dynamic and complex social networks fulfil most essential functions for newcomers, regarding not only their socio-emotional well-being but also access to housing, the labour market, education and healthcare.

For an effective integration process, it is important that new migrants can build social networks that provide sufficient social capital to support social mobility and allow them to make use of their own economic, cultural or human capital and to undertake activities to accumulate such capital. This means that engaging in social bridging relations (relations with members of communities other than their own) and social linking relations (relations with organizations and public services) is of the greatest importance for new migrants. But even so, social bonding relations (relations with members of their own community) remain vital for the social well-being and identity construction of newcomers. Especially in a social and political context where active citizenship is identified as an essential instrument to establish social cohesion and democratic participation, integration policies should help new migrants to build social bridging and linking relations.

In the following parts of this contribution we will report on the impact of Flemish integration programmes on the opportunities provided for new migrants to engage in social participation and build social networks.

## 4 Research questions and methodology

Before discussing the research questions and the methodology used, the research context is briefly described. In most western European countries, new immigrants have to take an integration course that consists of a language course and a course in societal knowledge referred to as the norms and values of the host society (Pulinx, Van Avermaet and Extramiana 2014). In Flanders, this course is called *inburgering*, literally meaning 'becoming a citizen'. These integration courses provide newcomers, as defined by the Flemish government, with an accompanied trajectory towards integration. The courses consist of a specific and personalized program aimed at increasing newcomers' self-reliance as well as their professional, educational and social participation. In other words, stimulating social participation has been made an explicit objective of Flemish integration policies, but always closely linked to increasing proficiency in the dominant language: "An important aspect in realizing proportional participation is Dutch. Someone who speaks Dutch, understands, reads, can find information, will find a job more easily, has increasing access to education and social services, will participate more in public debate and the democratic process. Good knowledge of the Dutch language increases self-reliance, makes them less dependent of others" (Policy brief, Flemish Minister of Integration, 2014).

By conducting a small-scale, exploratory, qualitative research project in Flanders, the impact of language and integration policies on the social participation of adult migrants is being looked at. Nine in-depth interviews were conducted, based on semi-structured interviews and the use of an instrument for mapping social networks. All the respondents were female, lived at the time of the interview in the same Flemish city, migrated three to five years ago from an eastern European country, and had school-age children. The interviews were mainly conducted in Dutch; only two were conducted in English. Excerpts from the interviews conducted in Dutch have been translated into English.

The research questions were: What social networks do adult newcomers have? What kind of social contact do newcomers have (bonding, bridging, linking)? What was the impact of participating in integration courses and Dutch language courses on building social networks? How and when are social networks being used?

# 5 Main findings

## 5.1 What social networks do adult newcomers have?

The social networks of all the respondents who participated in this research project were very limited. Most of their social contacts included members of the nuclear family (whether or not in the home country or a third country) and a few close friends, often with a migration background as well and originating from the same home country as the respondents. The main social contacts, as reported by the respondents, were social bonding relations.

> "I am living now for two years in [name of city]. I have one friend, she is also Polish. Sometimes I go shopping, or walking or drinking coffee, but I always speak Polish. I don't have any contact with Belgian people."

Social bridging relations, relations with members of other communities, and more specifically with members of the Flemish community, seem to be absent in the social networks of the respondents. The absence of these relations is mainly explained – by the respondents themselves – by referring to their insufficient proficiency in the Dutch language.

> "You can meet a lot of Romanian people and speak your own language. But in the beginning I didn't speak another language. And then it is very hard to make connections."

## 5.2 What kind of social contact do newcomers have (bonding, bridging, linking)?

In addition, participating in organized leisure-time activities, e.g. sports clubs or other associations, was hardly mentioned by the respondents. It was also striking that social linking relations (i.e., relations with organizations and public services) were only reported to a limited extent. These social linking relations included for the most part Dutch language teachers, teachers at their children's school, and career orientation counsellors.

> "The school of the children, the teachers. I can always ask them for help. They always help me. At first, I didn't understand all the notes the children brought home. I tried to translate via Google translate, but it wasn't always correct. I asked the teachers and they helped me. They are always very friendly."

## 5.3 What was the impact of participating in integration courses and Dutch language courses on building social networks?

The respondents indicated that social contacts were made during integration and Dutch language courses, but in most cases these contacts did not last beyond the duration of the integration and language courses.

> "After [the course], I have to work every day. I have two children. My husband works. I only go to school [the course] two times a week. I don't have time for friends."

Respondents expressed a need to engage in social bridging relations, making social contacts with members of Flemish society. They were offered few opportunities to do this during the integration courses.

> "Here at school is fine. I want to come every day to school. Here you can talk to people as friends. I want more contact, know more people. But I have to speak Dutch better in order to do that."

Because of the limited social contacts of the participating newcomers, it was impossible to answer the last question on how and in which situations these social networks are used.

# 6 Conclusions

These findings clearly show that it cannot be taken for granted – at least for the respondents involved in this study – that participating in a compulsory *inburgering* program has a positive impact on immigrants' inter-ethnic social networks.

Given that this is a small scale study with a non-random sample, one has to be careful in generalizing the findings that were summarized in section 5. As an exploratory study, however, it allows us to formulate hypotheses for further qualitative and quantitative research.

In most (mainly quantitative) research on this topic the voice of the immigrants is absent. This exploratory study shows the value of a more qualitative approach in researching immigrants' social networks. At the start of the study we encountered obstacles and fears when contacting the respondents directly. This in itself is an interesting finding. The assumption that people can automatically and independently build strong social networks after attending an integration course, ignores the real dynamics and complexities of processes of social bridging. It took us quite some time to get in touch with the respondents, approaching them indirectly via local NGOs. Based on the methodology used to conduct this study, we see the potential for the development of a tool for (self-)monitoring of social participation processes.

Building new social networks is not an individual but a shared process, including both newcomers and members of the host society. New migrants expressed the need for bridging relations, but do not appear the be able to engage in these relations without support and guidance from, e. g., integration services and counsellors. This means that facilitating social relations (bonding, bridging and linking relations) is an essential part of an "active" policy aiming at social participation and active citizenship of all members of society.

# References

Odé, Arend & Guido Walraven. 2013. *Binding en burgerschap: Buurtbetrokkenheid in Rotterdam en Den Haag* [Binding and citizenship: Neighbourhood involvement in Rotterdam and The Hague]. Antwerp & Apeldoorn: Garant.

Pulinx, Reinhilde, Piet Van Avermaet & Claire Extramiana. 2014. *Linguistic integration of adult migrants: Policy and practice. Final report on the 3rd Council of Europe Survey.* Strasbourg: Council of Europe. https://rm.coe.int/CoERMPublicCommonSearchServices/DisplayDCTMContent?documentId=09000016802fc1ce (accessed 9 August 2016).

Shohamy, Elana. 2006. *Language policy: Hidden agendas and new approaches.* London: Routledge.

Van Avermaet, Piet. 2009. Fortress Europe? Language policy regimes for immigration and citizenship. In Gabriella Hogan-Brun, Claire Mar-Molinero & Patrick Stevenson (eds.), *Discourses on language and integration: Critical perspectives on language testing regimes in Europe,* 15–44. Amsterdam: John Benjamins.

Van Avermaet, Piet & Sara Gysen. 2009. One nation, two policies: Language requirements for citizenship and integration in Belgium. In Guus Extra, Massimiliano Spotti & Piet Van Avermaet (eds.), *Language testing, migration and citizenship: Cross-national perspectives on integration regimes,* 107–124. London: Continuum.

Verhoeven, Imrat & Marcel Ham (eds.). 2010. *Brave burgers gezocht: De grenzen van de activerende welvaarstaat* [Good citizens wanted: The boundaries of the activating welfare state]. Amsterdam: Van Gennep.

François Grin, Guillaume Fürst
# Quels sont les facteurs qui renforcent l'exigence d'apprentissage par les migrants de la langue du pays d'accueil ?

Analyse multivariée des attitudes envers l'altérité linguistique de 40 000 jeunes hommes suisses

**Résumé :** Cette étude montre, sur la base d'une enquête auprès de plus de 40 000 jeunes gens, que la nécessité de l'apprentissage de la langue du pays d'accueil fait l'objet d'un consensus social quasi unanime, que le capital culturel et l'expérience des voyages tendent à renforcer, mais qui transcende largement les différences sociales et inter-régionales. L'attente d'apprentissage reste compatible avec des attitudes positives envers l'immigration, suggérant qu'il existe, chez les citoyens, une demande pour des politiques d'intégration, dont la langue est une composante essentielle.

**Abstract:** This study shows, based on a survey carried out among more than 40,000 young people, that there is an almost unanimous social consensus concerning the need to learn the language of the host country, a consensus which tends to be reinforced by cultural capital and experience gained from travelling but largely transcends social and inter-regional differences. This learning expectation remains compatible with positive attitudes towards immigration, which suggests that citizens see a requirement for integration policies of which language is a vital component.

## Introduction

L'apprentissage de la langue du pays d'accueil est en général considéré, sur le plan positif, comme une nécessité incontournable de l'intégration et, sur le plan normatif, comme une dimension légitimement attendue de cette intégration.

Toutefois, une telle vision suppose, tout d'abord, d'aller au-delà des visions minimalistes de l'intégration, par exemple celles qui postulent que l'intégration se résume à respecter la loi du pays d'accueil. Elle incorpore au contraire des

---

**François Grin, Guillaume Fürst**, Observatoire Économie—Langues—Formation, Université de Genève

facettes linguistiques et culturelles et elle voit plutôt l'intégration comme « une dynamique d'échange, dans laquelle chacun accepte de se constituer partie d'un tout où l'adhésion aux règles de fonctionnement de la société d'accueil, et le respect de ce qui fait l'unité de la communauté n'interdisent pas le maintien des différences » (*La Documentation française* 2011 citant Van Eeckhout 2007).

Deuxièmement, cette vision récuse diverses voix critiques aux termes desquelles l'accent mis sur l'apprentissage de la langue du pays d'accueil serait excessif, voire discriminatoire, au motif que cet apprentissage ne garantit pas le succès socio-économique, puisque les migrants se retrouvent souvent confinés à des emplois mal considérés. Elle renvoie au contraire aux chiffres montrant que si l'apprentissage de la langue locale n'est pas une condition *suffisante* de la réussite sur le marché du travail elle en est, statistiquement, une condition *nécessaire* (voir par ex. Adserà et Pytliková 2016).

On sait cependant fort peu de choses sur les attentes effectives de la société d'accueil : dans quelle mesure les résidents réclament-ils un tel apprentissage par les migrants ? De quoi dépend l'importance qu'ils y attachent ? Les attitudes à cet égard sont-elles très différenciées ou au contraire assez uniformément réparties ?

Cette étude entend fournir quelques éléments de réponse à ces questions, grâce à une enquête détaillée et de grande envergure portant sur les compétences linguistiques et interculturelles, ainsi que sur les attitudes et représentations de plus de 40 000 jeunes gens à l'égard de l'altérité linguistique et culturelle. Cette enquête comportait des items posant précisément ce type de questions.

Les questions méthodologiques sont abordées dans la section 1, tandis que la section 2 présente les résultats. La section 3 propose une brève conclusion.

# 1 Méthode

Les analyses présentées dans cet article se basent sur des données récolées en 2008–2009 dans le cadre de l'étude *Suisse – Société multiculturelle* (Grin *et al.* 2015). Il s'agit d'un échantillon de 41 240 jeunes hommes (19–21 ans) de nationalité suisse. Ces données ont été recueillies dans le cadre d'une série de tests précédant l'incorporation au service militaire, toujours obligatoire en Suisse ; cette étape étant obligatoire, l'échantillon qui en résulte constitue un relevé quasi exhaustif de ces jeunes gens. Les données ont été recueillies à l'aide d'un questionnaire de 60 pages (version originale en français et traduction en allemand et italien).

Dans cet article, nous utilisons une échelle basée sur le modèle *Tolérance et Tolérabilité* (Grin 2007). Parmi ses 48 items, huit traitent d'enjeux liés à la diversité des langues. Les analyses reportées ici sont basées sur ces huit items, qui proposent différentes affirmations telles que « Il est indispensable que les immigrants apprennent la langue d'ici » (l'intégralité des items utilisés ici figure dans le tableau 1). Pour chacune de ces affirmations, les répondants étaient invités à indiquer leur degré d'accord ou de désaccord à l'aide d'une échelle à quatre points (1 = « pas d'accord », 2 = « plutôt pas d'accord », 3 = « plutôt d'accord », 4 = « d'accord »).

# 2 Résultats

Dans les analyses ci-dessous, nous commençons par présenter des statistiques descriptives de ces items (moyennes), pour la Suisse dans son ensemble et par région linguistique. Dans un deuxième temps, nous proposons une analyse multivariée permettant de mettre en évidence divers facteurs qui sont en lien avec ces items. Pour ce faire, nous construisons une variable *exigence d'apprentissage de la langue locale* (EALL) qui est la moyenne de ces différents items, après avoir inversé le score de certains d'entre eux afin d'éviter l'annulation réciproque des items à teneur sémantique positive et négative. L'alpha de Cronbach de cette échelle est de 0,67. Dans un modèle de régression multiple, nous analysons quels sont les prédicteurs significatifs de cette variable EALL, comme par exemple les compétences linguistiques des répondants, l'origine de leurs amis ou encore leur ouverture à d'autres cultures (sur la base d'un questionnaire classique en psychologie, le *Multicultural Personality Questionnaire* [MPQ], dont nous avons utilisé ici la traduction française ; voir Faniko *et al.* 2015).

## 2.1 Statistiques descriptives

La moyenne de chaque item, pour la Suisse entière et par région linguistique, figure dans le tableau 1. On note un fort consensus autour de chaque affirmation, dans le sens d'une opinion qui manifestement attend de la part des migrants l'apprentissage de la langue locale. Par exemple, l'item 16, qui porte explicitement sur cette question, a une moyenne de 3,52, très proche du maximum de 4, qui indique une exigence forte ; les items 25 et 39 présentent des résultats similaires. Pour les items qui sont formulés dans le sens d'une *faible* exigence, les moyennes sont, à l'inverse, très basses. Par exemple, pour les items 3 et 44 –

qui portent sur la possibilité de passer le permis de conduire dans une langue étrangère et sur l'inclusion de cours de langues spécifiques pour les étrangers – le degré d'accord des répondants est très faible (moyenne autour de 1,8). Ces chiffres révèlent le refus d'aménagements particuliers pour les personnes ne parlant pas la langue locale et renvoient donc, par symétrie, à une forte exigence d'apprentissage de cette langue.

Par ailleurs, les moyennes par région linguistique montrent que les différences d'opinion entre régions sont minimes. Pour les items formulés dans le sens d'une forte exigence (n° 16, 25 et 39), les différences entre régions sont généralement de l'ordre de 0,1 point ou moins, ce qui montre bien l'homogénéité de l'opinion sur ce plan. Si d'autres items révèlent des différences entre régions légèrement plus marquées, comme par exemple l'item 23, celles-ci restent anecdotiques.

**Tableau 1.** Moyenne par item (Suisse entière et par région linguistique), échelle de 1 à 4

| | CH | CH-D | CH-F | CH-I |
|---|---|---|---|---|
| [3] « on devrait pouvoir passer l'examen théorique du permis de conduire dans les principales langues de l'immigration (p. ex. en espagnol, en serbo-croate, en turc, etc.) » | 1.87 | 1.83 | 2.05 | 1.95 |
| [6] « au travail, il n'est pas acceptable que les collègues étrangers parlent entre eux dans leur langue devant des collègues suisses » | 2.72 | 2.78 | 2.44 | 2.69 |
| [16] « il est indispensable que les immigrants apprennent la langue d'ici » | 3.52 | 3.48 | 3.66 | 3.69 |
| [23] « si l'enseigne d'un magasin chinois dans une ville suisse est en chinois, il est indispensable qu'elle soit aussi en français, allemand ou italien (selon la région) » | 2.8 | 2.79 | 2.72 | 3.17 |
| [24] « c'est une bonne chose de pouvoir entendre les langues étrangères dans la rue, les transports publics, etc. » | 2.49 | 2.44 | 2.77 | 2.4 |
| [25] « les étrangers qui vivent en Suisse ne devraient pas s'attendre à ce que les administrations cantonales ou fédérales s'adressent à eux dans leur langue » | 3.36 | 3.39 | 3.23 | 3.19 |
| [39] « les Américains venant s'établir en Suisse doivent apprendre la langue de leur nouveau domicile » | 3.47 | 3.48 | 3.49 | 3.38 |
| [44] « les programmes scolaires devraient inclure des cours de portugais, albanais, turc, etc. pour les élèves dont c'est la langue maternelle » | 1.82 | 1.86 | 1.62 | 1.6 |

## 2.2 Analyses multivariées

Considérons maintenant les résultats de l'analyse multivariée, afin d'avoir une meilleure vue d'ensemble sur cette exigence d'apprentissage, puis de mettre en évidence les facteurs qui tendent à la renforcer ou à l'atténuer. Les résultats de la régression linéaire multiple, qui inclut divers prédicteurs dont l'effet est discuté en détail ci-après, figurent dans le tableau 2. Pris conjointement, ces prédicteurs expliquent 21 % de la variance de la variable EALL définie plus haut, ce qui est non-négligeable. De plus, chaque prédicteur est significatif, ce qui indique que chacun d'eux explique une part de variance unique de EALL. Enfin, certains effets sont positifs (traduisant un *renforcement* de l'exigence) et d'autres négatifs (traduisant un *affaiblissement* de cette exigence). Examinons de plus près l'effet de chacun d'eux[1].

**Tableau 2.** Résultats de la régression linéaire multiple sur la variable EALL ($R^2$ = 0,21)

|  | Coeff. brut | Erreur std | t | p |
|---|---|---|---|---|
| (Constante) | 3.778 | 0.013 | 285.3 | <.001 |
| Nombre de livres | 0.043 | 0.002 | 18.4 | <.001 |
| Origine des amis en Suisse | −0.21 | 0.004 | −49.2 | <.001 |
| Nombre de pays visités | 0.02 | 0.003 | 6.2 | <.001 |
| Ouverture à d'autres cultures (MPQ) | −0.2 | 0.004 | −56.4 | <.001 |
| Compétences linguistiques totales | −0.032 | 0.002 | −14 | <.001 |

L'effet positif le plus marqué est celui du nombre de livres au domicile familial du répondant, qui constitue un bon indicateur de niveau socio-culturel. Plus la famille possède de livres, plus le répondant adhère à l'idée que les migrants doivent s'adapter linguistiquement. L'effet du nombre de pays visités est analogue ; il s'agit aussi d'un effet positif, quoique de moindre ampleur. Plus une personne a voyagé, plus elle attend des efforts d'apprentissage de la part des migrants.

---

[1] Les détails des modalités des prédicteurs dans la régression sont les suivantes : *nombre de livres*, cinq modalités (1 = « 0–10 [livres] », 2 = « 11–50 », 3 = « 21–200 », 4 = « 201–400 », 5 = « plus de 400 ») ; *origine des amis en Suisse*, trois modalités (1 = « en majorité suisse », 2 = « autant suisse qu'étrangère », 3 = « en majorité étrangère ») ; *nombre de pays visités*, cinq modalités (1 = « aucun », 2 = « 1 ou 2 », 3 = « 3 à 5 », 4 = « 6 à 10 », 5 = « plus de 10 ») ; *ouverture à d'autres cultures*, scores continus de 1 à 5 (moyenne de plusieurs questions) ; compétences linguistiques totales, scores continus de 0 à 7 (moyenne de plusieurs questions portant sur plusieurs compétences [lire, parler, comprendre, écrire] et plusieurs langues [L2, L3, L4]).

L'effet négatif le plus marqué est celui de l'ouverture à d'autres cultures (MPQ). Ce résultat implique que plus une personne est « ouverte » (en termes de la mesure psychométrique de ce trait de personnalité que fournit le MPQ), moins elle exige d'adaptation linguistique de la part des migrants. De même, plus on a d'amis d'origine étrangère, moins on est enclin à exiger une adaptation linguistique de la part des immigrants. Enfin, plus le niveau de compétences linguistiques totales est élevé, moins on réclame une telle adaptation. On rappellera toutefois que l'effet de ces variables est minime, car l'apprentissage de la langue locale par les migrants reste considéré comme indispensable par l'immense majorité des répondants.

## 3 Conclusions

Les considérations positives (sur l'utilité objective de l'apprentissage de la langue du pays d'accueil pour l'intégration, notamment sur le marché du travail) et normatives (sur le caractère légitime d'une telle attente, en termes d'une analyse ancrée dans la philosophie politique) s'adossent donc à des attitudes largement partagées par les citoyens. Mis à part leur caractère novateur (car les données à ce sujet sont rares), nos résultats permettent d'aborder en meilleure connaissance de cause la problématique de l'intégration, et cela pour deux raisons.

Premièrement, on a vu que l'attente d'apprentissage est quasi unanime. Elle transcende non seulement les différences présentées plus haut, mais aussi d'autres qu'il n'est pas possible d'aborder ici faute de place, notamment l'orientation politique et les attitudes envers la présence même des migrants. En d'autres termes, l'attente, voire l'exigence d'apprentissage est compatible avec des attitudes globalement favorables à l'immigration.

Deuxièmement, les chiffres indiquent qu'il n'y a pas lieu de chercher, dans cette attente, quelque intention discriminatoire. L'item 39 (tableau 1) révèle que cette attente ne s'adresse pas qu'à l'archétype du migrant en quête d'emploi et venant d'un pays économiquement moins favorisé. Elle s'adresse également à ceux qu'il est convenu d'appeler les « expats », qui sont en fin de compte également des migrants, même s'ils sont particulièrement prospères. Cette égalité dans les attentes est d'autant plus plausible qu'à l'heure de la mondialisation, les distinctions entre profils s'estompent au profit d'un *habitus* de mobilité de plus en plus généralisé.

Les tensions politiques et sociales qui entourent actuellement les enjeux migratoires doivent nous conduire à accorder une attention toute particulière à la sélection et à l'élaboration des politiques publiques en la matière. Les résultats présentés ici nous rappellent opportunément que les citoyens tiennent à ce que la mobilité, dans ses différentes formes, s'accompagne d'une démarche d'intégration véritable, et que dans celle-ci, l'apprentissage de la langue du pays d'accueil reste un principe incontournable.

## Références

Adserà, Alicia & Mariola Pytliková. 2016. Language and Migration. In Victor Ginsburgh & Shlomo Weber (dir.), *The Palgrave Handbook of Economics and Language*, 342–372. Basingstoke : Palgrave.

Faniko, Klea, François Grin & Paolo Ghisletta. 2015. Assessing multicultural effectiveness among Swiss young people: Factor structure and consistency in the French adaptation of the Multicultural Personality Questionnaire. *Swiss Journal of Psychology*, vol. 74. 5–15.

Grin, François. 2007. Tolérance et tolérabilité. *Éthique publique*, vol. 9, n° 1. 9–20.

Grin, François, Jacques Amos, Klea Faniko, Guillaume Fürst, Jacqueline Lurin & Irene Schwob. 2015. *Suisse – Société multiculturelle. Ce qu'en font les jeunes aujourd'hui.* Zurich : Éditions Rüegger.

Van Eeckhout, Laetitia. 2007. *L'immigration.* Paris : Odile Jacob. Citée par *La documentation française* : http://www.metiseurope.eu/immigration-integration-assimilation-de-quoi-parle-t-on_fr_70_art_29650.html.

Furio Bednarz
# Professional and social integration of migrants and language learning: convergences and challenges at the European level

**Abstract:** Based on the "Vintage" project, this article reports the results of research focused on policies and practices regarding the language training of migrants. It deals with common trends informing policies, linking the certification of linguistic skills with the duties and rights of migrants, making linguistic training more of an obligation than an opportunity for social and professional development. The article shows how policies influence language training and provide opportunities or obstacles, defines the stakeholders supporting effective training, and highlights methodological and pedagogical lessons emerging from good practices.

**Résumé :** L'article présente, en partant du projet « Vintage », les résultats d'une étude sur les politiques et pratiques mises en œuvre pour promouvoir les formations linguistiques pour les migrants. Il analyse les tendances communes qui servent de base à l'élaboration des politiques, à la corrélation entre certification des compétences linguistiques et devoirs et droits des migrants, à la formation linguistique considérée comme une obligation plutôt que comme une opportunité de développement social et professionnel. Il explique également en quoi ces politiques influencent les formations linguistiques et créent des opportunités ou des obstacles en définissant les acteurs qui soutiennent une formation efficace et valorisent les méthodologies et les pédagogies tirées des bonnes pratiques.

## 1 Introduction

This article is based on a Lifelong Learning Programme project ("Vintage") that includes research on national policies and practices in language training, with a particular focus on four key contexts: France, Germany, Italy and Switzerland. A combination of quantitative and qualitative methodologies characterized the study. Policies and good practices were analyzed through focus groups and inter-

---

**Furio Bednarz**, ECAP Foundation – Responsible Research & Development, Via Industria, 6814 Lamone, Switzerland, E-mail: furio.bednarz@ti.ch

DOI 10.1515/9783110477498-010, © 2017 Furio Bednarz, published by De Gruyter.
This work is licensed under the Creative Commons Attribution-NonCommercial-NoDerivs 3.0 License.

views with experts and practitioners, as well as by exploiting the literature, informal contacts and observations. The study took into account three dimensions of analysis, considering the policy level, stakeholders and actors involved in training, and concrete practices.

## 2 Macro dynamics: language mastery as a gatekeeper

Immigration trends, together with the evolution of policies and job markets, are producing a wider need for language learning. Policies converged a lot during the last decades, aiming at establishing shared frames for regulating migration flows, permits, and access to citizenship. EU citizens enjoyed freedom of mobility, while restrictive norms regulated immigration from third-world countries. Controls and compulsory measures, including language courses, have been set up, producing further fragmentation. In addition, at least before the refugee crisis of 2015, specific regulations have been applied to asylum seekers, in order to limit their recognition as refugees, postponing active measures fostering integration.

Assessment of language mastery became in this context a "gate keeper" for selecting access to basic rights of non-EU migrants. They must make efforts to integrate, according to the philosophy of "promoting and demanding" (*fordern und fördern*). This policy defines obligations, foreseeing optional or even compulsory training: in 29 out of 36 countries responding to a Council of Europe survey, adult migrants are legally required to take a language course and/or a language test prior to entry, for residence or for citizenship (Pulinx, Van Avermaet, and Extramiana 2014). Obligations and supportive measures are expected to speed up integration processes, fostering integration in the job market, according to evidence of a positive link between language proficiency, access to the job market and social integration (de la Rica, Glitz, and Ortega 2013).

Certification of language mastery corresponding to a certain level of the *Common European Framework of Reference for Languages* (CEFR) became a key learning driver for migrants. Used as a reference tool for classifying linguistic skills to be certified in order to gain a stable permit or additional rights, the CEFR finally influenced methodological approaches to language learning, fostering the appraisal of languages "in action" and the assessment of communicative skills.

## 3 Meso level: emerging stakeholders and actors

In order to implement policies, almost all European countries developed a mixed system of language training, based on public and private provision. Supportive measures and financing are defined by public authorities, and conditions vary a lot. Cooperation between public institutions and private providers (both NGOs and profit companies) characterizes central and north European countries. Non-profit organisations and associations work on behalf of public bodies offering training to lower qualified migrants, asylum seekers and refugees. An unstructured mix of actors and funds – often distributed on the basis of projects and special initiatives (which works against continuity) – characterizes Mediterranean countries; sometimes (see Italy) it is also the public sector which directly provides language training facilities and social integration courses, working independently of charitable organizations.

Certification is normally delivered by accredited institutions, on the basis of diverse regulations provided by norms, syllabi and standards aligned with the CEFR, and established by independent competence centers supervising the assessment of language learning. Practices of validation of non-formal and informal learning – using portfolios and passports – are slowly gaining some respect, but they are still rare.

## 4 Micro dimension: lessons learned from practice

### 4.1 Focus of the study

Innovative practices have been evaluated against the following criteria:
- respect for adult learning principles;
- balanced mobilisation of learning drivers, considering cognitive, emotional and relational dimensions (Illeris 1999);
- presence of key elements of inclusive learning, such as *proximity*, in terms of content and learning objectives close to the concerns and needs of the learners, a *holistic approach to learning*, and *participative design of learning outcomes and learning paths.*

## 4.2 Balanced learning drivers

At first glance, innovative practices seem to ensure a good balance between learning drivers. Practices try to cope with constraints deriving from policies. Language training is often planned under the pressure of time constraints, according to objectives defined by administrative obligations. Practices identify realistic solutions in order to make training more profitable: free choice of participation and flexible intake arrangements; involvement of stakeholders in orienting participants and facilitating access; activation of exchange face to face and at distance (social networking), enhancing motivation and relational dimensions of learning.

A certain level of proximity is always considered. Courses aim at helping learners deal with everyday life, complementing language training with basic civic notions. Communicative skills needed at the workplace are taken into account; however, practices very rarely focus on more ambitious learning objectives in which the acquisition of linguistic skills could be seen as a driver towards professionalization or personal development.

## 4.3 Language in action

Practices define a shared approach for innovative learning settings and outcomes. Learning activities are designed on the basis of scenarios and considering recurrent events characterizing specific fields of action. Outcomes are defined by "can do" descriptors. Flexible didactic resources are made available to trainers and learners: web tools are exploited in order to create communicative settings and to find examples and didactic solutions; structured libraries of artifacts, documents, exercises are developed in order to link language training to a specific professional context.

Despite the focus on communicative skills, practices take into account the four dimensions of language mastery (listening, reading, speaking, writing), trying to integrate oral and written communication. They define personalized learning objectives, moving from the simple evidence that a communicative task can be accomplished exploiting diverse resources and reaching different levels of complexity. Sometimes assessment procedures also follow this approach: learners are asked to deal with communicative situations, instead of passing a test aimed at verifying learning outcomes corresponding to a specific level.

## 4.4 New didactic frameworks

Practices provide examples of innovative didactic strategies. Books and exercises are replaced by the use of authentic materials (such as forms, manuals, leaflets, magazines, etc.), valuing the familiarity of the learners with sectoral micro-languages. Learning is facilitated by the use of visual glossaries. *Chunks* and *scripts* are gaining momentum. Learning occurs in groups, but also at distance, valuing new technologies: posting, answering, exploiting blogs and other social networking tools. These strategies pave the road to an inductive approach to grammar and language structures. Learning by practising and by exposure to a diverse language context does not represent an alternative to achieving a solid mastery of the language, but is intended as a route for reaching accuracy of expression, including intonation, without causing blocks and obstacles to communication, due to anxiety and refusal attitudes arising from the sanctioning of grammatical errors.

## 4.5 Assessment as a means of promoting learning

Self-assessment, peer-to-peer revision and formative feedback emerge as powerful resources to cope with the risks of *pidginization* of language learning, valuing at the same time the specific linguistic repertoires of the learners and informal learning. The use of portfolios facilitates formative evaluation by teachers, helping learners gain awareness of their progress as well as recurrent errors. At the same time, continuous assessment of communicative performance, based on evidence and proof, enhances the capacity of the learners to make their linguistic proficiency visible and updated.

# 5 Linking language learning and qualifications: an open challenge

Work-related language learning plays a role of growing relevance. However, language mastery is still conceived as a prerequisite rather than a component of a qualification. The challenge remains related to the higher level of linguistic skills required for participating in a formal qualification procedure, with respect to the skills needed to do the same work and communicate at the workplace. And despite much innovation, the world of language training shows persistent difficulties in dialoguing with the world of vocational education and training (VET). This reality frustrates the learners, whose motivations are both social and professional.

Interesting progress can be gathered from some experiences. In Germany, the recruitment of foreign apprentices (MobiPro Program) helped to integrate language learning and VET content, valuing informal learning by immersion and also complementary e-learning opportunities, in order to speed up the acquisition of a sufficient mastery of the German language to enable learners to follow VET lessons. In Switzerland *fide*-oriented courses provide examples of goal-oriented language learning. In France and Italy, at a local level, it is also possible to find examples of courses addressing specific professional environments, improving linguistic skills as a component of a qualification.

## 6 Final remarks

Over the past few years, policies have placed much emphasis on language learning as a key to integration but have underestimated the role of vocational qualifications in fostering social inclusion, professional mobility, active citizenship and participation of the learners. Structured practices aimed at developing the linguistic skills needed for participation in a formal qualification process are still very rare. On the other hand professional trainers are more and more faced with the challenge of making their communication appropriate to non-native speakers, imagining the use of glossaries and the assignment of tasks as an integral part of their teaching, facilitating the development of linguistic skills in parallel with the acquisition of vocational content.

Constraints have emerged. Interdisciplinary work seems to be difficult, the shift towards personalisation of learning and tailor-made didactic planning implies huge investments in time, often felt to be incompatible with the achievement of short-term learning outcomes. Therefore teachers and trainers should be supported accordingly. The feasibility and effectiveness of innovative methods and models should be demonstrated through effective piloting. Adequate resources should be provided, including training of trainers, libraries, materials and tools ready to be activated along the process.

(For more information on the results of the study: http://www.vintage-language.eu)

# References

de la Rica, Sara, Albrecht Glitz & Francesca Ortega. 2013. *Immigration in Europe: Trends, policies and empirical evidence*. IZA DP No. 7778, Bonn, November 2013.

Illeris, Knud. 1999. *Laering*. Roskilde: Roskilde University Press. English translation: Illeris, Knud. *How we learn: Learning and non-learning in school and beyond*. London & New York: Routledge, 2007.

Pulinx, Reinhilde, Piet Van Avermaet & Claire Extramiana. 2014. *Linguistic integration of adult migrants: Policy and practice*. Final report on the 3rd Council of Europe Survey. Strasbourg: Council of Europe. https://rm.coe.int/CoERMPublicCommonSearchServices/DisplayDCTMContent?documentId=09000016802fc1ce (accessed 6 June 2016).

Brian North, Enrica Piccardo
# Mediation and the social and linguistic integration of migrants: updating the CEFR descriptors

**Abstract:** The notion of mediation has been studied in psychology, pedagogy and the social sciences. The emerging vision of language acquisition as socialization into communities of practice through the mediation of material signs and its implications in the field of language education informed a Council of Europe project that has produced CEFR illustrative descriptors for mediation. The team conducted a three-phase developmental, mixed methods research. The paper concludes by pointing out the relevance of mediation to the integration of migrants.

**Résumé :** La psychologie, la pédagogie et les sciences sociales ont étudié la notion de médiation. Le nouveau concept d'acquisition de la langue comme compétence de « socialisation au sein des communautés de pratique par la médiation de signes matériels » et ses implications dans le domaine de l'apprentissage des langues a contribué à un projet du Conseil de l'Europe visant à élaborer des descripteurs de la médiation pour le CECR. L'équipe a réalisé une étude développementale en trois phases combinant plusieurs méthodes. En conclusion, l'article insiste sur l'importance de la médiation pour l'intégration des migrants.

# 1 Introduction

The notion of mediation, crucial for casting light on phenomena implying contact between the social and the individual and bridging between different elements and spaces, has been widely studied in psychology, pedagogy and the social sciences. In professional circles, mediation describes arbitration in disputes and counselling activities. In child development the notion is core both in child/adult interaction and in the way children employ tools and symbols creatively to

---

**Brian North** (corresponding author), Eurocentres Foundation and Eaquals,
E-mail: bjnorth@eurocentres.com
**Enrica Piccardo**, OISE, University of Toronto, Canada/Université Grenoble-Alpes, France,
E-mail: enrica.piccardo@utoronto.ca

make sense of their environment. In the Vygotskian view, semiotic mediation is central to all aspects of knowledge (co-)construction.

This paper reports on a Council of Europe project to develop mediation descriptors for the *Common European Framework of Reference for Languages* (CEFR; Council of Europe 2001). The emerging vision of language acquisition as "[s]ocialization into communities of practice through the mediation of material signs" (Kramsch 2002: 6) and its implications in the field of language education informed the approach adopted in the project. The interpretation of mediation taken led to descriptors potentially relevant to all contexts of language use, not just to the foreign/second language classroom.

## 2 Mediation in the CEFR

The CEFR pioneered the introduction of mediation, alongside interaction, to indicate communicative language activities which are not covered by reception and production. The change in terminology recognizes the role of the social dimension in language. Interaction is not just the sum of reception and production, but introduces a new factor: the co-construction of meaning. Mediation integrates and takes this further by underlining the constant link between the social and individual dimensions in language use and learning. Although the CEFR does not develop the concept of mediation fully, it emphasises the two key notions of co-construction of meaning in interaction and constant movement between the individual and social level in language learning, mainly through its vision of the user/learner as a social agent (Piccardo 2012). Both these concepts are central to the socio-constructivist/socio-cultural view of learning in which mediation is a key concept.

CEFR Section 4.4 states that "[i]n **mediating activities**, the language user is not concerned to express his/her own meanings, but simply to act as an intermediary between interlocutors who are unable to understand each other directly, normally (but not exclusively) speakers of different languages" (CEFR 4.4.4; English p.87, French p.71). The CEFR does not confine the concept to cross-linguistic mediation. The social agent and his/her interlocutor share the same situational context but may well maintain different perceptions and interpretations. The gap between these may be so great as to require some form of mediation, perhaps even by a third person (CEFR Section 4.1.4; English version p.50; French version p.44).

## 3 Mediation: a developmental notion

We can identify four types of mediation: linguistic, cultural, social and pedagogic.

**Linguistic mediation** comprises both the interlinguistic and the intralinguistic dimension, which could be in the target language (e.g. summarise an L2 text in L2) or in the source language, including mother tongue. Another form of linguistic mediation is the flexible use of different languages, for example in multilingual classrooms or in everyday professional life.

**Cultural mediation** is involved in any linguistic mediation that tries to facilitate understanding (Zarate et al. 2003). Mediation is the linchpin to the notion of cultural awareness, which applies within a language as well as across languages and cultures, with consideration of styles, genres and the different sub-cultures, social and professional, within a society.

**Social mediation** involves playing the role of intermediary and in the CEFR seems to be limited to helping persons to communicate who are unable to understand each other. But language is not the only reason why people cannot understand one another. The "mediator" helps to bridge gaps and overcome misunderstandings. The multifaceted nature of social mediation is shown by Kramsch (1993: 238) with the concept of "third space" in which a user/learner might take some distance from his/her cultural norms by "reading against the grain" and becoming more aware of loaded connotations. This last aspect is very close to Byram's (1997) *critical cultural awareness/political education.*

**Pedagogic mediation** is the process by which teachers and parents try to mediate knowledge and above all the ability to think critically for oneself – which together constitute **cognitive mediation.** However, a lot of time in a classroom context is spent establishing rapport, organizing work, keeping people on task, preventing and resolving problems – which together constitute **relational mediation.**

## 4 Towards a richer "model" of mediation

As we have seen, mediation can mean many things. The use of mediation in relation to diplomacy, conflict resolution and commercial transaction has more recently expanded to include a range of arbitration, counselling and guidance activities. Our deeper reflection on the nature of mediation, though, is rooted in German idealism and dialectical materialism. The work of Vygotsky then enabled the transition of this notion to psychology and education by explaining how social interaction plays a fundamental role in the development of cognition. Being at the core of knowledge (co-)construction, mediation occurs where there is bridging and exchange between different elements and spaces, where the individual and the social interact. According to Vygotsky, it is the process of mediation which allows one to break out of the dichotomy between the individual and the social dimension and to see individual processes as completely embedded in and structured by social processes. Mediation however is not exclusive to the sociocultural theory rooted in Vygotsky's work; it comes into play in ecological and complex views of language education as well. No matter where and how mediation is theorized though, the whole language acquisition process can be defined as "socialization into communities of practice through the mediation of material signs" (Kramsch 2002: 6).

Seeing mediation as an interdependent duality of individual and social echoes Halliday's "basic distinction between an ideational (representational, referential, cognitive) and an interpersonal (expressive-conative, social, evocative) function of language" (1975: 52). Halliday underlines in his model the difference between an idea of language as representation of thought and use of language as a communication tool for expressing social and personal relations. Action that allows one to make sense of things and structure learning through language is accomplished through the mediation of the mental processes involved in the completion of a task (Piccardo 2012).

## 5 Development and validation of illustrative descriptors

Mediation, then, is an all-embracing notion, striking in its richness, variety, layers and lack of structure. How can one capture this in a practical descriptive scheme? In addition, in discussing linguistic, cultural, social and pedagogic mediation, one sees an overlapping and intermeshing between these categories. Nowadays we understand that all categorisation in the social sciences is conventional rather than intrinsic. The fact that we bring one aspect into focus in order to describe it does not imply that we believe it enjoys a separate existence in an atomistic model. Using the current scholarly discussion on mediation as its conceptual framework, the team conducted a Type 1 developmental research (Richey and Klein 2005). The validation methodology adopted replicated the three-phase, "mixed methods" approach (Cresswell 2003) used to develop the original CEFR descriptors (North and Schneider 1998).

Firstly, in the *intuitive phase* a team reviewed source material, drafting, editing and discussing descriptors in an iterative process. Secondly, in the *qualitative phase*, with some 990 respondents, the categories were validated, individual descriptors evaluated and proposals for reformulation made. Finally, in the *quantitative phase* (c. 1250 respondents), the best descriptors were calibrated with two independent Rasch Rating Scale model analyses. A detailed paper, together with technical reports, is available on the Council of Europe's website. The categories for the resulting descriptor scales are given below. The "other new scales" concern aspects that might well not be considered to be mediation, but in which an element of mediation is involved.

## Mediation activities

***Relational mediation (spoken):*** Establishing a positive atmosphere; Creating pluricultural space; Facilitating collaborative interaction with peers; Managing interaction in plenary and in groups; Dealing with delicate situations and disputes

## Cognitive mediation

***Constructing meaning (spoken):*** Collaborating to construct meaning; Stimulating the development of ideas

***Conveying received meaning (spoken):*** Relaying specific information; Explaining data; Processing text; Interpreting; Spoken translation of written text

***Conveying received meaning (written):*** Relaying specific information; Explaining data; Processing text; Translating

## Mediation strategies

Linking to previous knowledge; Amplifying text; Streamlining text; Breaking down complicated information; Visually representing information; Adjusting language

## Other new scales

Multimodal online conversation and discussion; Goal-oriented online transactions and collaboration

Expressing a personal response to literature (including film); Analysis and criticism of literature (including film)

Exploiting pluricultural repertoire in intercultural encounters; Plurilingual comprehension; Exploiting plurilingual repertoire

## 6 Relevance to the LIAM context

Mediation is an everyday occurrence in public, academic, and professional life and in today's globalised world it is frequently cross-linguistic. In knowledge-based societies, an ability to sift through and process information – perhaps in more than one language – to identify and pass on what is relevant, is also of constantly increasing importance. Then of course there are second language learners who find themselves, as immigrants, despite their possibly partial competences, operating as more formal or less formal mediators between representatives of a host community and newer arrivals. Indeed, both migrants and professionals who work with migrants often find themselves in situations in which they need to help to create pluricultural space, facilitate discussion, deal with misunderstandings and delicate situations, relay or summarise information, interpret and elaborate on what is said, and above all increase their pluricultural awareness. The core vision of the CEFR is to value the dynamic and collaborative nature of user/learners' trajectories. We hope that the provision of CEFR descriptors will help raise awareness of the need for mediation skills in a migration context, and contribute to the efforts of those involved to improve mutual understanding.

## References

Byram, Michael. 1997. *Teaching and assessing intercultural communicative competence.* Cleveland: Multilingual Matters.

Council of Europe. 2001. *Common European Framework of Reference for Languages: Learning, teaching, assessment.* Cambridge: Cambridge University Press. http://www.coe.int/t/dg4/linguistic/Source/Framework_EN.pdf (accessed 9 August 2016).

Cresswell, John W. 2003. *Research design: Qualitative, quantitative and mixed methods approaches*, 2nd edn. Thousand Oaks, CA: Sage.

Halliday, Michael A. K. 1975. *Learning how to mean: Explorations in the development of language*. London: Arnold.
Kramsch, Claire. 1993. *Context and culture in language teaching*. Oxford: Oxford University Press.
Kramsch Claire. (ed.). 2002. *Language acquisition and language socialization: Ecological perspectives*. New York: Continuum.
North, Brian & Günther Schneider. 1998. Scaling descriptors for language proficiency scales. *Language Testing* 15(2). 217–262.
Piccardo, Enrica. 2012. Médiation et apprentissage des langues: Pourquoi est-il temps de réflechir à cette notion? *ELA: Études de Linguistique Appliquée* 167. 285–97.
Richey, Rita C. & James D. Klein. 2005. Developmental research methods: Creating knowledge from instructional design and development practice. *Journal of Computing in Higher Education* 16(2). 23–38.
Zarate, Genviève, Aline Gohard-Radenkovic, Denise Lussier & Hermine Penz. 2004. *Cultural mediation in language learning and teaching*. Strasbourg: Council of Europe Publishing.

Kate Hammer
# Sociocultural integration and second language proficiency following migration

**Abstract:** This presentation reports on an investigation into the links between proficiency level in the second language and degree of sociocultural integration in the host country following migration. Participants were 149 highly-educated young-adult sequential Polish-English bilinguals who had been resident in the UK for an average of eight years. Statistical analyses backed up with interview data show that the degree of acculturation and sociocultural integration are strongly linked to the ultimate proficiency level in the new language following migration.

**Résumé :** L'article examine la corrélation possible entre le niveau de compétence dans la langue seconde (L2) et le niveau d'intégration socioculturelle des migrants dans le pays d'accueil. Une étude a été réalisée auprès de 149 jeunes adultes très qualifiés, tous bilingues polonais-anglais, qui résidaient au Royaume-Uni depuis huit ans en moyenne. Les analyses statistiques et les données recueillies en entretien montrent que le niveau d'acculturation et d'intégration socioculturelle est étroitement lié au niveau de compétence acquis dans la langue seconde après la migration.

## 1 Background

Migration is one of the most widely debated topics in the modern world. Movement of people across national borders is a subject of negotiation in international relations; it also sparks discussions about cultural and linguistic integration, as well as social cohesion within individual nation states. There is a strong link between migration, integration and language (Esser 2006). The ability to use the official language of the new country of residence is a crucial component of successful integration into the new society. Language enables communication between members of the society; it is also a carrier of sociocultural values and norms. Language is a medium in the processes of sociocultural integration. The level to which the new language (L2) is attained by a new language user is linked to the user's ability to participate in the social, cultural and organiza-

---

**Kate Hammer,** Birkbeck, University of London, United Kingdom, E-mail: k.hammer@bbk.ac.uk

DOI 10.1515/9783110477498-012, © 2017 Kate Hammer, published by De Gruyter.
This work is licensed under the Creative Commons Attribution-NonCommercial-NoDerivs 3.0 License.

tional life of the new society (Esser 2006). Higher levels of L2 proficiency enable a more engaged character of settlement, for the language user is able to understand the surrounding sociocultural reality to a deeper level directly from authentic sources, as opposed to translation. Linguistic attainment is thus an important factor in sociocultural integration, as it helps the new language user to become an independent member of the new society.

Second language acquisition (SLA) is a complex process which engages various mental faculties, and which has been linked to different SLA-oriented variables including motivation, age of onset and context of L2 acquisition (Cook and Singleton 2014). Immersion in the target language for a prolonged period of time has also been linked to successful language attainment due to increased exposure to the new language in a variety of contexts (Singleton, Regan, and Debaene 2013). In addition, levels of attainment in L2 have been linked to the acquisition of the target culture. Acculturation is defined as a "process of cultural and psychological change" (Berry 2005: 698). The Acculturation Model for SLA (Schumann 1986) combines sociocultural and psychological factors in respect to the acquisition of a new language following migration. The model predicts that the L2 learner will acquire the target language to the level to which they acculturate to the new culture. According to Schumann (1986), successful acquisition of the L2 in the circumstances of migration is tightly linked to the extent to which the L2 learner assimilates to the new culture. Acculturation has been described as one of the most causal variables in SLA, and it has been employed in poststructuralist approaches to L2 learning and use (Pavlenko 2002).

This summary presents the results of the study, which investigated self-reported proficiency level in L2 following migration in native Polish L1 speakers who migrated to the UK in early adulthood. The independent variables included sociolinguistic and language acquisition factors, namely: acculturation level; frequency of L2 use; social network profile; age at migration; length of residence; age of onset of second language acquisition (AoA); current age; context of L2 acquisition; education level; gender; and motivation behind migration (Hammer 2012; Hammer and Dewaele 2015).

## 2 Research question

To what extent is self-reported proficiency in L2 following migration linked to:
(a) Acculturation level
(b) Frequency of L2 use following migration
(c) Social network profile
(d) Age of onset of L2 acquisition

(e) Age at migration
(f) Context of L2 acquisition
(g) Current age
(h) Length of residence
(i) Education level
(j) Gender
(k) Motivation behind migration

# 3 Methodology

Participants were 149 native speakers of Polish who migrated to the UK in early adulthood. The average age at migration was 23 (range 18–41, mean = 23.6, SD = 3.8), and the average current age was 31 (range 23–45, mean = 31.1, SD = 4.7). The majority of the participants (128) had migrated by the age of 26. All participants were university or college graduates, of whom 86% were female and 14% male. 45.6% of the respondents rated themselves as proficient users of English L2; 38.3% admitted native-like proficiency; 14.1% declared an advanced level of L2 use and 2% self-rated as intermediate level L2 users.

Participants completed an online questionnaire which consisted of both closed and open-ended questions (Hammer 2012). In addition, 14 participants were interviewed by the researcher. The design included both quantitative and qualitative approaches. A one-sample Kolmogorov-Smirnov test revealed that the values for self-reported proficiency level in L2 were not normally distributed ($Z = 2.9$, $p < .0001$); therefore Spearman's rank correlation, Kruskal-Wallis and Mann-Whitney tests were used in statistical analyses.

# 4 Results

Quantitative data analyses revealed:
(a) A significant effect of acculturation level on self-reported proficiency level in L2 (Kruskal-Wallis test; $\chi^2 = 11.1$; $p < .004$); completely and highly acculturated participants had significantly higher levels of self-reported proficiency than moderately and slightly acculturated participants.
(b) A significant effect of frequency of L2 use on self-reported proficiency level in L2 (Kruskal-Wallis test; $\chi^2 = 10$; $p < .018$); participants who used the L2 more frequently attained higher levels of L2-proficiency than those who used predominantly L1.

(c) A significant effect of social network profile on self-reported proficiency level in L2 (Kruskal-Wallis test; $\chi^2 = 7.9$; $p < .019$); higher levels of self-reported proficiency were recorded for participants whose social networks included both L1- and L2-speaking interlocutors, or majority L2-speaking interlocutors, as opposed to those whose social networks were predominantly L1-speaking.
(d) A significant effect of AoA on self-reported proficiency level in L2 (Kruskal-Wallis test; $\chi^2 = 6.3$; $p < .042$); participants who started learning the L2 at a lower age attained a higher level of L2-proficiency.
(e) No significant effect of age at migration on self-reported proficiency level in L2 (Kruskal-Wallis test; $\chi^2 = 2.4$, $p = .303$).
(f) No significant effect of context of L2 acquisition on self-reported proficiency level in L2 (Kruskal-Wallis test; $\chi^2 = 4.3$; $p = .116$).
(g) A significant link between current age and self-reported level of proficiency (Spearman's Rank Correlation; Rho = .176; $p < .032$); older participants felt more proficient in L2 than younger participants.
(h) A significant effect of length of residence on the self-reported proficiency level in L2 (Kruskal-Wallis test; $\chi^2 = 7.1$; $p < .029$); there was a monotonic increase in L2 proficiency levels between participants whose length of residence was under five years, those whose residency ranged from five to ten years, and those whose residency reached or exceeded ten years.
(i) No significant effect of education level on self-reported proficiency level in L2 (Kruskal-Wallis test; $\chi^2 = 2.25$; $p = .324$).
(j) No significant effect of gender on self-reported proficiency level in L2 (Mann-Whitney test; U = 1342; $p = .991$).
(k) No significant effect of motivation behind migration on self-reported proficiency level in L2 (Kruskal-Wallis test; $\chi^2 = .492$; $p = .782$).

Qualitative data analyses and the feedback from the interviews and open questions confirmed the statistical findings.

## 5 Discussion

The findings revealed that the effect of acculturation level on self-reported proficiency in L2 had the strongest statistical effect when compared to all other variables (Hammer and Dewaele 2015). Participants with higher acculturation levels were found to have higher levels of proficiency in English L2. Other variables which were found to have an effect on the level of attainment in L2 following migration were, in decreasing order of statistical significance: frequency of L2 use;

social network profile; length of residence; current age and AoA. Participants who used English L2 more frequently and whose social networks included more English-speaking interlocutors were found to have higher levels of L2 proficiency when compared to participants whose frequency of L2 use was low, and whose social networks were predominantly L1-oriented. Two temporal variables were also found to be linked to proficiency level in L2 namely, length of residence and current age. Participants with greater length of residence in the host country, as well as older participants, were found to have higher self-reported proficiency levels as opposed to younger participants, and those whose length of residence was shorter than five years. Participants whose length of residence reached or exceeded ten years were found to have the highest levels of L2 proficiency (Hammer and Dewaele 2015). Also AoA was found to be linked to proficiency levels; participants who started learning the L2 earlier in life recorded overall higher levels of proficiency in L2, which links with previous studies investigating the effects of AoA on L2 attainment (cf. Cook and Singleton 2014). No links were established between self-reported proficiency and education level, gender, age at migration, context of L2 acquisition and motivation behind migration.

The findings showed that L2 proficiency following migration is tightly linked to acculturation level, which links with the Acculturation Model for SLA (Schumann 1986). Acculturation is understood as a crucial component in L2 attainment in the circumstances of migration, which supports the notion that migration, integration and language are significantly interconnected (Esser 2006). The findings provide empirical evidence that linguistic acquisition develops alongside and in relation to cultural acquisition (cf. Singleton, Regan, and Debaene 2013). The present study provides support for the notion that acculturation is a powerful causal variable in processes of SLA (Pavlenko 2002).

# 6 Conclusion

Acculturation proved to be tightly linked to L2 attainment following migration; the statistical significance of the effect of acculturation level on self-reported proficiency in L2 was higher than any other variable tested as part of the study. The findings suggest that linguistic integration of adult migrants in the host country is tightly linked to acculturation levels, and that linguistic attainment does not happen independent of sociocultural integration.

# References

Berry, John W. 2005. Acculturation: Living successfully in two cultures. *International Journal of Intercultural Relations* 29. 697–712.

Cook, Vivian J. & David Singleton. 2014. *Key topics in second language acquisition*. Bristol: Multilingual Matters.

Esser, Hartmut. 2006. *Migration, language and integration*. AKI Research Review 4. Programme on Intercultural Conflicts and Societal Integration, Social Research Centre Berlin.

Hammer, Kate. 2012. Web questionnaire on language use and language choice in bilinguals (E-PLUS). Unpublished manuscript, University of London.

Hammer, Kate & Jean-Marc Dewaele. 2015. Acculturation as the key to the ultimate attainment? The case of Polish-English bilinguals in the UK. In Fanny Forsberg Lundell & Inge Bartning (eds.), *Cultural migrants and optimal language acquisition*, 179–202. Bristol: Multilingual Matters.

Pavlenko, Aneta. 2002. Poststructuralist approaches to the study of social factors in L2. In Vivian Cook (ed.), *Portraits of the L2 user*, 277–302. Clevedon: Multilingual Matters.

Schumann, John H. 1986. Research on the Acculturation Model for second language acquisition. *Journal of Multilingual and Multicultural Development* 7(5). 379–392.

Singleton, David, Vera Regan & Ewelina Debaene (eds.). 2013. *Linguistic and cultural acquisition in a migrant community*. Bristol: Multilingual Matters.

Monika Jezak, Encarnacion Carrasco
# Integration trajectories of adult (im)migrants in minority and minoritized contexts: Ottawa and Barcelona

**Abstract:** To investigate the impact of policies on the integration trajectories of adult (im)migrants, we conducted a study in two urban bilingual contexts, Ottawa and Barcelona, where one of the languages is a minority or minoritized language (French and Catalan). Despite the differences between these two sociolinguistic realities, our study highlights the unpredictability of integration pathways as well as the need to revise, from a plurilingual perspective, the epistemological framework of the field.

**Résumé :** Afin d'étudier l'incidence des politiques sur les parcours d'intégration des (im)migrants adultes, nous avons conduit une enquête dans deux contextes urbains de sociétés bilingues, Ottawa et Barcelone, où l'une des langues est minoritaire ou minorisée (français et catalan). Malgré les différences entre ces deux réalités sociolinguistiques, notre étude a mis en exergue l'imprévisibilité des retombées des politiques d'intégration ainsi que la nécessité de réviser, depuis une perspective plurilingue, le cadre épistémologique du domaine de recherche invoqué.

## 1 Introduction

In government, civil society, and research circles there is an agreement that proficiency in the host-society language is an important factor in the integration and retention of (im)migrants. However, few have studied the specific impact of this factor and those that have done so, insist that it is difficult to grasp. The present paper reports on a study conducted concurrently in Barcelona and Ottawa that looks at a hundred adult newcomers who take, respectively, Catalan and French language classes aimed at their social and labour market integration. Once registered in these advanced language courses, they are beneficiaries of settlement policies within the two communities. They are also likely to become members of

---

**Monika Jezak,** University of Ottawa, Canada, E-mail: mjezak@uottawa.ca
**Encarnacion Carrasco,** Université J. Fourier de Grenoble, France/University of Barcelona, Spain, E-mail: encarnicarrasco@ub.edu

DOI 10.1515/9783110477498-013, © 2017 Monika Jezak, Encarnacion Carrasco, published by De Gruyter.
This work is licensed under the Creative Commons Attribution-NonCommercial-NoDerivs 3.0 License.

the Francophone community in Ottawa and the Catalan community in Barcelona. Our study aims to trace the linguistic profile and language practices of recent (im)migrants, their attitudes and motivations towards French and Catalan, as well as their contact with the two communities in order to bring to light the impact of language factors on the integration trajectories in a minority and minoritized context.

# 2 Ottawa

## 2.1 Demolinguistic context and rationale

In 2015, the Francophone population represented approximately seven million out of 35 million Canadians, with just over a million native French speakers residing outside of Québec. Moreover, a certain number among this population no longer use French in their daily lives. The integration of newcomers in minority Francophone contexts is therefore essential not only because it maintains the demographic weight of these communities but also in order for the Canadian Francophonie to benefit from immigration. Yet, presently, the vast majority of immigrants outside of Québec are settling in Anglophone communities (Fraser and Boileau 2014).

Ottawa's demolinguistic situation presents certain similarities with the rest of Canada but also some particularity. The Anglophone population constitutes the majority (almost 64%) while Francophones represent about 15% and – like in the rest of Canada – the progressive decline of the number of Anglophones and Francophones to the benefit of allophone speakers is apparent. In fact, the number of allophones climbed from 10.5% in 1981 to 21.3% in 2011 (Office of the Commissioner of Official Languages 2015).

With respect to particularity, even though Ottawa has no official bilingual status, *de facto* bilingualism is very much present since the city is an emblem of Canada and hosts a bilingual federal government – the most important employer in the region. Situated at the boundary between Ontario and Québec, the Ottawa region contains all the Canadian linguistic groups: minority Francophones in Ontario and majority ones in Québec, majority Anglophones in Ontario and minority ones in Québec, as well as various allophone groups integrating either in English or French, in either a majority or a minority context. According to Gilbert and Veronis (2010: 35), "the region has a unique linguistic environment because the French presence is strongly rooted on both sides of the border. However, concomitantly, the region's bilingualism is highly valued because it provides the population with access to the rest of Canada and North America".

In this context of linguistic to-and-fro, more than 37% of Ottawa's population is estimated to be bilingual and this proportion is rising steadily. Similarly, a quarter of immigrants declare being able to communicate with ease in English and French, on top of one or more languages that they already possessed before arriving in Canada (Office of the Commissioner of Official Languages 2015).

## 2.2 Linguistic practices and integration trajectories of French speakers in Ottawa: principal results

Our sample consists of an almost equal number of men and women between the ages of 20 and 65, with strong representation in the 30–50 bracket, which is dependent on immigration policy. The sample is comprised of recent immigrants: 32 participants have resided in Canada less than a year. Moreover, they are an educated group, with the vast majority of participants having a post-secondary diploma.

At the linguistic level, it is a Francophone or Francophile population. Even if 23 different mother languages were declared, 11 participants have French as their mother language, 14 have Haitian Creole, and 36 originate from countries where French is one of the official languages. Furthermore, 43 participants finished their education in French in their country of origin (in Francophone Africa or the Maghreb).

### 2.2.1 Linguistic practices and attitudes towards the French language and community

Even if the tendency to live in two languages remains strong (for example, in French and English, in French and Creole, or in French and Arabic), the majority of our participants declared primarily using French in their daily social interactions and with their family (socializing, watching television, reading, surfing the web, etc.). Likewise, these immigrants mostly consider themselves as having a good or very good level of French, whereas 36 participants declared a "functional" or "weak" level of English. Finally, they seem keen on living in French in Ottawa. To that effect, the participants stated a preference for French in terms of integration aims (to live in French in a bilingual environment, to create a Francophone social network), economic goals (to find employment in a Francophone network, or even a bilingual job), and for personal reasons (an affinity with the language, to help their children with school, or to be introduced to a new Francophone culture).

### 2.2.2 Contact with Ottawa's Francophone community

However, notwithstanding a good command of French, a social and family life lived in French, positive attitudes towards the local Francophonie and its language, as well as a positive disposition to integrate into the French speaking community, the results suggest that other than social services (notably Francophone schools and hospitals), new immigrants are not familiar with institutions, organisms, and cultural events of the Francophone network established in Ottawa, and attend them even less. The same is true of numerous settlement services of which only three were recognized, and even then, only by ten participants.

# 3 Barcelona

## 3.1 Catalonia: a paradigm shift

From the beginning of the 21st century, Catalonia has experienced an unprecedented inflow of international migrants that poses a veritable challenge. In a single decade, the foreign-born population in the region has climbed from 2.9% in 2000 to 15.7% in 2011. In parallel with this demographic phenomenon, migrant settlement and integration legislation has progressively evolved within a double legislative framework: that of the Spanish state and that of the autonomous Catalan government. In 2011, the Generalitat of Catalunya agreed to take responsibility for, among other things, the *degree of integration* of migrants in relation to the granting of residency permits.

As Branchadell (2015) highlights, the local legislation envisions host-society language learning as an indispensable fact for migrants on the path to acquiring citizenship. Yet, if learning Catalan constitutes a measure of symbolic integration, it is perceived as a process for which only the migrant bears the responsibility. This unequal distribution of capital is rarely called into question, nor is the plurilingual repertoire of learners partially and impartially recognized (Garrido 2015).

The new Catalan sociolinguistic landscape impacts the acquisition and use of Catalan and, by extension, the linguistic integration of migrants. The territorial and official bilingualism encompasses two languages etymologically close as both are romance languages. This relationship increases translinguistic phenomena specific to contexts of language contact such as code-switching or hybridization. At the same time, there is a clear contradiction between, on one side, the official discourse that places the learning of Catalan as a central endeavour in the integration of newcomers and, on the other side, the practices that consist of addressing the very same newcomers in Spanish. Authors like Pujolar (2010, in Caglitutuncigil 2014) qualify this phenomenon of "interposition" of Spanish in bilingual exchanges and note the use of this language as a *lingua franca* in many Catalan language courses (Caglitutuncigil 2014).

Finally, from the beginning of the 21st century, new waves of migration have also prompted a profound change in the orientation of Catalan sociolinguistic research which passed from subscribing to a paradigm of *distribution* and *conflict* – of North American origin – to one of *multilingualism,* where the new directions and perspectives would be, according to Vila (2015), the sociolinguistics of mobility and resources, the socio-economic integration of migrants in the era of globalization, and the impact of these new migration flows on a fragile linguistic ecosystem.

## 3.2 Linguistic practices and integration trajectories of Catalan migrants: principal results

The Barcelonan sample was composed of thirty participants representing 14 different countries and, virtually in equal parts, the European continent and Latin America. The age bracket of those surveyed fell between 23 and 66 years. Despite the high qualifications of almost half the sample who possessed a university diploma, the rate of unemployment was 16%.

### 3.2.1 Catalan language practices

Our sample's language practices demonstrate a clear specialization by domain-of-use of three principal languages: Castilian, Catalan, and English. The first stands out as the most used in private, social, and professional domains. It is followed by Catalan in private and social domains, while English occupies the third place and is used mainly in professional contexts. In terms of Catalan in the workplace, the participants reported that they do indeed make use of it for interacting with clients and for reading.

### 3.2.2 Contact with Catalan and motivation for its learning

The distribution between Catalan and Spanish in the official settlement institutions remains relatively balanced. We found as many centers where our sample interacted more in Catalan, more in Spanish, or equally across both languages.

Nonetheless, Catalan asserted itself as being the most used language across municipal services and in the Consortium for Linguistic Normalisation.

With regard to the motivation to learn Catalan, the participants primarily pointed to their socio-professional integration and for many among them it was the primary and only reason stated. The second most cited reason was the desire (necessity?) to further the use of this language and to do so in the most correct and efficient manner possible.

## 4 Conclusion

Our data was collected in Ottawa and Barcelona, two cosmopolitan cities characterized by significant (im)migration rates, where the Catalan and the French-Canadian communities' identities are an important issue. In fact, these two communities (minoritized and minority respectively) remain preoccupied with the appeal that Spanish and English have for newcomers and with the power struggle facing their respective co-official languages, which affects the choice of language use and acquisition by (im)migrants. Hence our project tackles the integration process in a situation of relative fragility of the host society, where the newcomers are subjected to a double minority status.

In this context, in spite of the structural and environmental differences between the two sites, the project has highlighted, on either side of the Atlantic, a gap between the results expected by the various settlement and integration policies (that frame migrants in a homogenising vision) and the real directions finally taken by migrants, which prove to be multiple, varied, and often surpass the preconceived frame. Those results call as well for an epistemological shift in the field.

## References

Branchadell, Albert. 2015. Language education for adult migrant in Catalonia: Nation-state ambitions without nation-state resources. In James Simpson & Anne Whiteside (eds.), *Adult language education and migration: Challenging agendas in policy and practice*, 82–93. London & New York: Routledge.

Caglitutuncigil Martínez, Tulay. 2014. La construcció de desigualtats en espais bilingües: l'ensenyament del català a dones immigrants. *Digithum* 16. 33–41. http://journals.uoc.edu/index.php/digithum/article/view/n16-caglitutuncigil/n16-caglitutuncigil-en (accessed 25 March 2016).

Fraser, Graham & François Boileau. 2014. *Time to act for the future of francophone communities: Redressing the immigration imbalance*. Ottawa: Government of Canada.

Garrido Sardà, Maria Rosa. 2015. La gestió del multilingüisme en els serveis d'acollida de les ONG: un estudi de cas. In Franscesc Xavier Vila & Eulàlia Salvat (eds.), *Noves immigracions i llengües*, 97–118. Barcelona: Agrupació d'editors i autors universitaris.

Gilbert, Anne & Luisa Veronis. 2010. The best of both worlds: The geographic experience of Francophone immigrants from Central Africa in the Ottawa-Gatineau Region. In *Current research compendium on francophone immigration in Canada*, 35–37. Montreal: Heritage Canada – Metropolis.

Office of the Commissioner of Official Languages. 2015. *Portrait des groupes de langues officielles de la région d'Ottawa*. Ottawa: Government of Canada.

Pujolar, Joan. 2010. Immigration and language education in Catalonia: Between national and social agendas. *Linguistics and Education* 21(3). 229–243.

Vila, Francesc Xavier. 2015. De "l'etapa autonòmica" a la "sociolingüística del multilingüisme": una dècada de recerca sociolingüística sobre les noves immigracions. In Franscesc Xavier Vila, Eulàlia Salvat (eds.), *Noves immigracions i llengües*, 11–28. Barcelona: Agrupació d'editors i autors universitaris.

Jamel Sarraj
# L'intégration linguistique des migrants adultes : la mise en œuvre des politiques publiques dans la région suisse alémanique de Zurich

**Résumé :** Les pays industrialisés et surtout européens attirent les migrants par leur qualité de vie, leur respect des droits de l'homme, leur système d'assurance sociale, leur relative prospérité économique et leur enseignement moderne. L'intégration du migrant peut se faire grâce à l'apprentissage de la langue d'intégration, au travail, à une formation, à un mariage mixte, entre autres. L'intégration nécessite une volonté et un engagement du migrant mais aussi des moyens du pays d'accueil. Plusieurs pays membres du Conseil de l'Europe rencontrent des difficultés diverses pour mettre en place leur politique d'intégration linguistique des migrants.

**Abstract:** The industrialised countries, especially in Europe, appeal to migrants because of their quality of life, respect for human rights, social security systems, relative economic prosperity and state-of-the-art education systems. A migrant can integrate through learning the integration language, work, training, a mixed marriage, and so on. Integration requires determination and commitment from the migrant, but also resources from the host country. A number of Council of Europe member states are experiencing different kinds of problems in implementing their linguistic integration policies for migrants.

## Introduction

Ce travail concerne la région suisse alémanique de Zurich. Il dresse un état des lieux, relève les éventuelles difficultés et leurs origines et il propose des solutions en fonction du contexte. Il précise le degré de conformité du processus d'intégration linguistique des migrants adultes dans cette région aux recommandations du Conseil de l'Europe. Les difficultés sont d'ordre administratif, socio-culturel, politique et didactique. Celles-ci pourraient concerner les 17 cantons suisses alémaniques, dont le contexte peut être comparé à celui de

**Jamel Sarraj**, DILTEC, Université Sorbonne Nouvelle – Paris 3, E-Mail : jamelynsCH@gmx.ch

Zurich. Autrement dit, ces observations pourraient concerner 65 % de la population suisse. L'environnement sociolinguistique suisse se caractérise par la présence de 4 langues nationales : l'allemand qui représente 64,9 % des locuteurs de la population suisse, le français 22,6 %, l'italien 8,3 % et le romanche 0,5 %. Les diverses langues de migration représentent 21 % des locuteurs migrants résidant en Suisse selon les publications de la Confédération suisse de 2015 (37[e] édition, *Langues et religions* : 2). La langue anglaise est le plus souvent la langue des affaires ou du tourisme voire, parfois, une langue de compromis, lorsque deux citoyens suisses ne parlent pas la même langue.

Mon statut de migrant à Zurich depuis 2000, mon apprentissage de la langue allemande en 2001, ma fonction d'enseignant de langue française et arabe aux adultes dans plusieurs institutions de langue, mes relations avec des collègues enseignants de langue allemande et avec des migrants vivant à Zurich et ma recherche de thèse en doctorat (2015) sur la didactique des langues/cultures m'ont beaucoup aidé à réaliser ce travail.

À Zurich, les différentes institutions de langue sont publiques, soutenues et subventionnées par le Canton et les mairies. Elles sont aussi de statut privé et se présentent comme des coopératives, des fondations, des entreprises, des clubs et des agences. Celles-ci sont suisses, allemandes ou américaines et il existe des classes de langue dans des centres d'accueil pour réfugiés. Je vais surtout m'intéresser à ces institutions qui seront identifiées par une lettre majuscule (A, B...) et une ville pour respecter leur anonymat. Je renverrai aussi à des entretiens anonymes, réalisés avec des enseignants, des migrants et des réfugiés (renvoi au moyen de lettres minuscules : a, b, c...). Ils sont caractérisés en fin de texte. J'ai en outre analysé 9 manuels de langue auxquels il sera renvoyé par des chiffres et dont les références se trouvent en fin de texte.

# 1 Méthodologie de la collecte des données[1]

La collecte des données a eu lieu au mois de décembre 2015 pour les observations de classe et les entretiens avec les enseignants et les apprenants et en janvier 2016 pour les migrants. Les entretiens et les observations de classes n'ont pas été enregistrés conformément aux exigences des personnes interviewées, mais ils ont donné lieu à des prises de notes. Les migrants interrogés travaillent comme techniciens et cadres moyens dans des entreprises suisses et internationales. Ils sont originaires du Portugal, d'Italie, d'Espagne, du Maroc (une

---

[1] Les références aux données utilisées figurent en annexe.

femme), de Belgique, d'Angleterre, de France (une femme) et de Taiwan. Ils ont entre 28 à 46 ans. Les réfugiés sont originaires d'Afghanistan, de Syrie, du Pérou (une femme), du Nigéria et de Libye et ils ont entre 24 et 38 ans.

Les apprenants sont des débutants et de niveau A2. Ils sont originaires de Turquie, d'Irak, du Vietnam (une femme), de Bolivie (une femme), du Nigéria, du Ghana, de Pologne et de Libye. Ils ont entre 22 et 44 ans. Les enseignants qui ont accepté l'entretien sont au nombre de 7 : 4 hommes, 2 femmes suisses et 1 allemande. Ils travaillent dans des institutions de langue : A (Winterthur), B (Altstetten), C (Zurich), D (Wallisellen), E (Dübendorf), F (Zurich) et G (Oerlikon). Ils ont entre 32 et 56 ans. J'ai essayé de choisir des personnes le plus représentatives possible pour être le plus proche de la réalité et du contexte suisse alémanique. Mais celui-ci est diversifié. Cependant on peut espérer que cette enquête présente une certaine valeur qualitative.

## 2 État des lieux et analyse des données

### 2.1 Hétérogénéité

Les institutions organisent des classes avec le nombre maximal d'apprenants possible, sans toujours prendre en considération les différences entre les niveaux des apprenants/migrants (A, B, C, D, E, F et G) qui n'ont ni le même rapport avec la langue/culture cible, ni le même parcours scolaire, ni le même contexte familial, ni les mêmes attentes. Ceci crée des difficultés aux apprenants et à l'enseignant. Les différences individuelles et culturelles freinent ceux qui ont un bon niveau et démotivent ceux qui sont moyens. Comme les langues n'ont pas les mêmes systèmes phonétiques et morphologiques, ceci est à l'origine d'interférences grammaticales, sémantiques et phonologiques (Sarraj 2015 : 99–120) qui sont difficiles à traiter dans des classes hétérogènes. Selon les recommandations du *Regionales Arbeitsvermittlungszentrum* (Office régional de placement), de l'*Asyl Organisation Zentrum* (Centre d'organisation de l'asile) et du service social des mairies, les réfugiés qui trouvent du travail sont priés d'arrêter leur cours de langue (d.1 à d.5). Les observations de classe (A, B, C, D, E, F et G) ont montré des difficultés de compréhension et de production.

### 2.2 Choix des manuels de langue d'intégration

J'ai constaté que les thèmes de 7 manuels sur 9 s'intéressent uniquement au contexte allemand (manuels 1, 2, 3, 4, 5, 7 et 8). Or l'apprenant/migrant vit dans un contexte suisse alémanique. Par ailleurs, mis à part *Deutsch in der Schweiz* (manuel 6 : 30–31, 52, 64, 82–83), les autres manuels ne retiennent pas de situations valorisant la culture du migrant. L'altérité n'y figure pas. Le migrant y est aussi parfois présenté comme un simple employé, bruyant et bavard (manuel 1 : 8–10, 56 et manuel 3 : 40, 66). Or, il est évident que les migrants ne sont pas tous coursiers pour des pizzerias ou chauffeurs de taxi. Il y a aussi des migrants médecins, ingénieurs, stylistes et d'autres ayant réussi leurs études et occupé des postes de grande responsabilité. Les manières de gérer les conversations diffèrent d'une culture linguistique/communicative à une autre, mais il n'est pas dit que les migrants sont « naturellement » extravertis, communiquent facilement et d'une façon spontanée et parlent à haute voix en gesticulant, comme cela apparaît dans un manuel (6 : 75). De tels comportements peuvent être considérés dans les cultures des pays d'accueil comme agressifs et peu respectueux. Certains ne présentent aucune situation de communication ni personnage (manuels 4, 5 et 9). Dans le manuel 9, les apprenants n'ont pas de CD à disposition. Parfois les textes et les photos sont en noir et blanc (manuels 4 et 5), ce qui n'est pas très motivant.

## 2.3 Formation et compétence des enseignants

Les enseignants de langue d'intégration pour adultes rencontrés sont, en grande majorité, des chômeurs qui se sont reconvertis en suivant le stage de formation de la Fédération suisse pour la formation continue (*Schweizer Verband für Erwachsenenbildung*, stage *SVEB1*), (a.2, a.3, a.4, a.6 et a.7). Le candidat ne doit pas nécessairement être titulaire de la maturité (baccalauréat suisse) et il est formé en très peu de temps. Outre une quinzaine de cours théoriques, il doit effectuer un travail individuel en autonomie durant 3 mois, pendant lesquels il peut imaginer des séquences d'enseignement et proposer des solutions en se référant au cours théorique (a.2, a.3, a.4, a.5 et a.6). Il apprend au fur et à mesure qu'il enseigne. Ceci le met dans des situations difficiles (B, C, D, E et F). Le coût d'un stage de formation *SVEB1* s'élève en moyenne à 3 000 francs suisses et 7 enseignants sur 7 ne comptent pas poursuivre leur formation avec le *SVEB2* (7 000 Fr.) et le *SVEB3* (14 000 Fr.). Dans les entretiens avec les enseignants (a.1 à a.7), j'ai remarqué que 6 sur 7 travaillent à temps partiel et que leur salaire n'atteint pas le seuil qui leur permet d'avoir droit aux indemnités et allocations salariales. Certains s'inscrivent dans les caisses de chômage pour obtenir un complément de salaire.

## 2.4 Système d'évaluation

À la fin du cours, les apprenants reçoivent une fiche d'évaluation sous forme de questionnaire (c.2, c.4 à c.6). L'enseignant ne reçoit pas une copie des évaluations de ses apprenants, ce qui lui permettrait d'améliorer ses pratiques pédagogiques. Si des apprenants abandonnent le cours, l'administration tend à tenir l'enseignant pour responsable. Ce dernier peut alors devenir un enseignant remplaçant (a.2, a.4 à a.6), ce qui constitue une lourde sanction. Souvent, la majorité des migrants d'une classe ont un niveau inférieur à celui du manuel (b.1, b.5 à b.7), malgré le test de placement. Ceci oblige l'enseignant à faire des rappels, à avancer lentement et à ne pas « finir » le programme à temps. Six migrants sur les 8 interrogés n'ont pas fini leur cours de niveau B1, qui leur permettrait une intégration fonctionnelle et professionnelle satisfaisante (c.2 à c.6, c.8).

## 2.5 Alternance des codes

Plusieurs collaborateurs et cadres migrants essentiellement européens et asiatiques parlent anglais sur leur lieu de travail, car ils ne maîtrisent ni le dialecte zurichois ni l'allemand standard (c.1 à c.4, c.6). Leurs collègues zurichois s'adaptent à cette alternance de code et parlent aussi anglais. Les migrants italiens et portugais travaillant dans des commerces et sur des chantiers dirigés par leurs compatriotes et vivant en communauté n'ont pas besoin d'apprendre la langue d'intégration (c.7-8). Certains réfugiés africains parlent la langue de l'ancien pays colonisateur, l'anglais ou le français, lorsqu'ils se trouvent en difficulté pour communiquer en allemand ou en dialecte zurichois (d.5, d.7-8).

# 3 Propositions

## 3.1 Langue d'intégration adaptée à la nature du migrant

Les migrants n'ont ni les mêmes acquis antérieurs, ni le même niveau scolaire, ni le même objectif, ni la même formation professionnelle, ni le même répertoire linguistique. Pour ces raisons et comme il n'y a pas un modèle unique de cours d'intégration linguistique, il est possible de rendre le cours de langue mieux adapté au contexte des apprenants, en prenant en considération les éléments qui suivent.

**3.1.1** Une formation d'enseignants issus de la migration pour enseigner la langue d'accueil aux nouveaux migrants qui sont proches d'eux culturellement est souhaitée. Ceci aide à comprendre les difficultés, à trouver la solution adéquate et contextuelle et à assurer la compétence linguistique. Le migrant développe sa langue d'accueil comme sa langue d'origine et son intégration peut devenir co-identitaire. Le Conseil de l'Europe a souligné cette compétence plurilingue du migrant dans *L'intégration linguistique des migrants adultes. Guide pour l'élaboration et la mise en œuvre des politiques* (2014b : 12–13).

**3.1.2** La formation des enseignants à concevoir des activités dans des contextes professionnels : enseigner la langue aux apprenants/migrants adultes dans le cadre de leur profession les motive. En effet, le migrant qui a une expérience suffisante dans un domaine est prédisposé grâce à ses compétences professionnelles à mieux apprendre la langue de son travail et de son intégration, d'où la formation des enseignants de langues spécialisés (Faure 2014 : 50–65). La langue professionnelle traduit une vision collaborative et axée sur un dispositif de travail et la situation de communication suppose des compétences professionnelles spécifiques. Pour cela, il faut une terminologie spécialisée, un contenu et des tâches choisis. Le Conseil de l'Europe a prévu cela dans son document *L'intégration linguistique des migrants adultes : d'un pays à l'autre, d'une langue à l'autre* (2014a : 33–37).

## 3.2 Valorisation du métier d'enseignant

L'enseignant de langue d'intégration est faiblement rémunéré. Il ne peut pas être sanctionné et tenu pour responsable des abandons ou de l'arrêt du cours par les apprenants. Les institutions sont en mesure de prendre en charge les frais de formation de leurs enseignants. Pour assurer la qualité du cours de langue et un retour raisonnable sur investissement, il suffit d'engager des enseignants professionnels et expérimentés et d'améliorer la formation *SVEB*. Enfin, une grande majorité des responsables de l'enseignement/apprentissage dans les institutions de langue (A, B, C, D et E) ont besoin de recycler leurs connaissances, d'écouter davantage leurs enseignants et leurs apprenants. L'enseignement/apprentissage des langues fait partie du domaine de la recherche qui évolue et se développe chaque jour. C'est un investissement qui se fait à long terme.

## 3.3 Le système d'évaluation

À la fin de 2015, les listes des cours de langue d'intégration dans toutes les institutions visitées (A à G) montrent une régression constante du nombre des classes de langue d'intégration par rapport aux années précédentes. Les apprenants se démotivent et abandonnent plus vite qu'auparavant (c.3 à 5, c.7–8). L'évaluation ne doit pas affecter la motivation des apprenants et de l'enseignant mais doit répondre à leurs objectifs. Les responsables des institutions de langue ont besoin de recycler leurs connaissances dans l'enseignement/apprentissage de la langue d'intégration. Le *Cadre européen commun de référence pour les langues* (2001) et le *Portfolio européen des langues* (2000) insistent sur l'aspect continu du processus d'évaluation au niveau du résultat mais aussi au niveau de la progression de l'apprenant. La co-évaluation permet à l'enseignant d'aider l'apprenant dans sa prise de conscience et sa réflexion sur la construction de son savoir.

## 3.4 Le rôle de la société d'accueil et le respect de l'altérité

Les thèmes des manuels de langue peuvent être interculturels et valoriser le migrant. La politique suisse des 3 puis 2 cercles, datant de 1998 et favorisant les voisins de la Suisse sur le marché du travail helvétique, est souvent jugée discriminatoire. L'alinéa 3 de l'article 72 de la constitution interdisant la construction des minarets et l'article 25 sur le renvoi des migrants sont contraires aux valeurs du Conseil de l'Europe qui garantissent la liberté de croyance et la protection des faibles. La génération montante des *Secondos* (personnes nées en Suisse dont les parents sont migrants) peut jouer un rôle de « médiateur » entre la part non-négligeable de Suisses xénophobes et les migrants, apaiser les tensions et favoriser le respect de la langue/culture des migrants. Aujourd'hui, les autorités traitent le phénomène de la migration d'un point de vue davantage économique qu'humanitaire. Les migrants qualifiés dont le marché du travail a besoin sont prioritaires. Les réfugiés requérants d'asile sont de moins en moins nombreux (SEM, statistiques sur l'immigration, 2016 : 5–6). Pourtant, l'intégration, c'est aussi la formation du migrant et la facilité de son accès au marché du travail.

# Références

Conseil de l'Europe. 2001. *Portfolio européen des langues*. Strasbourg.
Conseil de l'Europe. 2001. *Cadre européen commun de référence pour les langues : apprendre, enseigner, évaluer*. Paris : Didier.
Conseil de l'Europe. 2010. *Politiques d'intégration des migrants adultes. Principes et mise en œuvre*. Strasbourg : Conseil de l'Europe.
Conseil de l'Europe. 2014. *L'intégration linguistique des migrants adultes : d'un pays à l'autre, d'une langue à l'autre*. Strasbourg : Editions du Conseil de l'Europe.
Beacco, Jean-Claude, Hedges, Chris, Little, David. 2014. *L'intégration linguistique des migrants adultes. Guide pour l'élaboration et la mise en œuvre des politiques*. Strasbourg : Conseil de l'Europe.
Faure, Pascaline. 2014. Enjeux d'une professionnalisation de la formation des enseignants de langues spécialisées. *Cahiers de l'Association des Professeurs de Langues des Instituts Universitaires de Technologie*. XXXIII, 1, 50–65.
Jost, Cyril & Vincent Jucholl. 2007. *Économie suisse*. Lausanne : Loisirs et pédagogie.
Office Fédéral des Statistiques Suisse. 2014. *Édition OFS 2014*. Neuchâtel : Office Fédéral des Statistiques.
Sarraj, Jamel. 2015. *Didactiques des langues/cultures (arabe, anglais, français) et contexte sociolinguistique dans les monarchies du Golfe Arabique*. Paris : Université Sorbonne Nouvelle – Paris 3, thèse de doctorat.
SEM (Secrétariat d'État suisse aux migrations). 2016. *Statistiques sur l'immigration 2016*. Berne : SEM.

# Annexe

## Manuels analysés

1 *Schritte plus 5, Niveau B1/2*. 2010. München : Hueber.
2 *Themen aktuell 2, Niveaustufe A2, Lektion 6–7*. 2004. München : Hueber.
3 *Schritte plus 1, Niveau A1/1, Kursbuch + Arbeitsbuch*. 2011. München : Hueber.
4 *Aspekte, Mittelstufe B2, Arbeitsbuch 2*. 2008. Berlin : Langenscheidt.
5 *Aspekte, Mittelstufe B1, Arbeitsbuch 1*. 2007. Berlin : Langenscheidt.
6 *Deutsch in der Schweiz, für Erwachsene A1–1, Kursbuch*. 2014. Zoug : Klett.
7 *Tangram aktuell 3, B1/2, Lektion 5–8, Kursbuch + Arbeitsbuch*. 2010. München : Hueber.
8 *Mit Erfolg zum Zertifikat Deutsch, Übungsbuch*. 2004. Stuttgart : Klett International.
9 *Vorstufe Deutsch 2, Niveau A1–2, Lehr- und Arbeitsbuch, für fremdsprachige Erwachsene*. 2006. Widnau : Büchler Verlag.

## Caractéristiques des entretiens réalisés

a : Entretiens avec 7 enseignants de langue d'intégration réalisés en janvier 2016 (a.1 à a.7).
b : Entretiens avec des migrants et des réfugiés/apprenants (8) dans des institutions de langue réalisés en janvier 2016 (b.1 à b.8).
c : Entretiens avec des migrants travaillant en Suisse alémanique (8) réalisés en décembre 2015 (c.1 à c.8).
d : Entretiens avec des réfugiés ayant arrêté leur cours de langue (5) et travaillant dans le canton de Zurich réalisés en janvier 2016 (d.1 à d.5).

3 **Linguistic repertoires and integration**
Répertoires linguistiques et intégration

Thomas Laimer, Martin Wurzenrainer
# Multilingualism as a resource for basic education with young migrants

**Abstract:** In the MEVIEL[1] project partnership, linguistic insights into multilingualism were adapted for educational and counselling practice, with the aim of improving educational opportunities for young migrants in Austria. The project employed a dynamic concept of multilingualism and regarded the use of more than one language as a process in which experience with language (learning) and competence constitutes a two-way relationship. The inclusion of multilingualism mainly meant acknowledging, making visible and using the learners' own linguistic repertoires.

**Résumé :** Dans le cadre du partenariat de projet MEVIEL, les connaissances linguistiques sur le multilinguisme ont été adaptées à la pratique pédagogique et au conseil, en vue d'améliorer l'accès des jeunes migrants à l'éducation en Autriche. Le projet a appliqué un concept dynamique du multilinguisme et considéré l'utilisation de plusieurs langues comme un processus où l'expérience de la langue (et de son apprentissage) et les compétences entretiennent une relation bilatérale. L'intégration du multilinguisme a surtout impliqué la reconnaissance, la visibilité et l'utilisation des répertoires langagiers propres aux apprenants.

## 1 Introduction

For years we have been observing in basic education courses[2] that participants want to use their many languages in class. That is why we take a critical view of

---

1 ESF/BMBF: E-1.2–190, http://www.integrationshaus.at/meviel
2 Basic education with young migrants in our institutions means working with people aged between 15 and 25 who had no or only infrequent opportunities to attend school. The aim of these courses is to allow young migrants to catch up on the education they may have missed so they can get an Austrian secondary school leaving certificate. For that reason, in the courses the focus

---

**Thomas Laimer** (corresponding author), Die Wiener Volkshochschulen, Vienna, Austria,
E-mail: thomas.laimer@vhs.at
**Martin Wurzenrainer**, Integrationshaus Wien, Vienna, Austria,
E-mail: m.wurzenrainer@integrationshaus.at

DOI 10.1515/9783110477498-015, © 2017 Thomas Laimer, Martin Wurzenrainer, published by De Gruyter.
This work is licensed under the Creative Commons Attribution-NonCommercial-NoDerivs 3.0 License.

Austria's "German above all" language policy. Learning languages should be perceived as something positive and not experienced as something compulsory. For this reason, we decided to consider how multilingualism could be integrated into our courses.

In 2012 we responded to a European Social Fund (ESF) call to tackle this very important social and educational policy issue and set up a special team of cooperation partners: a development partnership consisting of a large adult education institution, the Wiener Volkshochschulen (VHS Wien), two smaller NGOs, the Verein Projekt Integrationshaus and Piramidops, and a research institution, the University of Vienna, represented by the Unit for Language Learning and Teaching Research, which had provided input that formed the basis for further deliberation. This form of cooperation facilitated critical reflection on developments from different perspectives. In this way we managed to make ourselves and our fields of work more aware of the issues of multilingualism, to reflect on our own teaching practice, and to develop appropriate ideas and materials for basic education courses.

Statements by participating teachers, such as "Integrating multilingualism into my classes is like switching on an extra light. We're actually dealing with the same topics as ever, but the room we're doing that in is brighter" and "The learners are the experts!" reveal a new dimension of multilingualism that is becoming the framework for classroom learning. Recognising that course participants are the experts alters the teacher's attitude in that the roles of teacher and learner become interchangeable: Every learner is a teacher, and every teacher is a learner, too.

Multilingualism in basic education can increase interest in language(s) and create a positive attitude towards your own language repertoire. When we integrate multilingualism, the languages of the participants are appreciated and recognised and used as resources (e.g. seeing connections between languages by comparing words and structures), and by doing that further resources for learning can also be generated.

Within the MEVIEL project we created several products:
- a low-threshold multilingual learning space (the so-called Market Learning Café);
- materials and activities to make multilingualism visible and to make use of it in basic education classes;

---

is placed not only on developing linguistic competence in German but also on learning subjects such as mathematics, biology, geography, etc.

- a model of multilingual learning support where young learners worked together in tandem with adult learning partners;
- guidelines with approaches for the practical use of multilingualism in counselling practice;
- and further training for teachers on the topics of diversity and multilingualism.

## 2 Theoretical background

The MEVIEL project embraced a dynamic concept of multilingualism. A wide range of different terms are used in the scientific literature for this state; indeed there seems to be some terminological disagreement. However, they all describe the same phenomenon: that language is in a state of permanent change, that speakers use words and structures from other languages and mobilise all of their linguistic resources when communicating (e.g. Busch 2014; García and Wei 2014; Herdina and Jessner 2002; Shohamy 2006). All of these developments reveal a radical change in our perception of language.

> Language is open, dynamic, energetic, constantly evolving and personal. It has no fixed boundaries, but is rather made of hybrids and endless varieties resulting from language being creative, expressive, interactive, contact-and-dialogue-based, debated, mediated and negotiated. (Shohamy 2006: 5)

This key concept of language formed a starting point in our project for a dynamic concept of multilingualism. It refers to the use of more than one language in everyday life – and in educational contexts – as a process in which experiences of language learning and language competence are mutually interrelated. According to this view, a language is not to be seen as a discrete entity but as a network of means of communication. If this is the case, then our educational context has to adapt to this linguistic reality.

These concepts and approaches show that, although available language resources, or those the learners already have, are not always useful in the same way, they contribute to raising people's awareness of their own multilingualism. Dealing with the diversity of ways people use language can actually help them make use of learning and educational opportunities and develop metalinguistic skills in particular. The integration of multilingualism into the classroom mainly means acknowledging, making visible and using the learners' own repertoires of languages. Our project mainly aimed to answer the question which materials and activities are instrumental for this purpose in the context of basic education.

## 3 Development of materials and activities for basic education courses

The project was divided into four phases. Phase I consisted of research and the adaptation and development of materials. In Phase II materials were piloted in courses for basic education and reflective workshops were held with teachers. Phase III focused on the adaptation and re-piloting of materials, followed by reflection on these. Finally, in Phase IV we edited, collected and published materials and activities.

There may have been many events and projects on the subject of multilingualism over the past few years but, when you observe what actually happens in the classroom, the multilingualism that is going on there is often simply due to the fact that there are multilingual individuals sitting in these classes. Similarly, there is also a large amount of multilingual teaching material available, but this has either only been designed for very specific contexts or has not yet found its way into many institutions.

At the beginning, it was our aim to find out more about existing ideas of language education in diverse cultural and linguistic circumstances, enabling learners to acquire knowledge and use different languages and language styles for different life contexts. We intended to adapt these ideas for use with our own target group in our basic education courses or to develop our own new activities. We started by looking through the material available – be it from our own resources (many things had already been developed but this was not known among the teams) or from others (there are plenty of excellent materials available) – and adapted it for use in our courses. However, it turned out to be surprisingly difficult to recruit course teachers to try out the adapted materials in their classes, to reflect on them with us and develop them further. When approached on the issue of multilingualism, many reacted defensively or sceptically at first. It proved to be a challenge to convince the teachers to participate and to make them important partners in our project.

In the ensuing reflection workshops, the trainers' responses showed that by incorporating the languages the learners bring with them their motivation and interest in the lessons could be increased. This opened up opportunities for the course participants, enabling them to bring into the lesson the competences they already had. For example, it was only possible for some young people to bring their basic knowledge of mathematics into the lessons when they were given the opportunity to do that in their first language. However, not all of the languages the young people brought with them enjoy a similar status in society. Conversations with participants have shown that some of them have had negative experiences with their multilingualism and therefore hide their languages or are even ashamed of them. For this reason, it can often feel uncomfortable or strange when their first language is integrated into the lessons. The next step was to add important teaching tips to descriptions of classroom tasks and to make it clear that it is the job of the teacher to create a positive atmosphere for the use of first languages, using great care and their skill as a teacher. In further reflection workshops the group discussion among the trainers became more productive, and their responses became more positive.

Finally, we put together a handout of activities (Laimer and Wurzenrainer 2014) that make multilingualism visible, to be used in lessons as a motivational tool for learning and to increase the status of the first languages of the participants.

## 4 Results and perspectives

The project has shown that exploiting multilingualism on a broader basis is seen for the most part as something positive and that a respectful atmosphere can be created in the way people behave towards each other. It has demonstrated that the emotional aspect of your own ability to express yourself in different contexts can come to the fore, and that using your first language, and your experience of being competent in it, is relevant and significant.

In conclusion, we can say that our experiences in the project have shown that multilingualism can be a resource if it is taken into account in lessons. But ideas and materials can only be a first step. Above all, it is the teachers' attitudes and their approaches towards teaching – which have to be constantly adapted to the target group – that create opportunities to exploit multilingualism for learning purposes and to experience it as a valuable part of how we deal with each other.

Linguistic diversity is a fixed part of our social reality, and it is the task of adult education in a migration society to tackle the challenges of linguistic heterogeneity in education and educational processes caused by migration and to deal constructively with multilingualism. In particular, the current refugee situation shows that multilingualism is continuing to develop and that different languages are used and needed, opening up different perspectives on migrants and their multilingual socialisation, which we still have to find ways of exploiting.

Based on what we have achieved so far, we will continue to follow these principles in our work in the form of a new project, where we go on to react to the challenges of superdiversity (e.g. Blommaert 2013; Vertovec 2007) to focus on a subject-oriented approach, primarily to utilise existing multilingual resources and to be able to create new ones.

# References

Blommaert, Jan. 2013. *Ethnography, superdiversity and linguistic landscapes: Chronicles of complexity.* Bristol: Multilingual Matters.

Busch, Brigitta. 2014. *Mehrsprachigkeit.* Vienna: Facultas.

García, Ofelia & Li Wei. 2014. *Translanguaging: Language, bilingualism and education.* London: Palgrave Macmillan.

Herdina, Philipp & Ulrike Jessner. 2002. *A dynamic model of multilingualism.* Clevedon: Multilingual Matters.

Laimer, Thomas & Martin Wurzenrainer. 2014. *Mehrsprachigkeit im Basisbildungsunterricht. Materialien und Aktivitäten für jugendliche und junge erwachsene MigrantInnen.* Vienna: Die Wiener Volkshochschulen. http://www.vhs.at/meviel_handreichung/ (accessed 28 May 2016).

Shohamy, Elana. 2006. *Language policy: Hidden agendas and new approaches.* London & New York: Routledge

Vertovec, Steven. 2007. Super-diversity and its implications. *Ethnic and Racial Studies* 30(6). 1024–1054.

Büşra Hamurcu Süverdem
# La place de la L1 dans les familles bilingues franco-turques en Alsace

**Résumé :** Cette année, la communauté turque fête les 50 ans de son arrivée en France (1965–2015). En 50 ans de présence en France, de nombreuses études ont été réalisées sur l'intégration sociale, culturelle et linguistique de cette communauté, dont certaines (Akıncı 1996 ; Irtis-Dabbagh 2003 ; Mortamet 2005) confirment le fort maintien du turc et l'attachement de la communauté à sa langue et à sa culture d'origine. Notre objectif est de mieux comprendre les raisons de ce maintien au sein de la communauté turque en Alsace.

Pour ce faire, nous avons réalisé, dans le cadre d'une thèse de doctorat (Hamurcu Süverdem 2015), des entretiens semi-dirigés avec 12 familles originaires de Turquie. Ces familles se distinguent par leurs pratiques langagières, à savoir essentiellement le turc pour certaines (Type 1) et indifféremment le turc et le français pour d'autres (Type 2).

L'analyse de ces entretiens montre que, malgré la divergence de leurs pratiques langagières, toutes ces familles tiennent un discours valorisant sur le turc (langue 1, L1). La plupart relate également les effets positifs d'une bonne acquisition du turc (L1) sur l'acquisition du français (langue 2, L2) pour leurs enfants.

**Abstract:** This year the Turkish community is celebrating the 50th anniversary of its arrival in France (1965–2015). During these 50 years numerous studies have been conducted on the social, cultural and linguistic integration of this community. Some of them (Akinci 1996; Irtis-Dabbagh 2003; Mortamet 2005) confirm its strong maintenance of Turkish and attachment to the language and culture of origin. The author's aim is to gain a better understanding of the reasons for this language maintenance within the Turkish community in Alsace.

With this aim in mind, in the context of a doctoral thesis (Hamurcu Süverdem 2015), the author carried out semi-guided interviews with 12 families originating from Turkey. These families differed in their language usage, with some essentially using Turkish (Type 1) and others alternating between Turkish and French (Type 2).

The analysis of these interviews shows that, in spite of the differences in their language practice, all these families speak in favourable terms about the

---

**Büşra Hamurcu Süverdem**, Laboratoire Dynamique du Langage in Situ (DYLIS), Université de Rouen, E-mail : busrahamurcu@gmail.com

DOI 10.1515/9783110477498-016, © 2017 Büşra Hamurcu Süverdem, published by De Gruyter. This work is licensed under the Creative Commons Attribution-NonCommercial-NoDerivs 3.0 License.

use of Turkish (language 1, L1). Most of them also mention the benefits their children derived from a good degree of proficiency in Turkish (L1) when it came to learning French (language 2, L2).

## 1 La communauté turque : 50 ans de vie en France

L'année 2015 était une année importante pour la communauté turque en France, car elle a célébré les 50 ans de l'immigration turque en France. C'était à la suite de la signature de la convention de la main d'œuvre entre la France et la Turquie en 1965 que la communauté turque avait commencé à se former en France. L'immigration turque est le dernier grand courant migratoire en France. Il s'agit donc d'une population qui a une organisation migratoire plus récente que celles des courants précédents, comme les Polonais, les Marocains, les Portugais, etc. Aujourd'hui, selon les derniers chiffres donnés par le ministère turc du Travail et de la Sécurité Sociale, du mois de janvier 2014, ils seraient 611 515, dont près de la moitié aurait la nationalité française.

La population turque est reconnue pour sa forte sociabilité communautaire autour de la famille élargie et du cercle de voisinage (Rollan & Sourou 2006 ; De Tapia 1995). En revanche, elle est également caractérisée par la faiblesse des échanges avec des personnes extérieures à la communauté turque (Armagnague 2008). De plus, étant donné que le processus migratoire se renouvelle sans cesse, la communauté turque continue à vivre repliée sur elle-même. Ce repli aboutit à un taux de maintien de la langue et de la culture d'origine plus fort que pour les autres communautés immigrées en France. Dans cette étude, nous avons observé le cas particulier de 12 familles turco-alsaciennes.

## 2 L'Alsace : un terrain propice

Le terrain que nous avons choisi pour cette recherche est assez particulier, car la commune de Bischwiller est la deuxième commune alsacienne accueillant le plus grand nombre de Turcs parmi la population étrangère : 72 % des étrangers y sont Turcs. Il faut préciser que ce n'est pas la seule commune en France à présenter cette particularité. Environ 3 500 Turcs vivent à Bischwiller, à savoir 27 % de la population de la commune. Chacune des 12 familles franco-turques avec lesquelles nous avons travaillé appartiennent à la deuxième génération issue de l'immigration turque. Certaines familles sont composées d'un parent né et scolarisé en France et l'autre en Turquie. Toutes ces familles font partie de la population défavorisée de Bischwiller et la majorité des parents a suivi un parcours scolaire professionnalisant, que ce soit en France ou en Turquie, c'est-à-dire qu'ils se sont plutôt dirigés vers des diplômes professionnels. Dans ces 12 familles, nous remarquons, d'une part, qu'il y a une homogénéité quant aux catégories socio-professionnelle des parents et, d'autre part, que les hommes sont le plus souvent ouvriers non qualifiés et les femmes sans profession.

## 3 Méthodologie de collecte des données

Afin de collecter nos données, nous avons réalisé des entretiens semi-directifs dans chaque famille avec les deux parents réunis (très souvent accompagnés d'autres membres de la famille, même élargie) en juin 2013. Nous avons interrogé les parents sur leurs pratiques langagières.

Dans le point suivant, nous ne détaillerons pas les réponses fournies par les parents à chacune de ces questions mais nous ciblerons leur discours sur la place de la L1 au sein de leur famille, d'après leurs réponses.

## 4 Analyses

En ce qui concerne la place du turc dans les familles, ces 12 entretiens que nous avons analysés indiquent quelques points communs dans les discours des parents. En effet, nous avons pu observer qu'ils attribuent tous 4 valeurs au turc :
- une valeur identitaire
- une valeur culturelle
- une valeur affective
- et une valeur « didactique ».

Nous allons maintenant détailler chacune de ces valeurs en les illustrant avec des discours de parents.

### 4.1 La valeur identitaire

La première valeur attribuée à la langue d'origine est la valeur identitaire, ce qui n'est pas surprenant car nous savons que la langue est très souvent directement liée à l'identité, notamment dans les communautés immigrées. D'après un parent né et ayant grandi en Turquie, puis arrivé en France suite à son mariage, il est important que les enfants continuent à parler le turc pour éviter le risque de perte de la langue d'origine quelques générations plus tard. Il affirme : « Si on parle uniquement français et qu'on ne parle pas turc du tout, nos enfants ne pourront pas le transmettre à leurs enfants. La génération de nos petits-enfants va donc complètement perdre le turc. Ils oublieront qu'ils sont Turcs[1]. » Cet extrait souligne la relation étroite entre langue et identité. D'après ce parent, la perte de la langue d'origine est synonyme de perte d'identité.

Un autre aspect de cette valeur identitaire se présente sous la forme d'une comparaison entre le turc et l'alsacien que les parents établissent souvent. Nous pouvons prendre l'exemple de cette mère qui déclare :

> Mais ma collègue nous dit « si aujourd'hui j'ai un gamin il parlerait que l'alsacien ». Elle est très ouverte d'esprit mais elle se fâche beaucoup contre le comportement des enseignants envers l'enfant, le fait qu'ils mettent la pression et qu'ils disent « il ne parle pas, il y a un problème ». Donc elle dit « moi je parlerai alsacien à mon enfant, c'est sa langue maternelle ». Elle ne veut pas faire oublier la langue maternelle aussi. C'est comme nous[2].

Nous avons observé ce type de comparaison dans la majorité des familles. En effet, les parents turcs semblent chercher à confirmer et à rendre légitime leurs politiques linguistiques familiales en indiquant des cas semblables, notamment celui de l'alsacien en Alsace. D'après eux, si les Alsaciens parlent alsacien à leurs enfants, ils ont également le droit de parler turc aux leurs. Nous pouvons constater que dans les deux cas, il s'agit d'une affirmation d'identité.

## 4.2 La valeur culturelle

Une autre valeur attribuée au turc est la valeur culturelle dans le sens où les parents, même s'ils parlent généralement français avec les enfants, préfèrent parler turc lorsqu'ils abordent des sujets liés à la culture turque, dont les coutumes, les fêtes, la religion, ainsi que lorsqu'ils souhaitent dire certaines expressions propres au turc, n'ayant pas d'équivalents en français. L'exemple suivant illustre bien cette deuxième valeur :

> ... par exemple hayırlı günler[3] même quand je parle avec le petit günün bereketli olsun oğlum[4]... günaydın oğlum[5]... je vais pas lui dire bonjour (rires). Ce bonjour pour moi c'est

---

1 Extrait de la transcription de l'entretien avec le père d'Isa, traduit du turc vers le français.
2 Extrait de la transcription de l'entretien réalisé avec la mère de Yusuf.
3 Que ta journée soit bénie (traduction littérale, notre traduction).
4 Que ta journée soit riche mon fils (notre traduction).

vraiment... ça reste professionnel et c'est très distant c'est vraiment (en écartant les mains) comme ça alors que si je vais te prendre dans mes bras j'ai pas envie de te dire bonjour j'aurai envie de dire günaydın hoş geldin[6]. Tiens essaye de traduire hoş geldin. Hoş geldin... bienvenue? La richesse que je ne trouve pas en français eh bah je la trouve en turc[7].

En même temps, cette mère révèle aussi qu'elle parle le plus souvent français à la maison et qu'elle regrette que ses enfants aient des problèmes de compréhension en turc, alors que c'est leur langue d'origine. Le maintien du turc est primordial, car d'après cette mère, contrairement aux sujets quotidiens, certains aspects de la culture turque ne peuvent être exprimés en français. La perte du turc provoquerait donc la perte de la culture d'origine.

## 4.3 La valeur affective

La troisième valeur qui ressort des discours des parents est affective. Par « affectif » nous entendons tout ce qui concerne les sentiments et les émotions, ce qui est le plus souvent exprimé en turc d'après la déclaration des parents. Ces derniers disent être incapables d'exprimer leurs sentiments en français, même s'ils le parlent très couramment et même plus souvent que le turc. Parmi les sentiments évoqués, la colère est au premier rang. Toujours d'après leurs déclarations, même les parents qui sont nés et qui ont été scolarisés en France ne peuvent se disputer qu'en turc, que ce soit avec le conjoint ou avec les enfants. L'extrait ci-dessous illustre bien cette fonction particulière du turc :

Mère :   Non... non moi c'est plus en turc quand j'engueule
Père :   Les mots turcs sont plus efficaces
Mère :   Voilà (rires) c'est ça, c'est ce que j'allais dire. Le français est très poli. Ce n'est vraiment pas une langue de dispute. Ils ne font même pas de dispute les Français.
Père :   Ils font ils font mais...
Mère :   Ça nous convient pas. Ça ne donne pas le même effet[8].

Dans cet extrait, après un court débat, les deux parents découvrent qu'ils préfèrent se disputer en turc en raison de l'efficacité des expressions utilisées. En

---

5  Bonjour mon fils (notre traduction).
6  Bonjour, c'est agréable tu sois là (notre traduction).
7  Extrait de l'entretien réalisé avec la mère de Sinan. Partiellement traduit du turc vers le français.
8  Extrait de l'entretien réalisé avec les parents de Sinan. Partiellement traduit du turc vers le français.

plus de la colère, d'autres sentiments sont également exprimés le plus souvent en turc, notamment l'amour et la nostalgie, qui sont aussi beaucoup cités par les familles.

### 4.4 La valeur « didactique »

Enfin, nous aborderons la dernière valeur attribuée à la L1 par les familles franco-turques : la valeur didactique. Nous employons le terme « didactique » dans le sens où le turc, lorsqu'il est bien acquis, peut être un avantage dans l'acquisition d'une seconde langue qui est le français dans leur cas. Une bonne acquisition de la première langue favorise donc d'après les parents l'acquisition de la seconde langue. Et ils affirment cela en partant de leurs propres expériences ou de l'expérience vécue par leurs premiers enfants. Ils constatent aussi que cette idée est souvent confirmée par les pédiatres ou des spécialistes du sujet, ce qui les encourage. Un parent déclare : « Je n'ai jamais parlé français à mon enfant jusqu'à ce qu'elle aille à l'école. J'ai dit d'abord notre langue maternelle. Le français arrivera de toute façon. En général les pédiatres le disent aussi, une fois que l'enfant a bien appris sa langue maternelle, il est plus facile d'apprendre une deuxième langue. Je suis complètement d'accord avec ça[9]. » Cette idée se base probablement sur l'hypothèse de l'interdépendance des langues de Cummins (1980) d'après laquelle les connaissances acquises en L1 peuvent être positivement transférées pendant l'acquisition d'une L2.

Le discours des parents semble montrer qu'ils approuvent l'hypothèse de l'interdépendance des langues de Cummins. Or, bien qu'ils soient conscients de la nécessité d'une bonne acquisition de la L1 pour que la réalisation du transfert soit possible, les parents admettent ne pas accorder suffisamment d'efforts à la L1, au profit du français.

## 5 Discussion et conclusion

Pour conclure, nous avons constaté que pour chaque famille, le turc reste dans la sphère familiale. Les enquêtés déclarent ne pas parler turc en dehors de la maison « par respect pour les Français[10] ». D'ailleurs, ils acceptent également

---

9 Extrait de l'entretien réalisé avec la mère d'Eda. Traduit du turc vers le français.
10 Extrait d'entretien.

que l'emploi du turc ne soit pas encouragé à l'école[11], car sinon leurs enfants ne parviendront jamais à apprendre le français s'ils ne sont pas dans un bain linguistique. Cela semble contradictoire vis-à-vis du propre vécu des parents qui ont pourtant rencontré les mêmes difficultés à l'école.

De plus, le turc est considéré comme une *langue de transmission*, c'est à dire que les parents souhaitent transmettre cette langue à leurs enfants, alors qu'ils ne ressentent pas le même souhait ou la même responsabilité envers le français. D'après eux, c'est à l'école de transmettre le français. Tôt ou tard, les enfants finiront par l'apprendre, car ils seront toujours dans la société d'accueil. Toujours d'après le discours des parents, la langue qui est en danger, et donc qu'il faut sauver, est plutôt le turc.

## Références

Akıncı, Mehmet-Ali. 1996. Les pratiques langagières chez les immigrés turcs en France. *Écarts d'Identité* 76. 14–17.

Armagnague, Maïtena. 2008. Processus d'intégration des jeunes d'origine turque en France et en Allemagne. *Trajectoires* 2. 79–88.

Cummins, Jim. 1980. Psychological assessment of immigrant children: Logic or intuition? *Journal of Multilingual and Multicultural Development* 1. 97–111.

De Tapia, Stéphane. 1995. Le champ migratoire turc et l'Europe. In Paul Dumont, Alain Jund & Stéphane de Tapia (dir.), *Enjeux de l'immigration turque en Europe. Les Turcs en France et en Allemagne*, 15–38. Paris : CIEMI/L'Harmattan.

Hamurcu Süverdem, Büşra. 2015. *Le développement du turc et du français en situation de bilinguisme précoce. Le cas d'enfants d'origine turque scolarisés en maternelle*. Rouen : Université de Rouen, thèse de doctorat.

Irtis-Dabbagh, Verda. 2003. *Les jeunes issus de l'immigration de Turquie en France : état des lieux, analyses et perspectives*. Paris : L'Harmattan.

Mortamet, Clara. 2005. Situations de plurilinguisme en France : transmission, acquisition et usages des langues. *Glottopol* 5. www.univ-rouen.fr/dyalang/glottopol/.

Rollan, Françoise & Benoît Sourou. 2006. *Les migrants turcs de France, Entre repli et ouverture*. Pessac : Maison des Sciences de l'Homme d'Aquitaine.

---

[11] Il faut préciser, ici, que nos observations portent sur deux écoles maternelles de la ville où la collecte de données a été réalisée. Nous ne pouvons nous prononcer sur l'attitude des enseignants et des parents vis-à-vis de la place de la L1 à l'école dans les autres écoles maternelles de la ville ou dans d'autres écoles en France.

Salih Akin
# La loyauté linguistique au sein des membres de la communauté kurde en France

**Résumé :** Comment une langue minorée, privée d'enseignement public, peut-elle être transmise dans le contexte de diaspora ? C'est à cette question que cette contribution tente d'apporter des réponses à travers la situation du kurde en France. Les données d'une enquête menée au sein des membres de la communauté kurde mettent en évidence une forte loyauté linguistique, qui se traduit par une transmission intergénérationnelle de la langue au sein de la famille. Les représentations de la langue maternelle montrent que la loyauté est une expression identitaire du groupe qui renvoie à ses liens avec sa culture, ses origines et son vécu langagier.

**Abstract:** How can a minority language which is not taught in the public education system be passed on in a diaspora situation? This is the question that this article attempts to answer by looking at the situation of the Kurdish language in France. A survey conducted among members of the Kurdish community reveals the existence of strong linguistic loyalty, which results in the language being passed down from generation to generation within the family. The representations of the mother tongue show that language maintenance is an expression of the group's identity, reflecting its links with its culture, origins and linguistic experience.

## 1 La problématique

Cet article a pour objet d'étudier le degré de loyauté linguistique des Kurdes installés en France. Les données de cette étude proviennent d'une recherche internationale qui a associé des chercheurs des universités de Rouen et de Potsdam de 2011 à 2013. Intitulée « Évaluation contrastive des implications sociales de la langue kurde comme langue d'immigration en France et en Allemagne », la recherche a été financée par l'Allemagne et la France au sein du programme Procope. Le programme s'est fixé trois objectifs : le premier objectif est d'évaluer le processus de transmission intergénérationnelle et d'acquisition

---

**Salih Akin**, Université de Rouen, France, E-mail : salih.akin@univ-rouen.fr

du kurde dans deux contextes sociolinguistiques et au sein de deux systèmes éducatifs différents ; il s'agit d'analyser le degré de *loyauté linguistique* (Fishman 1991) des Kurdes vis-à-vis de leur langue maternelle dans le contexte migratoire. Le deuxième objectif concerne l'examen du rôle de la maîtrise de L1 dans les acquisitions scolaires par les enfants issus de l'immigration kurde en Allemagne et en France. Enfin, le troisième objectif, suivant l'hypothèse de l'interdépendance des langues (Cummins 1979), consiste à mesurer les compétences langagières de ces élèves en L1 et en langue de scolarisation.

Dans le cadre de cette contribution, nous n'aborderons que l'un des enseignements majeurs de la recherche, à savoir l'attitude, consciente ou non, qu'une communauté sans État peut développer vis-à-vis de sa langue maternelle et le rôle de cette attitude dans le maintien et/ou la transmission intergénérationnelle de la langue dans le contexte diasporique. Nous présenterons dans un premier temps la méthodologie de l'enquête ainsi que quelques données sur la langue et la communauté kurdes.

## 1.1 Méthodologie de l'enquête

Les données de la recherche ont été recueillies en France par un questionnaire écrit. Le questionnaire comprenait 48 questions (46 questions ouvertes et 2 questions fermées) et était constitué de 5 sections (informations sur le sujet, éducation, profil langagier, compétences langagières et pratiques langagières). Il a été administré en français et en kurde auprès de 177 enquêtés.

## 1.2 Langue et communauté kurdes

Le kurde est une langue indo-européenne parlée par environ 30 millions de locuteurs répartis dans quatre États (Irak, Iran, Syrie et Turquie) et les anciennes républiques de l'Union soviétique. Les aléas de l'histoire des Kurdes n'ont pas permis l'émergence d'une langue standard et la langue s'est développée sur une structure polydialectale. Les deux dialectes principaux, nettement apparentés, sont le *kurmanji* (parlé par la majorité des Kurdes de Turquie, de Syrie et par une partie des Kurdes d'Iran et d'Irak) et le *sorani* (parlé par des Kurdes en Irak et en Iran).

La situation sociolinguistique du kurde reflète la reconnaissance des Kurdes dans les États où ils sont répartis. Ainsi, le kurde est, avec l'arabe, la deuxième langue officielle de l'Irak. Dans le Kurdistan irakien, le kurde, qui est la langue de l'éducation, des médias, du marché, connait un développement remarquable.

En revanche, la situation est nettement contrastée dans les autres États. Après une politique linguistique répressive de 80 ans, la Turquie a levé les interdits sur l'usage de la langue au début des années 2000, mais n'a pas institué un enseignement public en kurde (Akin & Araz 2014). En Iran et en Syrie, l'usage oral et écrit du kurde est toléré, sans bénéficier d'une reconnaissance officielle, ni d'un enseignement public.

### 1.3 La communauté kurde en France

D'installation relativement récente en France, la communauté kurde est estimée à 200 000 personnes environ[1]. Cette estimation, réalisée en 2014, ne comprend pas des milliers de Kurdes ayant fui le conflit syrien et les exactions de l'organisation État islamique en Irak. Les Kurdes résident essentiellement dans les grandes villes et capitales régionales françaises (Paris, Marseille, Lyon, Strasbourg).

La communauté kurde en France s'est formée à partir des années 1960. Au début, il s'agissait essentiellement de l'arrivée de Kurdes de Turquie comme travailleurs immigrés. Mais les événements politiques ont transformé la nature de cette migration. À la suite de la Révolution islamique en Iran en 1979, du coup d'État militaire de septembre 1980 en Turquie, du long et meurtrier conflit Irak-Iran et de la campagne d'extermination des Kurdes (Anfal) lancée par le régime irakien, des vagues successives de réfugiés politiques kurdes sont arrivées dans les pays d'Europe occidentale. De nos jours, les statistiques les plus courantes font état de la présence d'environ 1,2 million de Kurdes en Europe occidentale.

## 2 Résultats

### 2.1 Profil sociologique

Les enquêtés se répartissent entre 75 femmes (42,37 %) et 102 hommes (57,63 %). 148 enquêtés, qui constituent l'écrasante majorité (83,62 %), sont nés en Turquie et constituent la première génération de réfugiés et de migrants. 29 enquêtés (16,28 %) sont nés en France et constituent la deuxième génération. Les autres enquêtés (7,34 %) sont nés en Iran, en Syrie, en Iran et en Arménie. L'origine des enquêtés fait apparaître le poids démographique de la population kurde selon

---

[1] http://www.institutkurde.org/kurdorama/

les pays. En effet, la Turquie abrite à elle seule environ 18 millions de Kurdes. Les tranches d'âge des enquêtés révèlent un large panel. D'un côté, les membres de la première génération, dont l'âge varie entre 60 et 30 ans et de l'autre, ceux de la deuxième génération, dont l'âge moyen est de 20 ans. Les principales activités professionnelles sont le bâtiment (24,86 %), les professions libérales (3,95 %), la restauration (2,82 %). Une petite partie des enquêtés (14,12 %) fait des études et les femmes au foyer représentent 11,3 % des enquêtés. Une grande partie des enquêtés (67,8 %) a été scolarisée.

## 2.2 Profil linguistique

Le profil linguistique des enquêtés révèle une grande variété de répertoires linguistiques. L'écrasante majorité des enquêtés (95,48 %) déclare parler le kurde, 64,97 % le français, 78,53 % le turc, 11,3 % le persan et 9,04 % l'arabe. Le répertoire linguistique traduit une réelle situation de plurilinguisme dans le pays d'origine. Avant de quitter leur pays, les enquêtés sont au moins bilingues (kurde et langue de scolarisation). Dans le contexte migratoire, le répertoire linguistique se diversifie avec le français et d'autres langues qui viennent s'y greffer.

L'immense majorité des enquêtés (89,83 %) considère le kurde comme sa langue maternelle. Cette appropriation est également attestée pour les 29 enquêtés (16,28 %) nés en France : 21 d'entre eux déclarent le kurde comme langue maternelle, 4 enquêtés le turc et seulement 1 le français. Le principal dialecte parlé est le kurmanji (74,01 % des enquêtés), ce qui semble cohérent par rapport aux 72,88 % d'enquêtés qui sont originaires de Turquie.

## 2.3 Pratiques langagières déclarées

Comment ce riche répertoire linguistique est-il mobilisé dans les pratiques langagières ? Nous avons souhaité connaitre la pratique des langues dans les interactions quotidiennes des enquêtés. Comme dans beaucoup de situations sociolinguistiques, le choix d'une ou plusieurs langues de communication dépend du profil de l'interlocuteur.

Le kurde, le français et le turc apparaissent comme les trois principales langues des interactions. Ce répertoire trilingue révèle une « hétérogénéité fonctionnelle » (Montaut 2001) dans la mesure où chaque langue du répertoire a une fonction spécifique et un domaine d'usage défini socialement et culturellement. Ainsi, le kurde domine les interactions au sein de la famille restreinte. Les enquêtés s'adressent très majoritairement en kurde à leur mère (73,45 %) et à leur père (68,93 %). Cette vitalité de la langue d'origine se maintient dans les interactions avec les proches (63,28 %), mais diminue au sein de la fratrie (55,37 %) et avec les amis (50,85 %). Le turc et le français occupent les espaces communicatifs où le kurde est moins présent. Les enquêtés ne sont que 9,6 % à parler en turc et 6,21 % à parler en français avec leur mère. Cependant, le turc est la deuxième langue de communication avec les proches (28,81 %), alors que le français occupe une place significative avec les amis (41,81 %). En même temps, une diversification des langues de communication est observée. Ainsi, les locuteurs utilisent assez souvent plusieurs langues avec leurs frères et sœurs (12,99 %), mais beaucoup plus souvent avec leurs proches (17,51 %) et leurs amis (24,29 %).

Les déclarations des enquêtés mettent en évidence la gestion d'un répertoire linguistique adapté aux situations de communication. Ce répertoire linguistique varié facilite la socialisation avec la langue du pays d'accueil. La pratique du français, moins attestée dans la famille, concerne surtout la sphère des relations sociales et professionnelles. Selon H. Bozarslan, cette socialisation linguistique s'expliquerait surtout par le profil sociopolitique des enquêtés :

> [...] l'immigration kurde a une certaine propension à mieux s'intégrer dans son environnement français. Les raisons pour cela sont relativement faciles à comprendre : avant de s'installer dans l'immigration, les Kurdes connaissent déjà une expérience minoritaire. Cette situation les pousse à mieux évaluer les chances et les risques que représente l'immigration. Par ailleurs, l'installation en Europe s'impose plus facilement comme une stratégie assumée, car les conditions du pays d'origine ne laissent que peu de perspective de retour (Bozarslan 1995 : 126).

Cependant, le répertoire plurilingue des enquêtés favorise aussi la socialisation linguistique, dans la mesure où ils sont déjà familiarisés avec l'apprentissage et la pratique de plusieurs langues dans leur pays d'origine.

## 2.4 Langue maternelle et loyauté linguistique en diaspora

Les déclarations des enquêtés mettent également en évidence le maintien et la pratique de la langue d'origine dans le contexte de la diaspora. La loyauté linguistique est considérée comme l'attitude consciente et explicite ou le sentiment d'une communauté à maintenir l'usage de sa langue maternelle dans des situations mettant en contact des communautés linguistiquement différentes (Fishman 1991). Dans un contexte de diaspora, elle se traduit par l'attachement qu'une communauté peut manifester à sa langue d'origine et sa volonté de maintenir sa pratique et de la transmettre aux générations suivantes.

L'étude montre que la loyauté est forte dans la communauté kurde de France. L'immense majorité des enquêtés de la première génération (93,24 %) et de la deuxième génération (72,41 %) considèrent en effet le kurde comme leur langue maternelle. Quels sont les facteurs qui conduisent les membres de la communauté à développer une telle loyauté linguistique ? Pour comprendre ces facteurs, nous allons analyser les représentations linguistiques que les enquêtés ont construites de l'expression « langue maternelle ». Nous avons en effet souhaité connaitre la façon dont les enquêtés perçoivent et représentent leur langue maternelle. Les représentations permettent de comprendre comment des enjeux affectifs, identitaires et existentiels peuvent être investis dans la langue maternelle.

### 2.5 Les représentations de la langue maternelle

La première représentation est celle d'une langue reçue en héritage de la part de la famille et des ancêtres. Les enquêtés rattachent la langue maternelle à la famille (29 enquêtés), aux parents (24), à la mère (15 enquêtés) et aux ancêtres (6). Cet héritage familial est reçu par filiation : « la langue que j'ai apprise de ma famille », ou par transmission : « la langue que mes parents m'ont transmise », « la langue que ma mère m'a transmise ». Constitutive de la construction langagière, la langue maternelle est aussi une partie de l'individu : « une partie inséparable de l'homme », « c'est ma personnalité ». Cette représentation existentielle est amplifiée par certains enquêtés qui associent la langue maternelle à « la vie », à « la raison de l'existence d'un peuple », à « la raison de vivre ». À ce vecteur qui fait exister s'ajoute la fonction véhiculaire : « la première langue dans laquelle nous nous exprimons », « un moyen de communication qui permet aux gens sur la terre de se parler et de se comprendre ». Ce véhicule est « la langue dans laquelle j'exprime ma culture », « la langue que notre culture nous fait parler ».

On le voit, les représentations sont révélatrices d'enjeux investis dans la langue maternelle et conduisent les membres de la communauté à s'approprier la langue maternelle. La loyauté est une expression identitaire du groupe qui renvoie aux liens avec sa culture, à ses origines et à son vécu langagier.

## 3 Quelques conclusions

Notre recherche montre comment une langue minorée, coupée de ses territoires d'origine, peut maintenir une vitalité dans le contexte migratoire. Il semble que seule une forte loyauté linguistique peut expliquer cette vitalité linguistique d'une langue soumise à des politiques répressives dans le pays d'origine et non transmise didactiquement dans le pays d'accueil. Les résultats montrent, par ailleurs, que la loyauté linguistique ne semble pas être incompatible avec la socialisation avec la langue du pays d'accueil. Le français, dont l'acquisition est facilitée par le parcours plurilingue des enquêtés, est aussi une réalité linguistique de la communauté.

## Références

Akin, Salih & Selda Araz. 2014. Kürtçe seçmeli dil eğitimi : sorunlar ve öneriler [L'enseignement du kurde comme langue optionnelle : problèmes et propositions], *Radikal*, 14/06/2014.
Bozarslan, Hamit. 1995. L'immigration kurde, un espace conflictuel. *Migrants – Formation* 101. Paris : 115–129.
Cummins, James. 1979. Linguistic interdependence and the educational development of bilingual children. *Review of Educational Research* 49. 222–25 l.
Fishman, Joshua. 1991. *Reversing Language Shift: Theoretical and Empirical Foundations of Assistance to Threatened Languages.* Clevedon : Multilingual Matters.
Montaut, Annie. 2001. Diaspora des langues en contexte multilingue : l'Asie du Sud. *Faits de langue* 18. 53–64.

Isabelle Bambust
# Le résident européen percevant sa propre aptitude linguistique dans un contexte judiciaire – une première recherche empirique sans prétention

**Résumé :** Ma recherche concerne la communication transfrontalière européenne de documents judiciaires. J'encourage une protection linguistique en faveur de la langue comprise par le destinataire et l'instauration d'une publicité linguistique européenne. Chaque personne devrait préalablement déclarer sa ou ses langues employable(s) dans un contexte judiciaire. En 2015, j'ai interrogé 310 personnes afin de vérifier la valeur qu'elles attribuent à leur propre langue dans un contexte judiciaire. Il me semble éclairant de présenter quelques résultats de cette enquête illustrative.

**Abstract:** My research concerns the cross-border communication of judicial documents in Europe. I favour a form of linguistic protection which involves using a language which the addressee understands, and I advocate the establishment of a European linguistic publicity. Each person should declare in advance the language(s) he or she can use in a judicial context. In 2015, I interviewed 310 people to check the value they attribute to their own language in a judicial context. My article presents some results from this illustrative survey.

## 1 Le point de départ

Ma recherche doctorale toujours en cours comprend quatre parties. La première partie parle de la friction entre la langue officielle du lieu où la personne a son centre d'intérêts et la langue propre à cette personne (c'est-à-dire la langue dans laquelle elle se sent le plus à l'aise). Il me semble qu'il faut protéger davantage la langue comprise par le destinataire. Une deuxième partie concerne la détermination concrète de la langue comprise par le destinataire. Je promeus la thèse que le destinataire lui-même devrait fixer la langue qu'il comprend. Dans une troisième partie, je défends la position selon laquelle, lorsqu'un acte est communiqué à son destinataire, un droit autonome à la traduction dans une langue

---

**Isabelle Bambust,** Université de Gand, Belgique, E-mail : Isabelle.Bambust@UGent.be

comprise doit exister, c'est-à-dire sans que ce droit ne soit minimisé par la présence d'un avocat. Enfin, la quatrième partie propose un Registre Linguistique Judiciaire Européen (RLJE). Toute personne présente dans l'Espace européen devrait préalablement déclarer sa langue ou ses langues employable(s) dans un contexte judiciaire oral ou écrit.

## 2 Les tables de conversation dans le Nord de la Belgique

En 2015, j'ai interrogé 310 personnes. J'ai contrôlé la valeur qu'elles attribuent à leur propre langue dans un contexte judiciaire. À l'exception d'une table de conversation à La Haye (Pays-Bas) et d'une autre à Bruxelles (capitale bilingue de la Belgique), toutes ces personnes participaient à des tables de conversation volontaires pour allophones, organisées sur le territoire néerlandophone de la Belgique. Suivant les quatre catégories de personnes interrogées reprises dans le schéma n° 1, j'ai interrogé des non-néerlandophones ainsi que des néerlandophones aidant les non-néerlandophones à apprendre la langue néerlandaise. Certaines personnes interrogées parlaient une autre langue d'une autre région linguistique du même pays. Par exemple, la 36[e] personne interrogée est née à Verviers, en Belgique (partie francophone). Elle est mariée avec une personne d'Anvers (partie néerlandophone). Pendant 29 ans, elle donne des cours sur le littoral belge (partie néerlandophone) à des enfants francophones. Je l'ai rencontrée à Ostende (partie néerlandophone), où elle a participé à la table de conversation. Dans la région bilingue de Bruxelles, j'ai interrogé deux personnes parlant une autre langue de la même région linguistique.

La présence féminine majoritaire (206 femmes (66 %) pour 104 hommes (34 %)) s'explique partiellement par le fait que certaines tables de conversation sont uniquement destinées aux femmes. Ce phénomène n'existe pas pour les hommes.

Le schéma n° 2 montre que j'ai surtout interrogé des trentenaires, puis des quadragénaires, des sexagénaires et des quinquagénaires.

## 3 Le contenu du questionnaire

Le questionnaire contient les informations suivantes : le numéro d'ordre de la personne interrogée, ses initiales, son sexe, sa nationalité et son âge ; la date, l'heure et le lieu de l'entretien et la langue dans laquelle celui-ci se déroule. J'ai

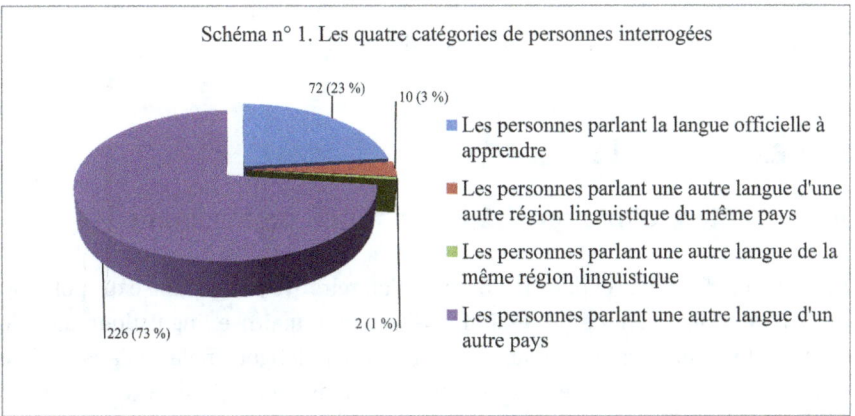

**Schéma n° 1.** Les quatre catégories de personnes interrogées

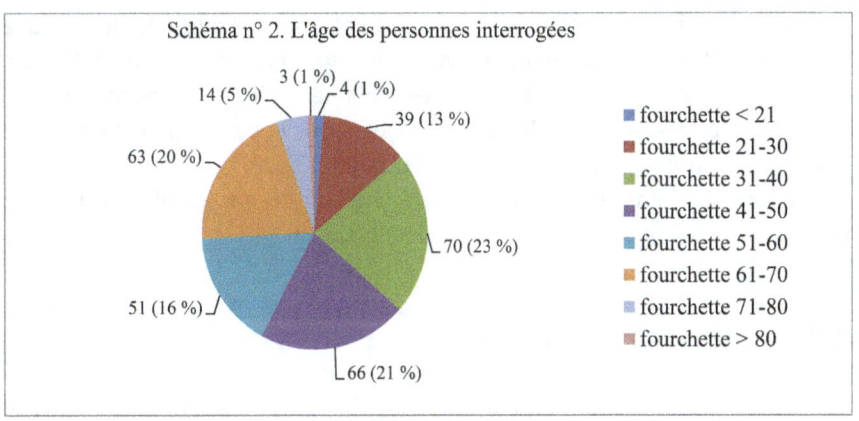

**Schéma n° 2.** L'âge des personnes interrogées

porté une attention particulière à la formation et à la profession, actuelle ou passée, ainsi qu'à la durée du séjour en Belgique. Au niveau linguistique, je me suis concentrée sur les données suivantes : la langue maternelle (la première langue du nid familial) ; la langue personnelle actuelle (la langue employée avec le plus de facilité) ; l'autre langue ou d'autres langues parlée(s), la langue lue avec le plus de facilité ; la langue ou les langues dans laquelle ou lesquelles la personne voudrait parler à un juge ; la langue ou les langues dans laquelle ou lesquelles la personne voudrait recevoir des documents judiciaires ; la personne accepterait-elle de faire connaître ce choix linguistique via une sorte de passeport linguistique électronique ? La personne trouverait-elle suffisant que seul son avocat comprenne les documents judiciaires et pas elle ?

## 4 Les résultats

### 4.1 Le critère d'une qualité linguistique professionnelle

Dans la jurisprudence et dans la doctrine, l'on retrouve parfois une extrapolation de la qualité linguistique professionnelle vers une maîtrise linguistique dans le contexte judiciaire. Par exemple, un acteur parle la langue anglaise dans un film et on en déduit que cet acteur va comprendre un document judiciaire en anglais. À mon avis, seule la personne concernée devrait décider une éventuelle extrapolation. Par exemple, la 7[e] personne interrogée, pensionnée, a donné des cours de néerlandais et d'anglais. Sa propre langue est le néerlandais. Elle parle également le français, l'espagnol et un peu l'allemand. Pourtant, elle indique seulement la langue néerlandaise en vue de sa protection linguistique judiciaire. Un autre exemple est celui de la 159[e] personne interrogée, un Brésilien, qui a été traducteur portugais-anglais. Il opte seulement pour la langue portugaise quant à sa protection linguistique judiciaire. Par contre, la 137[e] personne interrogée, pensionnée, a donné des cours d'anglais pendant 40 ans et elle accepte une protection linguistique judiciaire dans cette langue.

### 4.2 La présence d'un avocat

Une grande majorité (274 – 88 %) trouve qu'il n'est pas suffisant que seul l'avocat comprenne la langue du dossier (voir le schéma n° 3). D'aucuns prétendront que j'enfonce une porte ouverte avec une telle question et qu'il est quand même tout à fait normal que les citoyens eux-mêmes doivent comprendre leur dossier. Or, et c'est là où le bât blesse, la Cour européenne des droits de l'homme semble compenser l'importance de la langue comprise par la présence d'un avocat.

La 78[e] personne interrogée a étudié le droit et a une expérience de 35 ans de barreau. Elle veut comprendre le dossier afin de le gérer, ensemble avec son avocat. La 277[e] personne interrogée a également étudié le droit, et elle dit : « Comme avocat, je ne peux me relier à une seule source. Je veux vérifier moi-même. » La 11[e] personne interrogée dit : « Il faut savoir où le bateau va aller. » La 39[e] personne interrogée énonce : « Il faut savoir où on met le pied. »

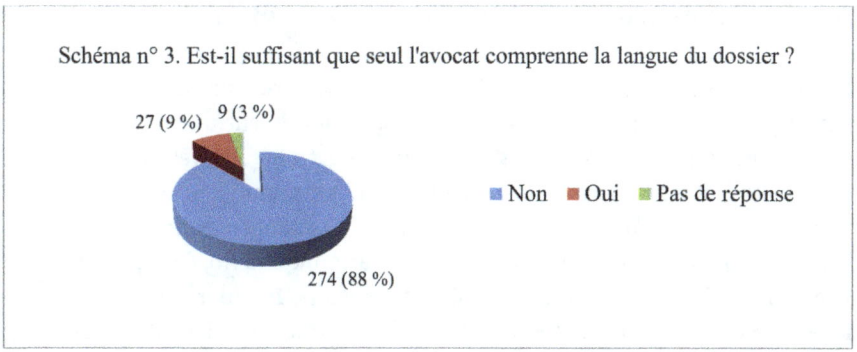

**Schéma n° 3.** Est-il suffisant que seul l'avocat comprenne la langue du dossier ?

## 4.3 La publicité linguistique européenne

Comme le montre le schéma n° 4, une grande majorité (293 – 94 %) est pour un RLJE.

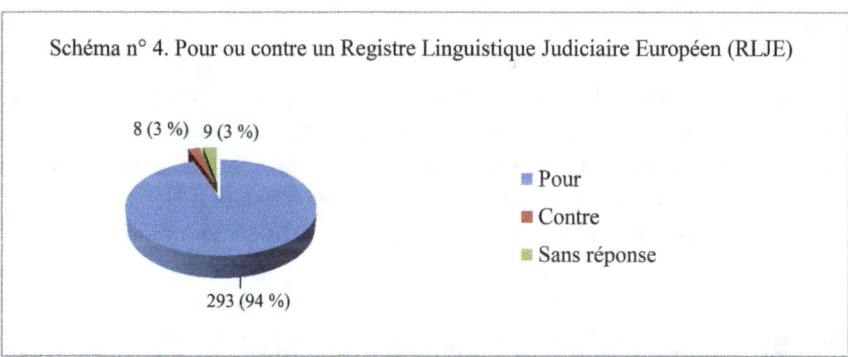

**Schéma n° 4.** Pour ou contre un Registre Linguistique Judiciaire Européen (RLJE)

La 17ᵉ personne interrogée précise que le RLJE « pourrait remédier à de nombreux inconvénients ». Elle se sentirait « plus à l'aise ». La 203ᵉ personne interrogée trouve que la proposition est une « condition préalable pour un respect linguistique réciproque ». La 287ᵉ personne interrogée me dit : « Il faudrait partager les choses. Être ensemble. Nous sommes les mêmes personnes. »

### 4.4 La différence entre l'expression orale et écrite

Les résultats vont dans deux sens différents. D'une part, il arrive souvent que les personnes, lors d'un contact oral avec le juge, choisissent une protection dans leur propre langue, parce qu'il s'agit d'un contact direct et véloce. Par contre, quand il s'agit de l'analyse d'un document, la personne peut prendre plus de temps ou peut chercher de l'aide. Ou encore, elle peut opter pour une langue qui est davantage littérairement établie. La 12[e] personne interrogée a pour langues personnelles le peul et le soussou. Elle les choisit pour parler à un juge. Pour la réception des documents, elle choisit la langue française. La 16[e] personne interrogée a les langues russe et avare comme premières langues. Elle veut parler en russe, mais accepte de recevoir les documents en néerlandais. La 120[e] personne interrogée est originaire du Kazakhstan. Elle parle le russe et l'ouïghour. Elle veut s'adresser au juge dans ces deux langues. Pour recevoir les documents, elle préfère le russe. La 180[e] personne interrogée est Afghane. Elle veut parler la langue pashto au juge, mais accepte également l'anglais pour le volet écrit.

D'autre part, certaines personnes ne craignent pas ce contact oral direct avec le juge et y voient même un avantage. De plus, certaines personnes aiment leur autonomie au niveau de la réception des documents judiciaires, sans devoir déranger d'autres personnes. Une réfugiée de Guinée (294[e] personne interrogée) le formule ainsi : « Il ne faut pas exposer ses problèmes linguistiques. » La 265[e] personne interrogée a la langue turque comme langue personnelle. Elle veut parler en turc, en néerlandais et en allemand. Pour recevoir des documents elle opte seulement pour le turc et pour le néerlandais. La 121[e] personne interrogée, de nationalité arménienne, accepte de parler en arménien, en russe ou en néerlandais. Elle n'accepterait les documents qu'en russe ou arménien.

## 5 Les atouts d'un éventuel Registre Linguistique Judiciaire Européen (RLJE)

À mon sens, il y a 6 avantages à créer un RLJE. Tout d'abord, une déclaration linguistique correspondrait davantage à la réalité linguistique. L'actuelle appréciation externe par un juge sur la base d'un éventail de critères pourrait ainsi être évitée. On éviterait également d'éventuelles traductions superflues. Deuxièmement, la déclaration préalable du choix linguistique n'invite pas à abuser du système de la protection linguistique.

Troisièmement, la personne peut librement gérer les risques linguistiques. Soit elle déclare sa maîtrise linguistique d'une manière très restrictive (p. ex.

uniquement sa propre langue). Soit elle s'aventure à déclarer d'autres langues maîtrisées. La personne crée donc sa propre zone linguistique dans le monde judiciaire. La 40$^e$ personne interrogée vient de Finlande et c'est une ancienne employée auprès de la Commission européenne. Elle opte pour une protection dans sa propre langue, le finnois, bien qu'elle parle convenablement le néerlandais, l'anglais, le français, l'espagnol et le suédois. La 11$^e$ personne interrogée (d'origine africaine) a le français comme langue maternelle. Elle est également prête à choisir la langue néerlandaise. Elle trouve important que « les langues coïncident avec le milieu ».

Quatrièmement, le RLJE serait un instrument flexible. La personne concernée pourrait modifier sa zone linguistique dans le temps, par exemple en fonction d'une évaluation linguistique personnelle ou d'un changement géographique. Il y a également – et c'est un cinquième point – un argument économique. En effet, une plus grande protection linguistique sur la base d'un RLJE pourrait par exemple attirer des entrepreneurs. Et sixièmement, le RLJE formerait une base de données linguistiques considérable. Cette masse de données pourrait elle-même contribuer à la protection linguistique, par exemple dans le cas où on ne trouverait aucun interprète ou traducteur.

Pour moi, un tel mécanisme de publicité linguistique pourrait s'inscrire dans le cadre de la justice que nous recherchons tous.

Antonella Benucci
# Répertoires linguistiques des détenus étrangers en Italie et en Europe : premiers résultats des projets RiUscire et DEPORT.

**Résumé :** Le contexte pénitentiaire européen est devenu une réalité multiculturelle qui oblige à une réflexion pour repenser les programmes d'aménagement de peine en tenant compte de la communication interculturelle et de la médiation sociale. Les Projets DEPORT et RiUscire, dont on présente ici les premières données collectées sur les répertoires linguistiques des détenus étrangers, ont la vocation de contribuer à la création d'un modèle de communication à la fois linguistique et professionnel qui puisse contribuer à la réinsertion sociale des détenus étrangers.

**Abstract:** The European penitentiary context has become a multicultural reality that requires reflection on a re-thinking of programmes of penal management in terms of intercultural communication and social mediation. The *RiUscire* project, a continuation of the *DEPORT* project, aims to create a model of communication, both linguistic and professional, that can contribute to the social reinsertion of foreign inmates. This intervention presents the first data collected on the linguistic repertoires of foreign inmates, elaborated from questionnaires and semi-structured interviews.

## 1 Les projets RiUscire et DEPORT[1]

Dans les premières phases de RiUscire et DEPORT, on a mené une recherche visant à relever les aspects sociolinguistiques, culturels et professionnels qui forment le contexte au moyen d'un recueil d'environ 1 000 questionnaires

---

[1] RiUscire (Erasmus+) : Réseau Socio-culturel Universitaire pour l'Instruction et la Réinsertion en Prison 2014–1-IT02-KA204–003517 Key A2 – Cooperation for innovation and the exchange of good practice 2014–1-IT02-KA204–003517 CUP E62I14000310005s ; DEPORT : Au-delà des limites de la prison. Portfolio linguistique et professionnel pour détenus. PAR FAS REGIONE TOSCANA 1.1.a.3 – CUP E67E10000130006.

---

**Antonella Benucci,** Università per Stranieri di Siena, E-mail : benucci@unistrasi.it

remplis par les détenus, les enseignants et le personnel qui travaille en prison et d'environ 100 interviews semi-structurées.

DEPORT (2010–2014) était un projet national, avec plusieurs administrations pénitentiaires impliquées dans les régions italiennes, ses actions prévoyaient une collecte de données (questionnaires, interviews), une description et une analyse sociolinguistique, un mappage de la population étrangère présente dans le contexte pénitentiaire italien, des actions de formation linguistique et professionnelle pour prisonniers étrangers (syllabus, approches et méthodes, matériels d'enseignement), des activités de dissémination de l'approche et de sensibilisation à la communication interculturelle auprès du personnel des prisons et des enseignants d'italien L2, la délivrance d'un Portfolio linguistique et professionnel pour détenus étrangers.

RiUscire (2014–2017) est un Projet international coordonné par l'Italie avec les partenaires suivants : l'Institut Supérieur d'Études Pénitentiaires italien et la Fundação Pessoa au Portugal, les Universités Autonome de Barcelone en Espagne, de Bamberg en Allemagne et Paris Diderot en France. Ses actions comprennent une collecte de données et de bonnes pratiques éducatives en milieu pénitentiaire, la description et l'analyse sociolinguistique de la population étrangère présente dans le contexte pénitentiaire européen, des actions de formation linguistique et professionnelle pour les détenus, des parcours de sensibilisation à la communication interculturelle pour les enseignants et le personnel qui travaille en prison.

## 2 La situation italienne

Selon les données fournies par le Ministère de la Justice Italien (Département de l'Administration Pénitentiaire), en date du 31/01/2016, les détenus étrangers dans les prisons italiennes étaient 17 526, c'est-à-dire environ 34 % du total, ce qui en fait le deuxième pays par le nombre de détenus étrangers (à la première place, on trouve la Grèce, tandis qu'à la troisième il y a l'Espagne, suivie par le Portugal) venus de différentes zones géographiques : le continent le plus représenté est l'Afrique (45 %), ensuite l'Europe (42 %). Ces pourcentages indiquent que la communication linguistique et interculturelle dans le milieu pénitentiaire peut constituer un problème d'importance non négligeable, qui peut être traité grâce à la formation des détenus, du personnel des prisons et des enseignants. C'est ce que l'on voudrait obtenir avec DEPORT et RiUscire, en créant une synergie entre universités, entreprises et maisons d'arrêt, pour donner une valeur ajoutée à la fonction de réhabilitation de la prison, par le biais de la production d'instruments que le détenu pourra employer pour sa propre réinsertion dans la société : le *Portfolio linguistique et professionnel*.

Les objectifs des deux projets tiennent compte d'une série de questions étroitement liées aux considérations suivantes sur l'éducation en prison : en général, les détenus ont un bas niveau d'instruction, alors que l'instruction peut réduire l'activité criminelle et les taux de criminalité (Maculan, Ronco, Vianello 2013 et Lochner & Moretti 2004). Et donc l'implémentation des activités éducatives à l'intérieur des prisons pourrait offrir des opportunités pour « aider les détenus à réorganiser positivement leurs vies [...] et pour leur permettre de s'émanciper en tant que personnes » (Coyle 2009 : 94).

La méthodologie de DEPORT était quantitative-qualitative : questionnaire prisonniers administré dans 21 pénitentiaires italiens (de différentes typologies) et interviews semi-structurées, celle de RiUscire est plutôt qualitative avec des échantillons plus limités.

## 3 Super-diversité

Par le mot *super-diversité* on veut souligner le niveau, la typologie et l'interaction dynamique d'une complexité de variables des sociétés actuelles, plus réduites dans le passé, « qui conditionnent l'*où*, le *comment* et le *qui*, conséquences des migrations de nos jours et qui imposent de ne pas considérer la diversité uniquement du point de vue ethnique » (Vertovec 2007 : 1025). Les données DEPORT et les premières données RiUscire (qui les confirment) montrent que les prisons européennes sont un milieu plurilinguistique riche et productif ou, pour mieux dire, un contexte de super-diversité.

C'est surtout la situation italienne qui exemplifie la pluralité des langues d'origine des détenus et des autres langues ou dialectes parlés, qui incluent des variétés de la langue italienne elle-même : les langues recensées par DEPORT sont au nombre de 63, avec l'arabe à la première place (39 %), suivi par le roumain (13 %), l'anglais (11 %), le français (10 %) et l'albanais (8 %), mais il y a aussi le napolitain, le sicilien, le vénitien et le frioulan.

Ce qui est encore plus intéressant est que le panorama des langues en prison montre l'existence de répertoires non homogènes mais évolutifs, des répertoires de ressources communicatives dont le locuteur joue selon ses besoins propres et qui peuvent recevoir des fonctions différentes : il ne nous importe pas de relever la compétence effective dans une variété de langue, du moment qu'on sait bien que si les détenus affirment parler par exemple le napolitain, il ne s'agit pas du dialecte, mais de quelques mots ou expressions, de leur imaginaire linguistique, de l'idée qu'ils possèdent de leurs propres ressources.

De fait, les détenus étrangers utilisent toutes les langues qu'ils ont à leur disposition, comme on peut le voir d'après les données fournies par les questions sur les langues parlées avec les autres prisonniers, où prédomine l'italien (63,54 %), suivi des langues les plus représentées dans le répertoire parmi les 63 langues recensées (arabe, roumain, anglais, français, etc.), avec l'ajout du napolitain (0,2 %). Et on enregistre plus ou moins la même situation pour les langues parlées avec le personnel des prisons, où l'anglais remonte à la troisième place. C'est évidemment la langue la plus connue par le personnel et, avec le français, c'est aussi une langue de colonisation présente dans plusieurs régions de l'Afrique du Nord ou subsaharienne. Voici un exemple tiré d'une interview avec un détenu roumain qui montre un cadre fonctionnel du plurilinguisme dans sa famille et le sentiment d'appartenance à une communauté ; cet homme connait très bien les possibilités de choix qu'il possède :

I: la sua famiglia vive in
D: ca' in Sicilia
I: ah qui in Sicilia e con loro che lingua parla?
D: Con mia moglie parlo nella nostra lingua no con i miei figli italiano ogni tanto rumeno bisogna vedere in quale situazione siamo ora che siamo qui cerchiamo di imparare tutte e due le lingue no

[I: votre famille vit en
D: ici en Sicile
I: ah ici en Sicile et quelle langue parlez-vous avec eux ?
D: avec ma femme je parle dans notre langue non avec mes enfants en italien et quelquefois en roumain ça dépend de la situation à présent nous sommes ici et on cherche à apprendre les deux langues non] (notre traduction)

## 4 La situation en Espagne, en Allemagne et au Portugal par rapport à l'Italie

L'échantillon réduit choisi dans le cadre de RiUscire montre pour l'Italie 35 pays de provenance (56,9 % des membres de la famille vit en Italie, 43,1 % dans d'autres pays), 15 pour l'Allemagne, 12 pour l'Espagne, 9 pour le Portugal, avec 21 langues maternelles en Italie (arabe 39 %, albanais 24 %, roumain 14 % etc.), 10 en Allemagne (roumain 31 %, arabe 11 %), 5 en Espagne (espagnol 42 %, arabe 28 %, catalan 11 %) et 5 au Portugal (portugais 36 %, arabe 28 %, ukrainien 24 %). Ces taux sont étroitement liés à ceux de l'immigration, qui montrent l'Italie surtout comme un pays qui est le lieu d'arrivée des voyages depuis l'outre-mer, mais aussi celui où l'immigration est plus récente. Mais ils nous montrent aussi que l'Espagne et le Portugal incluent aussi dans leurs pourcentages les immigrés de pays tels que le Brésil ou l'Équateur, où l'on parle la même langue que dans le pays d'arrivée.

En général, les détenus qui affirment parler d'autres langues dépassent les 50 %, mais les pourcentages de ceux qui ont appris d'autres langues dans leur parcours scolaire est inférieur. En effet, ils sont passés par d'autres pays avant la détention, ce qui nous autorise à penser qu'ils en ont appris les langues d'une manière ou d'une autre (pourcentage le plus important en Italie, 43 %, où la langue du pays d'accueil est plus employée même en famille : 27,3 %). En Italie, qui est le pays dans lequel ils ont séjourné le plus de temps avant la détention, les détenus parlent en italien avec les gardiens (97,1 % – Allemagne 27 %, Portugal, Espagne 40 %). Avec les autres détenus, on emploie les langues des pays d'accueil (Italie 87,1 %, Allemagne 69,2 %, Portugal 60 %), sauf en Espagne (7,3 %) ; l'arabe prédomine, sauf en Allemagne, où c'est l'anglais qui est à la première place. En général, les détenus n'ont pas étudié les langues de ces pays chez eux mais, de ce point de vue, il est intéressant de voir le niveau d'auto-évaluation des connaissances en langue étrangère : le niveau est estimé entre *bon* et *suffisant* à 81 % en Italie et à 60 % en Espagne. Beaucoup d'entre eux ont appris une langue étrangère en prison, surtout en Allemagne (62 %).

Tous les détenus reconnaissent l'utilité de connaître la langue du pays d'accueil pour travailler (au total, seulement 6,4 % de *non*), avant tout pour communiquer avec les collègues et les supérieurs à propos du travail, mais aussi pour employer des mots professionnels spécifiques, pour *arriver à s'expliquer*. Donc ils reconnaissent l'utilité de fréquenter un cours de la langue du pays d'accueil pour communiquer sur le lieu de travail en Italie (85,9 %) et en Allemagne (80 %), mais non au Portugal, où il faut prendre en considération le fait que les activités de travail à l'intérieur des institutions pénitentiaires sont assez réduites, et un peu moins en Espagne (46 %) où, à l'exception de l'arabe, la plupart des langues étrangères parlées par eux permet un bon niveau d'inter-compréhension.

Donc, la prison devient la première école de langue étrangère pour les étrangers, en leur permettant d'employer en même temps plusieurs langues ou variétés de celles-ci dans un cadre dynamique et pratique et en tant que pratiques sociales. Elle constitue donc une opportunité qui contribue à la déconstruction d'une conception statique du plurilinguisme (le *translanguaging* de García & Li Wei 2014) où les positions hiérarchiques sont remplacées par des positions fonctionnelles qui impliquent une coexistence de mots et d'expériences. Les détenus étrangers emploient les multiples langues dont se compose leur répertoire selon les différentes dimensions de la communication et leurs identifications personnelles dans les différentes situations de communication. Pour une éducation linguistique en prison, il faut donc partir de ces répertoires mixtes et les prendre comme point de départ pour l'intégration et la réinsertion sociale.

La super-diversité dans le milieu pénitentiaire reposerait donc sur des dynamiques évidentes du contact linguistique : une cohabitation (forcée) d'individus de différentes nationalités, avec plusieurs langues d'origine et différentes identités religieuses, la corrélation entre le vécu personnel des individus, les parcours migratoires précédents et les répertoires linguistiques.

# Références

Benucci, Antonella & Giulia Grosso. 2015. *Plurilinguismo, contatto e superdiversità nel sistema penitenziario italiano.* Pisa : Pacini.

Coyle, Andrew. 2009. *A Human Rights Approach to Prison Management, International Centre for Prison Studies.* London : International Centre for Prison Studies.

García, Ofelia & Li Wei. 2014. *Translanguaging. Language, Bilingualism and Education.* Basingstoke : Palgrave Macmillan.

Lochner, Lance & Enrico Moretti. 2004. The Effect of Education on Crime: Evidence from Prison Inmates, Arrests, and Self-Reports. *American Economic Review* 94 (1), 155–189.

Maculan, Alessandro, Daniela Ronco & Francesca Vianello. 2013. *Prison in Europe: overview and trends.* Roma : Antigone Ed.

Morgan, Rod & Alison Liebling. 2007. Imprisonment: An Expanding Scene. In Mike Maguire, Rod Morgan & Robert Reiner (dir.), *The Oxford Handbook of Criminology*, 1110–1138. Oxford : Oxford University Press.

Vertovec, Steven. 2007. Super-diversity and its implications. *Ethnic and Racial Studies* 29 (6), 1024–54.

4 **Language teaching for integration: content, methods and materials**
Formations en langue pour l'intégration : contenu, méthodes et matériels

Émilie Lebreton
# Les besoins langagiers des adultes migrants : une notion complexe à appréhender

**Résumé :** Cette contribution a pour objectif de décrire et d'interroger la manière dont les acteurs des formations linguistiques pour adultes migrants appréhendent la notion de besoins langagiers. À l'appui d'une recherche-intervention menée dans deux dispositifs de formations situés dans l'agglomération rouennaise, nous mettrons en évidence l'absence d'explicitation de la notion et les confusions induites entre besoins langagiers, objectifs d'apprentissage et difficultés sociales. Il semble nécessaire de dépasser la notion de besoins pour se focaliser pleinement sur les projets d'appropriation.

**Abstract:** The purpose of this contribution is to describe and question the way in which those involved in the language education of adult migrants comprehend the notion of language needs. Drawing on an interventional research study being carried out in two training organisations located in the Rouen conurbation, the author will show that an explanation of the concept is lacking, which engenders confusion between language needs, learning objectives and social difficulties. It seems necessary to go beyond the notion of needs in order to focus fully on acquisition projects.

## Introduction

Depuis les années 1970, la notion de besoins langagiers est récurrente dès lors qu'il s'agit de favoriser l'intégration linguistique des adultes migrants. Or, cette notion reste souvent peu explicitée et la confusion entre les besoins objectifs et subjectifs d'une part, entre besoins langagiers et objectifs d'apprentissage d'autre part perdure. Les besoins langagiers constituent un des principes directeurs du projet ILMA[1] mis en place par le Conseil de l'Europe. Et l'identification des besoins langagiers des adultes migrants tend à refaire surface dans le

---
1 Intégration Linguistique des Migrants Adultes : www.coe.int/lang-migrants/fr

**Émilie Lebreton**, DySola EA 4701, Université de Rouen,
E-mail : emilie.lebreton.pro@hotmail.fr

DOI 10.1515/9783110477498-020, © 2017 Émilie Lebreton, published by De Gruyter.
This work is licensed under the Creative Commons Attribution-NonCommercial-NoDerivs 3.0 License.

champ des formations linguistiques. À l'appui d'une recherche-intervention menée dans deux structures de formations implantées dans l'agglomération rouennaise, nous interrogerons les différentes réalités que recouvre la notion de besoins langagiers selon les acteurs des formations, à savoir les représentants institutionnels, les formateurs et les adultes migrants. À partir des entretiens réalisés avec l'ensemble des acteurs, nous analyserons les conséquences des processus de réduction des besoins sur les pratiques de formation, et plus largement sur l'appropriation linguistique. Aussi, nous nous appuierons sur cette expérience de recherche afin de réfléchir à la manière dont on peut accompagner les formateurs à conduire une réflexion plus approfondie sur la notion elle-même.

# 1 Besoins langagiers, migrations et insertions

## 1.1 Une notion phare en didactique des langues

La notion de besoin langagier a été explorée par des didacticiens et des experts du COE[2] souhaitant garantir une formation de qualité en adéquation avec les besoins des publics spécifiques tels que les travailleurs migrants en insertion, lesquels ont besoin de communiquer en français. Dès les premiers travaux sur cette notion, Richterich (1985) soulignait que l'intérêt accordé aux besoins langagiers ne résultait pas tout à fait d'une préoccupation humaniste, mais avait des accointances avec la logique managériale. Quatre décennies plus tard, on constate que les politiques relatives à l'intégration des publics migrants alliées à l'évolution du champ des formations linguistiques ont renforcé la conception entrepreneuriale des besoins langagiers. L'identification de ces besoins s'élabore en fonction des situations de communication écrites et orales dans lesquelles les apprenants souhaitent ou doivent pouvoir s'exprimer. L'ambigüité et la complexité de la notion apparait alors, les besoins langagiers se composent de besoins subjectifs, exprimés par les apprenants, et de besoins objectifs, exprimés par un tiers. Afin d'éviter l'instrumentalisation de la notion, où les besoins objectifs imposés par un tiers prennent le pas sur les besoins subjectifs, Richterich (1979 : 56) proposait de s'interroger sur les modalités de l'identification, à savoir « qui identifie, pour qui, pour quoi, où, quand, comment ? ». Des travaux plus récents privilégient la négociation des besoins avec les apprenants en fonction de leurs profils et de leurs parcours antérieurs (Van Avermaet et Gysen

---

2 Conseil de l'Europe.

2008). Cependant, le caractère équivoque de la notion semble persister puisque les besoins langagiers sont encore définis par « les situations de communication (orale et écrite) que les migrants adultes concernés souhaitent devenir capables de gérer ou que l'on veut qu'ils soient capables de gérer » (Beacco, Little et Hedges 2014 : 19). L'identification demeure complexe.

## 1.2 Cadre de la recherche-intervention

Les éléments de réponses que nous tentons d'apporter dans cette contribution sont issus d'une recherche-intervention[3] menée dans deux structures de formation implantées dans l'agglomération rouennaise. L'organisme de formation La Fontaine est installé dans une commune en périphérie de la ville. Homologuée centre de formation et prestataire de services, cette structure propose trois types d'actions linguistiques prescrites par le Conseil Régional, Pôle Emploi et l'Office français d'immigration et d'intégration (OFII). Chacune des actions vise l'insertion socioprofessionnelle par l'apprentissage du français et toutes s'adressent aux migrants bénéficiaires du Contrat d'accueil et d'intégration (CAI) et aux demandeurs d'emploi. Ces actions prennent la forme de stage dont la durée varie entre 300 et 600 heures, en moyenne 35 heures de formation par semaine, mais avec des périodes de stage en entreprise. Le centre Senghor est une association située dans un quartier de la ville classé en zone urbaine sensible. Ancrées dans l'éducation populaire, les actions linguistiques de cette structure sont ouvertes à toutes les personnes désirant s'approprier le français. Selon les disponibilités de chacun, le volume horaire varie entre 2 et 5 heures de cours par semaine. Quelle que soit la structure, la diversité des profils des migrants, de leurs parcours migratoires, de leurs projets et de leurs expériences linguistiques, scolaires, professionnelles est omniprésente. Cette diversité induit des besoins langagiers qui peuvent varier d'une personne à l'autre.

---

3 Recherche-intervention menée entre 2012 et 2015 dans le cadre de notre recherche doctorale.

## 2 Les besoins langagiers selon les acteurs des formations linguistiques

### 2.1 Les représentants institutionnels

Pour les représentants institutionnels, les besoins langagiers pour les publics migrants sont liés aux objectifs d'apprentissage et, plus largement, à l'insertion socioprofessionnelle. Les besoins langagiers se rapportent à la communication, notamment à l'oral, et tendent à se confondre avec les besoins d'ordre sociétal. À leurs yeux, l'essentiel est d'accéder et de multiplier les formations pour pouvoir s'intégrer à la société. La prégnance de la mise en emploi par l'acquisition ou le renforcement des compétences linguistiques conduit les représentants institutionnels à ne pas détailler les besoins, et à les rapporter automatiquement à la finalité des formations. En outre, lorsqu'ils évoquent la difficulté de répondre aux besoins de chacun des apprenants, ils opèrent un glissement avec les objectifs d'apprentissage puis soulignent le risque d'instrumentalisation des besoins concrets. Pour ces acteurs, l'identification des besoins langagiers n'est pas de leur ressort, ce qui expliquerait pourquoi ces besoins tendent à se réduire à l'intégration, finalité première des formations.

### 2.2 Les formateurs

Au sein des dispositifs de formation, lorsque nous évoquons avec les formateurs la question des besoins langagiers, la discussion aboutit le plus souvent sur le positionnement qui a lieu à l'arrivée en formation. Pour le centre La Fontaine, les formateurs utilisent des documents communs. Il s'agit de quelques activités en conformité avec le Cadre européen de référence pour les langues (CECR) (compréhension, production écrite et entretien oral). En ce qui concerne le centre Senghor, rien n'est véritablement défini. Seule une formatrice explique s'appuyer sur des activités préparant à l'examen du Diplôme d'initiation à la langue française (DILF), surtout parce qu'elle estime avoir besoin d'un cadre. L'autre formatrice et la secrétaire en charge de la plateforme d'accueil déclarent privilégier un échange oral retraçant le parcours des personnes. Dans le cadre de cette structure, l'étape du positionnement permet de cibler les besoins langagiers et d'orienter les personnes dans le cours adéquat. Lors des entretiens individuels, leurs perceptions des besoins langagiers se précisent, dans un certain sens. La diversité des apprenants et les situations précaires auxquelles peuvent être confrontés les apprenants conduisent une des formatrices à déclarer que les besoins des publics migrants ne peuvent se résumer aux besoins langagiers. Certes, la communication orale et écrite est fondamentale, mais les difficultés sociales rencontrées par ces publics et l'urgence de l'insertion rendent prioritaires les besoins d'ordre sociétal. Il semble nécessaire de se demander quelles sont les priorités. S'agit-il de privilégier le développement des compétences langagières ou l'intégration ? Doit-on opposer ou articuler ces priorités ? Par ailleurs, la diversité, le flou des besoins et l'adaptation aux profils des apprenants sont discutés par l'ensemble des formateurs. Chacun fait en sorte de répondre aux besoins subjectifs, lesquels semblent être identifiés au travers des projets professionnels.

## 2.3 Les apprenants

La prise en compte régulière des besoins subjectifs devrait garantir aux apprenants une certaine satisfaction. Or, plusieurs d'entre eux soulignent des écarts entre ce dont ils jugent avoir besoin et ce qui leur est proposé. Ces écarts ne sont pas uniquement évoqués dans les entretiens, les apprenants les mentionnent au cours des séances ou en dehors, lors des pauses. À titre d'exemple, certains estiment que les ateliers proposés ne permettent pas de bien apprendre le français, faute d'attention portée à la langue et aux règles. D'autres déclarent ne pas progresser malgré la multiplication des formations, car on leur refuse l'accès au bon français, alors que ce bon français est nécessaire pour valider les tests d'entrées des formations qualifiantes. On peut alors se demander si les écarts exprimés sont à mettre en lien avec des besoins subjectifs ou si cela relève des représentations de l'apprentissage en France et en français. Il s'avère que Richterich (1985) apporte un élément de réponse intéressant lorsqu'il écrit que l'observation des représentations de l'apprentissage peut entrer dans le processus d'identification des besoins. Cela signifie qu'il serait judicieux d'entendre et d'interroger ce que disent les apprenants. Cette absence de considération n'est pas nécessairement malveillante, au contraire, que ce soient les formateurs, les didacticiens ou les experts du Conseil de l'Europe, le souci de garantir une formation de qualité est omniprésent. Les propos de Little (2008 : 12) sont éclairants à ce sujet lorsqu'il souligne que l'« objectif est de permettre aux migrants d'utiliser la langue de la communauté hôte pour communiquer de façon basique. Ce qui importe est donc qu'ils parviennent à faire passer leur message, et non que leurs phrases soient correctes sur le plan grammatical ou qu'ils arrivent à parler sans accent au bout de quelques semaines ou de mois de cours ». Ces propos illustrent la complexité de l'analyse des besoins langagiers et, plus largement, l'élaboration des contenus et des objectifs d'enseignement.

## 3 Des besoins aux projets d'appropriation

### 3.1 Réflexions, propositions et transformations

Les écarts ressentis par les apprenants ont conduit les formateurs à remettre en question leurs conceptions des besoins langagiers. En avril 2015, une rencontre entre les formatrices des deux structures de formation a permis de repenser la grille de positionnement perçue comme nécessaire mais insuffisante, notamment parce que les besoins sont seulement analysés à l'entrée en formation. Il s'agit de partir d'une grille commune qui serait renégociée avec les apprenants, d'abord d'une manière collective puis individuelle lors d'un entretien bilan de mi-parcours. Les besoins ne sont plus figés mais perçus dans une dynamique. Dans l'optique d'allier la communication à la perspective d'emploi, les formatrices décident de s'appuyer sur le CECR, et sur le référentiel *Compétences clés*. Aussi, elles proposent de partir des productions des apprenants dans le sens où celles-ci sont un lieu d'observation des besoins et permettent de construire des activités. En parallèle, des rencontres plus régulières avec les apprenants se réalisent à partir de leurs productions. Désormais, les formatrices souhaitent se diriger vers la prise en compte des projets des apprenants, et pas seulement en termes d'insertion professionnelle, mais en termes d'appropriation du français.

### 3.2 Poursuivre les recherches avec les acteurs des formations

Parler de besoins langagiers pour adultes migrants avec les acteurs des formations linguistiques rappelle l'urgence de l'intégration par la langue et la difficulté à répondre aux besoins exprimés par les apprenants. Malgré la volonté de satisfaire les besoins dits subjectifs, des confusions apparaissent entre besoins, objectifs d'apprentissage et difficultés sociales. Le souhait de prendre en compte les écarts perçus par les apprenants implique de dépasser la notion de besoin pour se diriger vers celle de projet d'appropriation. Si cela reste un projet ambitieux et complexe, il offre aux formateurs et aux apprenants la possibilité de travailler ensemble. Du reste, il convient de réfléchir activement à la manière dont le chercheur peut accompagner les formateurs dans leurs réflexions sur les pratiques de formation.

# Références

Beacco, Jean-Claude, David Little & Chris Hedges. 2014. *L'intégration linguistique des migrants adultes. Guide pour l'élaboration et la mise en œuvre des politiques.* Unité des politiques linguistiques. Strasbourg : Conseil de l'Europe.

Little, David. 2008. *Le Cadre européen commun de référence pour les langues et l'élaboration de politiques en faveur de l'intégration des migrants adultes.* Unité des politiques linguistiques. Strasbourg : Conseil de l'Europe.

Richterich, René. 1979. L'antidéfinition des besoins langagiers comme pratique pédagogique. *Le français dans le monde* 149. 54–58.

Richterich, René. 1985. *Besoins langagiers et objectifs d'apprentissage.* Paris : Hachette.

Van Avermaet, Piet & Sara Gysen. 2008. *Apprentissage, enseignement et évaluation des langues, et intégration des migrants adultes. Importance de l'analyse des besoins.* Strasbourg : Conseil de l'Europe.

Thomas Fritz, Dilek Donat
# What migrant learners need

**Abstract:** The analysis of a series of interviews carried out with young migrant learners shows that they like learning, are motivated and committed. But they also have a lot of problems that make it difficult for them to learn. They first of all need stability. This means family and friends, a secure residence status and realistic perspectives. Young migrants need to make new friends, to build and regain trust in order to achieve stability. Only then they can start learning.

**Résumé :** L'analyse d'une série d'interviews de jeunes apprenants migrants indique qu'ils aiment apprendre, sont motivés et attentifs, mais qu'ils sont aussi confrontés à de nombreux problèmes qui handicapent leur apprentissage. Ils ont surtout besoin de stabilité – une famille et des amis, une situation stable au regard du droit de séjour et des perspectives d'avenir réalistes. Les jeunes migrants doivent se faire de nouveaux amis, apprendre ou réapprendre à avoir confiance pour trouver la stabilité. Ce n'est qu'après qu'ils peuvent se mettre à apprendre.

## 1 Introduction

We see that young migrant learners are motivated but at times find it hard to learn. They seem to be distracted and find it hard to concentrate. At the same time they are full of aspirations and expectations as to how their future lives will be. Learning is both a chance and a problem for them. As one of the social workers at Volkshochschule Vienna stated: "If only their minds were free."

## 2 Methods and data

In the framework of a European funded learning partnership named "Enabling and Empowering Young Adult Migrants to fully Participate in Society", 15 interviews were carried out with migrant learners in three European cities: Gothenburg, Cologne and Vienna. The learners' ages ranged from 15 (6) to 30 (5) and

**Thomas Fritz** (corresponding author), Volkshochschule Vienna, Austria,
E-mail: thomas.fritz@vhs.at
**Dilek Donat**, Volkshochschule Vienna, Austria, E-mail: dilek.donat@vhs.at

DOI 10.1515/9783110477498-021, © 2017 Thomas Fritz, Dilek Donat, published by De Gruyter.
This work is licensed under the Creative Commons Attribution-NonCommercial-NoDerivs 3.0 License.

over 30 (2); 9 of them were male and 6 female. Their countries of origin were Syria (3), Spain (2), and Bosnia, Chechnya, India, Hungary, Iraq, Senegal, Pakistan, Greece, Bangladesh and Iran (1 each). It is interesting to note that reasons for migration were manifold, with a clear dominance of flight (7), followed by marriage/love (4), family reunification (2), the spouse's job (1) and their own job (1).

The interviews were carried out using an interview guideline produced by all project partners jointly; some interviews were conducted in Swedish, some in German, and some in English. Unfortunately, for financial reasons it was not possible to interview the learners in their first languages because that would have necessitated interpretation.

The analysis of the interviews was again carried out by the project team jointly in two meetings and resulted in four categories: family and friends; work (and job perspectives); stability and safety; education. In the following sections selected passages from the interviews are presented and analysed. A selection of the interviews (in German, English and Swedish) can be found in the project brochure at http://www.vhs.at/lernraum.wien.html. The translations into English try to represent the German or Swedish original versions with all the grammatical and lexical "mistakes" and hence do not always conform to Standard English. The interviewees have been anonymised and the interviews are coded.

## 3 Feeling safe/stability

There are several aspects of this category to be observed if we take a closer look at the interviews. A young female migrant from Chechnya reports about her coming to Austria and being moved around the country together with her parents. This is a result of the relocation policy in place in Austria.

> We lived in Poland for 10 months and then Slovakia, that's what it is called I think, there about a week or so and we went to Kirchberg, there is a bed and breakfast, like, and there we lived for a year. And then to Wagram, there we lived about three or four months and then again to Traismauer. And there we were for two years. And then to Melk we went and there also one and a half years and here for five years in Vienna. I hope that is it. (AT-B2)

The journey to Austria via two countries and two languages took quite some time. The interviewee is not even very certain what the countries were called, a fact that could have affected – or still might affect – her legal status as refugee, as her narrative does not conform to assumed patterns (see Blommaert, Spotti and Van der Aa 2015: 6). For a child, as she was at the time, this long journey also interrupted schooling. After having arrived in Austria the constant movement continues; she mentions five different locations. This permanently being on the move is a concrete threat to schooling, as she mentions herself: "Yes, I do not want any more [e.g. moving around], because of school. Each me I have to go to a new school. Everything is new. That is so difficult" (AT-B3).

We certainly cannot infer from this one interview how asylum policies foster or hinder educational careers and hence, perhaps, integration, but taken as an individual example we see that for B schooling was made very difficult and this is why she was in a Second Chance Training course for secondary school leaving exams at the time of the interview. Apart from producing demotivation these procedures or mishaps cost valuable time in the process of education and finding a place in society.

In this paper we use the term integration to describe a process much wanted by some policy makers responsible for migration and asylum policies, although we are aware that integration is a very opaque and politically loaded concept that is highly controversial. We are also aware that migrants are in fact integrated into many different networks and specific parts of society (see, for example, Blommaert 2016).

A different aspect of the category stability is the legal status that refugees have in a certain country and the lack of legal rights and the deterioration of opportunities this entails. E mentions that he has no residence permit:

> I have no proper residence permit. Every six months I have to renew my residence permit. You can't do anything with a temporary residence permit. And so for a long time goes on and I have no more hope. I see no future with this temporary residence permit. (GER-E1)

A temporary residence permit means that E cannot get a proper job, as there is no guarantee that he will still be available in six months. It also means no opportunity for an apprenticeship or a long-term educational programme or other training, and no long-term rent or loans, and hence no integration. But the stress and the feelings of obligation do not cease even after permanent residence permits have been granted: "When you get a permanent residency permit, you straight away feel like you have to build something to integrate yourself to the society" (SW-T16). In this passage we can discern a feeling of obligatory gratitude, of having to pay back something.

Lack of stability is present in many interviews and in the next quote J lists three aspects that actually mirror the demands of society, as for example presented in the materials for courses on Austrian values for newly arrived asylum seekers: the willingness to work, competence in German, and integration. He actually mentions these three aspects as the main obstacles in his life in Germany:

> The main aspect of living in Germany is uncertainty. In the moment there is no special positive aspect for me in Germany. There are a few positive aspects for me: 1. Working permit 2. Learning the language 3. Communication build up with the German community. (GER-J13)

The aspect of security is mentioned in some of the interviews. The main aspects here are safety, freedom and a choice of opportunities, which do not exist in the learners' home countries: "Freedom. This is very, very important for me, I had no freedom in Iran. Here there is real freedom. This is great" (GER-E20). "To feel calm ... to start over ... and to leave all problems there ... It's important to feel at peace" (SW-T1).

## 4 Family and friends

In addition to the fact that general stability seems to play an important role, the networks of family and friends seem to be vital. Moreover, it seems very difficult to build up networks outside these and outside the learning environments where other learners and teachers become important parts of personal networks.

B states that she feels "at home" in Austria, "because my parents are here, too, that's very important, my parents" (AT-B8). Support from the family is vital for learning and to overcome obstacles like the above-mentioned relocation policies and the resulting permanently interrupted educational paths. Looking at another quote from a young man from Syria who came to Austria on his own, we can clearly see what the statement in the introduction means – "if only their minds were free". The fact that the situation of the family is not clear, although there is contact through social media, is very much an obstacle to learning: "but sometimes I do not want to learn. My family in Syria and I am here. I don't know. I don't want to learn or to live. My heart in Syria and my head in Austria. So that's what I mean" (AT-Ri39). This situation not only constitutes a problem for learning but also results in depressive moods if not outright depression. When he mentions that he does not want to live, we see that there is an imminent danger to him, which cannot be solved by educational institutions alone but calls for a network of social workers and therapists.

It seems hard for migrants to build up networks outside their closest friends, if indeed it is possible. Contact with people living in the countries these young people ended up in is hard to establish. D states the he has "no network of friends" (SW-D18), "but sometimes I meet Swedish friends, but it's not often. I meet many Africans. Sometimes I meet a friend from Ivory Coast and we go to his friend. But I know Swedes because we play music together" (SW-D16).

## 5 Education

Education is a major issue with young migrants. Very often they have lost precious time by migrating to the country they are in at the moment. Due to the allocation policies in place in most countries, migrants end up in places where there are facilities to live, but sometimes these places do not offer any educational opportunities, as S mentions: "First it was a bit difficult as we were in a small village and there was no school and no German classes" (AT-S25).

In other cases, education that has already been successfully completed is not recognized in the receiving countries, an issue that is similar in all European countries and is in stark contrast to the oft mentioned need for more qualified people (Gächter and Smoliner 2010). Lack of certainty and information as well as very long periods of waiting for qualifications to be recognised are a major obstacle for many young, highly qualified migrants: "I would like to know what kind of German university degree equals the degree I already have" (GER-G12).

Lost or hard-to-retrieve documents from universities in countries in which wars are raging stop young people from continuing their academic careers. "I would like to continue with my studies and I have read the law. If I want to become a lawyer I need to be a Swedish citizen. I shall apply for Swedish citizen and after that I want to find a job" (SW-U1).

## 6 Work and job perspectives

Work perspectives are characterised by two features. One is continuity, i.e. going on doing the job people had before they had to migrate: "My wish is to return to my profession, even if it means to start from the beginning. But everything good will come" (SW-T3).

The second is the drive to help others who are going through the same procedures as they themselves had to undergo. Ri states that he wants to work as a lawyer to help people on their way to a secure country, to support them with legal advice: "And I want to work like this. I help these people when they come to Bulgaria then Slovenia and then come to Vienna or Germany. They need help and want to do it like that" (AT-Ri27).

# 7 Conclusion

At the LIAM conference 2016 Piet van Avermaet stated in his presentation that language is not a prerequisite for integration but its outcome. We would like to add that integration might be a result of stability; refugees and migrants in general need stability in the new country and environment. They need clear educational and professional perspectives as well as access to networks, whether of people with similar backgrounds and experiences to themselves or – even more important – of migrants and people who have lived in the receiving countries for a longer time.

To conclude we quote S on being part of society:

> I: It sounds as if you feel like a part of this society ...
> S: Well, we all are, aren't we? Important or less important, we all play our parts, don't we? As an electrician, you are part of a construction, each one in his own profession. A small part, but you do. (GER-S8)

# References

Blommaert, Jan, Massimiliano Spotti & Jef Van der Aa. 2015. *Complexity, mobility, migration* (Tilburg Papers in Culture Studies 137). https://www.tilburguniversity.edu/upload/25a7c347-6fa3-4ad1-9238-5c068f019476_TPCS_137_Blommaert-Spotti-VdrAa.pdf (accessed 2 July 2016).

Blommaert, Jan. 2016. *New forms of diaspora, new forms of integration* (Tilburg Papers in Culture Studies 160). https://www.tilburguniversity.edu/upload/ba515695-257b-4dd0-b030-b52a158c7a42_TPCS_160_Blommaert.pdf (accessed 2 July 2016).

Gächter, August & Stefanie Smoliner. 2010. *How well does education travel? Education and occupation with and without migration.* (ZSI report). https://www.zsi.at/users/153/attach/10fiwfinal.pdf (accessed 2 July 2016).

Myriam Schleiss, Margrit Hagenow-Caprez
# *fide* – On the way to a coherent framework

**Abstract:** *fide* – the innovative conceptual framework for the linguistic integration of migrants in Switzerland – is characterised by a systemic approach to questions of language learning, teaching and assessment. First presented to the public in 2012, the development phase of *fide* is now in its final stages. This contribution, based on mainly qualitative data collected among teachers, focuses on issues related to the implementation of the *fide* approach to teaching.

**Résumé :** *fide* – le cadre de référence pour l'encouragement linguistique des migrants en Suisse – se caractérise par une approche systémique des questions liées à l'apprentissage, à l'enseignement et à l'évaluation linguistique. Présenté au public en 2012, *fide* est entré dans sa phase finale de développement. L'article, qui repose principalement sur les données qualitatives recueillies auprès des enseignants, se concentre sur les questions liées à la mise en œuvre de l'approche *fide* à l'enseignement.

## 1 Linguistic integration policy

Switzerland has a population of eight million people, 23% of them holding a foreign passport. The Swiss Federal Law on Foreigners states that it is imperative for all foreigners to become familiar with Swiss society and the Swiss way of life, and that this includes the learning of the national language spoken in the area of residence.

In 2007, the Swiss Federal Council ordered the development of a national framework for the linguistic integration of adult migrants, with the aim of ensuring the quality and efficacy of language courses throughout the country. At the same time, the framework was to provide reliable tools to evaluate and certify the linguistic skills of adult migrants.

Against the background of heterogeneous structures and greatly varying traditions in the teaching of languages to migrants, the first step towards a national framework consisted in getting an overview of the various models of practice,

---

**Myriam Schleiss,** Swiss State Secretariat for Migration SEM, Switzerland,
E-mail: myriam.schleiss@sem.admin.ch
**Margrit Hagenow-Caprez** (corresponding author), *fide* Secretariat, Switzerland,
E-mail: margrit.hagenow@idea-ti.ch

DOI 10.1515/9783110477498-022, © 2017 Myriam Schleiss, Margrit Hagenow-Caprez, published by De Gruyter.
This work is licensed under the Creative Commons Attribution-NonCommercial-NoDerivs 3.0 License.

and in defining the features of "good practice". The resulting guidelines for a national framework were published in 2009, in an Outline Curriculum (Lenz, Andrey, and Lindt-Bangerter 2009).

## 2 *fide* – the national framework for the linguistic integration of migrants

*fide* stands for *français, italiano, deutsch* – the languages migrants have to learn in the various parts of Switzerland.[1]

In the Outline Curriculum, a close link to the learners' real communicative needs was identified as one of the key factors for successful learning. Therefore, frequent contact situations between migrants and Swiss residents were identified and analysed, in the various domains of everyday life, work contexts, contacts with authorities etc. These formed the basis for an inventory of "scenarios": descriptions of interactive situations, the interlocutors involved, their respective roles, the overall aim to be achieved by the interaction, the usual course of action, socio-cultural factors to be considered, and helpful linguistic resources to achieve the interaction aim.[2]

These scenarios, along with a set of pedagogical principles, constitute the "backbone" of the *fide* system. Numerous tools, guidelines and materials illustrating the system and the teaching approach have been added. As an overall system, *fide* now comprises:

- the aforementioned inventory of scenarios;
- videos and texts illustrating the performance of migrants at different levels of proficiency in L2 in various scenarios;
- a placement tool and recommendations to course organizers;
- guidelines for teachers and sample materials illustrating the teaching approach;
- a qualification profile for teachers as well as a training and qualification system;
- procedures for language competence assessment (both testing and portfolio-based approaches, operating as from 2017);
- a quality development system;
- a national secretariat as a reference point;

---

[1] All fide-publications are available at http://www.fide-info.ch.
[2] The contents and the structure of the scenario database are described in an article by Martin Müller and Lukas Wertenschlag (2013).

- a website (http://www.fide-info.ch) on which all products are freely available for download.

## 3 Implementing the *fide* system

The aim of the present study is to gain insights into the practical implementation of *fide* in the classroom: Has the *fide* system with its underlying didactic principles been successfully communicated? How are these principles interpreted by teachers, course organizers and decision makers? What elements of *fide* – both ideas and products – have been adopted with success? What elements of *fide* are "struggling" and need to be supported and promoted further?

The analysis is mainly based on a survey conducted among the users of the *fide* website in February 2016 (a short written questionnaire returned by 370 people, the large majority teachers, over 85% of them claiming to implement *fide* in their courses). The data obtained is also being compared to the written feedback received from nearly 600 teachers participating in the introduction events in 2013 as well as the feedback collected informally during meetings, information and training events.

## 4 Systemic coherence

The title of this contribution, "On the way to a coherent framework", reflects the working hypothesis that the coherence of the *fide* system is a key factor for its successful implementation. To gain the support and collaboration of teachers and schools, it has been crucial to ensure that all elements of the system are consistent and that they convey the same underlying assumptions and attitudes towards teaching, learning and assessment.

Analysing the teachers' feedback, however, it became evident, that the way *fide* is perceived and interpreted has even more importance in determining successful implementation, as these statements illustrate: "I really like the *fide* scenario approach, but my students need to pass the A2 exam"; "I have to work through the book in only 60 lessons, so I don't have the time for the fide scenarios".

A first conclusion, therefore, is that the coherence of the framework is a necessary but by no means sufficient condition. Consequently, the focus at this stage probably has to move from the "product" to the communication and the perception of the product.

## 5 Didactic principles of *fide*

The following principles constitute the core of the *fide* approach to teaching:
1. orienting teaching to the everyday Swiss context, applying an action-oriented and task-based approach to teaching: *scenario based teaching*;
2. developing learner autonomy by recording and evaluating the learning process: *portfolio approach*;
3. orienting teaching to the learners' needs: *co-construction of the learning curriculum.*

From the course entry procedures to the teaching methodology right through to the assessment procedures, all instruments and examples provided are largely coherent and in line with these underlying principles. But how successful have these elements been in the classroom? Which of these principles have actually been translated into teaching practice, and how? In the following sections, first findings will be summarized.

### 5.1 Scenario-based teaching

The aim of scenario-based teaching is the acquisition of action competence for everyday situations. These situations and the usually quite predictable course of events constitute the building blocks for the learning process: an initial discussion of the situation and the likely course of events allow the learners to build up knowledge about a specific aspect of everyday life in Switzerland on the one hand, and assess their own linguistic abilities with respect to the interactions to be expected and their learning needs on the other. These then form the basis for the definition of concrete and relevant learning targets, corresponding to the language competence level of the learners, and for the planning of the learning process.

For teachers, as well as for the non-language professionals concerned, e.g. decision makers at various levels, the scenario approach is intuitively appealing. It embodies the close link to the context in which second language learning takes place, and it also relates to what many teachers have done for years: taking up everyday situations their learners are confronted with, illustrating them with authentic materials, and practising them with role-plays and similar activities. In general, teachers are therefore open to adopt scenario-based teaching.

## 5.2 Portfolio approach

Collecting the products of lessons, such as sample texts or vocabulary lists on a specific topic, and regularly assessing learning outcomes form the basis for a continuing process of evaluation and planning. Creating records of learning promotes, especially with learners not used to formal education, the ability to self-assess their performance, to talk about their learning needs and thus become active partners in the co-construction of the learning process.

However, the structured documentation of learning is not popular with teachers and, as a consequence, with learners who feel that their teacher is not fully convinced of the usefulness of this practice. There are various reasons: portfolios are often perceived as "cumbersome", and they "take away time from learning". Another reason why teachers do not feel comfortable with portfolios might be that in the Swiss education system, group cohesion and moving forward as a group is highly valued, and this could appear to be contradicted by a practice that essentially promotes reflection on the individual learning process.

Although the portfolio approach has not been fully successful so far, one could say that it has been successful on a micro level: teachers put more emphasis on working towards "useful" learning outcomes and tend to include more formal and informal evaluation phases in the learning process.

## 5.3 Co-construction of the learning process

The principle of co-construction, in the *fide* system, not only includes negotiating meaning and constructing knowledge collaboratively but claims that the learning process as well, the content and learning aims, are continuously negotiated between teacher and learners. Co-construction in this sense is one of the key principles of *fide*, maybe the most characteristic – and at the same time it seems the most difficult one to implement.

Co-construction goes against the firm and fundamental convictions of many teachers. It contradicts what they believe to be their role and responsibility. It is also against the beliefs of many learners as regards the role of the teacher. Often, the teachers' resistance is also, explicitly or implicitly, backed up by school administrators, who see their careful planning jeopardized when the learning content of courses becomes less predictable.

On the basis of the data obtained, it seems clear that the key element of co-construction will need to be reinforced both in teacher training and in communicating information about *fide*. The changing role it involves for teachers will have to be explained and illustrated, e.g. with experiences like the following:

"My learners are much more motivated since they know that the course is modelled on their expressed needs."[3]

## 6 Conclusion: dialogue and negotiation

Most Swiss people would agree that in their country systems and frameworks cannot be introduced and implemented top down; they need to be negotiated and agreed upon by all partners involved – this is why innovative processes in Switzerland take time (but in general the results are accepted and not overruled the next day). Dialogue and negotiation, historically, can actually be seen as fundamental values of Swiss society.

In coherence with these values, the idea of partnership and dialogue is a key element of *fide*, and finds expression on all levels: from the Confederation and the Cantons agreeing on integration programmes, to teachers and learners negotiating learning content and aims in the spirit of co-construction.

Possibly in the course of developing products and introducing *fide*, the focus – also in communicating with teachers – has been, quite understandably, on the "material" side of *fide*. At the present stage, to ensure the successful implementation of the *fide* system, it might be appropriate to emphasize and promote the underlying principles and values, reinforcing partnership and dialogue between all stakeholders.

## References

Hagenow-Caprez, Margrit. 2013. Unterrichten mit Szenarien: "Aus der Praxis". *Babylonia* 1/2013. 47–50.

Lenz, Peter, Stéphanie Andrey & Bernhard Lindt-Bangerter. 2009. *Rahmencurriculum für die sprachliche Förderung von Migrantinnen und Migranten / Curriculum-cadre pour l'encouragement linguistique des migrants*. Bern: Bundesamt für Migration BFM.

Müller, Martin & Lukas Wertenschlag. 2013. "Meine Kinder möchten, dass ich auch zum Elternabend gehe". Anmerkungen zum Szenarienansatz und zur Entstehungsgeschichte der fide-Szenarien. *Babylonia* 1/2013. 28–34.

---

[3] The approach of sharing successful practice, rather than giving instructions on how to implement scenarios, is described in an article by Margrit Hagenow-Caprez (2013).

Enrica Piccardo, Danielle Hunter
# Settlement, integration and language learning: possible synergies. A task-based, community-focused program from the Region of Durham (Ontario, Canada)

**Abstract:** Task-based learning and the action-oriented approach have introduced a shift in second language education, opening new possibilities for anchoring language learning in real-life practice. The collaboration of over 80 partners in the Region of Durham (Ontario, Canada) led to the development of an online community-based immigration portal for newcomers, which served as a platform for a language program. This case study shows how this program has influenced immigrants' knowledge and access to essential services, motivation to learn, and confidence levels in the host language.

**Résumé :** L'apprentissage par les tâches et la perspective actionnelle ont introduit un changement dans l'apprentissage de la langue seconde et ouvert de nouvelles possibilités d'intégrer l'apprentissage d'une langue dans le vécu. Dans la région de Durham (Ontario, Canada), plus de 80 partenaires se sont unis pour développer un portail local sur l'immigration destiné aux nouveaux arrivants, qui sert de plateforme pour un programme d'apprentissage de la langue. Cette étude de cas montre en quoi ce programme a influencé la connaissance et l'accès des migrants à des services essentiels, leur motivation à apprendre et leur niveau de confiance dans la langue du pays d'accueil.

## 1 Introduction

As global mobility increases, the necessity of accelerating settlement and integration of newcomers is an ever-growing priority. This reality has challenged institutions to find innovative approaches to address the complex needs of a changing population, including language learning based on transparency and accountability, and to validate the results.

---

**Enrica Piccardo** (corresponding author), OISE, University of Toronto, Toronto, Canada/Université Grenoble-Alpes, France, E-mail: enrica.piccardo@utoronto.ca
**Danielle Hunter,** Durham District School Board, Whitby, Canada,
E-mail: danielle.hunter@ddsb.ca

DOI 10.1515/9783110477498-023, © 2017 Enrica Piccardo, Danielle Hunter, published by De Gruyter.
This work is licensed under the Creative Commons Attribution-NonCommercial-NoDerivs 3.0 License.

The availability of both conceptual and operational resources in the form of sound methodological options such as task-based learning and the action-oriented approach, and reference tools for assessment and planning, including the *Common European Framework of Reference for Languages* (CEFR; Council of Europe 2001) and the *Canadian Language Benchmarks* (CLB; Centre for Canadian Language Benchmarks 2012), show great potential for rethinking second language education. The synergies created between effective pedagogic support and terrain for experimentation can fuel innovation on a broader scale.

In this paper, we discuss an exploratory case study, conducted in the Region of Durham (Ontario, Canada), on the use of an online community-based immigration portal for newcomers as a platform for a language program. Starting from the potential of CEFR- and CLB-informed real-life tasks in renewing second language education among immigrants, this study investigated how this program influenced immigrants' knowledge of and access to essential services, motivation to learn, and confidence in the host language.

## 2 From task-based to action-oriented: opening doors to real life

Although task-based learning originated in the late 1980s (Prabhu 1987), more recent theoretical reflection has enriched its conceptual apparatus (Nunan 2004; Van den Branden 2006). A further step in this direction has been the action-oriented approach, which constitutes one of the pillars of the CEFR. This has led to a marked shift in the field of second language education, while opening new possibilities for anchoring language learning in real-life practice. In particular, there has been research on the following: the nature and typology of tasks; the distinction between tasks aimed at supporting learning and task-based learning where tasks are the backbone of the teaching/learning process; the sequencing of tasks and task cycles; the need for clear criteria for outcomes assessment, and the roles of teachers and learners. The action-oriented approach has moved away from an accumulation of knowledge and know-how toward an activation of competences (both general and communicative language competences) in order to achieve an objective. Action-oriented tasks make it possible to structure learning around moments, actions, and products that are vivid, defined, and concrete. Organizing learning around tasks also makes it possible to effectively link teaching and assessment (Piccardo 2014).

Canada's interest in task-based learning and the action-oriented approach is growing. With two official languages, communities rich with linguistic and cultural diversity, together with localized educational policies, there is a need to refine and/or adapt tools that support task-based learning and assessment and provide transparent criteria and proficiency level indicators. With this in mind, the CLB, the national standard for adult ESL/FSL in Canada, were updated in 2012. This coincided with the identification by researchers (Vandergrift 2006) and institutional stakeholders (CMEC 2010) of the potential value of the CEFR for Canada. The CEFR is presently contributing to language education policies, particularly curriculum development in FSL (French as a second language) and International Languages (K-12 curriculum). The resource which is at the centre of this study is informed by these approaches and aligns with the CLB and the CEFR.

## 3 Learning and living in English through action-oriented tasks: the case of the Region of Durham

The Region of Durham, 45 minutes east of Toronto, covers an area of 2,590 km$^2$ with a total population of 608,125 inhabitants of which 20.7% identify as immigrants, with over 30% in some municipalities (Statistics Canada 2013).

With an aging population and slow population growth, Canada requires immigrants to thrive. With this in mind, both the federal and provincial governments continue to invest in an immigration strategy to address the complex needs of communities and newcomers. One such example is the *Municipal Immigration Information Online Program* from the Ontario Government's Ministry of Citizenship, Immigration and International Trade (MCIIT). Through funding from this program, the Durham Immigration Portal (http://www.durhamimmigration.ca) was created, which aims to be "a one-stop community-based web portal, designed to welcome, support, attract and retain skilled newcomers, newcomer entrepreneurs, businesses and other new Canadians to [the Region]" (2016). Over 80 community partners representing diverse sectors developed and continue to share responsibility for content and the long-term sustainability of the portal.

The benefits of using the portal in educational settings lead to the development of support material for ESL instructors and further partnerships between the Regional Municipality of Durham and the Durham District School Board (DDSB). As task-based learning gained ground in Canada, support material was updated, resulting in the creation of a publicly available resource entitled *Exploring the Region of Durham through Task-based Learning. Living in English,*

*Discovering Durham* (Collins and Hunter 2013), funded by MCIIT. This resource provides community-centred, task-based scenarios, based on information from the portal, to support settlement and integration, as well as linguistic competence in the host language. Given that the target audience is adult newcomers to Canada learning English, the driving framework of reference in the document is the CLB (2012), presented alongside the CEFR to allow for a broader use.

## 4 A case study investigating synergy between language learning and settlement

With further funding from MCIIT, a small-scale case study was launched to explore the possible synergy between language learning and settlement through the use of an immigration portal. The following research questions were investigated:

Has this specific language program influenced Canadian adult newcomers'
i) knowledge of and access to essential services?
ii) motivation to attend English language classes and to learn English?
iii) confidence in the host language?

The study included three ESL instructors, the Department Head of Language Programs, and 36 learners from Durham Continuing Education, DDSB, as well as the Manager of Strategic Partnerships and Initiatives from the Regional Municipality of Durham. Over the three-month duration of the study, a variety of data collection tools were used with instructors, students, and Region management, including pre and post questionnaires and focus groups.

Instructors participated in four hours of training to deepen their understanding of task-based learning/the action-oriented approach and the portal. Next, instructors were provided eight hours of mentored co-planning time to develop activities that support learners in achieving the defined task. The activities, as well as the task, aimed to develop linguistic competence and to improve knowledge of, and access to, the community for newcomers. The instructors then delivered the learning block of approximately five days, consisting of the activities and the culminating task, to their respective ESL class.

## 5 Discussion of results

Data revealed that students highly appreciated being exposed to task-based learning/the action-oriented approach. Learners at CLB 3–4/CEFR A2 presented an average score of 8.9/10 when asked "how much did you enjoy task-based learning?" If we break down this score, comparing learners' pre- and post-intervention questionnaires, the perceived level of proficiency and comfort in the language increased considerably (20% and 18% respectively) together with the perceived ability to accomplish the real-life task (32%). Positive results, albeit less substantial, were observed at CLB 7/CEFR B1+ (5%, 12% and 8% respectively). We interpreted this difference as mainly due to resistance to change in methodological routines from learners who had been longer in the program.

Instructors observed that their students enjoyed using task-based learning/the action-oriented approach and reported increased interest in learning, improved attendance during the intervention, as well as an increase in confidence. They also declared that, overall, they enjoyed teaching this way and that lesson planning was improved. One instructor voiced: "[...] I stayed more focused [in lesson planning], I kept coming back to the question *how is this going to help my students perform the task?*" Instructors felt that the spiraling of learning through the intervention, which led to gradual release of responsibility on their side, was helpful in solidifying learning and building confidence in students. They also observed a transfer of knowledge to other contexts and noted the benefits of embedding grammar and vocabulary in context. Furthermore, they saw this approach as student-centred, and through this intervention, reinforced the necessity to ensure that learning encompasses practical, real-life connections that support community integration. Finally, instructors reported that students benefited from the authentic nature of the task, and their direct application in real-life situations. The application through classroom simulations took place in a safe, supportive environment, where students felt comfortable taking risks. Through the use of the portal, a greater awareness in the students of what their community offers of specific interest to newcomers was also observed.

Instructors identified challenges throughout the study including an increase of planning time and professional development, which currently is not allocated in their contract. The observation was also made by instructors that task-based learning/the action-oriented approach conflicted with some students' preconceived notion of teaching, especially the more traditional teaching of grammar. Another challenge reported related to classes being continuous intake and exit, resulting in missed instruction. Instructors did express that flexibility and a spiral approach to learning did help to alleviate this concern as there were other entry points for new students to catch up on missed learning.

## 6 Potential benefits and future developments

Although this was a small-scale case study, it yielded promising results. Task-based learning/the action-oriented approach brings together real-life tasks, strategic/autonomous decision-making in learning, and transparency of objectives and assessment. Targeted resources and professional development coupled with the availability of authentic, locally situated and community-relevant resources available on the same virtual space, maximize the language learning process and support action once learners (newcomers) leave the class, which in turn helps with settlement and community integration. Thanks to funds allocated by MCIIT, this study will be upscaled in the province as part of a wider immigration strategy.

## References

Centre for Canadian Language Benchmarks. 2012. *Canadian Language Benchmarks: English as a second language for adults.* Ottawa: Centre for Canadian Language Benchmarks. http://www.cic.gc.ca/english/pdf/pub/language-benchmarks.pdf

CMEC (Council of Ministers of Education, Canada). 2010. *Working with the Common European Framework of Reference for Languages (CEFR) in the Canadian context: Guide for policy-makers and curriculum designers.* http://www.cmec.ca/docs/assessment/CEFR-canadian-context.pdf (accessed 14 June 2016).

Collins, Geoff & Danielle Hunter. 2013. *Exploring the region of Durham through task-based learning: Living in English, discovering Durham.* https://www.durhamimmigration.ca/learning/Documents/Living-in-English_Discovering-Durham.pdf (accessed 14 June 2016).

Council of Europe. 2001. *Common European Framework of Reference for Languages: Learning, teaching, assessment.* Cambridge: Cambridge University Press. http://www.coe.int/t/dg4/linguistic/Source/Framework_EN.pdf (accessed 9 August 2016).

Nunan, David. 2004. *Task-based language teaching.* Cambridge: Cambridge University Press.

Piccardo, Enrica. 2014. *From communicative to action-oriented: A research pathway.* Toronto: Ontario Ministry of Education. https://www.coe.int/t/dg4/linguistic/Source/CSC605_Research_Guide_English.pdf (accessed 14 June 2016).

Prabhu, N. S. 1987. *Second language pedagogy.* Oxford: Oxford University Press.

Van den Branden, Kris. 2006. *Task-based language education: From theory to practice.* Cambridge: Cambridge University Press.

Vandergrift, Larry. 2006. *Proposal for a Common Reference Framework for Languages for Canada.* Ottawa: Canadian Heritage. https://www.caslt.org/pdf/Proposal_Common%20Framework_Reference_languages%20for%20Canada_PDF_Internet_e.pdf (accessed 14 June 2016).

George Androulakis, Anastasia Gkaintartzi, Roula Kitsiou and Sofia Tsioli

# Research-driven task-based L2 learning for adult immigrants in times of humanitarian crisis: results from two nationwide projects in Greece

**Abstract:** This paper reports on two nationwide projects implemented in Greece aiming at providing courses in Greek as a second language for adult immigrants. A qualitative approach was adopted using interviews, focus groups, ethnographic observation, and written reports. Based on a prior stage of needs analysis, we designed specialized courses using the research stages as a means of empowering immigrants. We discuss our most important results concerning the needs analysis and the implementation of the task-based approach.

**Résumé :** L'article fait référence à deux projets de portée nationale menés en Grèce en vue de proposer des cours de grec langue seconde aux migrants adultes. L'approche qualitative retenue a reposé sur des entretiens, des groupes de discussion, une observation ethnographique et des rapports écrits. Après avoir analysé les besoins, nous avons élaboré des cours spécialisés utilisant les étapes de recherche pour faire participer les migrants. Nous examinons nos principaux résultats concernant l'analyse des besoins et la mise en œuvre d'une approche par les tâches.

# 1 Introduction: the projects' identity

This paper reports on two nationwide research projects (ELMEGO and MATII-EME) implemented by the Greek Language and Multilingualism Laboratory of the University of Thessaly, Greece, from 2010 to 2015. ELMEGO is an acronym

---

**George Androulakis,** GreekLangLab, University of Thessaly, Volos, Greece, Hellenic Open University, Patras, Greece, E-mail: androulakis@uth.gr
**Anastasia Gkaintartzi,** GreekLangLab, University of Thessaly, Volos, Greece,
E-mail: againtartzi@gmail.com
**Roula Kitsiou,** GreekLangLab, University of Thessaly, Volos, Greece,
E-mail: roulakit@gmail.com
**Sofia Tsioli,** GreekLangLab, University of Thessaly, Volos, Greece, Hellenic Open University, Patras, Greece, E-mail: sofia.tsioli@gmail.com

DOI 10.1515/9783110477498-024, © 2017 George Androulakis, Anastasia Gkaintartzi, Roula Kitsiou and Sofia Tsioli, published by De Gruyter.
This work is licensed under the Creative Commons Attribution-NonCommercial-NoDerivs 3.0 License.

for Greek for Immigrant Parents, a small-scale project funded by the Research Committee of the University of Thessaly. The subject of this project was to plan and implement specialized courses in Greek language for immigrant parents with children attending compulsory education. The main objective was to facilitate immigrant parents' communication with teachers and schools attended by their children. The second project, MATHEME, is an acronym for Greek Courses for Immigrants. The subject was the design and implementation of Greek courses for immigrant target-groups. These target-groups were immigrants from non-EU countries who are unemployed; mothers; immigrants with disabilities; and illiterate immigrants. The main objective was to empower immigrants during their integration process in Greece by giving voice to their narratives and designing specialized Greek courses. It was funded by the European Integration Fund (EIF).

The two projects had four main characteristics. First of all, they took place in a particularly sensitive context. Greece is going through a deep financial and social crisis. Immigration flows have been the pretext for negative and even racist reactions. Additionally, bureaucracy issues are an important factor of adversity in the implementation of projects. For both projects, priority was given to social cohesion and to raising awareness about the rights of immigrants. Third, an emphasis was placed on research during all stages of the project. We conducted needs analysis (Long 2005), which was perceived in a more societal way; we implemented teacher training through research activities; and we carried out multilateral course evaluation. Finally, we adopted task-based learning (Van den Branden 2006) as the most appropriate methodology for the linguistic integration of adult immigrants. There were seven stages in the implementation of the projects: 1) recording of the target-group; 2) review of the relevant international literature and tracing of good practices concerning the linguistic training of immigrants; 3) language and communication needs analysis; 4) specification of the course objectives and development of a specialized syllabus; 5) design, development and adjustment of teaching material in printed form and multimedia – organizing educational activities; 6) implementation of free courses: Greek language, history and culture; and 7) evaluation and assessment of implemented courses and creation of a resource pack.

# 2 Methodology

Concerning the research methodology, both projects were team-based and interdisciplinary. The research teams were composed of social anthropologists, sociolinguists, applied linguists, and specialists on education. We adopted a qualitative approach, which involved open (unstructured) and semi-structured interviews, individual and group interviews, focus groups with prospective students and teachers, ethnographic observation of the courses, written reports (from teachers, mediators and researchers). As for the involvement of course participants in the research, 46 learners, five teachers and four mediators participated in the ELMEGO project, while 414 learners from non-EU countries, 28 teachers, and ten mediators participated in the MATHEME project. Our data analysis methods were qualitative thematic analysis and critical discourse analysis.

One of the most important modalities underpinning the interview design was approaching the interview as a tool to create deeper understanding of the experiences of others in all their complexity and multiple meanings (Mears 2009). The semi-structured interview was transformed into a critical instrument to understand immigrants' voices and the interview process was a stage towards the empowerment and integration of our immigrant participants (Androulakis et al. in press). Parts of interviews and focus group communication were held in three international languages. Specifically, Italian, English and French were used as auxiliary languages for communication with Albanian, Pakistani and Romanian immigrants respectively. We used mediation languages to conduct interviews. The working languages were Albanian, English, French, Greek, Italian, Urdu and Romanian.

# 3 Results

Our most important results relate to immigrants' communicative needs, which are connected with their everyday life and work. They expressed the importance of Greek language learning for finding a job and improving their economic condition (economic capital), as well as for their social integration and advancement of social capital. They stressed the need for effective formal communication with public services (objectified capital) and with their children's schools as public organizations. Their expectations from the language courses related mostly to knowledge and skills which they could not acquire from everyday language use. They identified the urgent role of acquiring writing skills and developing language competence in order to claim their rights in the professional domain, face up to their work obligations, and deal with bureaucratic issues concerning their legal status in the country, as shown in the following interview extract:

Εγώ περιμένω να μάθω ελληνικά, γράφω καλύτερα, να διαβάζω γιατί να έχει αύριο πιο εύκολα για μένα, αύριο για μένα πιο εύκολα η ζωή, όταν μάθω καλύτερα, καλύτερα είναι η ζωή εδώ Ελλάδα, αν δεν μάθω τίποτα, τίποτα, δύσκολα, άμα πάω κάπου δουλειά μου λέει φέρε αυτά, μπορεί να βρω δουλειά για ντελίβερι, πώς θα γράφω; πώς θα διαβάσω; Μου λέει πήγαινε αυτό το στενό, πώς θα ...; [...] Pakistani man, 13 years in Greece, 30 years old (interview language: Greek)

[I expect to learn Greek, write better, to read because to be more easily for me tomorrow, tomorrow for me more easily the life, when I have learnt more, better is the life here Greece, if I don't learn anything, anything, it is difficult, if I ask for a job somewhere they say bring me these, I may find a job as a delivery boy, how am I supposed to write? how to read? they tell me go to this street, how shall I ...?]

In addition, the immigrants' expressed needs were more relevant to processes and social skills than language itself (for example, how to search for a job in Greece or which documents are necessary to get an unemployment card, rather than how to use the language accurately in order to complete the document). The main domains which emerged from the analysis (school, home and family, movement/mobility, work, health, everyday communication) were explicitly or implicitly stated during the research process. The data revealed that immigrants lacked communicative language skills and intercultural understanding in the societal context, and were exposed to ethnocentric and xenophobic attitudes during the financial and socio-economic crisis. Based on these findings, we developed a multidimensional syllabus (analytic and not synthetic, process-based and not product-based, cultural, task-based). The task-based approach was chosen as the most appropriate since it refers to tasks which engage learners through communicative procedures in situations which require problem solving, decision making and negotiation of concepts (Van den Branden 2006).

The analysis of the teachers' written reports and the interview data revealed that the task-based approach was effective and resulted in team-building, identity investment and empowerment. It also gave opportunities for learners to share their experiences and feelings. They gradually became more involved in the teaching process and participated more actively. Drawing from their own voices: "No one wanted to talk about their school experiences but when the first one took the initiative, soon afterwards they all participated in the circle in order to show the corporal punishments that students suffer from in Nigeria" (Nigerian woman, 5 years in Greece, 29 years old, interview language: English).

In the final interview at the end of the courses, the learners stressed that the teaching materials and lessons were of interest to them and offered them opportunities for communication. Apart from developing their language confidence, they stated that they developed a more powerful will for learning in general, which would facilitate their integration process: "It is an investment in ourselves" (field notes). They particularly focused on their gains in language awareness and expressed their positive feelings towards the collaborative, supportive and friendly learning environment. This is evident in their own words: "They helped us overcome the block. To express ourselves without reservations. I will join a regular school afterwards. I learned to express myself. They talk to us well, they helped us fill in documents. They taught us to do it ourselves, to express ourselves confidently without feeling ashamed" (researcher's written report).

## 4 Discussion

The focus of these two projects in Greece was the empowerment of immigrants in their integration process. Therefore, priority was given to learners' needs prior to the lessons and these were explored using a qualitative methodology. The scope of the research process was to empower the participants through all the research stages (design, modality, analysis) by giving them space and a "voice" to share their experiences and realities. This was an innovation in the Greek context. Another point is that researching language needs using insiders led to the emergence of a mediated trilingualism (Androulakis 2013). We also dealt with issues of asymmetrical power relations as part of the methodological design. Specifically, through the interviews we aimed at challenging the researcher's power in order to break down the researcher–participant hierarchy and build a connection (Bourdieu et al. 1999) through empathy and an insider perspective (Cooper 2009).

Aspects of immigrants' identities were integrated in the teaching material. As a result, learners were helped to invest their identities in the learning process. The student participants were encouraged to talk, to tell about themselves, to share their stories and their realities; they "carved a space of their own" (Scheurich 1997: 71) in each classroom. The impact of the projects on the researchers and the participants was evident, at a local and a national level. Finally, the projects were experienced as a process of mutual empowerment, raising the researchers' multilingual awareness. The projects' added value was their impact on the local communities, which we tried to affect towards the transformation of the national landscape in times of societal and economic crisis.

## References

Androulakis, George. 2013. Researching language needs using "insiders": Mediated trilingualism and other issues of power asymmetries. *International Journal of Applied Linguistics* 23(3). 368–384.

Androulakis, George, Anastasia Gkaintartzi, Roula Kitsiou, Evi Markou & Zoi Liveranou. In press. Interviewing as understanding: Principles and modalities for transforming a qualitative research instrument into a stage of the integration process for immigrants. In *Proceedings of the Rethinking Language, Diversity and Education (RLDE) Conference*, Rhodes, 27–31 May.

Bourdieu, Pierre et al. 1999. *The weight of the world: Social suffering in contemporary society*. Cambridge: Polity Press.

Cooper, Robin. 2009. Entering into a "community" of experience and meaning: A review of interviewing for education and social science research: The gateway approach by Carolyn. *The Weekly Qualitative Report* 39(2). 229–232.

Long, Michael (ed.). 2005. *Second language needs analysis*. Cambridge: Cambridge University Press.

Mears, Carolyn. 2009. *Interviewing for education and social research: The Gateway approach*. New York: Palgrave Macmillan.

Scheurich, James. 1997. *Research method in the postmodern*. London: Falmer Press.

Van den Branden, Kris (ed.). 2006. *Task-based language education: From theory to practice*. Cambridge: Cambridge University Press.

Michel Gout
# Quatre approches didactiques pour la formation linguistique des nouveaux arrivants

**Résumé :** La communication expose ici quatre approches originales d'enseignement de la langue aux migrants. Il s'agit des « textes identitaires », de la pratique artistique, de la méthode communicative « de l'intérieur » et, enfin, de *l'empowerment* par la dynamique de projet.

**Abstract:** This article presents four original approaches to language teaching for migrants. They involve using "identity texts", artistic activities, the "from within" communicative method and, lastly, "empowerment" through the project process.

## Introduction

En 1994, John Schumann de l'université de Californie, neurolinguiste, spécialiste de l'évolution du langage, montre que « les cellules du cerveau, dans les sphères du système du traitement de l'information, modulent l'acte de cognition de telle façon que, dans le cerveau, l'affect et la cognition sont bien identifiés mais fonctionnent de manière inséparable. En conclusion, dans une perspective neurologique, on peut en déduire que l'affect fait bien partie de l'acte cognitif. » (Schumann 1994 : 232).

Quant à Earl Stevick, professeur de linguistique à l'Université du Maryland, il appuie cette thèse en affirmant que « le succès dans l'apprentissage des langues étrangères dépend moins des matériaux, des techniques et des analyses linguistiques que de ce qui se passe dans et entre les personnes pendant la classe » (Stevick 1980 : 4). En d'autres termes, la réussite dépendrait moins des « outils » que des liaisons interpersonnelles, des relations sociales et interculturelles, mais aussi, de toutes les activités qui font appel à l'hémisphère droit du cerveau : l'imagination, la créativité, le plaisir, l'émotion, etc.

C'est sur la base de ces considérations que nous avons orienté une grande partie de notre recherche qui s'est étalée dans quatre pays d'Europe entre 2012 et 2014 (Gout 2015). Elle avait pour objectif principal de découvrir des approches pédagogiques de formation linguistique aux nouveaux arrivants à la fois inno-

---

**Michel Gout,** Université d'Aix-Marseille, France, E-mail : michel.gout31@yahoo.fr

vantes et en même temps reconnues pour leurs résultats performants aux examens et tests linguistiques.

Parmi les approches didactiques que nous avons observées dans plusieurs pays, nous en citerons quatre que nous allons développer ici : les « textes identitaires », l'appropriation linguistique par la pratique artistique et culturelle, l'approche communicative « de l'intérieur », et l'*empowerment* par la dynamique de projet.

## 1 Les textes identitaires

Le migrant a une histoire, une culture propre : l'enseignant, en accordant de la considération à son histoire familière, lève des obstacles à l'apprentissage et établit ainsi la relation.

Jim Cummins (2011) de l'Université de Toronto, relate plusieurs expériences de textes identitaires menées au Canada, dont une, dans l'établissement scolaire de Thornwood (Canada), dans lequel plus de 40 nationalités étaient représentées parmi les élèves migrants. Les apprenants rédigeaient la propre histoire de leur vie en anglais et traduisaient le texte dans leur langue vivante 1 d'origine (LV1). Ils présentaient ensuite à la classe le texte dans leur propre langue. Les apprenants, ainsi, investissaient leur identité dans la création de ces textes qui pouvaient être écrits, lus, visuels, joués, ou la combinaison de toutes ces formes de communication. Ces travaux furent ensuite exposés dans le Centre de documentation et d'information (CDI) de l'établissement qui fut largement ouvert aux parents et membres de la famille. Cette expérience, menée sur le long terme, s'est révélée être un instrument d'apprentissage linguistique et d'intégration puissant.

Une autre pratique d'apprentissage par l'identité se développe aujourd'hui au Royaume-Uni, c'est la méthode « *language experience* », souvent utilisée comme méthode d'alphabétisation. L'apprenant raconte oralement son histoire ou un fragment de l'histoire de sa vie en présence de son professeur ; l'enseignant et l'élève écrivent le texte à deux. L'apprenant dispose ainsi du récit écrit de sa propre vie, qui devient un document de travail qui va remplacer le manuel scolaire, et c'est autour de cet écrit que s'élabore le cours d'alphabétisation. L'apprenant déchiffre les signes, prononce les syllabes, puis les mots, découvre la syntaxe, et reproduit les phrases par écrit, les mémorise, etc. L'objectif de la méthode est que l'appropriation du texte de l'histoire de vie doit conduire naturellement à l'appropriation de la langue du texte.

## 2 L'appropriation linguistique par la pratique artistique et culturelle

Une démarche culturelle très originale est actuellement à l'œuvre dans la Fédération Wallonie-Bruxelles depuis un décret de 2003[1].

Il s'agit de l'*appropriation* du français par le biais de l'expression artistique.

Ces actions d'apprentissage non formel mettent en jeu deux types d'intervenants complémentaires : une structure de formation et une structure d'animation artistique. C'est le cas par exemple d'une association théâtrale dans le centre de Bruxelles qui travaille de concert avec un organisme d'enseignement pour l'alphabétisation et le français langue étrangère (Alpha/FLE) pour enseigner le français à ses apprenants. C'est aussi le cas d'une ASBL[2] à Bruxelles dans laquelle une classe d'apprenants de niveau Alpha/FLE programme, grâce au soutien d'artistes locaux, des expositions de peinture dans une galerie en centre-ville. Il est possible de trouver aussi des institutions intégrées dans lesquelles interviennent des formateurs à double compétence.

L'approche d'*appropriation* qui fait travailler ensemble des structures de formation linguistique avec des structures d'animation artistique peut réunir dans un même cours des publics étrangers et francophones en alphabétisation. Cette mixité de public apprenant est intéressante car elle plonge les nouveaux arrivants dans un environnement linguistique « naturel » où tout le monde communique en français, peu importe son niveau, autour de l'élaboration d'un projet artistique commun.

Cette approche promeut un apprentissage à la fois cognitif et affectif. Comme le disent Alen et Manço : « le terme appropriation signifie avant tout aimer la langue, l'autre, sa culture et ce qui fait son identité, cela suppose la présence des dimensions de plaisir, de sensation et d'émotion. Mais pour que le plaisir puisse naitre, il faut d'abord qu'il y ait un désir » (Alen et Manço 2012 : 27).

---

[1] Décret sur l'autorisation permanente du 17 juillet 2003.
[2] Association Sans But Lucratif.

## 3 L'approche communicative « *speaking from within* »

L'apprentissage linguistique a recours depuis plusieurs décennies à la méthode communicative, qui est désormais adoptée dans la plupart des organismes de formation linguistique. Mais des recherches récentes, comme celles menées au Royaume Uni en 2013 pour le British Council (Esol Nexus Research), montrent que la plupart des méthodes communicatives sont peu motivantes pour les élèves, car elles n'utilisent que des moyens factices pour enseigner un langage standard. Constat : les sujets abordés sont éloignés des intérêts et des préoccupations des apprenants.

Les recherches menées par Cooke, Winstanley et Bryers (2013) du King's College de Londres montrent en revanche que lorsque les discussions portent sur des questions qui touchent à la vie personnelle des apprenants, alors, au contraire :
- les apprenants se délient de la peur de l'erreur linguistique, l'expression devient spontanée,
- ils parlent « *from within* », avec leur cœur et avec leurs « tripes »,
- ils s'investissent plus intensément et personnellement dans le débat,
- et, plus étonnant, les chercheurs ont remarqué alors qu'ils se mettent à produire un langage plus complexe, plus riche et plus fluide.

Dans leur pays d'accueil, les nouveaux arrivants sont interpellés par beaucoup d'aspects de la vie sociale. Les habitudes de leurs hôtes, les mœurs, les traditions, les étonnent, et même parfois, disent-ils, les « choquent ». Des comportements leur paraissent insolites, étranges, voire inquiétants chez les autochtones. Aborder ouvertement ces questions avec eux peut permettre de dissiper leurs doutes et d'éclairer leur compréhension et développer leur esprit critique.

Lors d'un cours, l'enseignant avait utilisé l'image d'un iceberg pour découvrir les causes d'un problème à partir d'un jugement sur l'attitude des autochtones. Le débat portait sur le problème suivant : les migrants sont parfois choqués par le fait que les familles britanniques ne s'occupent pas de leurs parents âgés. Les Anglais seraient-ils égoïstes (partie émergée) ? L'iceberg montrait la partie émergée et visible du problème et le groupe-classe devait découvrir la partie immergée de ce problème, trouver des explications au phénomène et arriver à un jugement juste. Des débats avaient lieu dans la classe, et les apprenants découvraient alors des raisons techniques à ce problème (partie immergée) : les couples anglais travaillent, problèmes de logement, tradition et culture, volonté des grands-parents de vivre à part, etc.

Dans une deuxième séance, une image montrait une femme musulmane portant le hijab, mais après quelque temps dans le pays, elle adoptait la tenue européenne et on la voyait, entourée d'amis européens, en terrasse de café, en train de boire une boisson alcoolisée. La question qui émergeait était la suivante : jusqu'à quel point les migrants doivent-ils rejeter leurs traditions culturelles pour être acceptés par la société d'accueil, et ont-ils des chances d'être acceptés s'ils ne le font pas ?

Face à ces questions qui le touchent, l'apprenant libère son expression car le sujet débattu rejoint ses préoccupations et son vécu profond. Il apprend en même temps à mettre à distance ses représentations, ses préjugés, et à exercer sa liberté de penser, de juger par lui-même. Ce faisant, il acquiert un début d'autonomie pour comprendre la société d'accueil qui peut faciliter son intégration.

## 4 *Empowerment* et dynamique de projet

Le verbe *to empower* signifie en anglais : « Donner à quelqu'un l'autorité ou le pouvoir de faire quelque chose. Rendre quelqu'un plus fort et plus confiant, notamment par le contrôle de sa vie et en lui donnant la possibilité de faire valoir ses droits[3] ».

En éducation, l'*empowerment* est basé sur la conviction que tout apprenant possède des aptitudes et des capacités, mais qu'il a besoin de circonstances favorables et d'opportunités pour les exprimer. Les adeptes de l'*empowerment* affirment que les compétences s'acquièrent beaucoup mieux lorsque l'on pratique une activité dans le contexte de la vie courante que dans des formations artificielles prodiguées par des experts professionnels.

Le processus de l'*empowerment* est donc une opération par laquelle on passe d'un état passif (« je subis ») à un état actif (« j'agis »). Mais la prise de conscience de ses capacités ne doit pas servir des intérêts individualistes, elle prend sa pleine mesure au service de ses pairs, de sa communauté, de sa localité.

Dans le quartier populaire de Tower Hamlets à l'Est de Londres, nous avons visité l'association *The Arbour*, structure sociale chargée de la formation linguistique et civique de femmes bangladaises et d'Asie du Sud. Cette association était réputée en Angleterre pour ses bons résultats aux tests linguistiques et pour

---

[3] « Empower: Give someone the authority or power to do something. Make someone stronger and more confident, especially in controlling their life and claiming their right. » Oxford Dictionaries 2014.

la qualité de sa formation (Hedges, 2013) ; elle utilisait largement la démarche d'*empowerment.*

Une partie des apprenantes migrantes participaient à un programme de formation linguistique et civique appelé *Empowerment and Leadership*[4]. Le programme visait à apprendre aux femmes migrantes à devenir des leaders au sein de leur communauté et à amorcer des changements à la fois en elles-mêmes et dans leur environnement. C'étaient des cours intensifs de 15 heures par semaine sur une durée de 6 mois centrés sur l'apprentissage du leadership sous toutes ses formes. Le projet culminait dans une action communautaire en fin de module : il s'agissait de créer, d'organiser et de publier un évènement local. Les cours d'anglais étaient orientés de manière à développer les compétences des apprenants dans l'art du débat et de la négociation et aussi à évaluer leurs sentiments et affirmer leurs opinions. Un cercle de paroles avait été créé dans le but d'aider les participantes à parler avec confiance et assurance d'elles-mêmes et de leurs projets.

Ces formations encourageaient l'engagement civique : des apprenantes chinoises avaient réalisé une brochure en deux langues (mandarin et anglais) et créé un site d'information à l'attention des sinophones récemment arrivés dans le pays. D'autres participaient à une campagne pour la défense de la gratuité des soins. Par ces types d'actions, les apprenantes acquéraient des compétences multiples :
- linguistiques (composer un texte dans la langue cible),
- discursives et argumentatives (exprimer son opinion, parler en public),
- organisationnelles (respect d'échéances, travail en équipe),
- mais aussi humaines (prises d'initiatives).

Les apprenantes quittaient ces formations avec un sentiment renforcé de capacité personnelle et collective.

## Conclusion

On constate que dans les approches didactiques de l'apprentissage linguistique aux migrants que nous venons de voir ci-dessus, ce n'est pas la connaissance de la langue qui est l'objectif affiché prioritairement. En effet, ces méthodes partent du principe que l'apprentissage cognitif ne peut se dérouler de façon satisfaisante que si l'apprenant se trouve dans une condition optimale de réception et

---

[4] http://www.thearbour.org.uk/portfolio/lead-to-inspire/.

de production. Les tenants de ces méthodes estiment qu'avant tout enseignement, une première phase est nécessaire durant laquelle sont affirmées la reconnaissance de l'identité et l'affirmation des capacités de l'élève. Ces méthodes s'inspirent en effet de la philosophie constructiviste qui affirme que c'est l'apprenant qui construit lui-même son savoir et qu'il ne peut y parvenir que s'il est en pleine maitrise de ses moyens et en capacité psychologique, intellectuelle et affective de le faire.

Ces méthodes promeuvent en outre l'aspect collectif de l'apprentissage dans un cadre collaboratif, par opposition à la forme individualisée de l'enseignement classique dans un cadre compétitif.

Enfin, au-delà de l'apprentissage linguistique, ces approches poursuivent un but qui va plus loin que le savoir lui-même : le migrant, au-delà de la connaissance de la langue d'accueil, découvre de nouvelles perspectives qui s'ouvrent à lui. Il apprend à renouveler son rapport au monde, à développer son autonomie, et aussi à amorcer son émancipation.

# Références

Alen, Patricia & Altay Manço. 2012. *Appropriation du français par les migrants*. Paris : L'Harmattan, collection « Compétences interculturelles ».

Cooke, Melanie, Becky Winstanley & Dermot Bryers. 2013. *English for Action*. ESOL Nexus, Final Report. British Council.

Cummins, Jim & Margaret Early. 2011. *Identity Texts: The Collaborative Creation of Power in Multilingual Schools*. Stoke-on-Trent : Trentham Books.

Gout, Michel. 2015. *Le rapport entre langue et intégration dans les dispositifs linguistiques pour migrants nouveaux arrivants en Allemagne, Belgique, France et Royaume Uni*. Aix-en-Provence : Université d'Aix-Marseille, thèse de doctorat.

Hedges, Chris. 2013. Conférence lors du séminaire « Reviewing reception measures for the integration of legal immigrants in the European Union ». Paris, 18 – 19 avril 2013.

Schumann, John H. 1994. *The Study of Second Language Acquisition*. Oxford : Oxford University Press.

Stevick, Earl W. 1980. *Teaching Languages: A Way and Ways*. New York : Newbury House Publishers.

Peter Lenz, Malgorzata Barras
# Does teaching chunks and fluency make a difference in migrants' language learning?
Results of an intervention study in intensive German courses for adult migrants

**Abstract:** A quasi-experimental study involving over 150 adult migrants in 12 beginner's German courses explored the consequences of a chunk-based and fluency-oriented teaching approach. The findings suggest that, overall, such an approach can be successfully implemented. An interesting pattern emerges from the language test results (pre- and post-tests): more fluency and less accuracy gains for the experimental classes in oral language use; no differences on the written test sections. The Trade-off Hypothesis and the "ballistic" nature of automatized chunks of language may provide explanations.

**Résumé :** Une étude (quasi)expérimentale portant sur 150 migrants adultes répartis dans 12 cours d'allemand pour débutants a passé au crible les effets d'un enseignement par *chunks* (formules) et axé sur l'aisance à l'oral. Les conclusions laissent penser que, globalement, ce type d'approche peut être mis en œuvre avec succès. Les résultats des tests de langue (pré-tests et post-tests) ont permis de faire émerger un modèle intéressant : une plus grande aisance et une précision moindre à l'oral dans les classes expérimentales ; aucune différence à l'écrit. La *Trade-off Hypothesis*, ainsi que la nature « balistique » des *chunks* automatisés sont proposés pour expliquer les résultats obtenus.

## 1 The study

In the Swiss context, newly arrived adult migrants often start learning the local language (e.g. German) in so-called low-threshold language courses. Often, a considerable proportion of the course participants have limited experience with school-based learning, particularly foreign-language learning. As a consequence, teachers of such courses frequently experience problems that arise when activities from the textbooks explicitly focus on language structures and

---

**Peter Lenz** and **Malgorzata Barras**, Research Centre on Multilingualism, Fribourg, Switzerland, E-mail: Peter.Lenz@unifr.ch, Malgorzata.Barras@unifr.ch

DOI 10.1515/9783110477498-026, © 2017 Peter Lenz, Malgorzata Barras, published by De Gruyter.
This work is licensed under the Creative Commons Attribution-NonCommercial-NoDerivs 3.0 License.

forms (e.g. use of grammar rules). However, widely available and accepted methodological alternatives seem to be rare.

The objectives of the present study were (1) to develop and implement a teaching concept, including a corresponding set of materials, that offers a methodological alternative for low-threshold German courses; (2) to explore the acceptance as well as perceived advantages and disadvantages of the concept; and (3) to compare classes using the alternative concept with classes using the more conventional approach taken by the official textbooks with regard to a number of language learning outcomes.

The alternative teaching concept chosen (i.e. our *intervention concept*) builds heavily on the Lexical Approach (Lewis 1993; Lewis 1997). The Lexical Approach favors language learning through *chunks,* i.e. multi-word lexico-grammatical units, partially with open slots (e.g. "I'd like ..."). It does not include the type of obviously problematic activities mentioned above. In particular, no explicit grammar instruction is to take place. Moreover, we complemented the set of chunk-oriented activities with regular (daily) fluency practice (Nation and Meara 2002) in order to ensure that the lexico-grammatical elements learned would be accessible to the learners for communicative use. Two frequently used textbooks were adapted to correspond to this approach, and then reprinted and distributed to the experimental classes.

A quasi-experimental design with an intervention and a control group (IG/CG) was implemented in order to enable valid comparisons. A total of six class pairs (twelve classes, subdivided into six pairs of classes, each pair formed in a principled fashion at the same school) worked their way through an entire textbook. One class of each pair followed the intervention concept, the other class served as a control and therefore used the original textbook and followed a concept that largely reflected the intentions of the original authors. The concepts and materials for both groups had an equivalent form and were introduced and accompanied in a comparable fashion.

At the end of the intervention, the teachers of both groups were interviewed to gain insight into the acceptance of the teaching concepts and their suitability for the target group, and to better understand the specific features of the teaching and learning processes in both groups.

In an initial examination (that took place before the second half of each beginners' course started), and a final examination (pre- and post-test), various written and oral language skills and competences were measured.

## 2 Results

The interviews with the teachers suggest that both concepts can be applied to good effect overall. Some learners in the IG with experience in school-based foreign language learning, as well as students specifically interested in improving accuracy, missed grammar instruction and exercises. Most learners in the IG considered fluency training a good learning opportunity, once they were used to it. According to the teachers, the IG concept is more suitable for students who have had less formal schooling, while the CG approach better meets the needs of students with more school experience. Teachers in the IG sometimes missed having a grammatical metalanguage at their disposal to identify and correct errors. Also, they found it unsatisfactory that they could not sufficiently intervene during the daily phases of fluency training due to class size because they feared that the frequent repetition of incorrect language, which they observed, might have undesirable effects.

The results on the item-based written examinations and on the (oral) elicited imitation task (Erlam 2009) were scaled using the Rasch model. This made comparisons between the results on the four test forms possible, which overlapped only partially (two forms adapted to two different textbooks for use on two occasions). The indicators calculated for spoken fluency could be compared directly, as they were based on the same oral production task. For statistical inference, a series of analyses of covariance (ANCOVAs) were conducted.

When evaluating the various test sections, data from slightly different numbers of participants were available. Of the 153 students who entered the second stage of the course, 141 participants could be successfully tested in at least one test section, 129 of these in all test sections.

The results on the skills and competences that were tested generally indicate an improvement between the initial test and the final test, with few exceptions on some fluency measures: the *articulation rate*, i.e. the number of syllables per second in those stretches of spoken production in which the speaker actually produces sounds, remained unchanged for either group. However, with regard to the two fluency indicators that include the sounding parts as well as the silent pauses (*speech rate* and *pruned speech rate*),[1] increase depends on group membership. Progress from time 1 to time 2 is observed for the IG but not for the CG. The corresponding difference in progress between the two groups is significant

---

[1] Speech rate: number of syllables per second of the total speaking time including all pauses; pruned speech rate: basically identical to the speech rate, but syllables in filled pauses, repetitions, and self-corrections are not counted.

at the 95% confidence level. When all three fluency measures are viewed together, it can be concluded that learners in the IG were able to (or simply *did*) produce speech with less planning and self-monitoring leading to pauses than learners in the CG. The results from another oral test section that was based on the elicited imitation technique, show that for the IG, progress in fluency is accompanied by less progress (than the CG) in the accuracy of morphosyntax and lexical form. In terms of function and content, the results on the elicited imitation test reveal no differences between the two groups. The same is true for the areas tested in the written test section: neither the integrative measure taken by means of a C-test nor the morphosyntax items showed differential growth for the two groups during the experimental phase.[2]

# 3 Discussion and conclusions

Based on the teacher statements from the guided interviews, it seems in order to conclude that the first objective of the study, developing and implementing a teaching approach, including materials, that builds on the Lexical Approach and a focus on fluency, was reached. Despite the fact that feedback on the intervention concept was predominantly positive, it met with some criticism from teachers and some of those learners who had different expectations due to previous experience in school-based (language) learning. One specific point in question was grammar teaching. Some IG teachers and learners would advocate at least some explicit dealing with grammar. Learners with a weaker educational background reportedly liked the lack of explicit grammar teaching because this reduced the learning load. What conclusions concerning this matter can be drawn from the test results? The results on the written test section give no reason to think that the intervention concept might hinder the development of learner grammar. But how should the clear group difference regarding grammar (and accuracy more generally) in the oral test section be interpreted?

Skehan's Trade-off Hypothesis (Skehan 2009) can provide a possible explanation. The basic tenet of this hypothesis is the generally recognized condition that our cognitive capacity is restricted; specifically, the capacity of our working memory and our attentional capacity are both limited. As a result, competition arises between complexity, accuracy and fluency (CAF) in spoken language pro-

---

[2] It should be noted that on the entry test that was administered before the second half of the German course, the CG *tended* to attain better results than the IG. The measured distance between the two groups basically remained the same on the final test.

duction. Complexity should not be an issue in our context as the test tasks were guided to a large degree. Neither accuracy nor fluency was explicitly asked for in the elicited imitation and the description (i.e. the spoken production) tasks. Given this leeway, it appears plausible that the learners chose to put emphasis on those aspects of their language production they usually focused on in class. If this is the case, the observed group differences may be attributed to performance rather than competence, at least to some extent.

The "ballistic" nature of automatized language as described by Segalowitz and Hulstijn (2009), could form the basis for an alternative explanation. As mentioned above, several intervention-group teachers observed critically that often faulty language was repeated over and over again in fluency practice activities. Frequent repetition could make chunks of language readily available which are not quite accurate. Under the relative pressure of the elicited imitation task, the learners might simply trigger such elements without monitoring and correcting them due to the "ballistic" nature these elements have taken on through automatization. The storing of deficient chunks of language as relatively stable and easily recalled pieces of procedural knowledge is arguably not desirable.

While the CG had better results with regard to oral grammar and accuracy, the IG was superior when spoken fluency (speech rate) was considered. Fluency is a key area of language competence, especially when it comes to oral language use. Therefore, it needs to be carefully developed, just like other areas of language proficiency. In this respect, the conventional approach could be improved.

Overall, the observations made in this project speak in favor of more balanced learning opportunities in either of the concepts. On the one hand, the findings indicate that the teaching concept in the IG requires at least a stronger emphasis on the accuracy of the chunks that are to be automatized. This does not necessarily have to be in the form of systematic grammar teaching but implies some kind of stronger emphasis on forms – possibly simply greater insistence on the accuracy of the target chunks that are actively learned and also practiced in fluency training. On the other hand, it appears that a conventional concept like the one used for the control group should be complemented by regular fluency training. Furthermore, it seems that both concepts should (re-)consider what (essential) grammatical terminology and linguistic concepts and forms they should introduce using explicit teaching methods. Internal differentiation in the classroom could further help optimize the amount of explicit teaching and focus on form(s) for different types of learners.

# References

Erlam, Rosemary. 2009. The elicited oral imitation test as a measure of implicit knowledge. In Rod Ellis, Shawn Loewen & Catherine Elder (eds.), *Implicit and explicit knowledge in second language learning, testing and teaching*, 65–93. Bristol: Multilingual Matters.
Lewis, Michael. 1993. *The lexical approach: The state of ELT and a way forward.* Hove, UK: Language Teaching Publications.
Lewis, Michael. 1997. *Implementing the lexical approach: Putting theory into practice.* Hove, UK: Language Teaching Publications.
Nation, Paul & Paul Meara. 2002. Vocabulary. In Norbert Schmitt (ed.), *An introduction to applied linguistics*. London: Arnold.
Segalowitz, Norman & Jan Hulstijn. 2009. Automaticity in bilingualism and second language learning. In Judith F. Kroll & Annette M. B. de Groot (eds.), *Handbook of bilingualism: Psycholinguistic approaches*, 371–387. Oxford: Oxford University Press.
Skehan, Peter. 2009. Modelling second language performance: Integrating complexity, accuracy, fluency, and lexis. *Applied Linguistics* 30(4). 510–532.

Christa Nieuwboer, Rogier van't Rood
# Progress in proficiency and participation: an adult learning approach to support social integration of migrants in Western societies

**Abstract:** Educational courses that exist to support migrants in their efforts to participate in a host society should be properly designed with pedagogical expertise. In this paper, we clarify basic principles of adult learning, using the Themis method as an example. Instead of a fixed curriculum which aims to teach dominant and stereotypical cultural habits, a participatory approach fosters the development of new kinds of awareness and new ways of coping with the differences between cultures, and leads to more profound results in terms of self-confidence, participation, empowerment and language proficiency.

**Résumé :** Concevoir les cours destinés aux migrants qui veulent s'intégrer dans le pays d'accueil exige une expertise pédagogique. Dans l'article, nous explicitons les principes de base de l'apprentissage des adultes, en prenant la méthode Themis comme exemple. En lieu et place d'un programme fixe pour l'enseignement des habitudes culturelles dominantes et stéréotypées, l'approche participative encourage le développement de nouvelles formes de sensibilisation et manières de concilier les différences culturelles ; les résultats sont plus significatifs en termes de confiance en soi, de participation, d'autonomie et de compétence langagière.

## 1 Courses for social integration

In accordance with the policy guidelines of the Council of Europe, language education for migrants in Western countries should be guided by an analysis of the needs of the learners, and targets should be functional and facilitative, rather than discriminatory (Beacco, Hedges, and Little 2014). However, the regulations of most European countries force both educators and learners to achieve high

---

**Christa Nieuwboer,** APPARENT R&D, The Netherlands,
E-mail: info@ideal-participation.eu
**Rogier van't Rood,** Utrecht University, Vantrood Educational Services, The Netherlands,
E-mail: R.A.vantRood@uu.nl

standards in both oral and written language proficiency (Pulinx, Van Avermaet, and Extramiana 2014). Recent research into the experiences of migrant students has pointed out that the current system demands high-level skills to be aware of all legal requirements, find a suitable course of good quality, be responsible for the course fees, know how to learn and study, and combine the course with obligations in everyday life (Besselsen and Hart 2015). Moreover, Krumm and Plutzar (2008) have argued that social integration encompasses such a broad range of competencies that it cannot be achieved in a course and in the target language alone. In fact, intercultural competency involves a dynamic and relational process, rather than a transfer between (fictional) stable cultural systems (Martin 2015). Paradoxically, the focus on language education for migrants in European countries may frustrate progress in social integration and fails to decrease tensions between cultural groups. Even more discouraging, the current political climate forces integration by negative sanctions, such as exclusion, fines and, ultimately, eviction. More effective approaches to civic integration involve intercultural communication and a learner-centred methodology.

## 2 Principles of adult learning

Regular civic integration courses are focused on in-classroom teaching in the target language in highly diverse groups of students in terms of gender and ethnicity. They provide a fixed curriculum with an instructive didactic style, taking a teacher-centred approach, using mono-didactic methods and the language of instruction of the host country. Contextualisation of language, using examples which are relevant to the learners, and sometimes combining the course with excursions or work, is seen as a way of enhancing the learning process.

However, such traditional teaching methods do not take into account the specific needs of adult learners, who are in the process of constructing a new life in an unfamiliar society. Basic principles of adult learning include learning about things that matter and learning by exposure to different perspectives. By focusing on what matters to individuals, instead of teaching a predefined and fixed model of culture, learners are encouraged to interact with others to explore their identity and the context of their own cultural group, which already holds different perspectives. Consequently, through encounters with locals and exposure to the habits and language of the receiving country, other perspectives will challenge the learning process even more. One of the results of such a pedagogical method is that learners will not only experience progress in language acquisition, but also in their ability to redefine themselves as individuals, capable of learning and interaction, and confident to take part in society. The students influence the content, speed and chosen activities of the course, while its main goal (namely, integration in a host society) is agreed upon and crucial topics are identified within the group of learners.

## 3 Design principles for migrant learning

Surprisingly, although participatory adult learning methods are well-known in developing countries (Chambers 2002; Freire 1994; Nieuwboer and Rood 2016; Rood 1997), they are lacking in the array of civic education programmes in European countries. Design principles of participatory methods are: 1) mapping relevant topics, 2) role model facilitation, 3) homogeneous groups of learners, 4) a multi-sensory, semi-structured curriculum, and for migrants: 5) a mother-tongue-based dual language approach.

At the start of the course and following each module, participants are invited to map the topics most pressing and stressful to them. For instance, on the topic of parenting, learners express their concerns about raising children in an unfamiliar culture, and tell about the way they guide and correct their children.

1. A similar-background role model facilitator shows feasible alternatives for perception and behaviour and serves as a cultural broker. In the case of parenting, the facilitator may expose the learners to positive parenting skills such as instruction and negotiation and encourage reflection on the consequences of rowing and spanking.
2. Forming a group of learners with similar backgrounds is advantageous, since too much diversity leads to stress and insecurity: women dare to speak about their bodies, health and parenting more freely without men present. Even in homogeneous groups mothers discover that peer learners have different solutions to everyday parenting challenges. They feel safe to experiment and accept change in the safety of the zone of proximal development (Vygotsky 1978).
3. By using many creative and playful didactic tools, the learning process is fun and leads to many experiences of success and encouragement. This is particularly important for first-time adult learners, who often have a history of failure in educational settings, resulting in low self-esteem and anxiety. Play is used as a means to learn the target language, allowing trial and error, very much in the same way as young children learn language.
4. Participants are encouraged to effectively express themselves in their native language (L1). In this way, they are understood by the facilitator and do not depend on interpreters. Their confidence to communicate with others is improved, instead of discouraged. At the same time, they are constantly chal-

lenged to learn the new target language (L2) in a functional way, mainly listening and speaking.

## 4 The IDEAL-programme

This approach has been successful in the Themis-programme (the Netherlands) from 2002 onwards, and the IDEAL-programme, Integrating Disadvantaged Ethnicities through Adult Learning, from 2011 onwards (Nieuwboer and Rood 2016; http://www.ideal-participation.eu).

Groups of migrant mothers choose topics like health, effective communication, parenting and taking part in Western society. These topics are used to design a curriculum with conversations, role play, story-telling and many other activating didactic tools. Out-of-class activities are organised as well, like using public transport, a visit to a library, education at a health centre, or talks with teachers at a school.

The participants reported progress in self-confidence and communications skills. They were able to prevent rows, they found themselves less impulsive in their reactions to others, they could criticize each other without feeling unsafe, and they were more likely to join in personal activities such as celebrations. One participant confessed that she used to punish her children by holding their hand over a lighter flame. She now learned how to use positive parenting skills like instructions, play and compliments, and reported that her behaviour prevented rows and arguments. We also measured progress in participation. After the programme, participants were able to structure their daily activities, become involved in school affairs, visit a doctor without an interpreter, and use public transport, visit public facilities and take up voluntary work. Finally, we assessed the language proficiency levels of the participants. They were reported to easily formulate correct full sentences, whereas others used correct words and created sentences with some minor mistakes. Most learners improved one level in oral communication.

Examples show that a standard language course, in which migrants pay per hour, can cost up to €10,000 with no guarantee of success. Some of the participants in IDEAL had previously followed standard courses for 3–5 years without making significant progress. In groups of 15 students, the cost of a participatory course (300–350 contact hours) is approximately €1500 per student. Evaluations show good results in terms of progress in language proficiency and participation, even for first-time learners.

# 5 Recommendations

Standard courses for civic integration focus on language acquisition only and do not aim at fundamental changes in cultural identity. As a consequence, by learning stereotypical habits and behaviours and language, the tensions between values and different cultural subsystems are not addressed. The result is that cultural groups withdraw into their own subculture, transferring tensions between marginal and dominant cultural systems to the next generation.

However, when these tensions are discussed in a safe and conducive learning environment, respecting the prior knowledge and beliefs of the learner, gradual change becomes feasible and acceptable. A participatory, social constructivist approach encourages participants to share observations, opinions, doubts, dilemmas, choices and solutions among individuals who are learning to live in a country which is not familiar to them, including topics which matter most and have a considerable impact on daily family life and future generations in the context of society. Effective adult learning programmes take these perspectives of learners into account and use them to encourage change. It is useful and feasible to reconsider and redesign a programme for social integration based on these insights. Such an approach is not contradictory to language acquisition and active participation, but instead enhances the learning process, even with first-time learners.

In Western societies, it is standard to invest 16 years of education in children. With the knowledge of adult learning processes, we suggest that, in order to relieve tensions caused by cultural discontinuity and to prevent problems arising from failed integration, participatory education should be provided as basic education for migrants, especially those without formal educational experience.

# References

Beacco, Jean-Claude, Chris Hedges & David Little. 2014. *Linguistic integration of adult migrants: Guide to policy development and implementation.* Strasbourg: Council of Europe. https://rm.coe.int/CoERMPublicCommonSearchServices/DisplayDCTMContent?documentId=09000016802fc1cd (accessed 9 August 2016).
Besselsen, Elles & Betty de Hart. 2015. *Verblijfsrechtelijke consequenties van de Wet inburgering. Een onderzoek naar de ervaringen van migranten in Amsterdam* ('Judicial consequences of Dutch law on migration'). Amsterdam: University of Amsterdam, Amsterdam Centre for European Law and Governance.
Chambers, Robert. 2002. *Participatory workshops. A sourcebook of 21 sets of ideas and activities.* New York: Taylor & Francis.

Freire, Paulo. 1994. *Pedagogy of hope: Reliving pedagogy of the oppressed*. New York: Continuum.

Krumm, Hans-Jürgen & Verena Plutzar. 2008. *Tailoring language provision and requirements to the needs and capacities of adult migrants*. https://rm.coe.int/Co-ERMPublicCommonSearchServices/DisplayDCTMContent?documentId=09000016802fc1c8 (accessed 9 June 2016).

Martin, Judith N. 2015. Revisiting intercultural communication competence: Where to go from here. *International Journal of Intercultural Relations 48*. 6–8.

Nieuwboer, Christa & Rogier A. van't Rood. 2016. Learning language that matters: A pedagogical method to support migrant mothers without formal education experience in their social integration in Western countries. *International Journal of Intercultural Relations 51*. 29–40.

Pulinx, Reinhilde, Piet van Avermaet & Claire Extramiana. 2014. *Linguistic Integration of Adult Migrants: Policy and practice. Final report on the 3rd Council of Europe Survey*. https://rm.coe.int/CoERMPublicCommonSearchServices/DisplayDCTMContent?documentId=09000016802fc1ce (accessed 9 June 2016).

Rood, Rogier A. van't. 1997. *Empowerment through basic education: A foundation for development*. CESO Paperback no. 26. The Hague: CESO/Nuffic.

Vygotsky, Lev S. 1978. *Mind in society: The development of higher psychological processes*. Cambridge, MA: Harvard University Press.

Katherine Swinney
# Networks and super connectors

**Abstract:** This study addresses the linguistic integration of adult migrants by exploring English language provision in a super-diverse community in Sheffield, Northern England. The research was planned and developed in collaboration with English language students in response to cuts to adult community education. The study foregrounds the importance of dynamic local networks, English language classes linked to service provision, and engagement with local campaigns and activities.

**Résumé :** L'étude traite la question de l'intégration linguistique des migrants adultes et examine l'offre de cours d'anglais dans un district très diversifié de Sheffield, dans le Nord de l'Angleterre. Elle a été conçue et développée avec des étudiants en anglais en raison de la baisse des budgets alloués à l'éducation populaire pour adultes. Elle met en avant l'importance des réseaux locaux dynamiques, des cours d'anglais pour l'offre de services et la participation aux campagnes de sensibilisation et activités locales.

## 1 Introduction

In a period of cuts to public services the study focused on community education in Burngreave, a ward in the city of Sheffield. The legacy of radical community development work could be seen in key structures in the area which derived strength from organising and campaigning. Consistent with this ethos, "the community research approach aims to empower community members to shape and have some ownership of the research agenda" (Goodson and Phillimore 2010: 489). The research was conducted in three stages. Firstly 325 questionnaire interviews were conducted in 35 classes, generating baseline data about the student population and the English language classes. Collaborative analysis of the data with groups of students, teachers and providers informed the next stage of the research process. Three interviews were then conducted to explore community networks and the roles of key links or "super connectors" in relation to the networks.

Incumbent on researchers who embrace the concept of super-diversity is the acknowledgment that super-diverse areas face continual change, that each area

**Katherine Swinney,** University of Sheffield, United Kingdom, E-mail: kswinney1@sheffield.ac.uk is different, and a flexible and reflexive approach is integral to community research. "As scholars of humans in society and culture, our research instruments demand perpetual reality checking [...] methods that were adequate yesterday are not guaranteed to be adequate tomorrow" (Blommaert and van de Vijver 2013: 1). In practice this research in Burngreave was possible because of a flexible understanding and use of language as students, tutors and supporters engaged with each other and the process. Jufferman's (2015) use of the terms "Englishing" and "languaging" illuminated the processes which enabled communication in Burngreave; a flexible focus on meaning enabled people to "English" as a communicative tool. This article focuses on findings about community networks, exploring the importance of local concerns and community knowledge to develop and sustain appropriate connectors in local education and campaign networks.

## 2 What is a network?

"The network approach reduces complex systems to a bare architecture of nodes and links" (Caldarelli and Catanzaro 2012: 17). Network diagrams are visual tools and in a super-diverse community they support understanding. The network diagram of the tube in London has international resonance and is an example of when a reductive approach to information is useful. Conducting a census questionnaire and analysing the findings involved many people across the area. Information about the research travelled round at surprising speed and overlapping networks became apparent. This phenomenon is known as the "small world property" (Caldarelli and Catanzaro 2012: 49) and "super connectors" in Burngreave were found to link many diverse networks together.

How do networks relate to integration? "It is important to realize that it is the researcher – by choosing a set of nodes and a type of tie – that defines a network" (Borgatti and Halgin 2011: 3). I began to experiment with network diagrams of classes from information gained from visiting the community venues.

In Figure 1 the diagram on the left shows a tutor-centred class where the tutor controls the interactions, mediating student inputs. By contrast, the diagram on the right, a networked community class in Burngreave, shows students linked to other students and regular visitors to the classroom. Workers and volunteers, career officers, health and advice workers, and students were given space and time to network, to make links which had relevance outside. Students were involved in writing for the community newspaper in campaigns to prevent cuts to provision, then later in campaigns for the local adventure playground and the library. Three of the super connectors identified were women: Aram,

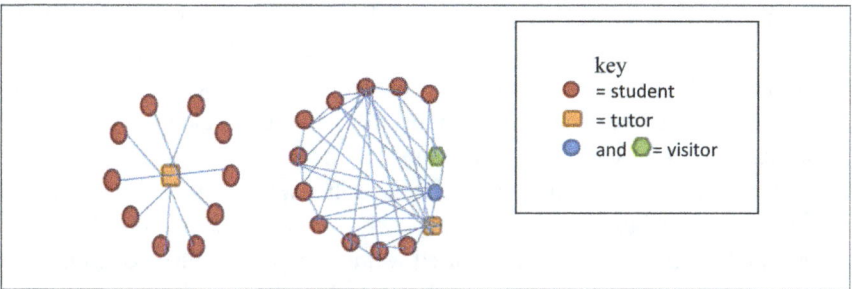

**Figure 1:** Network diagrams of English language classes

Isla and Aisha and the information which follows comes from three semi-structured interviews with them conducted in the summer of 2014.

The first super connector discussed was the Adult Learning Working Group (ALWG) and the following excerpts were from an interview with Isla, the editor of the community newspaper and chair of the working group. "The ALWG brings the different networks together. The extended schools network with the adult learning network and the community newspaper." It planned and co-ordinated provision, reviewed classes, supported recruitment, circulated information, organised the Adult Learning Guide, and fed into the citywide ESOL (English for Speakers of Other Languages) directory. "The meeting [...] has been continuous over 15 years. What gave it continuity and constancy is that the money was always there and the council development worker had the collaborative approach [...]. It was a very democratic, collaborative sharing of resources and the meeting had a very practical purpose."

The second super connector, the community newspaper, had explicit aims to be a tool for cohesion: to increase awareness of services and opportunities available to residents, increase their involvement in local groups and community activities, and build confidence and pride in the Burngreave community; to increase the capacity of Burngreave residents to identify and address problems in their community; and to increase understanding between different sections of the community. The newspaper was delivered free to every household in the Burngreave ward.

The third super connector was the Adult Learning Guide, which was published in print once a year and every term on-line. It publicised courses and classes. Isla explained: "The Adult Learning Guide is an incentive to keep in touch and submit details to both the printed version and the on-line version as it recruits students and everyone is aware of the scope of the provision."

The next three super connectors were the three women mentioned above, who lived and worked in Burngreave. Their networks were both formal and informal (Gilchrist 2009). They had paid roles which served the local community and in addition were active community members. Aram as coordinator of the extended schools provision said, "My job is to oil the wheels: for example there are lots of agencies that want to work in Burngreave. If I weren't there they wouldn't know who to talk to. They wouldn't get started until six months down the line." In addition she led and supported women to become involved in the life of the community through ESOL and family learning courses: "I'm a local mum. I live in the area. The children go to the local school. On every count I can speak with passion. I can encourage action without it being negatively construed."

Isla was editor of the community newspaper and chairperson of the Adult Learning Working Group; in a personal capacity she was a member of the local history group and a member of her Tenants and Residents Association. She worked to involve the schools and the community learning classes in the newspaper and to publicise local campaigns and interests: "What started it was the ESOL. Ever since the ESOL campaign, people are not afraid to campaign on issues they care about. A woman asked me 'Is it really OK to complain to a councillor?' I said, 'You don't need to worry, that is what they are there for. They are there to hear your complaints'."

In her interview Isla was critical of the city council and Aisha, the director of a community organisation, discussed the detrimental effect campaigning can have on relationships with potential supporters and funders. City councils have multiple roles: as funders, service providers, contract managers. Elected members are also representatives of individuals and areas and sometimes these roles can conflict. Aisha's role was to connect with wider city networks, legal networks and regional and national initiatives. At an individual and group level campaigning can have a positive impact on students' skills, but community organisations that scrutinize council policy and campaign can lose supportive mechanisms. Aisha said: "You get political strength from politicians but we challenge politicians. When we took the City Council to court for a judicial review, I lost supportive mechanisms from councillors. It is important to have councillors' support." Community organisations in the area had to compete at national level for funding because of a lack of access to local funding. The research enabled a process of analysis about the dynamics within and around the community and has contributed to change.

Van der Aa and Blommaert (2015: 13) discuss the value of long-term field work in areas of super-diversity. They argue for an understanding of what Bourdieu describes as a *sens pratique*, in other words, the experience or good practice of social workers. They explain that this can become "expertise" shaped by researchers' observations and understandings: "The ethnographic presence turned people's ideas, routines and beliefs into an epistemic tool that generates 'theory'. Knowledge was shaped by finding and co-constructing a logic for knowledge that was already there." In Burngreave, the process of the research had a similar effect for the people involved and enabled us to "formulate counter hegemonic knowledge" as Van der Aa and Blommaert (2015: 12) describe.

After the first dialogue, students initiated dialogue with another group of students. Network concepts enabled community members to analyse and identify their roles in relation to each other. Isla once said, "I'm not a hub but I know who the hubs are", and another community worker at a celebration event looked over and said, "The super connectors", and took their photo. These are small but clear examples of how research changed the way that people thought and spoke. Van der Aa and Blommaert (2015: 13) also discuss a false distinction between researcher and researched: "Creation of knowledge always takes place through a communicative process [...] we need to work in our respective fields with both immediate and long-term feedback." Immediately the research process began, I was concerned to share, verify and validate findings. Some had immediate impact for the provision, but I was also aware of an academic pressure to "get it right" and be polished in my ideas and words before I could speak. I was not constrained by the people in the community, and our dialogue has remained dynamic throughout the time of the research. The "process of co-constructing a logic for knowledge that was already there" (Van der Aa and Blommaert 2015: 12) is continuous for us. Network theory can be used to describe how integrative processes develop in areas of superdiversity, and there is also the possibility that by engaging in network dialogues within communities it can contribute to processes of integration.

# References

Blommaert, Jan & Fons van de Vijver. 2013. Combining surveys and ethnographies in the study of rapid social change. *Tilburg Papers in Cultural Studies* 108. Tilburg: Tilburg University.
Borgatti, Steve & Daniel Halgin. 2011. On Network Theory. *Organization Science* 22(5). 1168–1181.
Calderelli, Guido & Michelle Catanzaro. 2012. *Networks: A very short introduction*. Oxford: Oxford University Press.
Gilchrist, Alison. 2009. *The well-connected community: A networking approach to community development*, 2nd edn. Bristol: Policy Press.

Goodson, Lisa & Jenny Phillimore. 2010. A community research methodology: Working with new migrants to develop a policy related evidence base. *Social Policy and Society* 9(4). 489–501.

Jufferman, Klaus. 2014. Englishing, imaging and local languaging in the Gambian landscape. In Klaus Juffermans, Yonas Asfoha & Ashraf Abdelhay (eds.), *African literacies: Ideologies, scripts, education*. Newcastle upon Tyne: Cambridge Scholars Publishing.

Van der Aa, Jeff & Jan Blommaert. 2015. Ethnographic monitoring and the study of complexity. *Tilburg Papers in Cultural Studies* 123. Tilburg: Tilburg University.

Sabrina Machetti, Lorenzo Rocca
# Integration of migrants, from language proficiency to knowledge of society: the Italian case

**Abstract:** This paper presents the first results of a research project realized by the Universities for Foreigners of Perugia and Siena that created materials designed to promote social awareness. The materials consist of 24 video clips of approximately one hour in total, which are available to download free of charge onto tablet, smartphone or PC, and are accompanied by texts in five languages.

**Résumé :** Cette contribution présente les premiers résultats d'un projet de recherche mené par les universités pour étrangers de Pérouse et de Sienne en vue d'élaborer des aides multimédias pour expliquer et comprendre la société italienne. Les aides consistent en 24 vidéos de 60 minutes environ sur la connaissance de la société qui peuvent être téléchargées gratuitement sur tablette, smartphone, PC ; chacune est accompagnée d'un texte en cinq langues.

## 1 Introduction

This paper presents the results of a research project carried out in Italy in 2015 and 2016 by a group of researchers of the University for Foreigners of Perugia and the University for Foreigners of Siena, with funding from the Italian Ministry of Home Affairs. The main objective of the project was the design and production of didactic and training materials on Knowledge of Society (KoS), addressed to migrants living in Italy and also to teachers and trainers involved in Italian language courses. The paper describes the Italian context within the more complex European situation, then moves to the analysis of the construct and content of the KoS materials and identifies some critical issues related to the fairness and ethics of a KoS test.

---

**Sabrina Machetti** (corresponding author), University for Foreigners of Siena, Italy,
E-mail: machetti@unistrasi.it
**Lorenzo Rocca**, University for Foreigners of Perugia, Italy, E-mail: lorenzo_rocca@libero.it

DOI 10.1515/9783110477498-029, © 2017 Sabrina Machetti, Lorenzo Rocca, published by De Gruyter.
This work is licensed under the Creative Commons Attribution-NonCommercial-NoDerivs 3.0 License.

## 2 The KoS in Europe and in Italy

A recent report of the Council of Europe (Pulinx et al. 2014) on the linguistic integration of adult migrants describes the linguistic and KoS requirements laid down by 36 European countries; 18 of them require KoS both for residence and for citizenship. Building on two previous surveys (2007 and 2009), the report summarizes the European context by analyzing data from a survey carried out in 2013. The Italian data frames a scenario where KoS content is offered by Italian language teachers in non-compulsory language courses and without formal assessment.

The Italian language courses addressed to migrants and the KoS tests afterwards were officially introduced in Italy in 2012, when the Integration Agreement came into force. Their origin is linked to that of the language requirements for long-term residence permits in particular to the law of 4 June 2010, which defines the procedures of the Italian language test: "for the issuance of a permit for EU long-term residents, the foreigner must possess a level of knowledge of the Italian language that allows him/her to understand sentences and frequently used expressions in current areas, at Level A2 of the Common European Framework of Reference" (Masillo 2016: 210). The Integration Agreement is also linked to the agreement signed in November 2010 between the Italian Ministry for Home Affairs and the Ministry of Education, University and Research: "the latter developed official guidelines for test design and the assessment of performances of migrants. As explained in these guidelines, which contain basic test specifications and the required competence level (i.e. CEFR Level A2), the test must consist of three sections: Listening, Reading and Written Interaction. The Ministry of Education provided only these test specifications and guidelines which each educational center, located all across Italy, was to use to design their own tests and administer it" (ibid.).

Since March 2012, in order to fulfill the standards laid down by the Integration Agreement, KoS has been linked to knowledge of Italian at A2 level. According to the new guidelines, migrants who lack documentation confirming that they meet the requirements of the Integration Agreement must take a test to assess their proficiency in the Italian language and KoS. Considering the characteristics of migrants and their level of proficiency in Italian (usually very basic), the guidelines specify that the test must be oral, which recognizes the dominant role of the spoken language. As in the case of the Italian A2 level test, the guidelines also specify that the test should be designed by the teachers involved in adult education centers and administered by adopting specific strategies.

The content of the test refers to the following topics:

SECTION A: BASIC PRINCIPLES OF THE ITALIAN CONSTITUTION AND THE ORGANIZATION AND MODE OF OPERATION OF PUBLIC INSTITUTIONS IN ITALY
Basic principles of the Constitution:
- The form of government in Italy: the Republic
- Guarantee of fundamental human rights and duties of solidarity
- Equal social dignity and equality before the law
- Right to work
- Freedom of religion
- Legal status of foreigners
- The Italian flag

Organization and mode of operation of public institutions in Italy:
- Authority and power of the state government
- Regions, provinces and municipalities: local government

SECTION B: LIVING IN ITALY, WITH SPECIAL REFERENCE TO THE FIELDS OF HEALTH, SCHOOL, SOCIAL SERVICES, LABOUR AND TAX OBLIGATIONS
- Health: the right to health
- School
- Social services: the integrated system of interventions and social services
- Work: the right to work and labor rights
- Tax liabilities

SECTION C
- Rights and duties of foreigners living in Italy
- Rights and obligations attached to living in Italy
- The reciprocal rights and duties of married people
- Duties of parents towards their children according to the Italian legal system, also with reference to schooling
- Principal local projects that support the integration of foreigners and relevant regulations concerning health and safety at work

As we said, the test is a spoken test. It is conducted one-to-one: each candidate interacts with a test administrator and a second test administrator plays the role of observer (usually the test administrators are Italian language teachers). The test lasts for a minimum of seven and a maximum of 10 minutes, including the attribution of a level of proficiency. It consists of:

1. a brief presentation of the candidate, conducted by the test administrator;
2. on the basis of three different inputs (one for each of the three sections listed above), a spoken interaction between the candidate and the test administrator.

The brief presentation is conducted using a series of open-ended questions in order to introduce the candidate. All the inputs of the spoken tests refer to the personal experience of the candidate, without generalizations or cultural, conceptual or speculative abstractions. In any case, the linguistic formulation of the inputs should be related to the A2 level of proficiency in Italian. The test must be an interview and not an interrogation, and the test administrator can use a variety of different inputs, such as pictures or objects, aimed at facilitating the oral interaction. The test administrator should establish a relaxed mood, maintain a highly cooperative attitude, and speak clearly and with an accent not far removed from standard Italian.

The test results may be:

1. High: The test is carried out in an appropriate way; the candidate interacts with fluency and rarely requires the test administrator to repeat; he/she gives appropriate answers even if in a short form and with some hesitation; he/she uses a basic lexical repertoire and simple structures, even if his/her speaking includes some lexical and morphosyntactic errors and intonation and pronunciation are in some cases influenced by his/her L1.
2. Good: The test is carried out in an appropriate way; the candidate interacts but sometimes requires help from the test administrator; he/she gives appropriate answers even if in a short form and with some hesitation; he/she uses a basic lexical repertoire and simple structures, even if his/her speaking presents some lexical and morphosyntactic errors and intonation and pronunciation are influenced by his/her L1.
3. Sufficient: The test is carried out in a way that is not quite appropriate; the candidate interacts with some difficulty but is nevertheless able to orient him/herself to the issues addressed; he/she often requires the examiner to repeat; he/she does not always give appropriate answers; he/she uses a basic lexical repertoire and simple structures, though his/her speaking presents some lexical and morphosyntactic errors and intonation and pronunciation are strongly influenced by his/her L1.

Achieving at least a *Sufficient* level in KoS also entails the achievement of A2 level in spoken Italian.

## 3 The Italian project

The introduction of a KoS test in Italy had to deal with the lack of materials that migrants could use to learn the KoS content. As we suggested above, before the Agreement KoS was scheduled only as content to be included as part of the Italian language courses provided by adult education centers and in some cases proposed as the content of specific courses delivered in the L1 of the migrants. Before 2012, the KoS test was not compulsory, and in any case it was a written test, and in some cases computer-based. In these circumstances, there was a total lack of materials for autonomous study/training.

The project carried out in 2015 and 2016 was started precisely to satisfy the needs of migrants whether or not they are attending a KoS course and/or an Italian language course (Machetti and Rocca 2015). The aim was to design didactic materials in KoS that would be linguistically appropriate and easily accessible. There are two kinds of material:
- a guide to the KoS test, addressed to migrants;
- a series of video-materials (accompanied by a text in five languages – English, French, Spanish, Arabic and Chinese) that illustrate the KoS contents.

The guide is intended to present, in a clear and concise manner, the Agreement's aims and illustrate the characteristics of the test (content, duration, assessment criteria etc.). The 24 video-materials (one hour in total) are designed on the basis of the KoS contents; their purpose is to support migrants and their teachers as they prepare for the KoS test.

## 4 Critical issues

Finally, we want to offer some reflections concerning the issues of fairness and ethics with regard to the KoS test, taking into account the Italian context and the impact of the test in that context (Shohamy 2007). The total lack of a culture of evaluation and assessment in Italy is an incontrovertible fact, and very influential considering the impact that the KoS test could have in this country.

One of the main problems is that the KoS test is exclusively instrumental; it exists in order to fulfill an obligation and lacks any other function. Another critical point concerns the choice of level A2 for the language test required for long-term residence and the construct of the KoS test: is this choice ethical? Does it run the risk, already evident in language testing, of marginalizing migrants by demanding a language proficiency level well below the threshold of full communicative autonomy? And finally: is a test aimed at assessing both proficiency in Italian and KoS valid and reliable?

Looking at the issue of impact, the question that remains open is whether the introduction of the KoS test will have a positive impact in the educational context. In fact, we wonder whether migrants who access the test will also be more strongly motivated to attend a language course. We cannot forget that in Italy a large number of migrants are socially and linguistically very disadvantaged: the opportunity to access a language course in Italian could represent a valuable opportunity for them.

# References

Machetti, Sabrina & Lorenzo Rocca. 2015. Conoscenza della cultura civica e della vita civile: sussidi per il cittadino migrante. Paper presented at the conference *Integrazione linguistica: fra didattica dell'italiano L2 e certificazione delle competenze*, Rome, 29 May.

Masillo, Paola. 2016. Language assessment for migration and social integration: A case study. In C. Docherty & F. Barker (eds), *Language Assessment for Multilingualism. Proceedings of the ALTE Paris Conference, April 2014* (Studies in Language Testing 44), 209–228. Cambridge: Cambridge University Press.

Pulinx, Reinhilde, Piet van Avermaet & Claire Extramiana. 2014. *Linguistic integration of adult migrants: Policy and practice. Final report on the 3rd Council of Europe Survey*. Https://rm.coe.int/CoERMPublicCommonSearchServices/DisplayDCTMContent?documentId=09000016802fc1ce (accessed 10 February 2016).

Shohamy, Elana. 2007. Language tests as language policy tools. *Assessment in Education* 14 (1). 117–130.

Agnes Kukulska-Hulme, Mark Gaved, Ann Jones, Lucy Norris and Alice Peasgood
# Mobile language learning experiences for migrants beyond the classroom

**Abstract:** This paper summarises key findings from three recent research projects investigating how mobile technologies can support migrants in achieving greater language immersion through situated, informal and incidental language learning beyond the classroom. The research highlights the affordances and constraints of the city space as an emerging environment for semi-structured informal learning. Pedagogical models arising from this research emphasize the potential for learners' agency and engagement through self-directed, social and playful learning. Implications for policy and practice are discussed.

**Résumé :** L'article résume les principales conclusions de trois projets de recherche récents portant sur les technologies mobiles et la manière dont elles peuvent favoriser l'immersion des migrants dans la langue grâce à un apprentissage en situation, informel et fortuit – en dehors de la salle de classe. L'étude met en avant les *affordances* (potentialités) et les contraintes de l'espace urbain comme nouvel environnement favorisant un apprentissage informel semi-structuré. Les modèles pédagogiques proposés par l'étude soulignent le potentiel d'organisation et de participation des apprenants par le biais d'un apprentissage autodidacte, social et ludique. Les implications politiques et pratiques sont également examinées.

## 1 Introduction

Language learning can take place in a wide variety of settings, from formal language classes conducted by a teacher, to semi-formal language clubs and self-study materials, through to informal learning in everyday life and work. The advent of online learning has blurred the boundaries between these settings, and mobile learning has further modified the learning landscape through increased flexibility of access and new learning experience designs (Traxler and Kukulska-Hulme 2016). The designs are based around mobility and focus on learners inter-

---

**Agnes Kukulska-Hulme** (corresponding author), **Mark Gaved, Ann Jones, Lucy Norris** and **Alice Peasgood**, The Open University, United Kingdom,
E-mail: Agnes.Kukulska-Hulme@open.ac.uk

DOI 10.1515/9783110477498-030, © 2017 Agnes Kukulska-Hulme, Mark Gaved, Ann Jones, Lucy Norris and Alice Peasgood, published by De Gruyter.
This work is licensed under the Creative Commons Attribution-NonCommercial-NoDerivs 3.0 License.

acting with their physical and social environment, for example by getting involved in conversations in the target language or in media creation and data capture. Sensors on mobile phones and in the environment can also trigger learning content based on a person's location, perhaps combined with their interests or needs. This new learning landscape can be highly advantageous to migrants, enabling them to develop language competencies aligned to everyday tasks and encounters in life and work.

Mobile phones are in widespread use among migrants (Chib, Wilkin, and Hua 2013; Leite et al. 2014) and create opportunities for those who are not able or willing to attend classroom-based language courses. We report key findings from projects in which we have designed and evaluated mobile-supported language learning in city environments, incorporating mobile applications designed to support engagement with local information, services and people.

## 2 Researching migrant language learning beyond the classroom

There is growing research evidence that language learning beyond the classroom can promote greater language immersion through situated, informal and incidental learning (Chen and Li 2010; Lai and Gu 2011; Shao and Crook 2015). Research on language learning beyond the classroom also examines the affordances and constraints of the city space as an emerging environment for learning, where mobile technologies and applications, together with online social networking, can provide some structure and support for learners. Affordances of a town or city include the availability of a rich linguistic landscape in the form of public and commercial signs, advertisements and notices (Rowland 2013), and the chance to observe and record how language is used *in situ*. Constraints include distracting and noisy environments, intermittent internet connectivity, and ambiguities around the new social etiquette of mobile device use and media sharing.

## 3 MASELTOV, SALSA and Mobile Pedagogy projects

In the EU-FP7 MASELTOV project (Mobile Assistance for Social Inclusion and Empowerment of Immigrants with Persuasive Learning Technologies and Social Network Services; 2012–15), a prototype context-aware smartphone app was developed comprising an integrated suite of navigation, information, social interaction, language learning and game playing services for non-European immigrants, and it was trialled in four major cities across Europe (Gaved et al. 2012; Kukulska-Hulme, Norris and Donohue 2015). In the process of trying to understand how the app would be used in both planned and spontaneous ways in the city, we developed an Incidental Learning Framework as a way to map everyday tasks to dimensions of time, place, tools, social support and outcomes of the immigrant's learning journey. In the SALSA project (Sensors and Apps for Languages in Smart Areas; 2014–15) we delivered location-triggered mobile language lessons across the town of Milton Keynes, UK, as part of the local smart city initiative. Bluetooth beacons were deployed on streets, buildings and buses, constituting a treasure hunt or trail, and these beacons triggered lessons on learners' smartphones (Gaved, Greenwood and Peasgood 2015). In the Mobile Pedagogy for English Language Teaching project (2013–14), we interviewed language learners and teachers in Brighton, UK, to discover their informal language learning practices with their phones and tablets. This led to the development of a Mobile Pedagogy framework and a guide for teachers wishing to design mobile language learning experiences beyond the classroom (Kukulska-Hulme, Norris and Donohue 2015).

What these three projects had in common was a focus on learner empowerment and how that may lead to the development of more self-directed learning. Migrants were always involved in discussions about their real needs and requirements. Top level findings from the projects may be summarized as follows:

- Mobile learning creates opportunities to complement and enhance classroom-based learning (extending highly limited access to formal adult education language learning).
- Language teachers see increased informal use of mobile devices by their learners, and are keen to leverage this enthusiasm to extend learning beyond class time.
- Language teacher training is currently lacking with regard to mobile technologies for language learning both in and beyond class. There is a need for mobile policy setting and guidance for learners, teachers, and facilitators in community settings and institutions.
- Migrants are a highly diverse audience and bring a wide range of prior educational, cultural and technological experiences that should be considered when developing a learning intervention.
- Learning becomes locally and personally relevant, and content therefore needs to be reconsidered. Learning can be based around interests, contexts and locations; it can include language for reacting to unexpected events, being a helpful citizen and accessing essential services.

- Mobile learning encourages migrants to think about different strategies and approaches to learning. Shared usage of tools was observed highlighting social learning among friends and family. Effective application designs can also motivate and trigger learning.
- For many recent migrants, financial constraints and lack of familiarity with digital literacies may influence engagement with mobile technologies. It is necessary to consider developing for budget-range devices and interactivity that does not require frequent or large (i.e. expensive) data downloads.
- For many migrants, finding the time for learning is an issue. Even if not in employment, many have family or other responsibilities. Hence they need to fit learning into their daily routine (e.g. on the bus). Learning may occur in short episodes (15 minutes), even if the goal is longer (listening to an audio-book).
- Tracking of mobile learner movements around the city (e.g. to deliver useful language content specific to locations, or to give recommendations based on interests inferred from movements) raises ethical, trust and privacy issues.

## 4 Pedagogical models

Pedagogical models arising from this research foreground learners' agency, blending of formal and informal learning, the value of social interaction, and playful learning that may alleviate anxiety or build confidence. Three relevant pedagogical models may be identified on the basis of our research:

*Self-directed learning:* Learners are in a position to formulate their personal learning goals more freely than would typically be the case in a classroom setting. They may need considerable support with doing this if they have been used to exclusively teacher-led education.

*Social learning:* This focuses on bringing migrants and others together to facilitate sharing of experiences, questions, resources, language practice, peer support and mentoring.

*Gamified learning:* The SALSA project beacons illustrate a playful treasure hunt learning model, encouraging learners to explore and interrogate the city. The MASELTOV project's cultural mobile game was very popular with some users.

## 5 Implications for policy and practice

1. Be aware of the diversity of audience: there is not one "migrant profile" and engagement should be based upon an understanding of the expertise and

prior experiences of your target audience. Consider the need to support diverse languages; the diversity of migrant languages in current translanguaging initiatives might mean the ability to input other scripts (e.g. Arabic).
2. Recent migrants may be economically constrained and so applications should be developed that run on budget as well as high-end devices; applications also accessible on PCs and laptops would be welcomed. Interactivity should not depend on regular downloads from high-speed internet connections: data downloads can be expensive and will act as a barrier to uptake. Consider applications that run without network connections or can work with sporadic, occasional connectivity (e.g. connection made when there is free Wi-Fi).
3. Cultural sensitivities may affect how learners engage with resources: they may not be comfortable using phones in public places, visiting some places across the city, or contacting unknown local volunteers. In some places mobile use may be prohibited.
4. Be transparent in explaining what data is collected, and how it will be used. Learners may be cautious about sharing data but will be more likely to participate if the "contract" is made clear.

# 6 Conclusion

Migration can no longer be viewed as a linear move from home country to host country, without further links to the former, and it is partly due to portable digital technologies that migrant networks have become "more mobile and less anchored to the host country, rendering integration a flexible and dynamic activity" (Spotti and Kurvers 2015:197). Self-directed, yet supported language learning can enable the positive psychological benefits of social interaction within a mobile community (Shao and Crook 2015:416), reported by participants in the projects described in section 3.

# References

Chib, Arul, Holley A. Wilkin & Sri Ranjini Mei Hua. 2013. Migrant workers' use of mobile phones to seek social support in Singapore. *Information Technologies & International Development* 9(4). 19–34.
Chen, Chih-Ming & Yi-Lun Li. 2010. Personalised context-aware ubiquitous learning system for supporting effective English vocabulary learning. *Interactive Learning Environments* 18(4). 341–364.

Gaved, Mark, Ann Jones, Agnes Kukulska-Hulme & Eileen Scanlon. 2012. A citizen-centred approach to education in the smart city: Incidental language learning for supporting the inclusion of recent migrants. *International Journal of Digital Literacy and Digital Competence* 3(4). 50–64. http://oro.open.ac.uk/36648/ (accessed 20 June 2016).

Gaved, Mark, Richard Greenwood & Alice Peasgood. 2015. Using and appropriating the smart city for community and capacity building amongst migrant language learners. In Gabriela Avram, Fiorella De Cindio & Volkmar Pipek (eds.), *Proceedings of the 7th International Conference on Communities and Technologies*, 63–72. http://oro.open.ac.uk/43783/ (accessed 20 June 2016).

Kukulska-Hulme, Agnes, Mark Gaved, Lucas Paletta, Eileen Scanlon, Ann Jones & Andrew Brasher. 2015. Mobile incidental learning to support the inclusion of recent immigrants. *Ubiquitous Learning* 7(2). 9–21.

Kukulska-Hulme, Agnes, Lucy Norris & Jim Donohue. 2015. *Mobile pedagogy for English language teaching: A guide for teachers*. London: British Council.

Lai, Chu & Mingyue Gu. 2011. Self-regulated out-of-class language learning with technology. *Computer Assisted Language Learning* 24(4). 317–335.

Leite, Lorena, Megan Buresh, Naomi Rios, Anna Conley, Tamara Flys & Kathleen R. Page. 2014. Cell phone utilization among foreign-born Latinos: A promising tool for dissemination of health and HIV information. *Journal of Immigrant and Minority Health* 16(4). 661–669.

Rowland, Luke. 2013. The pedagogical benefits of a linguistic landscape project in Japan. *International Journal of Bilingual Education and Bilingualism* 16(4). 494–505.

Shao, Yinjuan & Charles Crook. 2015. The potential of a mobile group blog to support cultural learning among overseas students. *Journal of Studies in International Education* 19(5). 399–422.

Spotti, Massimiliano & Jeanne Kurvers. 2015. ICT based applications for civic integration in The Netherlands. In James Simpson and Anne Whiteside (eds.), *Adult language education and migration: Challenging agendas in policy and practice*, 187–199. Abingdon: Routledge.

Traxler, John & Agnes Kukulska-Hulme (eds.). 2016. *Mobile learning: The next generation*. London: Routledge.

Mariet Schiepers, Annelies Houben, Annelies Nordin,
Helga Van Loo, Helena Van Nuffel, Leen Verrote
and Kris Van den Branden

# Creating a dynamic and learner-driven online environment for practising second language skills: guiding principles from second language acquisition and online education

**Abstract:** Scientific research clearly states that people only learn a language after long and repeated practice in a variety of contexts. In reality, however, adult migrants trying to master the language of their new country often lack opportunities to practise their language skills outside the classroom. In this paper we will discuss six guiding principles for creating a dynamic, learner-driven online environment in which adult learners can autonomously practise the performance of tasks that meet their specific language learning needs.

**Résumé :** Les études montrent clairement que l'appropriation d'une langue se fait par une pratique longue et répétée dans des contextes variés. Or, concrètement, les migrants adultes qui s'efforcent de maîtriser la langue de leur nouveau pays ont rarement l'occasion d'exercer leurs compétences langagières en dehors de la salle de cours. Dans cet article, nous examinons six principes directeurs pour créer un environnement en ligne dynamique, axé sur les apprenants, qui permet aux adultes de s'entraîner en autonomie à la réalisation de tâches qui répondent à leurs besoins spécifiques d'apprentissage.

---

**Mariet Schiepers*** (corresponding author), **Annelies Houben***, **Annelies Nordin****, **Helga Van Loo****, **Helena Van Nuffel***, **Leen Verrote**** and **Kris Van den Branden***
*Centre for Language and Education, KU Leuven/University of Leuven, Belgium
**Leuven Language Institute, KU Leuven/University of Leuven, Belgium
E-mail: Mariet.schiepers@kuleuven.be, Annelies.houben@kuleuven.be, Annelies.nordin@ilt.kuleuven.be, Helga.vanloo@ilt.kuleuven.be, Helena.vannuffel@kuleuven.be, Leen.verrote@ilt.kuleuven.be, Kris.vandenbranden@kuleuven.be

## 1 Introduction

Empirical research on second language acquisition (SLA) (Doughty and Long 2003; Ellis and Shintani 2014) provides clear indications that adult second language learners need extensive and repeated practice in a variety of contexts to develop second language skills. In addition, learning opportunities need to be challenging and connected with what learners want and need to be able to do with language in real life. Furthermore, adults need access to rich and extensive input in the target language and need to be provided with opportunities to produce output themselves. Finally, feedback is of paramount importance in the learning process.

These conditions should be integrated as much as possible in classroom-based instruction and in technology-mediated environments. Moreover, empirical research on the impact of online education and technology-mediated language education (Nielsen and Gonzáles-Lloret 2010) has revealed that a sense of community is essential for participants in online environments. Also, the technological application needs to be easy to access and use.

This paper will describe how the above-mentioned principles were integrated in a dynamic, learner-driven online environment in which adult learners can practise their second language skills. More specifically, the paper will present the case-study of NedBox (http://www.nedbox.be), a digital platform developed with financial support from the European Integration Fund, which aims to offer adult learners of Dutch as a second language rich online practice opportunities in a fun, non-academic way during their leisure time. As such, it aims to promote the language proficiency adult migrants need to integrate and fully participate in their new society.

## 2 Guidelines for a powerful, task-based online learning environment

Given the specific goal of NedBox, the general requirements of effective online course design and principles of effective instructed SLA were translated into six guidelines underpinning the design of NedBox. A further challenge was to design a user-centred environment that could address the needs and integrate the feedback of the people who were meant to use the platform. Our main aim was to develop a tool that was maximally tailored to the needs and expectations of its potential users (Schiepers et al. 2015). Below, we will present the six guidelines and discuss how they were integrated in the actual design of NedBox.

## 2.1 Provide adult learners with a diversified corpus of appealing and authentic online input

Adults need access to extensive authentic input in the target language, including written and spoken texts produced by native speakers. Given the diversity of the target audience (including both low- and high-educated users), a one-size-fits-all approach was unlikely to work, so the corpus of texts on which NedBox would be built had to be sufficiently diverse. Moreover, since NedBox would typically be used by adults during their leisure time, the input had to captivate learners' interest and motivate them to learn on a voluntary basis.

To meet these conditions, NedBox was built around a diversified corpus of appealing and authentic news items. A pilot run involving a group of future users showed that working with topical, high-quality videos and newspaper articles (provided by the Flemish public broadcasting company and three leading Flemish newspapers) and using them as the starting point for meaningful tasks had great potential to attract a wide group of adult learners. Several strategies were adopted to make sure that the input was selected and offered in such a way that it would be closely related to the needs of adult learners. First of all, a varied mix of news items is selected on a weekly basis: on the one hand topical news items are selected, such as an article about the sales period at the beginning of January. In addition, the website features more timeless subjects and human interest stories, such as a video about people's search for work, including tips for people who are applying for a job. The news items also cover different themes that were derived from research into the specific language learning needs of learners of Dutch as a second language (Van Avermaet and Gysen 2006); these themes include "work", "children", "social contact", "living in Belgium". On the homepage of NedBox (Figure 1), users can choose freely the items and themes they consider most interesting, thus customizing the input maximally to their needs.

## 2.2 Make sure adult learners can perform meaningful tasks, tailored to their needs

Since adult learners are more motivated when they are interested in what they are learning and see a direct relationship between the instruction and their own language learning needs, each news item on NedBox forms the basis of a range of functional, real-life tasks from which the learners can choose according to their needs and level of proficiency. This creates a rich online learning environment in which practice opportunities are not restricted to traditional exer-

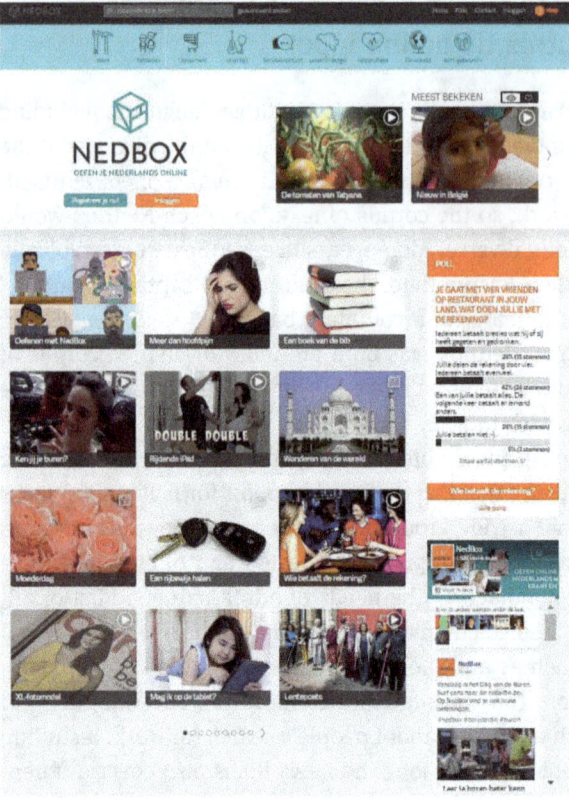

**Figure 1:** Homepage NedBox

cises which focus mainly on formal elements of the language such as grammar and vocabulary.

Figures 2 and 3 illustrate NedBox learning tasks. Figure 2 shows an article about (funny) things people lose on the bus. One of the accompanying real-life tasks consists of filling out the authentic form that passengers complete if they lose personal belongings on public transport. Figure 3 shows a video about a young job seeker, featuring a real-life task that consists of reading and assessing job vacancies. Again, the learner can navigate freely through the different types of exercises, as is further explained in 2.3.

**Figure 2:** Activity page: article

**Figure 3:** Activity page: video

## 2.3 Put the learner in control, not the system

To enhance learner motivation, the website puts the learner in control of items, level of complexity and task selection. The levels of task complexity are indicated with asterisks (Figure 3) which are the equivalent of CEFR levels A1, A2 and B1. The icons below the tasks represent the various skills – listening, reading, writing, speaking – and can also refer to vocabulary and grammar exercises. Learners select the tasks they consider useful and pleasant, thus constructing their own learning path. The learner also controls which supportive tools he wants to use when trying to cope with the tasks. These tools, which can be manipulated according to the learner's needs and level of proficiency, include the use of subtitles while playing the video (Figure 3), looking up word explanations in the articles (Figure 2), and some useful hints users can consult before they start performing the task (Figure 3).

## 2.4 Provide immediate online feedback

Feedback is of paramount importance in the learning process. NedBox provides immediate feedback that targets users' personal errors and contains suggestions for further improvement. For example, learners are automatically redirected to a specific fragment of the video which contains the answer to a comprehension question they failed to answer. Alternatively, the system provides the learner with additional information on why a particular answer was not correct, including hints about how to correct them (Figure 3). Thus the need for a tutor who provides feedback tailored to the learner is, to some extent, replaced by the sophisticated feedback options offered by NedBox.

## 2.5 Create task-based interaction by linking the online tasks to the real world

A sense of community is another imperative for the success and satisfaction of learners making use of online learning environments. Consequently, online second language instruction must include a social space so that learners can interact in the target language both with each other and with native speakers, through tasks that require collaboration.

To ensure that the learners on NedBox can interact with fellow users of the platform and with native speakers, the potential of social media is tapped by means of a lively Facebook community on which, for instance, written products can be posted and results of polls can be consulted. The Facebook community is also used by the designers as a channel to announce new items on the platform. These announcements are accompanied by teasing questions to provoke interaction among the target audience. Furthermore, a connection between the online and offline world is created in the tasks, by providing external links to organizations and activities that could be interesting for the learners. For instance, the above-mentioned video about the job seeker is linked to the site of the public employment service, where real job vacancies can be found. All these possibilities to interact can further be stimulated by teachers of Dutch as a second language who take up a role as ambassador of NedBox. Hints on how NedBox can be promoted in formal and non-formal educational contexts are provided through a specific link on the homepage.

## 2.6 Make sure the online environment is easily accessible

The group of adult learners is highly diverse, consisting of high- and low-educated learners, with high and low digital skills. Research in the field of the digital divide shows that the integration of ICT in learning can constitute an additional barrier for vulnerable groups such as lower-educated migrants (Mariën and van Audenhove 2010). Engaging in e-learning implies a high degree of self-regulation. Several studies indicate that people with limited literacy levels often lack this competence. To cope with this, the designers added additional support tools for low-educated adults with low digital skills (such as the subtitles and word explanations) and emphasize that for these learners the e-learning environment should be considered as complementary to, instead of a substitute for, existing classroom-based courses. For these groups in particular, the interface of NedBox was made as simple as possible, thus constituting an environment which is very easy and straightforward to use.

# 3 Conclusion

NedBox was developed on the basis of empirical research which has shown that any program intended to facilitate online SLA must not only meet the principles of effective online course design but also comply with the principles of effective instructed SLA. The key identifying features of NedBox are its wide range of appealing input that creates "enjoyable" practice opportunities during leisure time, and a user-centred design that is maximally tailored to the needs and expectations of its users. The overall satisfaction of the users during the pilot study and the high (returning) visitor numbers since the launch of the website are very encouraging in this respect. This seems to confirm the hypothesis that what motivates the learner in a face-to-face context is also of paramount importance in a digital environment. Nonetheless, continued user research will be conducted to gather feedback on the platform in use, next to specific user research on the experiences of lower-educated learners which has to unravel if and under which conditions technology-enhanced language learning can be a lever or an extra threshold for this group of learners.

# References

Doughty, Catherine J. & Michael H. Long (eds.). 2003. *The handbook of second language acquisition*. New York: Blackwell.

Ellis, Rod & Natsuko Shintani. 2014. *Exploring language pedagogy through second language acquisition research*. London & New York: Routledge.

Mariën, Ilse & Leo van Audenhove. 2010. E-learning and undereducated learners: Barriers and opportunities. Digitas conference *Digital natives, digital immigrants, digital asylum-seekers: The clash of cultures*, Sibiu, Romania, 22–24 June. https://www.academia.edu/861889/e-Learning_and_undereducated_learners_barriers_and_opportunities (accessed 20 June 2016).

Nielsen, Katharine B. & Marta Gonzáles-Lloret. 2010. Effective online foreign language courses: Theoretical framework and practical applications. *The EUROCALL Review* 17. 155–168.
https://www.academia.edu/9323949/Effective_Online_Foreign_Language_Courses_Theoretical_Framework_and_Practical_Applications.

Schiepers, Mariet, Annelies Houben, Annalies Nordin, Helga Van Loo, Helena Van Nuffel, Leen Verrote & Kris Van den Branden. 2016. How to create online practice opportunities for adult second language learners? NedBox, an online platform for practicing Dutch language skills. *INTED2016 Proceedings*, 2349–2357.
https://library.iated.org/publications/INTED2016 (accessed 11 August 2016).

Van Avermaet, Piet & Sara Gysen. 2006. From needs to tasks: Language learning needs in a task-based approach. In Kris van den Branden (ed.), *Task-based language teaching: From theory to practice*, 17–46. Cambridge: Cambridge University Press.

## 5 Language testing and assessment for integration
Evaluation des compétences en langues pour l'intégration

Jane Lloyd, Michaela Perlmann-Balme
# Language tests for access, integration and citizenship: an outline for policymakers from the ALTE perspective

**Abstract:** This paper is presented on behalf of the Language and Migration Special Interest Group (LAMI SIG) of the Association of Language Testers in Europe (ALTE). Our position paper aims to clarify the role of assessment in the context of migration. It focuses on the ethical use of assessments and test results. We contextualize this position by considering evidence of assessment requirements across Europe, such as language and knowledge-of-society tests, and our concerns over assessment use as a barrier to entry and integration.

**Résumé :** Cet article est présenté pour le compte du *Language and Migration Special Interest Group* (LAMI SIG / Groupe d'intérêt sur Langue et Migration) d'ALTE (*Association of Language Testers in Europe / Association des organismes certificateurs en Europe*). Dans notre document de fond, nous nous proposons de clarifier la place de l'évaluation dans le contexte de la migration. Se concentrant sur l'utilisation éthique des évaluations et des résultats des tests, il est contextualisé par l'analyse des preuves des exigences d'évaluation en Europe, tels que les tests de langue et de « connaissance de la société », ainsi que par nos préoccupations quant à l'utilisation de l'évaluation pour faire barrage à l'entrée et à l'intégration des migrants.

## 1 ALTE

The Association of Language Testers in Europe (ALTE) is an international non-governmental organisation with participatory status in the Council of Europe. It is an association of institutions within Europe, each of which produces examinations and certification for language learners. Each member provides examinations in the language which is spoken as a mother tongue in their own country or region. ALTE was formed in 1990, with eight founder members. There are now more than 30 full members, and two associate members, representing 26 lan-

---

**Jane Lloyd** (corresponding author), Association of Language Testers in Europe, Cambridge, United Kingdom, E-mail: lloydj@cambridgeenglish.org
**Michaela Perlmann-Balme**, Goethe-Institut, Germany, E-mail: perlmann-balme@goethe.de

DOI 10.1515/9783110477498-032, © 2017 Jane Lloyd, Michaela Perlmann-Balme, published by De Gruyter.
This work is licensed under the Creative Commons Attribution-NonCommercial-NoDerivs 3.0 License.

guages. ALTE's aims are to establish common levels of language proficiency in order to promote transnational recognition of certification in Europe, to establish common standards for all stages of the language testing process, and to exchange expertise in the field of language testing.

## 2 LAMI Publications for the CoE

The Language and Migration (LAMI) Special Interest Group within ALTE explores the use of tests in a political context, and advises the Council of Europe (via the Linguistic Integration of Adult Migrants, or LIAM, project) on issues of language exam content, purpose and quality. Its work involves collecting data on language exam requirements and knowledge-of-society tests across Europe, with reference to the following types and purposes of entry: initial entry, family reunion, employment, study, permanent residence, and citizenship.

The ongoing data collection by members of the LAMI group was done via questionnaires, and collated into tables and posters. It also resulted in the completion of a booklet, at the request of the Council of Europe. This booklet formed the basis of *Language tests for social cohesion and citizenship – an outline for policymakers* (Balch et al. 2008). A second edition of the booklet, now greatly expanded in terms of advice and content, was produced in 2016 (ALTE 2016), and its contents and ethos formed the core of this presentation at the symposium.

The presentation gave an overview of the seven main sections of the updated booklet ("Background", "Formal entry requirements", "Concepts in assessment", "Levels and profiles", "Deciding what to test", "The test production cycle", and "Conclusion"), which are explained in more detail in the booklet introduction, reproduced below. The aims of the updated booklet are to support policy makers, to make the complex area of language assessment accessible to a non-specialist audience, and to focus on practical advice and current information. Our recommendation for the future is that language policy should help to promote multilingualism and work towards the best outcome for all stakeholders.

## 3 Future collaboration

Moving forward, ALTE has an online edition of the booklet available on its website (http://www.alte.org/resources) and hopes to have it also available on the LIAM website, both versions of which can be regularly updated to reflect current policy. ALTE, as part of its commitment to multilingualism, intends to translate the complete booklet into the languages of all its members. As a first step, the introduction of the booklet is included after this brief summary of the presentation, in English and French.

In addition to presenting the new booklet, the presentation contextualized the work of the LAMI group by outlining two collaborative projects, a multinational research project on the use of language by migrants in the workplace in Germany, Portugal, and Italy, and the development of a national test for migration purposes, which was the result of collaboration between two German ALTE members, namely the Goethe-Institut and telc.

In terms of upcoming work for the LAMI group, we plan to continue the political discussion, and contribute by supporting the Council of Europe in its development of a toolkit for volunteer teachers of refugees. We shall also continue to collect data on current assessment practices and policies, produce valid and reliable language exams, and develop exams specifically for migrants.

# References

ALTE (Association of Language Testers in Europe). 2016. *Language tests for access, integration and citizenship: An outline for policymakers.* http://www.alte.org/attachments/files/alte_lami_language_test_policy_booklet_web_en_0 m4wh.pdf (accessed 9 August 2016).

Balch, Andrew, Michael Corrigan, Sara Gysen, Henk Kuijper, Michaela Perlmann-Balme, Shalini Roppe, Heinrich Rübeling, Steffi Steiner, Piet Van Van Avermaet & Beate Zeidler. 2008. *Language tests for social cohesion and citizenship – an outline for policymakers.* Strasbourg: Council of Europe. https://rm.coe.int/CoERMPublicCommonSearchServices/DisplayDCTMContent?documentId=09000016802fc1b9 (accessed 9 August 2016).

# Appendix

## A: Introduction to the booklet *Language tests for access, integration and citizenship: An outline for policymakers*

This booklet is an expanded and detailed second edition of a previous publication on the use of assessment in the migration context. The aim of this booklet is to support policy makers by enabling them to make informed decisions in the area of language policy and language testing policy. The booklet presents an overview of key issues, concepts and processes in language testing and the related fields of language learning and language competence, with particular reference to the context of migration. For ease of reference it is divided into sections.

The first section, "Background", explains the involvement and relationship between the Association of Language Testers in Europe (ALTE), the Language Assessment for Migration and Integration (LAMI) Group and the Council of Europe (CoE). It discusses the assessment work carried out by ALTE and the LAMI Group, and in broad terms, how test results should be used, and for what purposes.

The second section, "Formal entry requirements", gives an overview of the current situation across Europe in terms of different types of language requirements for the purposes of entry, residence and citizenship, and how these have changed over time. It describes tests which assess knowledge of society. It illustrates why different types of planning and policies are necessary for different types of migrant or different circumstances. It ends with a discussion of the importance of plurilingualism and the linguistic repertoire of the migrant.

This is followed by an overview of terms in "Concepts in assessment", which highlights the fundamental importance of needs analysis. It includes a discussion of how good testing practice underpins test fairness, a glossary of common terms in assessment, and an overview of how the test validation process is used to provide evidence that tests are fit for purpose.

Section 4, "Levels and profiles", outlines how policy makers and assessment professionals can work together to decide on the relevant level and skills profile to target for different migrant groups. It discusses issues of literacy and how migrants are likely to progress through different levels and profiles, and what factors may affect this.

Section 5, "Deciding what to test", describes how a needs analysis can establish the real-life linguistic demands on migrants and inform what should be included in a valid test, and how these demands can be translated into the design of the test in terms of linguistic requirements and tasks. It discusses different types of assessment and tasks, and how to decide which are appropriate to different contexts and test takers.

Section 6, "The test production cycle", presents an overview of the test production cycle, followed by more detailed information about each of the main stages, such as producing test specifications, item writing, pre-testing, exam administration, inclusion of candidates with special requirements, marking, monitoring, and conducting impact research.

The final section, "Conclusion", acknowledges the complexity of assessing language use for the purposes of entry, residency, integration and citizenship, and the burden of responsibility placed on policy makers. It concludes with a summary of how policy makers and test providers can work together to shape a language testing policy and assessment system that is valid, reliable, practical and fair.

## B : Introduction (en français)

Ce livret est la seconde édition, revue et augmentée, d'une publication relative à l'utilisation de l'évaluation dans un contexte d'immigration. L'objectif de ce livret est d'assister les décideurs institutionnels dans leurs prises de décision en matière de politiques langagières et des politiques d'évaluation en langue. Le livret présente une vue d'ensemble des problématiques, concepts et processus clés de l'évaluation en langue ainsi que des champs associés de l'apprentissage des langues et de la compétence langagière, en focalisant sur le contexte de l'immigration. Il est subdivisé en plusieurs parties.

La première partie, « Background », décrit les relations entre l'Association ALTE (Association des centres d'évaluation en langue en Europe, le *LAMI group* (groupe de travail sur l'évaluation en langue pour l'immigration et l'intégration) et le Conseil de l'Europe. Elle évoque le travail d'évaluation mené par ALTE et le LAMI group et, dans les grandes lignes, la façon dont les résultats aux tests devraient être utilisés et dans quel but.

La deuxième partie, « Formal entry requirements », donne une vue d'ensemble de la situation actuelle à travers l'Europe, en termes de types d'exigences langagières requises à des fins d'accès au territoire, de résidence et de citoyenneté, et de la manière dont ces dernières ont évolué dans le temps. Elle évoque également l'existence de tests de connaissance de la société. Elle illustre en quoi différents types d'organisation et de politiques sont nécessaires selon les différentes catégories de migrants et des circonstances de leur présence. Elle exprime enfin l'importance d'une prise en considération du plurilinguisme et du répertoire linguistique du migrant.

S'ensuit une vue d'ensemble des principales notions dans la partie « Concepts in assessment », qui met en évidence l'importance fondamentale d'une analyse des besoins. Elle met en évidence la manière dont les bonnes pratiques d'évaluation renforcent l'équité des tests, propose un glossaire des termes courants de l'évaluation et donne un aperçu de la façon dont le processus de validation des tests permet d'apporter des preuves de leur adéquation à l'usage prévu.

La partie 4, « Levels and profiles », souligne la façon dont les décideurs institutionnels et les professionnels de l'évaluation peuvent travailler de concert pour décider du niveau pertinent et du profil langagier cible pour différents groupes de migrants. Elle aborde les questions relatives à la littératie, la façon dont les migrants sont susceptibles de progresser à travers les niveaux et les profils, et les facteurs susceptibles d'affecter cette progression.

La partie 5, « Deciding what to test », décrit comment une analyse des besoins permet d'établir des exigences linguistiques de la vie réelle pour les migrants, de renseigner sur ce qui devrait figurer dans un test valide, et comment ces exigences peuvent être transcrites dans l'élaboration du test en termes d'exigences linguistiques et de tâches. Elle présente différents types d'évaluations et de tâches en donnant des indications pour déterminer lesquels sont adaptés aux différents contextes et aux différents candidats.

La partie 6, « The test production cycle », présente une vue d'ensemble du cycle de production d'un test, puis des informations détaillées concernant chacune des principales étapes, comme la rédaction des spécifications du test, la conception d'items, le pré-testage, l'administration des tests, la prise en considération des candidats ayant des besoins particuliers, la notation, le monitorage et la conduite d'une recherche d'impact.

La dernière partie, « Conclusion », reconnaît la complexité de l'évaluation de la langue d'usage à des fins d'accès au territoire, de résidence, d'intégration et de citoyenneté, et la lourde responsabilité qui pèse sur les décideurs institutionnels. Elle conclut en rappelant comment les décideurs institutionnels et les concepteurs de tests peuvent travailler ensemble pour modeler une politique d'évaluation et un dispositif d'évaluation qui soit valide, fidèle, faisable et équitable.

Boris Printschitz
# All a question of the "right" capital? Subjectification – the hidden mechanism behind language tests for residence permit in Austria

**Abstract:** Impossible to detach from its political, cultural and social context, language is used to determine practical and symbolic membership (Dirim 2013), including citizenship. Language tests play an essential role in this practical and symbolic regulation. With this philosophical approach to the field "language tests for residence permit" in mind, the aims of my study are to analyse the (hidden) mechanism behind the use of language tests in the case of residence permits (theoretical approach) and to analyse their impact on test participants using empirical quantitative methods (empirical approach).

**Résumé :** Etroitement liée à son contexte politique, culturel et social, la langue est utilisée pour déterminer l'appartenance symbolique et pratique (Dirim 2013) y compris la citoyenneté. Les tests de langue jouent un rôle essentiel dans cette régulation symbolique et pratique. Gardant à l'esprit cette approche philosophique de « l'obtention d'un titre de séjour conditionnée par la réussite à un test de langue », mon étude analyse le mécanisme (caché) derrière le recours aux tests de langue pour accorder un titre de séjour (approche théorique) et leur impact sur les participants, en utilisant des méthodes quantitatives empiriques (approche empirique).

## 1 Theoretical part

### 1.1 Regime of integration – test regime

The terms "regime of integration" or "test regime" refer to Foucault's "regime" and "governmentality". According to Foucault (2013), it is the nature of a state to get control over everything in form of a contract to regulate the relation between state and people. If we see language tests from this point of view, we can see tests as instruments of power – they serve as gate-keepers. For example,

---

**Boris Printschitz**, Österreichisches Sprachdiplom Deutsch, Vienna, Austria, E-mail: boris.printschitz@osd.at

Shohamy (2001) described language tests as tools of a policy of exclusion because only the applicants who pass a test are selected. McNamara and Roever (2006) call such tests instruments for regulating migration because not all who have to pass are able to pass. Another point criticised by Van Avermaet, Extra and Spotti (2009) and Hogan-Brun (2009) is the arbitrary nature of language requirements and criteria: the levels demanded to pass such tests differ from country to country. There is in any case a very doubtful connection between proficiency in the language of the host country and integration (Krumm 2011).

The next section will focus on Austria's integration regime, its language requirements and its gate-keeping activities.

## 1.2 Example: test regime in Austria

According to the *Niederlassungs- und Aufenthaltsgesetz* (NAG; Settlement and Residence Act) executed by the *Bundesministerium für Inneres* (BMI; Federal Ministry of the Interior) and supported by the *Österreichische Integrationsfonds* (ÖIF; Austrian Integration Fund), a certain politically constructed group of people called *Drittstaatsangehörige* (third-country citizens) have to prove their German language skills via standardised tests (e. g. Goethe-Institute, ÖSD, telc). Different needs require different levels of proficiency. Level A1 is required for the first visa application before entering Austria, while level A2 needs to be passed within the first two years in order to get a temporary residence permit. For a permanent residence permit and application for citizenship after 10 years' residence in Austria, level B1 is required, while applicants for "faster" citizenship, after 6 years' residence in Austria, need to pass level B2. In the case of applications for citizenship, beside German language skills, applicants have to fulfil a long list of other criteria, including a certain level of socio-economic status. These are obvious mechanisms of power. According to Gomolla and Radtke (2009) we can call this a "direct institutional discrimination". Of course, there are a number of mechanisms of power that are more or less hidden.

## 1.3 (Hidden) mechanism of power in test regimes

Some examples of important mechanisms in these regimes are identified in this section such as follows. Krumm (2011) sees a triple discrimination. There is discrimination by nationality (e. g. "third-country citizens"), by social standing (e. g. the cost of courses, the times when they take place, and the exams that must be taken) and by language (e. g. different languages enjoy different levels of prestige). Plutzar (2010) criticises the argument that tests may be seen as motivating; in many cases so-called positive effects on better integration are predicted. Dirim (2010), on the other hand, criticises the "enable and deny" power of the authority which enables applicants to take an exam by providing a standardised test, but denies them the relevant resources (e. g. knowledge and courses) needed to acquire the hegemonic language. And McNamara and Roever (2006) criticise the claim that tests can be objective at all and that, for example, the status of residence depends on apparently non-objective results.

At this point we can come to a first assumption that language tests for residence are an instrument of power that reproduces social discrimination. Especially individuals lacking in specific capital (Bourdieu 1987) suffer from this discrimination. According to Gomolla and Radtke (2009) we can call this "indirect institutional discrimination". The question then arises: If we are aware of those criticisms, why are test regimes still in use, so widely accepted and even on the increase?

## 1.4 *Dispositif* of integration – (re-)production of "we" und "not-we"

To answer this question another term introduced by Foucault is necessary – the *dispositif*. Very briefly, a *dispositif* is a structured method, a strategy to balance power within a group, an area, a state etc. (Foucault 1978). Mecheril (2011) uses the term to analyse methods and strategies within the discourse of integration and calls it "dispositif of integration". According to Mecheril a dispositif of integration:
– differs between the national-ethno-cultural "we" und "not-we" and makes these constructed differences understandable;
– turns individuals into certain subjects, a process known as "subjectification" (Foucault 2013; Butler 2013);
– generates political, cultural and social order which then becomes institutionalized, systematically differentiated and hierarchic;
– and is therefore socially realized and authorized (Mecheril 2011; Mecheril et al. 2010).

Within the dispositif of integration and focused on language tests, we come to the second assumption that language tests for residence permissions are an essential tool to support the dispositif within the regime of integration.

And these two assumptions – alongside others – I aim to prove in a large scale quantitative study.

# 2 Empirical part

## 2.1 Empirical study – design

Due to the very political nature of the topic and in order to get representative data, I've chosen the quantitative empirical paradigm in order to prove my theory. I've therefore designed a standardized questionnaire to collect socio-economic and sociocultural data from test participants. The questions used are based on Bourdieu's types of capital (Bourdieu 1987) as well as on several large scale studies which collect socio-economic and sociocultural data from specific populations. It is planned to administer the questionnaire to participants in B1 German language courses in the week before the test. The questionnaire will be devised in German and translated into the five languages which are the most common among the random sample of participants. To collect language data from these participants I shall use a standardised German test often used for the purpose of getting a residence permit (ÖSD B1 ZDÖ).[1]

In order to validate the questionnaire (n = 50), I have conducted a pre-pilot study, of which I'd like to share the first results in section 2.2.

The study itself will hopefully take place in the autumn of 2016. A representative number of participants in B1 courses (n > 500) is aimed for. After the data collection, the test results will be compared with the results in the questionnaire and analysed using the statistical program SPSS.

### 2.1.1 Empirical study – main questions

– Do language tests used to grant or refuse residence permits (re-)produce social inequality? If so, how?
– Which characteristics of heterogeneity, according to Bourdieu's types of capital (1987), have a significant impact on individuals' performance in standardised language tests?

### 2.1.2 Main hypotheses

Following Settinieri et al. (2014) and Albert and Marx (2014) main hypotheses are as follows:

---

[1] http://www.osd.at/default.aspx?SIid=32&LAid=2&ARid=388 [accessed: 30.4.2016].

- Alternative hypothesis
  - $H_A$: There is a significant impact of economic factors (independent variable, IV) on the individuals' performance in standardised German language tests (dependent variable, DV).
- Distinctive hypothesis
  - $H_{A1}$: Economic factors (IV1) of individuals have a greater influence on their German language test performance than cultural factors (IV2).
  - $H_{A2}$: Economic factors (IV1) of individuals have a greater influence on their German language test performance (DV) than social factors (IV3).

Certainly, some of the theories presented above might appear quite obvious, and we already have reliable figures on the impact of socio-economic status and segregation in the school system on children's test results. Examples are PIRLS and PISA studies as well as Gomolla and Radtke's (2009) study of institutional discrimination within the German educational system. But as far as I know, there is still a lack of at least quantitative data focused on the impact of test regimes on adult participants. Also, since this topic is very political, data are very important to prove these claims.

## 2.2 First results (pilot study) and conclusion

Before presenting some preliminary unofficial data, I should emphasize that they were collected in a pre-pilot study. The aim was simply to confirm the relevance of the questions and how the participants used the questionnaire in the first place. The data were collected as part of the piloting of an ÖSD B1 test (piloting followed by statistical analysis is a standard feature of test production). In other words, personal data about the participants and language data were collected at the same time.

The selected parameters according to Bourdieu's theory of capital (1985, 1987) were as follows:
- net income (economic capital);
- level of education (cultural capital);
- number of social contacts (social capital) outside the course and family.

The pre-pilot-study questionnaire included more parameters for each of Bourdieu's capital types, and the final questionnaire may include even more. Nevertheless, the characteristics of the participants in the pre-pilot study may be summarized as follows:
- 50% vocational training/high school degree, 30% academic degree;

- 3–5 languages (even more if Bosnian, Croatian and Serbian are counted as separate languages);
- 90% had a regular income of less than €1000 per month;
- 70% lived within a solid social network.

In a second step, I used a scale with a range from 0 to 4 in each of the chosen parameters to get ordinal data and to calculate Spearman Rho to see if there is any significant association. The chosen range also represents the points (or level of capital) participants can reach. Although this procedure might appear a little arbitrary, even with a small sample of 50 people, I got some interesting results:
- There is a strong association between "total capital" and test result: R = 0.57 (Spearman Rho). Participants with higher "capital in total" reached higher results, even in this small pre-pilot-study.
- There is only weak evidence for an association between income and test result: R = 0.47. A possible explanation might be that most of the participants were on the same income level (only 10% of them had employee status). Therefore, I'll need more parameters to collect economic data (economic capital).
- There is also only weak evidence for an association between number of social contacts and test result: R = 0.35. Of course, the data tell us nothing about the quality of the contacts. The challenge here is to find parameters which measure the quality of social contacts.
- But there is no evidence of an association between level of education and test result: R = 0.26. This was slightly surprising even within this small pre-pilot study. But also here, more parameters to collect cultural data (cultural capital) are needed.

So far, the following tendencies have become visible: If test results differed, it was a matter less of educational level than of financial status and number of social contacts.

# References

Albert, Ruth & Nicole Marx. 2014. *Empirisches Arbeiten in Linguistik und Sprachlehrforschung*. Tübingen: Narr.
Bourdieu, Pierre. 1987. *Die feinen Unterschiede*. Frankfurt am Main: Suhrkamp.
Bourdieu, Pierre. 1985. *Sozialer Raum und Klassen*. Frankfurt am Main: Suhrkamp.
Butler, Judith. 2013. *Psyche der Macht. Das Subjekt der Unterwerfung*. Frankfurt am Main: Suhrkamp.

Dirim, Inci. 2013. "Deutsch als Zweitsprache" als Fachgebiet. http://dafdaz.univie.ac.at/fileadmin/user_upload/lehrstuhl_daf/Definition_DaZ.pdf (accessed: 30.4.2016].
Dirim, Inci. 2010. "Wenn man mit Akzent spricht, denken die Leute, dass man auch mit Akzent denkt oder so." Zur Frage des (Neo-)Linguizismus in den Diskursen über die Sprache(n) der Migrationsgesellschaft. In Paul Mecheril, Inci Dirim, Mechtild Gomolla, Sabine Hornberg & Krassimir Stojanov (eds.), *Spannungsverhältnisse: Assimilationsdiskurse und interkulturell-pädagogische Forschung*, 91–112. Münster: Waxmann.
Foucault, Michel. 2013. *Analytik der Macht*. Frankfurt/Main: Suhrkamp.
Foucault, Michel. 1978. *Dispositive der Macht*. Berlin: Merve.
Gomolla, Mechthild & Frank-Olaf Radtke. 2009. *Institutionelle Diskriminierung. Die Herstellung ethnischer Differenz in der Schule*. Wiesbaden: VS.
Hogan-Brun, Gabrielle (ed.). 2009. *Discourses on language and integration: Critical perspectives on language testing regimes in Europe*. Amsterdam: Benjamins.
Krumm, Hans-Jürgen. 2011. Deutsch für die Integration – notwendig aber nicht hinreichend. In Barbara Haider (ed.), *Deutsch über alles?*, 7–26. Wien: VHS GmbH.
McNamara, Tim & Carsten Roever. 2006. *Language testing: The social dimension*. Malden, MA: Blackwell.
Mecheril, Paul. 2011. Wirklichkeit schaffen. Integration als Dispositiv. *Aus Politik und Zeitgeschichte* 43. 49–54.
Mecheril, Paul, María do Mar Castro Varela, Inci Dirim, Annita Kalpaka & Claus Melter (eds.). 2010. *Migrationspädagogik*. Weinheim & Basel: Beltz.
Plutzar, Verena. 2010. Sprache als "Schlüssel" zur Integration? In Herbert Langthaler (ed.), *Integration in Österreich*, 123–142. Innsbruck: Studien Verlag.
Settinieri, Julia, Sevilen Demirkaya, Alexis Feldmeier, Nazan Gültekin-Karakoç & Claudia Riemer (eds.). 2014. *Empirische Forschungsmethoden für Deutsch als Fremd- und Zweitsprache: eine Einführung*. Paderborn: Schöningh.
Shohamy, Elana. 2001. *The power of tests: A critical perspective on the uses of language tests*. Harlow: Longman.
Van Avermaet, Piet, Guus Extra & Massimiliano Spotti (eds.). 2009. *Language testing, migration and citizenship: Cross-national perspectives on integration regimes*. New York: Continuum.

Coraline Pradeau
# Les évaluations « Français langue d'intégration » (France, *FLI*) et « Français en Suisse – apprendre, enseigner, évaluer » (*fide*) : une alternative aux tests de langue certifiés pour la naturalisation française et suisse

**Résumé :** Cet article présente une perspective comparée entre deux dispositifs d'évaluation linguistique pour l'accès à la nationalité française et suisse : les attestations « Français langue d'intégration » (*FLI*) et « Français en Suisse – apprendre, enseigner, évaluer » (*fide*). Cette étude empirique porte sur la conception et la validation de ces instruments d'évaluation. L'enjeu est de s'assurer de leur fiabilité, validité et équité.

**Abstract:** This article compares two methods of assessing the language capabilities of applicants for French and Swiss nationality, leading to the certificates *FLI* (French as a language of integration) and *fide* (French in Switzerland – learn, teach, evaluate). This empirical study looks at the design and validation of these assessment tools. The challenge is to ensure their reliability, validity and fairness.

## Introduction

Comme le soulignent Evelyne Pochon-Berger et Peter Lenz, il existe encore peu d'études empiriques portant sur la validation et la conception de tests de langue à des fins d'immigration (2014). Un réel besoin existe pourtant, puisque la recommandation 2034 (2014) *Tests d'intégration : aide ou entrave à l'intégration* adoptée par l'Assemblée parlementaire du Conseil de l'Europe a mis en évidence que la finalité de certaines pratiques en matière d'évaluation conduirait à exclure des migrants de la collectivité nationale plutôt qu'à les y intégrer.

Ces lectures m'ont incitée à proposer une étude autour de deux dispositifs d'évaluation linguistique des populations migrantes pour l'accès à la nationalité française et suisse : les attestations Français Langue d'Intégration (*FLI*) (Vicher 2011) et « Français en Suisse – apprendre, enseigner, évaluer » (*fide*) (Lenz. *et al.* 2009).

Présentons rapidement les contextes. En France, depuis le 1er janvier 2012, les candidats à la nationalité doivent justifier du niveau B1, rubriques « écouter », « prendre part à une conversation » et « s'exprimer oralement en continu » du *Cadre européen commun de référence pour les langues* (CECR)[1]. Les organismes de formation labellisés *FLI* sont accrédités par le Ministère de l'Intérieur pour apporter la preuve du niveau de langue des candidats à la nationalité, après leur avoir délivré une formation obligatoire de 20 h. Chaque organisme produit ses propres tests. Les différents tests ne sont pas standardisés : il n'y a pas de directive officielle quant au contenu et au format des épreuves.

En Suisse, en 2009, l'Office fédéral des migrations a confié à l'Institut de plurilinguisme de l'Université de Fribourg la conception d'un concept-cadre pour l'apprentissage des langues par les migrants. De là est né le projet *fide* qui compte, entre autres, de nombreuses ressources didactiques, une formation de formateurs conduisant à un certificat, un concept qualité en cours de pilotage et, pour ce qui nous intéresse, un projet « évaluation de langue *fide*[2] ». Il doit être lancé dans toute la Suisse courant 2017/début 2018 pour la mise en vigueur de la nouvelle loi sur la nationalité, qui prévoit un minimum requis pour les exigences linguistiques fixé au niveau A2 écrit et B1 oral.

L'évaluation de langue *fide* ne vaudra pas pour la seule procédure de naturalisation, mais pourra également servir pour justifier de son niveau de langue lors d'une recherche d'emploi ou d'une formation professionnelle continue. L'organisme *The European Language Certificates* (telc) a emporté l'appel d'offres pour concevoir le test pilote, dont la première phase s'est achevée fin 2015[3]. À la différence des attestations de langue *FLI*, les tests *fide* seront standardisés. Le secrétariat *fide* centralisera à l'avenir l'élaboration des tests, et communiquera aux centres de formation, qui auront reçu le concept qualité, les procédures d'administration et de correction des tests.

---

[1] Décret n° 2011–1265 du 11 octobre 2011 relatif au niveau de connaissance de la langue française requis des postulants à la nationalité française (JORF n° 0237 du 12 octobre 2011).
[2] Les ressources *fide* sont accessibles sur le portail web : <http://www.fide-info.ch> (consulté le 20 juin 2016).
[3] Le test est modulaire (6 modules couvrant les niveaux A1 à B1) et se compose de deux parties : « Parler et comprendre » et « Lire et écrire ». Je ne considèrerai que la partie « Parler et comprendre » pour pouvoir la comparer aux épreuves de compréhension et de production orales des évaluations de langue *FLI*.

Ces deux dispositifs ont en commun d'offrir aux candidats à la naturalisation une alternative aux tests de langues certifiés : diplôme élémentaire de langue française (DELF), test de connaissance du français (TCF), test d'évaluation de français (TEF), etc. L'enjeu de cette étude comparative sera de s'assurer de leur garantie de qualité. Il s'agira de reprendre trois aspects de l'équité : l'équité en tant qu'absence de biais, l'équité en tant que traitement équitable dans le processus de l'évaluation, et enfin l'équité en tant qu'égalité dans les résultats de l'évaluation *(Association of Language Testers in Europe* [ALTE] 2011 : 19).

Alors que chaque organisme labellisé *FLI* élabore ses propres tests, ce système peut-il garantir l'équité des attestations à l'échelle nationale ? Quels avantages y aurait-il à standardiser les évaluations *FLI* sur le modèle du projet *fide* ?

Pour réaliser cette étude, j'ai recueilli entre février et mars 2016 différents scénarios d'évaluation *FLI* dans quatre organismes labellisés à Paris, nommés par les lettres A, B, C et D. Pour ce qui est du projet « évaluation de langue *fide* », j'ai rencontré Myriam Schleiss, du Secrétariat d'État aux migrations, et Christine Grand, du secrétariat *fide*, qui m'ont présenté le test pilote.

# 1 L'équité en tant qu'absence de biais

Pour tenter de minimiser les biais dans les tests de langue, il s'agit de s'assurer que les items proposés n'avantagent ou ne désavantagent pas certains groupes de candidats (ALTE 2011 : 19). Ce facteur d'équité fait partie intégrante du critère de fiabilité des tests (ALTE 2011 : 19). ALTE associe la fiabilité à la cohérence : un test fiable produira des résultats similaires et classera un groupe de candidats pratiquement de la même façon lors de différentes sessions (2011 : 18). Pour s'assurer de la fiabilité d'un test, les phases d'expérimentation et de contrôle sont essentielles.

## 1.1 Les phases d'expérimentation et de contrôle des tests

Tous les centres labellisés *FLI* visités ont expérimenté leurs tests auprès de leur équipe de formateurs et des apprenants présents en formation, mais le centre A est le seul à avoir été particulièrement attentif à la pré-évaluation des items, et à concevoir un étalonnage des épreuves par niveau. C'est aussi le seul centre visité à procéder à une analyse de contrôle des tests.

Pour ce qui est du projet « évaluation de langue *fide* », les items du test pilote ont subi une épreuve de calibrage en 2015. Le rapport d'expérimentation est en cours d'écriture.

### 1.2 Le traitement de l'écrit

En comparant les épreuves de compréhension orale des scénarios d'évaluation *FLI* récoltés, il apparaît que le biais principal se rapporte à l'équité de traitement des candidats avec de faibles compétences en réception écrite, et des candidats peu scolarisés.

Parce que le niveau B1 oral est exigé pour la procédure de naturalisation française, la mobilisation de compétences relevant de l'écrit ne devrait pas être de mise dans les évaluations de langue *FLI*.

Pourtant, seuls les centres A et C prennent soin de dissocier l'évaluation des compétences orales de celle des compétences écrites. Les centres B et D proposent des QCM dans lesquels des compétences de réception écrites entrent en jeu.

Même si l'épreuve de compréhension orale de l'évaluation *fide* repose sur un support papier, le choix des réponses repose sur des images et les informations écrites y sont volontairement très limitées.

## 2 L'équité en tant que traitement équitable dans le processus d'évaluation

Cet aspect se réfère à tout ce qui relève de la validité du test. Comme ALTE le souligne, « un test est valide s'il mesure ce qu'il a l'intention de mesurer » (2011 : 16). En d'autres mots, pour juger de la validité d'un test, il est nécessaire d'identifier ce qui est attendu d'un candidat lorsqu'il utilise la langue dans la vie réelle, puis de s'assurer que le test apporte la preuve de cette compétence. Il est donc question de déterminer les besoins langagiers des candidats dans le monde réel, puis de les traduire en exigences linguistiques dans le test.

### 2.1 Le format des épreuves

Considérons les différents scénarios d'évaluation des épreuves de production orale.

Les tests des centres A et D et l'évaluation de langue *fide* privilégient l'évaluation de compétences en « situation réelle ». Ici, la preuve de la validité du test se rapporte à l'utilisation de la langue selon différents objectifs de communication. La dimension sociale et culturelle prime sur la dimension purement linguistique.

Les scénarios d'évaluation des centres B et C ne reproduisent pas une mise en situation quotidienne. La preuve de validité porte sur la « capacité potentielle » des candidats à utiliser la langue (ALTE 2011 : 16). La préoccupation est essentiellement linguistique.

En regardant de plus près le format des épreuves, les mêmes centres A et D proposent deux épreuves de production orale, qui portent chacune sur l'évaluation des deux compétences distinctes à évaluer selon le décret de 2011 : « prendre part à une conversation » et « s'exprimer oralement en continu ».

Les candidats sont évalués sur leur capacité à faire face sans préparation à des situations un peu inhabituelles de la vie courante, à exprimer leur point de vue, et à pouvoir échanger sur un sujet familier, comme il est attendu d'un niveau B1 selon les grilles de référence du CECR. C'est le cas aussi pour l'évaluation de langue *fide* (de niveau B1).

Quant aux centres B et C, ils ne proposent qu'une seule épreuve, dans laquelle sont évaluées (a priori) les deux compétences citées ci-dessus. L'objectif n'est pas de pouvoir réagir à une situation un peu inhabituelle, mais plutôt de pouvoir exprimer son point de vue et/ou de répondre aux sollicitations et questions de l'examinateur.

## 2.2 Quels domaines d'utilisation de la langue évaluer ?

Un choix se pose aux organismes labellisés *FLI*. Considérant l'enjeu de l'attestation, s'agit-il de donner une « teinte » résolument civique et citoyenne aux épreuves ou d'évaluer indifféremment les compétences langagières selon les 4 domaines indiqués par le CECR (public, personnel, professionnel et éducationnel) ?

Les organismes labellisés visités ont tous fait le choix d'orienter les épreuves des tests autour de thématiques citoyennes (telles que le droit de vote, les valeurs de la République, les impôts, etc.). Les centres A, B et D proposent également des épreuves de production et de réception orales portant sur des situations plus générales (l'école, le vivre-ensemble, l'espace public, etc.) dans lesquelles sont évaluées des connaissances socioculturelles.

Quant au centre C, il axe délibérément toutes ses épreuves autour de la citoyenneté. L'épreuve de production orale se présente comme un simulé d'entretien d'assimilation à la préfecture, et porte sur *Le livret du citoyen*, un document récemment édité par le Ministère de l'Intérieur qui présente le « socle commun » de connaissances à acquérir sur l'histoire, la culture et la société françaises.

Il n'est pas question de prendre part à une conversation : seul l'examinateur conduit l'échange interactionnel. Certaines questions permettent aux candidats de s'exprimer oralement en continu (ex : « Pouvez-vous définir la laïcité ? ») ; d'autres ne leur permettent de répondre que par des informations factuelles (ex : « Pouvez-vous me citer la devise de la France ? »). Finalement, l'examinateur dispose de peu de matière pour évaluer le niveau B1 en production orale des candidats. Il y a une confusion certaine entre le rôle que doit jouer un spécialiste en didactique du français et celui d'un agent de préfecture.

Contrairement à l'approche *FLI*, la démarche *fide* n'a pas pour objectif de présenter aux apprenants les valeurs citoyennes suisses. Le projet s'appuie sur un recueil des besoins communicatifs des migrants dans la vie quotidienne, recueillis en consultant des spécialistes d'intégration cantonaux, et des prestataires de formation. L'évaluation de langue *fide* s'aligne bien sur les recommandations d'ALTE puisque ces besoins ont été traduits en exigences linguistiques. Les domaines d'utilisation de la langue ont été dissociés en 11 champs d'action (logement, travail, enfants, administration, recherche d'emploi, etc.), découpés en plus de 100 scénarios, eux-mêmes détaillés en différentes étapes et tâches communicatives. Chacun des six modules du test porte sur un champ d'action.

## 3 L'équité en tant qu'égalité dans les résultats de l'évaluation

Plusieurs facteurs font que l'égalité dans les résultats de l'évaluation de langue *FLI* n'est pas assurée :
– Le niveau évalué : un centre a choisi d'évaluer la seule recevabilité des candidats au niveau B1. Les trois autres centres évaluent le niveau linguistique réel des candidats, indépendamment de leur recevabilité au niveau B1.
– Le poids des différentes épreuves par rapport au résultat global : les centres visités n'accordent pas tous une importance égale aux épreuves de réception et de compréhension orales.

## Conclusion

Au vu du fort enjeu social que représente l'évaluation de langue *FLI* pour les candidats à la naturalisation, la procédure de labellisation des centres devrait être plus rigoureuse. Il faut noter le désengagement du gouvernement actuel concernant le dispositif. Tous les labels – délivrés entre 2012 et 2013 pour une durée de 3 ans – ont été automatiquement reconduits jusqu'en 2017, sans nouvelle procédure d'audit[4]. Les centres sont donc en totale autonomie depuis quelques années.

Quel avenir pour le dispositif *FLI* en 2017 ? Pour assurer un traitement équitable des candidats au niveau national tout en proposant un test spécifiquement conçu pour les populations issues de la migration, faudrait-il s'aligner sur l'exemple allemand du *Deutschtest für Zuwanderer* (DTZ) (basé sur le *Cadre de référence* du Goethe-Institut, 2007) et celui du projet suisse « évaluation de langue *fide* » ?

Deux choix se présentent aux décideurs politiques pour assurer un dispositif d'évaluation équitable et éthique pour tous les candidats à la naturalisation française : accréditer une instance permettant une élaboration centralisée des épreuves et une standardisation des épreuves selon des critères d'administration et de correction uniformisés ; ou inciter les centres à se coordonner pour faire converger les bonnes pratiques.

## Références

ALTE. 2011. *Manuel pour l'élaboration et la passation de tests et d'examens de langue*. Strasbourg : Conseil de l'Europe. https://www.coe.int/t/dg4/linguistic/Source/ManualLanguageTest-Alte2011_FR.pdf (consulté le 17 mai 2016).

Goethe-Institut. 2007. *Rahmencurriculum für Integrationskurse – Deutsch als Zweitsprache*. München : Bundesamt für Migration und Flüchtlinge. https://www.goethe.de/lhr/prj/daz/pro/Rahmencurriculum_online_final_Version5.pdf (consulté le 20 juin 2016).

Lenz, Peter et al. 2009. *Curriculum-cadre pour l'encouragement linguistique des migrants*. Fribourg : Office fédéral des migrations. https://www.fide-info.ch/doc/01_Projekt/fideFR01_CurriculumCadre.pdf (consulté le 20 juin 2016).

Pochon-Berger, Evelyne & Peter Lenz. 2014. *Les prérequis linguistiques et l'usage de tests de langue à des fins d'immigration et d'intégration : une synthèse de la littérature académique*. Fribourg : Institut de plurilinguisme. http://www.centre-plurilinguisme.ch/

---

4 Décret n° 2015–870 du 16 juillet 2015 modifiant le décret n° 2011–1266 du 11 octobre 2011 relatif à la création d'un label qualité intitulé « Français langue d'intégration » (JORF n° 0163 du 17 juillet 2015).

documents/Documentation/Resid_IPL_FR_05%2006%202014_web.pdf (consulté le 20 juin 2016).

Vicher, Anne (dir.). 2011. *Le Référentiel Français Langue d'Intégration (FLI)*. Paris : Direction de l'Accueil, de l'Intégration et de la Citoyenneté. http://www.immigration.interieur.gouv.fr/content/download/38544/292981/file/FLI-Referentiel.pdf (consulté le 20 juin 2016).

Paola Masillo
# Linguistic integration and residence policies in Italy: issues and perspectives

**Abstract:** This paper reports on the development of policies and practices designed to support the linguistic integration of adult migrants in Italy. The focus is on the use of language requirements: in order to secure a permanent residence permit, non-EU citizens must pass a compulsory Italian language test. The purpose is to highlight the lack of coherence and effectiveness of Italian policy with regard to the issues of *fairness* and *ethics*.

**Résumé :** L'article informe sur le développement des politiques et pratiques italiennes pour favoriser l'intégration linguistique des migrants adultes. L'accent est mis sur le recours à des conditions de connaissances linguistiques, via la réussite du test d'italien obligatoire exigé des ressortissants non-UE qui demandent un titre de séjour permanent. Le but est de mettre en avant l'incohérence et l'inefficacité des politiques italiennes, dues à leur manque d'équité et d'éthique.

## 1 Introduction

Language assessment has a long history of use as an instrument of social policy and practice, in particular in the role of "linguistic gate-keeping" (Hogan-Brun, Mar-Molinero, and Stevenson 2009). Language tests and their results always have consequences for test takers in educational, professional or social contexts, but sometimes tests may be used to take high-stakes decisions in respect of migration, such as permission to migrate to a new country and receiving an official document to stay there (Shohamy 2001).

**Paola Masillo,** University for Foreigners of Siena, Italy, E-mail: masillo@unistrasi.it

## 2 Research context

The starting point of this study was reflection on the concept of integration as it is defined in some fundamental European documents.[1] In particular, the focus was on one of the most frequently used parameters for measuring the level of integration in a host country, proficiency in its language. The research investigated testing regimes in which language tests are both assessment tools with a diagnostic purpose and "powerful tools" because they are required to access residence rights (McNamara 2000; Shohamy 2001). The research was also concerned with the impact of the *Common European Framework of Reference for Languages* (CEFR; Council of Europe 2001) on language policies, mostly in Europe. Since its publication, the CEFR has become the main reference document in the fields of language learning, teaching and assessment. Nowadays it has even assumed an operational function, being used to justify choices in language policies of integration and immigration (Extra, Spotti, and Van Avermaet 2009).

## 3 Overview of the study

In the last decade, successive surveys have demonstrated that language and cultural knowledge play a central role as prerequisites for obtaining residence permits and/or citizenship in many countries, particularly in Europe. As demonstrated by the most recent survey (Pulinx, Van Avermaet, and Extramania 2014), many European countries are increasingly requiring adult migrants to attain certain minimum levels of proficiency in the language of the country before they are granted the right to long-term residence. Consequently, an increase in the use of language tests based on the CEFR descriptors has been found across the whole of Europe. In Italy, non-EU citizens who apply for a permanent residence permit are asked to take an official language test in order to demonstrate that they have reached CEFR level A2 (Law no. 94/2009; MD 4 June 2010).

### 3.1 Aims and objectives

Good practice in test design requires that test developers meet the following conditions: "results are standardised and reliable, which means that it is easy to

---

[1] See among others: Resolution 68 (18); Resolution 1437 (2005); Resolution 1511 (2006); COMM (2003) 336.

compare candidates across the same or different administrations; candidates are assessed with a high degree of independence and objectivity; large numbers may be tested in a short space of time; test validity helps to ensure fairness" (Council of Europe/Language Policy Unit, Project LIAM). Starting from these theoretical preconditions, the scope of this study is to highlight the lack of coherence and effectiveness of Italian policy with regard to the issues of fairness and ethics. The study also aims to investigate *test usefulness* (Bachman and Palmer 1996), taking into account three factors: *validity, reliability* and *impact*.

## 3.2 Research questions

The crux of the matter underpinning the research questions concerns the issue of ethics in adopting a test not only as a tool to measure linguistic competences, but also as an instrument to discriminate and even exclude.

Based on this preliminary observation, three research questions were developed. The first one arises from the Italian government's decision not to use a national standardised test, but to leave test development and administration in the hands of each adult education centre, which raises questions of fairness, validity and reliability.

The second research question takes into account test reliability, in terms of comparability of test structure, content, and results, considering the uneven score distribution obtained in the first year of administration.

The third research question focuses on test design: the construct is mainly based on receptive and written skills[2] and the assessment criteria focus on accuracy, consistency and appropriateness. The test design makes no reference to speaking or effective communication, which raises problems of test validity.

## 3.3 Study procedures and sample characteristics

This PhD study was carried out over three years. In the first year, a database was established of 83 potentially equivalent test forms developed for migrants throughout Italy. Following a survey of outcomes, we selected two test forms developed by the two most representative areas, according to the pass rates: Piemonte (90.2%) and Veneto (71.6%).

---

[2] The test content consists of three sections: listening, reading and written interaction (MIUR 2010).

In the second year, we administered the two selected tests to a representative sample of test takers, following the official guidelines given by the Italian Ministry of Education (MIUR 2010).

In the third year, we focused on data analysis. In the first stage, a content analysis was carried out via correlation with the CEFR descriptors, according to the *Standard Setting* method. In the second stage, a selection of statistical analyses was run in order to measure test reliability following *Classical Test Theory* and focusing on the two receptive skills, listening and reading. In the last stage, the focus was on the validation of the assessment scale by assessing a sample of written performances and running a judgment analysis.

# 4 Findings and discussion

The aim of this paper is to show the main results reached during the three-year project, followed by a discussion and final considerations.[3]

## 4.1 Unfair testing

The first research question can be confirmed, first of all, in the light of the results obtained through the *standard setting* process, in particular the *specification stage*[4] (Table 1). Looking at the mean values obtained, there is a difference in the level of item difficulty recognised, in particular between the Reading 1 components of the two tests.

**Table 1:** Standard setting – specification

| Mean | Test 1 | Test 2 |
| --- | --- | --- |
| Listening 1 | 2.38 | 2.7 |
| Listening 2 | 2.2 | 2.78 |
| Reading 1 | 1.54 | 3.09 |
| Reading 2 | 2.3 | 2.3 |

Secondly, if we look at the *frequency distribution* (Table 2), the outcome confirms the unfairness of the two tests. 63.7% of the test takers achieved the maxi-

---

[3] For research purposes, we named the two tests Test 1 (Piemonte) and Test 2 (Veneto).
[4] For research purposes, we named the CEFR levels 1 (A1), 2 (A2), and 3 (B1).

mum score (10) for listening in Test 1, while only 28.7% of the same sample achieved the maximum score (10) in Test 2.

**Table 2:** Frequency distribution

| Test 1 | | Test 2 | |
|---|---|---|---|
| Listening | 63.7% | Listening | 28.7% |
| Reading | 28.7% | Reading | 17.8% |

*Descriptive statistics* (Table 3) gave us the third confirmation of the *unfairness* of the two tests. The difference between the mean values of the two tests confirms that Test 1 is easier than Test 2.

**Table 3:** Descriptive statistics – mean

| Test 1 | | Test 2 | |
|---|---|---|---|
| Listening | 9.31 | Listening | 8.46 |
| Reading | 8.20 | Reading | 7.13 |

## 4.2 Non-equivalent testing

The first confirmation of low test reliability is the *Cronbach's alpha* value (Table 4), since it appears generally below the minimum threshold of acceptability (.7).

**Table 4:** Cronbach's alpha

|  | Listening 1 | Reading 2 |
|---|---|---|
| Test 1 | .388 | .566 |
| Test 2 | .512 | .627 |

*Correlations* are weak (.390) between the listening tests and moderate (.483) between the reading tests. In addition, a very low value was detected for *shared variance:* there is a degree of overlap of 15% for listening and 23% for reading.

The final confirmation of the second hypothesis is given by the *paired-samples t-tests* and the *Wilcoxon signed rank tests*, since they confirm that the correlations and differences found between the mean values of the two tests were statistically significant.

### 4.3 The low validity and low reliability of the assessment scale

As regards the third research question, we selected a sample of 20 written performances by test takers who took both tests. The *standard deviation* value for Test 1 indicates more similar and more clustered scores around the mean; by contrast, for Test 2, it confirms a greater spread both above and below the mean. For both tasks, the *range* is very low, considering the 35-point assessment scale, as if the judgment process takes into consideration only one third of the scale (Table 5).

**Table 5:** Rating process (statistics)

| Written interaction | | Test 1 | Test 2 |
|---|---|---|---|
| N | Valid | 20 | 20 |
| | Missing | 0 | 0 |
| Mean | | 29.80 | 29.25 |
| Mode | | 27 | 29 |
| Std. Deviation | | 2.707 | 3.810 |
| Range | | 10 | 16 |

The outcome obtained by the judgment analysis was the following: 11 raters out of 11 considered the scale slightly acceptable and they stated the need to focus on other assessment criteria to achieve the assessment task.

## 5 Final considerations

In line with the recent Recommendation 2034 (Strik 2013), the research attempted to provide scientific evidence about the (mis-)use of language tests for purposes of integration, and to share potential good practice to support the linguistic integration of adult migrants.

The crux of the matter is the lack of a language testing and assessment culture in Italy, which is reflected in the choices that underpin the activated procedures (Barni 2012). Test developers should ensure that they follow appropriate testing procedures, considering the high-stakes decisions that will be based on their test (Van Avermaet and Rocca 2011).

A second critical point concerns the lack of fairness and transparency caused by decentralised procedures and the involvement of test developers who lack appropriate training. Test fairness is relevant to all types of language test and all test takers, but it is especially important when used for migration purposes (ALTE 2016).

Our case study confirms that Italy's *testing regime* uses tests as instruments of power and only apparently to support integration. As regards new perspectives to focus on, the first is the need to monitor the assessment tools and carry out validation studies, in order to ensure that the tools measure the abilities they claim to measure in a valid and reliable way. A collaborative effort is needed to guarantee the quality of assessment procedures so that they meet current professional standards (validity, reliability, and transparency). Finally, it is necessary to promote studies that focus on the impact of language policies on the social integration and social inclusion of adult migrants in the host country (Pulinx, Van Avermaet and Extramiana 2014).

# References

Bachman, Lyle F. & Adrian S. Palmer. 1996. *Language testing in practice*. Oxford: Oxford University Press.
Barni, Monica. 2012. *Diritti linguistici, diritti di cittadinanza: l'educazione linguistica come strumento contro le barriere linguistiche,* 213–23. Roma: Bulzoni.
Council of Europe. 2001. *Common European Framework of Reference for Languages: Learning, teaching, assessment.* Cambridge: Cambridge University Press.
Council of Europe/Language Policy Unit (Strasbourg) – Project LIAM. Tests (language test). https://rm.coe.int/CoERMPublicCommonSearchServices/DisplayDCTMContent?documentId=0900001680494490.
Extra, Guus, Max Spotti & Piet Van Avermaet (eds.). 2009. *Language testing, migration and citizenship: Cross national perspectives on integration regimes.* London: Continuum.
Hogan-Brun, Gabrielle, Clare Mar-Molinero & Patrick Stevenson (eds.). 2009. *Discourse on language and integration.* Amsterdam: John Benjamins.
McNamara, Tim. 2000. *Language testing.* Oxford: Oxford University Press.
MIUR – DG IFTS. 2010. *Vademecum. Indicazioni tecnico-operative per la definizione dei contenuti delle prove che compongono il test, criteri di assegnazione del punteggio e durata del test.* http://hubmiur.pubblica.istruzione.it/alfresco/d/d/workspace/SpacesStore/d6686cab-4f36–4c32-acb3–97f2090ead92/vademecum.pdf (accessed 20 June 2016).
Pulinx, Reinhilde, Piet Van Avermaet & Claire Extramiana. 2014. *Linguistic integration of adult migrants: Policy and practice. Final report on the 3rd Council of Europe survey.*

Strasbourg: Council of Europe. https://rm.coe.int/CoERMPublicCommonSearchServices/DisplayDCTMContent?documentId=09000016802fc1ce (accessed 28 July 2016).

Shohamy, Elana. 2001. *The power of tests: A critical perspective on the use of language tests.* Harlow: Pearson.

Strik, Tineke. 2013. Integration tests: Helping or hindering integration? Report of the Committee on Migration, Refugees, and Displaced Persons. Strasbourg: Council of Europe, Parliamentary Assembly, Doc. 13361.

Van Avermaet, Piet & Lorenzo Rocca. 2011. Language testing and access. LAMI forum at the 4th ALTE International Conference, Kraków, 8 July, 2011). https://biblio.ugent.be/publication/4284783/file/6809549 (accessed 20 June 2016).

Jitka Cvejnová, Kamila Sladkovská
# Examens en vue de l'obtention du titre de séjour permanent en République tchèque

Un bilan des expériences, 2009–2014

**Résumé :** La présente contribution résume le développement des examens mis en place en vue de l'obtention du permis de séjour permanent et cherche à comprendre si ces examens ont favorisé l'intégration linguistique dans la période concernée ou si, au contraire, ces derniers ont constitué un obstacle à l'intégration des migrants en République tchèque, devenue récemment un pays d'immigration. Nos recherches représentent la première tentative de traiter les données acquises dans le cadre de la réalisation des examens. Elles soulignent surtout la nécessité d'une conception cohérente et réfléchie de l'enseignement de la langue tchèque aux immigrés.

**Abstract:** This article discusses the examinations introduced for granting a permanent residence permit and attempts to understand whether these examinations have been conducive to linguistic integration during the period under consideration or whether, conversely, they have constituted an obstacle to the integration of migrants in the Czech Republic, which has recently become a country of immigration. Our research is the first attempt to process test data, and it emphasizes the need for a coherent and carefully reflected approach to teaching Czech to immigrants.

## 1 Hésitations entre A1 ou A2

Depuis le 1er janvier 2009, la République tchèque a mis en place des examens en vue de l'obtention d'un titre de séjour permanent. Toute la période avant la mise en place des examens (2008) et la période concernée ont été accompagnées de discussions quant au niveau adéquat de compétence du CECR à choisir pour ce type d'examens. En 2008, les experts en matière d'enseignement des langues et les représentants de certains organismes sans but lucratif ont demandé que le niveau requis pour les examens soit A2. Ils ont fait remarquer que la compétence linguistique au niveau A1, conformément au CECR, a un potentiel d'insertion

---

Jitka Cvejnová, Kamila Sladkovská, Institut National pour l'Éducation, Prague,
E-mail : cvejnova@a-contact.cz, kamila.sladkovska@nuv.cz

sociale très faible. Au contraire, les employeurs et les décideurs politiques ont plutôt favorisé le niveau A1, et c'est pourquoi c'est ce niveau qui a finalement été adopté par l'arrêté n° 348/2008 Sb. du ministère de l'Éducation, de la Jeunesse et des Sports qui a introduit ces examens sur le plan législatif. Néanmoins, la résolution gouvernementale n° 99 du 9 février 2011 sur la Conception de l'intégration des étrangers sur le territoire de la République tchèque prévoit d'augmenter le niveau de compétence pour passer au niveau A2, ce qui ne s'est toujours pas réalisé. En tout cas, ces hésitations de l'administration de l'État concernant le niveau des examens ont passablement compliqué, et compliquent encore, leur développement, qui doit toujours garder une certaine avance.

## 2 Création des tests

Pendant toute la période de leur développement, l'élaboration des examens a été assurée par l'Institut National pour l'Éducation de Prague. Les concepteurs impliqués dans l'élaboration des tests se sont largement inspirés des textes publiés sur le site de l'Unité des politiques linguistiques du Conseil de l'Europe et des travaux de l'organisation Association of Language Testers in Europe (ALTE). Il a fallu assurer un grand nombre de variantes des examens individuels, parce que l'administration exige depuis 2012 que les examens aient lieu cinq fois par mois pour répondre aux besoins des demandeurs de séjours permanents. L'équipe des rédacteurs des items a élaboré un total de 37 versions originales de tests, et environ 70 versions combinées ou bien modérément modifiées. Ce développement intensif des épreuves a permis d'adapter de plus en plus ces dernières aux principes de validité et de fiabilité d'une part, aux besoins des migrants d'autre part. Cette expérience acquise a abouti à la création d'une banque de données électronique d'items individuels qui a été créée à la fin de la période en question. Cette banque de données facilitera désormais la combinaison et la modification des items individuels et deviendra un outil utile pour tous les rédacteurs d'items.

## 3 Création d'un référentiel spécial pour le niveau A1-A2 en tchèque

Lors de la création des premières épreuves, il s'est avéré nécessaire d'ancrer les épreuves individuelles non seulement sur l'inventaire des compétences et des activités présentées par le CECR, mais aussi sur des inventaires spécifiant concrètement le niveau de référence A1, le cas échéant A2, pour la langue tchèque langue seconde[1]. Les rédacteurs des premières épreuves se sont appuyés sur les descriptions de référence pour le tchèque langue étrangère (Hádková 2005). Malheureusement leur contenu ne correspond pas suffisamment aux besoins linguistiques des immigrés. Ce fait a été sévèrement critiqué à la conférence de l'Université de Plzen organisée en 2010, et dédiée à la langue tchèque au niveau A1. Les avis des experts ont amené l'Institut National pour l'Éducation de Prague à créer et publier le référentiel spécial du niveau A1-A2 pour le tchèque (Cvejnová 2014). Ce manuel constitue désormais un inventaire d'appui pour la création des épreuves pour toutes les compétences langagières. Sa version électronique est munie d'un inventaire lexical en ligne dans lequel il est possible de rechercher le vocabulaire des deux niveaux selon différents critères.

## 4 Reproductibilité des processus de passation et des résultats des examens

Pour qu'on puisse garantir la reproductibilité des processus de passation et des résultats des examens dans un grand nombre de centres d'examen (environ 50 au début), il a fallu élaborer des règles détaillées pour la logistique et l'administration des examens. En rédigeant ces règles, les auteurs ont tenu compte surtout de la liste des questions de contrôle contenues dans le manuel *Alte Quality Assurance Checklist Unit 2 – Administration and Logistics* (ALTE 2013). Mais les auteurs ont dû prendre aussi en considération les textes réglementaires tchèques et les conditions spécifiques des centres d'examen, la fréquence des sessions et le nombre de candidats. Ces règles, sous le titre *Directives pour l'organisation de l'examen*, sont devenues un outil indispensable pour les examinateurs qui, selon l'enquête réalisée auprès des centres, apprécient leur structure logique et concise ainsi que leur approche pratique. Les règles ont été plusieurs fois modifiées pour mieux répondre aux besoins des centres de passation et des candidats. Elles sont accessibles sur le site Internet grâce à un mot de passe. Les auteurs ont préparé également un extrait des instructions utiles pour les candidats en plusieurs langues.

Puisque les centres d'examens doivent prévoir un personnel nombreux (surveillants, correcteurs des épreuves écrites, évaluateurs des épreuves orales), l'Institut National pour l'Éducation de Prague a préparé une formation en ligne pour ces personnes. Toute personne impliquée dans la réalisation des examens

---

[1] Nous reprenons la définition de « langue seconde » donnée par Richards & Schmidt (2010).

doit disposer d'un certificat de l'Institut confirmant la validation de la formation en ligne. C'est l'Institut qui gère le registre des titulaires. Le certificat doit être renouvelé et le personnel participant à la réalisation des examens est appelé à renouveler sa formation en cas de besoin. Cette formation en ligne a fait l'objet d'une analyse de Kamila Zelinková, de la Vysoká škola technická a ekonomická v Českých Budějovicích (Zelinková2012). Elle a permis de découvrir de nombreux points faibles des premiers cours. Les autres améliorations et modifications sont dues aux commentaires des participants. Le développement du cours continue et son contenu est sans cesse adapté aux mises à jour des examens.

## 5 D'un envoi sécurisé du matériel au système sophistiqué de contrôle et de distribution électronique

Au début, le matériel était envoyé aux centres d'examens sur un support papier et les exemplaires n'avaient pas d'éléments de sécurité, bien que l'Institut ait utilisé un dispositif de transport sécurisé. Ces mesures n'ont pas suffi, parce que les candidats, et même certaines personnes impliquées dans les examens, ont fraudé aux examens. Il a donc fallu créer un système de distribution électronique hautement sécurisé capable de contrôler en même temps certaines étapes de la passation des examens.

## 6 Résultats des examens

La réussite moyenne aux examens est de 78,84 % dans la période allant du 1$^{er}$ juin 2009 au 30 avril 2015. Le résultat moyen des examens est donc assez stable, il ne présente aucun écart inattendu dans toute la période suivie. La légère dégradation des résultats vers la fin de la période, en 2014, est certainement due aux mesures anti-corruption introduites cette année-là.

Sur le plan de l'intégration, les résultats sont moins satisfaisants. Alors que chaque étranger peut demander un titre de séjour permanent au bout de 5 années de séjour sur le territoire du pays, il s'avère que presque un quart des étrangers n'ont pas de compétences langagières au niveau A1 après avoir vécu plus de 5 ans de manière continue sur notre territoire. Les causes de cette situation ont été examinées partiellement par une étude sociologique de l'Académie des sciences tchèque (Leontieva et al. 2013) qui souligne, entre autres, l'absence d'une préparation aux examens de la part des étrangers. Les mêmes faits ont été signalés par les organismes sans but lucratif (OBNL) venant en aide aux étrangers. Malheureusement, l'Institut n'a pas pu déterminer le nombre d'essais nécessaires à la réussite à l'examen, parce que la réglementation ne le permet pas et que le nombre d'essais n'est pas limité. Les résultats obtenus ne sont donc pas en mesure de refléter exactement la situation concrète des candidats de ce point de vue.

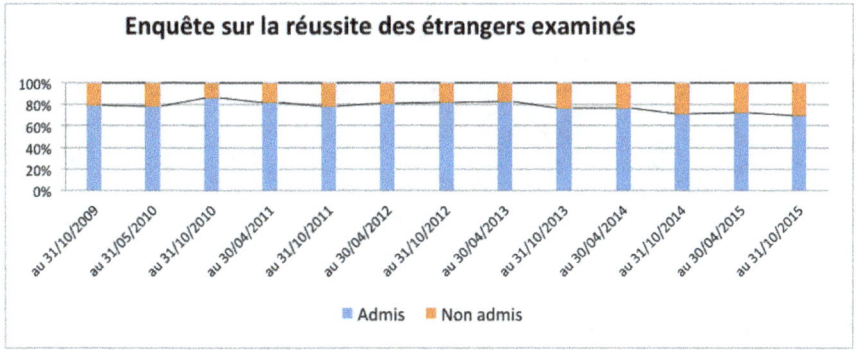

**Figure 1 :** Données statistiques sur la réussite aux examens (Sladkovská 2009 – 2015)

## 7 Préparation aux examens

Les immigrés devraient se préparer aux examens par eux-mêmes, étant donné que l'État, en établissant ce type d'examens, n'a déterminé aucun type de préparation. En se basant sur l'analyse sociologique des immigrés ukrainiens et vietnamiens (les nationalités les plus fréquentes parmi les candidats) (Leontieva 2013), l'Institut a mené sa propre enquête en 2015 auprès de 42 institutions (34 écoles de langues, 8 organismes sans but lucratif) pour vérifier si les immigrés se préparent aux examens et comment ils s'y préparent.

Le but de cette enquête était de vérifier si les écoles qui sont autorisées à réaliser les examens et les organismes sans but lucratif (OBNL) sont impliqués dans la préparation de l'examen. L'Institut s'est adressé à 42 institutions au total, dont 19, soit près de la moitié, ont confirmé qu'elles assurent la préparation aux examens. Néanmoins, toutes les institutions qui ont répondu positivement ne font pas de cours à proprement parler, mais offrent une consultation pour les examens de l'ordre de 0 – 4 heures. En ce qui concerne les OBNL, cette consultation est souvent menée par un travailleur social. Il ne s'agit donc pas d'un enseignement proprement dit. Nous avons pu constater que 6 373 candidats avaient assisté à ces brèves consultations dans la période concernée, sur un total

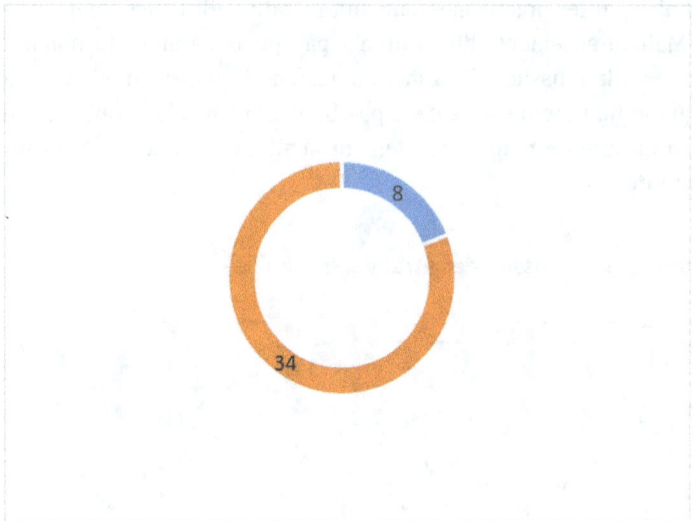

**Figure 2 :** Type des institutions sondées

d'environ 55 000 candidats ayant passé les examens, ce qui signifie qu'environ 12 % de tous les candidats ont recherché une assistance institutionnelle pour préparer leurs examens. Ce chiffre montre nettement qu'aucune préparation intensive pour les examens n'est organisée et que les candidats ne cherchent que des renseignements sur l'examen. La préparation reste individuelle mais comme nous l'avons déjà constaté, presque un quart des candidats aurait besoin d'une préparation fournie par un spécialiste.

L'enquête a révélé, entre autres, les difficultés des candidats en ce qui concerne les compétences langagières individuelles, voir la Fig. 3. Dans ce contexte, il faut souligner que ces constatations des institutions ne correspondent pas tout à fait aux résultats des examens, où beaucoup de candidats ne réussissent pas à l'expression orale. Nous voudrions cibler les enquêtes à venir sur ce fait.

# 8 Stratégie des candidats en échec

Dans le cadre de l'enquête relative à la préparation aux examens et à partir de l'étude sociologique, nous avons suivi aussi les stratégies des candidats en situation d'échec. Les candidats qui n'ont pas réussi utilisent surtout la possibilité illimitée de repasser l'examen, bien que les essais suivants soient déjà payants. En conséquence, certains d'entre eux dépensent beaucoup d'argent en payant

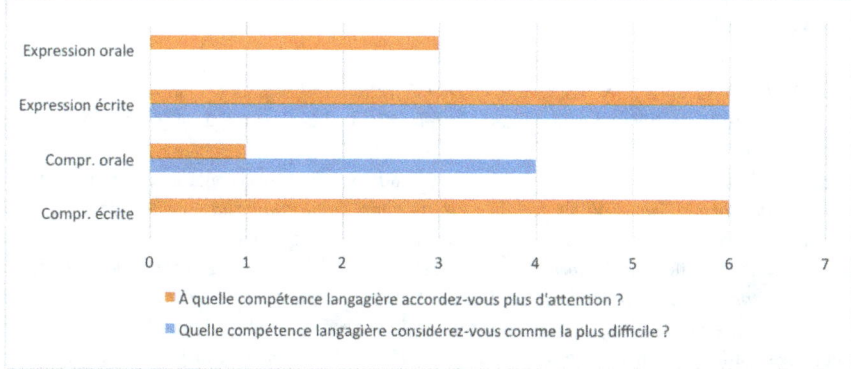

**Figure 3** : Difficultés des candidats quant aux compétences langagières individuelles

différents intermédiaires, au lieu de se préparer ou de s'inscrire à un cours linguistique. Certains candidats qui n'ont pas réussi s'inscrivent immédiatement à une autre session d'examens sans penser à un cours de préparation. Certains candidats recherchent différents moyens de frauder, au lieu de se préparer sérieusement aux examens. Malheureusement, nous avons dû constater que certaines écoles organisatrices d'examens étaient impliquées dans des pratiques de corruption. Il a donc fallu les exclure du système. La stratégie des candidats en échec révèle clairement que l'examen ne correspond pas aux intérêts réels des candidats quant à l'intégration linguistique des immigrés dans la société tchèque. L'examen n'est considéré que comme un obstacle administratif à surmonter afin d'obtenir le titre du séjour permanent.

# Conclusion

L'examen au niveau A1 ne constitue pas un grand obstacle pour un immigré qui veut obtenir le titre de séjour permanent, étant donné son niveau très bas et la possibilité illimitée de repasser l'examen. D'autre part, l'examen n'a qu'un effet minimal sur l'intégration linguistique, car les examens ne sont pas liés à l'apprentissage réel de la langue. À l'heure actuelle, les spécialistes et les décideurs politiques commencent à discuter de la possibilité d'augmenter le niveau des examens. Dans ce contexte, nous soulignons le fait qu'aucune augmentation du niveau ne mènera automatiquement à l'intégration linguistique, tant que l'obligation de passer l'examen ne sera pas liée à une conception réfléchie et cohérente de l'enseignement du tchèque aux immigrés.

# Références

*ALTE Quality Assurance Checklist Unit 2 – Administration and Logistics.* (sans date) : https://www.testdaf.de/fileadmin/Redakteur/PDF/TestDaF/ALTE/ALTE_unit2.pdf (consulté le 11 juin 2016)

Cvejnová, Jitka. 2014. Vývoj a další perspektivy zkoušek z českého jazyka pro migranty, in *Čeština jako cizí jazyk VII materiály z VII. mezinárodního sympozia o češtině jako cizím jazyku*, 341–351. Praha : Univerzita Karlova v Praze, Filozofická fakulta.

Cvejnová, Jitka et al. 2014. *Referenční popis češtiny pro účely zkoušky z českého jazyka pro trvalý pobyt v ČR – úrovně A1, A2*. Praha : Národní ústav pro vzdělávání.

Hádková, Marie et al. 2005. *Čeština jako cizí jazyk. Úroveň A1*. Praha : Tauris.

Leontieva, Yana, Petra Ezeddine & Andrea Plačková. 2013. *Životní styl, jazykové znalosti a potřeby ukrajinských a vietnamských migrantů v ČR*. Praha : Sociologický ústav AV ČR.

Richards, Jack C. & Richard Schmidt. 2010. *Longman Dictionary of Language Teaching and Applied Linguistics*. 4e édition. London : Pearson Education Limited.

Sladkovská, Kamila. 2009, 2010, 2011, 2012, 2013, 2014, 2015. *Statistika zkoušky pro trvalý pobyt*. Praha : Národní ústav pro vzdělávání.

Zelinková, Kamila. 2012 Reflexe e-learningového školení pro examinátory zkoušky z českého jazyka pro trvalý pobyt v České republice. In Zdeněk Caha, Jindřiška Šulistová (ed). *Sborník příspěvků 1. Jazykové a pedagogické e-konference s mezinárodní účastí na VŠTE*. 1. vyd., 78–86. České Budějovice : Vysoká škola technická a ekonomická v Českých Budějovicích.

Sari Ohranen, Heidi Vaarala and Taina Tammelin-Laine
# Developing placement assessment in integration training for adult migrants in Finland

**Abstract:** As part of integration training in Finland, migrants are provided with Finnish or Swedish language courses. The linguistic objective is to provide migrants with the basic language skills required in daily life. To find the most suitable teaching group for learners in integration training, a placement assessment is carried out. This includes assessment of learners' current proficiency level in the target language and study skills/experience. In this article we describe a project to develop a national test system for placement assessment (see Ohranen et al. 2015).

**Résumé :** En Finlande, des migrants adultes suivent des cours de finnois ou de suédois dans le cadre d'une formation pour l'intégration. L'objectif est de les doter des compétences langagières de base nécessaires dans la vie de tous les jours. Une évaluation est réalisée en amont afin de trouver le groupe d'enseignants le mieux adapté aux apprenants inscrits à la formation d'intégration. Elle inclut l'évaluation du niveau de compétence dans la langue cible et du niveau de qualification/d'expérience. Dans cet article, nous décrivons les objectifs d'un projet destiné à concevoir un système national pour l'évaluation de placement (voir Ohranen et al. 2015).

# 1 Immigration in Finland

The number of foreign citizens living permanently in Finland has increased rapidly in the last decade. As far as language background is concerned, at the end of 2014 there were 310,000 people with a foreign language background living in Finland. Russian was the most common foreign language, followed by Estonian, English, Somali and Arabic (Statistics Finland).

The year 2015 was exceptional in terms of the number of asylum seekers in Europe in general. In Finland the number of asylum seekers was 32,476. Relative

**Sari Ohranen** (corresponding author), **Heidi Vaarala** and **Taina Tammelin-Laine**, Centre for Applied Language Studies, University of Jyväskylä, Finland, E-mail: sari.ohranen@jyu.fi, heidi.vaarala@jyu.fi, taina.a.tammelin-laine@jyu.fi

DOI 10.1515/9783110477498-037, © 2017 Sari Ohranen, Heidi Vaarala and Taina Tammelin-Laine, published by De Gruyter.
This work is licensed under the Creative Commons Attribution-NonCommercial-NoDerivs 3.0 License.

to Europe overall this number is not high, but proportionally the increase in Finland has been considerable, as the number of asylum seekers in 2014 was 3,651 (Finnish Immigration Service).

## 2 Policy documents

Integration and integration training have been promoted through legislation and work on national core curricula in various ways. The Act on the Promotion of Integration (1386/2010) and Decree on an Initial Assessment for Promoting Integration (570/2011) came into effect at the beginning of the 2010s. Furthermore, the National Core Curriculum for Integration Training for Adult Migrants and the National Core Curriculum for Literacy Training for Adult Migrants came into effect in 2012.

## 3 Integration training

Integration training is considered key to becoming a part of Finnish society since it includes Finnish/Swedish language and communication skills, civic and working life skills, and guidance counselling. The length of integration training is most commonly approximately ten months, taking place five days a week and for seven hours per day. Integration training is free of charge and the participants receive an integration allowance based on their active and regular participation. The number of students in this training in 2015 was 14,742.

Teachers are usually professional Finnish as a second language (L2) teachers with a master's degree in Finnish language and pedagogical studies. After integration training, the target for language proficiency is quite high, CEFR level B1.1 (according to the Finnish adaptation of the CEFR levels), and the goal is to move on to working life or continue studies in preparatory education for migrants.

## 4 Typical pathways through integration training

Figure 1 shows typical pathways through integration training and other possible education for migrants.

When a migrant is registered in a municipality they are usually guided to employment services for an integration plan. This includes placement assessment, which usually consists of an initial interview, a test of language skills

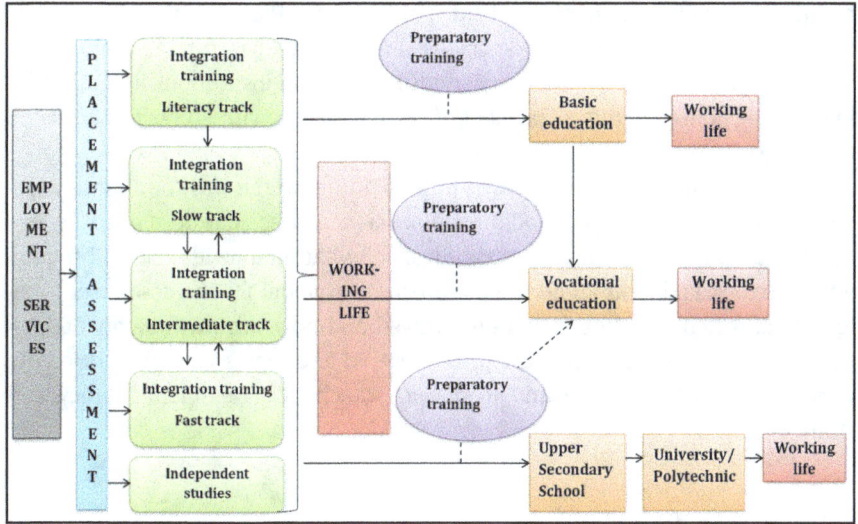

**Figure 1:** Typical pathways through integration training for adult migrants in Finland

and an assessment of study skills. Following this, the migrant is most often guided to a suitable form of integration training.

According to the placement assessment, the most suitable type of integration training is chosen – slow, intermediate or fast-track – depending on the student's motivation and readiness for study. If it turns out that the recommended course is inappropriate, it is possible to switch track during training. The literacy track is chosen if a migrant is non-literate or needs to improve his/her literacy skills (e.g., by learning the Latin alphabet), after which he/she may proceed to regular integration training. Migrants also have the possibility to find suitable education on their own and receive the same benefits, i.e., the integration allowance as in regular integration training.

Naturally after the training there are different possibilities depending on the motivation and life goals of the migrant, such as moving on to basic education/vocational education/upper secondary school (via preparatory training), and then to polytechnic or university level education.

# 5 Our project and its aims

The project was funded by the Ministry of Employment and the Economy during 2014–2015. It was carried out by the Centre for Applied Language Studies (CALS) and Testipiste. CALS has a long history in language testing through coordinating and developing the National Certificates of Language Proficiency testing system, and as a research institution it specialises in research-based test development. Testipiste, a unit formed by four major adult education institutions in the Helsinki area, specialises in the assessment of adult migrants with Finnish as a second language (L2).

The main aim of the project was to plan and pave the way for a more widespread, national use of the model for placement assessment developed by Testipiste. The plan would include an analysis of what nationwide use will require and a recommendation about the administrative model for the assessment system (e.g., which institutions will be involved and how work will be divided between them). A further aim of the project was to develop assessment carried out during integration training and to develop teachers' assessment literacy and skills.

# 6 Data collection

There was no previous information gathered at the national level in the field of placement assessment. Our data collection included
1) contacting 15 Centres for Economic Development, which are responsible for placement assessment in their own regions;
2) a questionnaire addressed to the institutions organizing placement assessment;
3) teacher interviews;
4) school visits.

# 7 Results

## 7.1 Variation in placement assessment

In our data we found that the tests are administered by different kind of institutions, both public (schools) and private (businesses). The data also revealed that there is one major organizer of placement assessment tests (4000 test takers per year), though most institutions organize tests for 100–500 test takers per year. There are also organizers who only have one hundred or fewer test takers. The largest provider organizes tests non-stop and other organizers offer testing only on certain days. Moreover, the duration of placement assessment varies significantly: between half an hour and 70 hours during one to ten days. Through a national model, quality of testing could be assured also for those who do not organize tests on a daily basis, and the length of testing would be equal for all test takers.

Language tests typically take all sub-skills into account. However, the duration of testing sub-skills varies greatly, from five to 90 minutes in different skills.

When it comes to testing readiness for study and learning, all institutions who answered the question used some kind of reading aloud/mechanical reading test and dictation test. Mathematics, visuo-spatial functions and hand-eye coordination, as well as morphological reasoning were also often tested. However, other test types were also mentioned, adding to the huge variation in what skills institutions test.

As we can see, the methods of testing utilised vary greatly nationwide. This is probably as a result of lack of clear coordination at the national level, as there are also different needs in different regions. The regions are also quite independent in how they implement placement assessment. Even though legislation and curricula are current, it seems that there is a need to examine how they are interpreted and implemented at the regional level in different parts of Finland.

From the point of view of migrants it would be beneficial to have a unified system in placement assessment so that when people move within the country, the information "follows" them, and there is no need to take yet another test. There would also be equal opportunities to be guided to the most suitable training and proceed to employment.

## 7.2 Placement assessment procedure

One outcome of the project is the placement assessment procedure, which is currently based on the model developed by Testipiste. Over time the model will undergo research-based development in CALS. The current model is illustrated in Figure 2.

The test day starts with an interview where background information is elicited, such as gender, age, L1, previous education, number of languages known and studied, length of residence in Finland etc. During the interview there are also tests in mechanical reading, word dictation and speaking. If a test taker appears to have low literacy it is possible to guide them to literacy tests.

After that there are tests in morphological reasoning and basic mathematics for all. If a person already knows some Finnish, they take language tests (writing, reading and listening). The end result is the track and module recommendation of suitable integration training for employment services. From employment services a person is then guided to training. This requires functional cooperation

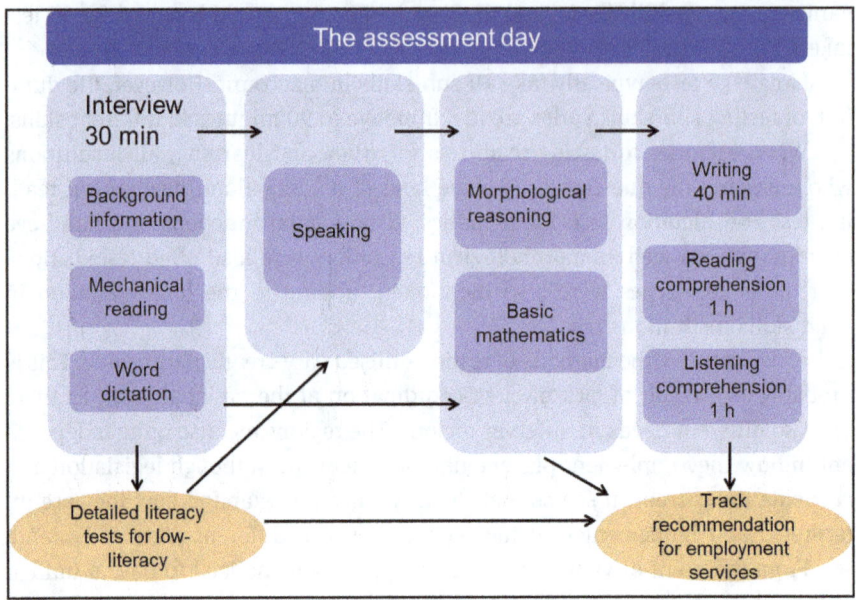

**Figure 2:** Placement assessment procedure

between employment services, the test administrator and schools/integration training teachers.

However, during the project we got the impression that it is possibly not always so clear if all the tests used are in fact useful or needed. More research-based information is needed, so for Georgetown University Round Table (GURT) we undertook a small-scale study which indicates that, e.g., word dictation in the Finnish language does not seem to be a good predictor of the suitable study track (Tammelin-Laine et al. 2016). We still need more data to verify this, but this is an example of the kind of research-based information that is needed to find out which tests are the most important.

Furthermore, from research (e.g., Tarone, Bigelow & Hansen 2009) we know that literacy in L1 has an effect on the development of both oral and written skills when learning a new language. Therefore, we are looking into the possibility of adding a test of reading in L1 to the test model.

# 8 Discussion

After the planning project presented in this article, a new project has started with the goal of implementing the national model. A network of interested administrators of tests has started to take shape, the existing test package is undergoing careful scrutiny, and training of test administrators will start in the near future. The ultimate goal is to extend these activities from their initial project base to permanent interventions.

During the planning project it became clear that general assessment literacy needs attention. The Centres for Economic Development need to be more aware of issues related to placement assessment because those who administer it are chosen based on competitive tendering in different regions. The quality of assessment should be the priority criterion for tendering rather than financial cost. If there is a national model for assessment then criteria like the competence of the testers (experience), how well testers know the region and its integration training, and whether the testers cooperate with the trainers/teachers in interpreting test results, are of paramount importance.

Finally, the goal of the national test system is to assure equality to all test takers and to develop assessment literacy in general.

# References

Finnish Immigration Service. http://www.migri.fi/tietoa_virastosta/tilastot/turvapaikka-_ja_pakolaistilastot (accessed 19 May 2016).

Ohranen, Sari, Heidi Vaarala, Ari Huhta, Kristel Kivisik, Marja Feller & Elina Stordell. 2015. *Selvitys aikuisten maahanmuuttajien suomen/ruotsin kielen taidon arvioinnista: suunnitelma kotoutumiskoulutuksen lähtötason arviointimallin valtakunnallistamisesta* [A report on assessment of Finnish/Swedish language skills of adult migrants: A plan for a national model of placement assessment in integration training]. Soveltavan kielentutkimuksen keskus: Jyväskylän yliopisto. https://www.jyu.fi/hum/laitokset/solki/tutkimus/julkaisut/pdf-julkaisut/kotoarviointimalli (accessed 19 May 2016).

Statistic Finland. https://www.stat.fi/tup/maahanmuutto/index.html/maahanmuuttajat-vaestossa/vieraskieliset (accessed 19 May 2016).

Tammelin-Laine, Taina, Ari Huhta, Sari Ohranen, Reeta Neittaanmäki, Tuija Hirvelä & Elina Stordell. 2016. Predicting placement accuracy and language outcomes in immigrants' L2 Finnish education. Paper presented at Georgetown University Round Table (GURT), 11–13 March.

Tarone, Elaine, Martha Bigelow & Kit Hansen. 2009. *Literacy and second language oracy.* Oxford: Oxford University Press.

6 **Language and the workplace**
Les langues sur le lieu de travail

Anke Settelmeyer
# What management assistants of retail services and medical assistants need to read, write, speak and listen to in the workplace

**Abstract:** Requirement analysis is an empirical method to achieve systematically detailed information about the written and oral requirements employees have to master in the workplace. A few examples may illustrate that they contribute to the transparency of linguistic and communicative requirements. They provide an empirical base to develop language proficiency systematically in courses or in the workplace.

**Résumé :** Les analyses des besoins sont une méthode empirique qui permet d'obtenir de façon systématique des informations détaillées sur ce que les salariés doivent maîtriser sur leur lieu de travail à l'oral et à l'écrit. Quelques exemples montrent qu'elles contribuent à la transparence des besoins langagiers et de communication. Elles constituent une base empirique pour développer de façon systématique les compétences langagières en cours ou sur le lieu de travail.

## 1 Introduction

The European Commission highlights linguistic and communicative skills as key competencies, for learning in education, training and in a profession, for social inclusion and employment. Research has therefore been done on skills and competences needed in the workplace. Some of the studies reveal competences that individuals possess or should possess. Others are requirement analyses and focus on situations revealing what employees or trainees need to read, write, speak and listen to in the workplace. This article endeavours to demonstrate that requirement analyses may contribute to the transparency of linguistic and communicative requirements in the workplace and constitute therefore an empirical base to reflect on linguistic integration of migrants.

**Anke Settelmeyer,** Federal Institute for Vocational Education and Training, Bonn, Germany,
E-mail: settelmeyer@bibb.de

## 2 Requirement analyses and the linguistic integration of adult migrants

Lessons for the linguistic integration of adult migrants in the workplace can be learned from two categories of requirement analyses – those with a migrant-specific and those with a non-migrant-specific approach.

### 2.1 Requirement analyses with a migrant-specific approach

These studies mainly focus on jobs with a high percentage of migrant employees, especially on jobs with low qualification requirements in industry or in the cleaning sector (Grünhage-Monetti 2010). In addition, there are studies that focus on potential job opportunities for migrants. In Germany, the intention is that doctors and nurses recruited from abroad should fill the growing shortage of employees in this branch. Since linguistic and communicative competences are indispensable for these professions, migrants must pass a language test if they wish to access to one of these occupations. Requirement analyses are a prerequisite for the development of such tests. In any case, requirement analyses are also used to develop language courses.

### 2.2 Requirement analyses with a non-migrant-specific approach

Alongside research on writing in the workplace, such as that performed by police officers or lawyers (Jakobs 2005), and on specific types of conversation, e.g. in the medical sector, there are more recent studies that examine oral and written requirements trainees need to fulfil at the learning venues of the company and the vocational school. Research on vocational training is carried out because the poor levels of literacy and communicative competences revealed by PISA and other studies in schools could have a negative impact on training outcomes.

While migrant-specific requirement analyses focus on a narrow range of occupations, studies with a non-migrant-specific approach widen the range of occupations investigated to include, for example, design draughtsmen, industrial mechanics, electronics technicians, and occupations in the medical and the retail sector. Studies with a non-migrant-specific approach thus might open up new vistas for the linguistic integration and, moreover, for the employment of migrants in general.

The findings presented in this article are based on a study of the linguistic and communicative requirements trainees need to manage at companies and vocational schools. The study was carried out by the Federal Institute for Vocational Education and Training. Data was collected using document analysis, participant observation and qualitative interviews with stakeholders. Investigating management assistants for retail services (clothes), motor vehicle mechatronics technicians, and medical assistants (general surgery), the sample covers different branches and occupations with high participation rates (Settelmeyer, Widera, and Efing 2014). Since this article omits linguistic and communicative requirements that relate exclusively to training situations, such as record books, the results are applicable both to trainees and employees.

# 3 Describing linguistic requirements

After outlining the daily operations that comprise linguistic and communicative requirements, the requirements of some typical and relevant operations will be described in more detail.[1]

## 3.1 Management assistants for retail services

Management assistants for retail services need to master the following tasks:
- merchandise management – e.g. control stock, check incoming merchandise, and transfer stock;
- communication with customers – e.g. sell, reserve and exchange goods, deal with complaints, and work at the checkout service area;
- communication within the company – e.g. deal with letters from management, new suppliers or trade unions, organise and improve daily work;
- training activities in some companies – informal activities such as reading journals and sometimes formal training such as communication with customers.

Checking incoming merchandise is one typical operation within merchandise management. Trainees/employees need to read attentively delivery notes (highly structured texts, often set out as a table, with long numbers and technical terms in some cases) and tick off articles or make short notes if an article is missing or

---

[1] I would like to thank Kerstin Schneider for her many suggestions.

damaged. The requirements with regard to transferring stock from one branch office to another in a chain store are very similar.

One of the predominant activities of a management assistant is communication with customers in order to sell clothes and accessories. They need to welcome customers in a polite and adequate manner. When the customer asks for help, the management assistant starts a consultation following a conventional sequence, probably using the wording of the company. Enquiring about the demands of the customer, they listen attentively to what the customer says, both explicitly and non-explicitly. Management assistants need to use an adequate register regarding the stock, the department – young fashion or exclusive clothes – and the customer. In any case, utterances should be respectful, polite, diplomatic and confidential, sometimes humorous or calming, if the customer is under stress. Moreover, management assistants need to reveal their expertise by using technical terms, if this is appropriate, to provide information on the product. In addition, interviewees highlight the importance of being authentic in conversations: "Because if we say that you [the trainee] have to tell it the customer this way, it won't work. The conversation would be artificial. Not authentic." Hence management assistants have to create their own style of communication with customers in order to get in touch with them.

## 3.2 Medical assistants

The daily work of medical assistants covers the following:
- receiving and guiding patients – e.g. welcome patients, organise workflows and monitor time schedules;
- carrying out diagnostics and treatment – e.g. assist in examinations, treatment and emergency cases, conduct laboratory work;
- working "backstage" – e.g. perform administrative work, procure and manage materials requirements;
- communication in a common space – e.g. pick up or give instructions, ask questions currently. This space is indispensable in order to delegate special tasks rapidly and to reorganise work as the need arises.

*At reception* – At reception, medical assistants enquire about the demands of the patients arriving for surgery. If necessary, they complete personal data of the patient in the computer and note whether there are any problems. They then ask the patient to sit down in the waiting room or in front of the surgery. When patients enter the surgery just to pick up a prescription, the medical assistant makes out the prescription by opening the data sheet of the patient and choosing the drugs needed. The prescription is generated and printed out by the computer. All this work has to be done rapidly in order to avoid queues of patients at reception. Moreover, medical assistants need to monitor appointments in the time schedule accurately, arrange a doctor's appointment with the patient, and write down the name of the patient or erase names when appointments are cancelled.

Conversation with patients needs to be polite and friendly. Because of the great number of patients, medical assistants have to avoid longer conversations with patients. This means that short utterances dominate. Medical assistants need to master a lot of routine tasks with recurrent wording and sometimes special tasks, such as rejecting the demand of a patient. All day long, they make short notes with to do's in order to record things that they need to deal with later.

*Working "backstage"* – In contrast to the requirements described above, working "backstage" comprises a lot of writing and reading. Medical assistants need to complete the data sheet of patients after a hospital stay or treatment by a specialist. They fill in information they ascertain from the doctor's letters, e.g. diagnosis or new drugs the patient needs to take, although this type of text full of technical terms primarily addresses the physician rather than a medical assistant. Moreover, they need to document treatment procedures by entering technical codes into the data sheet of the patient, a standardised and structured form. They therefore sometimes need to consult a manual to find the right number. In order to ask for further information, they phone specialist surgeries, hospitals or pharmacies. They have to fill in a great variety of prescription forms, sometimes with special needs, e.g. orthopaedic shoes. Finally, medical assistants procure and manage material requirements by writing e-mails to suppliers to requisition articles such as toner cartridges or bandage material. They use an adequate register and meet the formal and content-related conventions of this type of text. All the work needs to be done very carefully and correctly, faults can damage the health of patients.

The work processes in the surgeries visited were organised efficiently so that the work could be done rapidly. Short oral and highly formalized written utterances perfectly complemented the organisation of work in these settings.

# 4 Conclusions for the linguistic integration of adult migrants

The main purpose of the symposium on the linguistic integration of adult migrants organised by the Council of Europe in 2016 was to discuss to what extent and in what ways scientific evidence can be used to support the linguistic integration of adult migrants. In this article, the substantial contribution of requirement analyses was described.

Requirement analyses reveal systematically and in a differentiated way what written and oral utterances are like. The examples illustrate that the linguistic requirements management assistants for retail services and medical assistants need to manage vary enormously both within the occupation and between occupations. Requirement analyses provide an empirical basis for conceptualizing occupation-specific language courses and developing learning materials, such as scenarios, that fit closely to the wide range of linguistic needs at the workplace.

Linguistic requirements in the workplace can be interpreted as a meaningful and relevant input to improve linguistic competences. Managing requirements in the workplace also means acquiring occupation-specific language proficiency. From this point of view, the company is one important learning venue to develop these competences. Up to now in Germany, improving linguistic competences and working in the company have often been seen separately. Firstly, migrants need to participate in a language course, partly via internships in companies, then they have to look for work. Only a few training models promote combinations of work and language learning in the workplace. Unfortunately, employees do not usually acquire in the workplace the occupation-specific theoretical knowledge that is indispensable to a better understanding of workplace procedures. Training models that support language acquisition and theoretical instruction in the workplace should be developed and tested.

# References

Grünhage-Monetti, Matilde. 2010. *Sprachlicher Bedarf von Personen mit Deutsch als Zweitsprache in Betrieben*. Bonn: Deutsches Institut für Erwachsenenbildung.

Jakobs, Eva M. 2005. Texte im Berufsalltag: Schreiben, um verstanden zu werden. In Hardarik Blühdorn, Eva Breindl & Ulrich H. Waßner (eds.), *Text – Verstehen: Grammatik und darüber hinaus*, 315–331. Berlin: De Gruyter.

Settelmeyer, Anke, Christina Widera & Christian Efing. 2014. Linguistic and communicative requirements in vocational education and training. Poster presented at the *Applied Linguistics and Professional Practice Conference*, Geneva, 10–12 September. https://www2.bibb.de/bibbtools/tools/dapro/data/documents/verweise/so_22304%20Poster.pdf (accessed 23 May 2016).

Aurélie Bruneau
# Langues et insertions : pluralité des parcours et des perceptions

Appropriations langagières, sociales et professionnelles de femmes migrantes

**Résumé :** La plupart des discours relatifs à l'intégration des migrants mettent en exergue la nécessité de « maîtriser » la langue du pays d'accueil, qui devient un sésame préalable à toute intégration. Or, il semble que ce n'est pas tant un code linguistique que des phénomènes sociolinguistiques qui permettent de donner sens à des formes d'affiliation, d'appartenance et de participation sociale. Ce texte a pour objectif d'interroger des processus d'appropriation sociolangagière de femmes migrantes visant des projets d'insertion professionnelle pluriels.

**Abstract:** Most discussions about the integration of migrants highlight the need for them to "master" the language of the host country, which becomes an "open sesame" for their subsequent integration. In actual fact, it seems that it is not so much a linguistic code but socio-linguistic factors which help give a meaning to forms of affiliation, belonging and social participation. The purpose of this article is to examine the processes involved in socio-linguistic acquisition by female migrants with diverse employment integration projects.

Cette contribution s'articule autour de deux questionnements issus d'une réflexion portée sur les processus d'appropriation sociolinguistique de femmes migrantes (étrangères ou naturalisées) souhaitant travailler, au carrefour des phénomènes migratoires, développés par ailleurs dans une recherche doctorale au sein d'une collectivité locale française (Bruneau 2015). D'une part, dans quelle mesure le prisme dominant de la « maîtrise du français » induit-il aujourd'hui des formes de contrôle, de mise en concurrence et d'exclusion des individus cristallisant une conception unilatérale de l'intégration ? D'autre part, dans quelle mesure la part biographique et sensible influe-t-elle sur les processus d'appropriation langagière ?

---

**Aurélie Bruneau,** Université François Rabelais, Tours, EA 4246 PREFics-Dynadiv, E-mail : bruneauaurelie@orange.fr

DOI 10.1515/9783110477498-039, © 2017 Aurélie Bruneau, published by De Gruyter.
This work is licensed under the Creative Commons Attribution-NonCommercial-NoDerivs 3.0 License.

## 1 De l'accueil au contrôle sociolinguistique des individus : une injonction paradoxale ?

En regard des offres de formation linguistique, dans lesquelles les processus d'apprentissage sont relativement codifiés, il s'agissait de réfléchir à partir de récits d'expériences sociolinguistiques, d'histoires de pratiques langagières en contexte de migration afin d'entendre et comprendre des parcours *chaotiques* d'apprentissage du français en regard de projets de vie multiples (souvent mis sous silence par les personnes elles-mêmes). Cette perception contraste avec une idée communément répandue qu'il suffirait de suivre nombre d'heures d'apprentissage pour ensuite accéder à un emploi, être autonome dans ses démarches sociales et être intégré.

La notion d'accueil mobilisée couramment (société d'accueil, accueillir les étrangers) requiert une idée d'ouverture, voire d'adaptabilité. Or dans les faits, nous constatons que cette conception est plutôt figée. Il n'est qu'à lire les lois relatives à l'immigration et à l'intégration depuis 2007 pour souligner le caractère de contrôle et la place de la langue comme facteur d'exclusion. Autrement dit, aujourd'hui l'action publique considère l'acquisition du français tout à la fois comme un devoir pour accéder à une situation administrative pérenne et un préalable à une intégration pensée et normalisée par la société elle-même. Le Contrat d'Accueil et d'Intégration (CAI) en est une illustration. La langue est alors un moyen d'accéder à des statuts administratifs et non une manière d'être aux autres, de s'émanciper. À ce propos, Van der Meulen (2012 : 66) met en évidence qu'entre 2003 (expérimentation du CAI) et 2007 (généralisation en France), l'apprentissage du français est passé d'une « nécessité » à une « exigence de l'intégration ». En résumé, le CAI s'inscrit au cœur de présupposés idéologiques posant le risque d'une menace de la cohésion sociale par le défaut d'intégration – linguistique – des étrangers. De plus, ce dernier exclut de fait les Européens, comme si ces derniers, du fait de leur appartenance européenne, étaient intrinsèquement prêts à vivre dans le pays et déjà compétents en langue.

Debono (2013) rappelle que la contractualisation des rapports sociaux est une tendance forte qui irrigue l'ensemble des politiques sociales visant à responsabiliser les individus. Dans ce processus, l'étranger doit prouver sa bonne volonté de venir résider en France, il doit montrer un engagement personnel. Ce parcours est construit sur des obligations, des éléments prescriptifs et quantifiables, *a priori* maîtrisables, prédictibles et stables. Or les parcours de vie explicités par les femmes rencontrées sont plus aléatoires et soulignent des projets de vie complexes. Cette mise en exergue de gage « de bonne volonté d'intégration » interroge de surcroît une société qui doute de sa capacité à intégrer

(Debono 2013). Des questions restent en suspens face à un État en voie de désengagement en termes d'accueil, comme celles notamment de la place accordée aux personnes non signataires, aux ressortissants de l'Union européenne. « La langue », en tant qu'objet stable, prédictible, aux contours homogènes, décontextualisé est désormais la clé de voûte de la politique d'intégration. Or, les récits des femmes rencontrées lors d'une formation de français langue professionnelle, répondant à certaines de leurs attentes en termes de projection professionnelle (dans le secteur de la petite enfance) et entrant en résonnance avec certaines expériences vécues, mettent en évidence le fait qu'elles peuvent investir le processus d'appropriation linguistique parce qu'elles se projettent dans un temps défiant le temps politique et institutionnel. De ce fait, je pose comme *a priori* le fait que les situations sociales et les phénomènes linguistiques ne sont pas prédictibles, donc ne peuvent être maîtrisables et maîtrisés.

## 2 Des affiliations socio-professionnelles à travers le prisme d'appropriations sociolinguistiques

En regard des contraintes et injonctions institutionnelles, les individus composent pour parvenir, de gré voire de force, à accéder à des cours de français, en situation formelle. Dans cette partie, je mettrai en évidence dans un premier temps les types de parcours d'apprentissage linguistique, puis à partir de ces éléments de contextualisation, j'interrogerai la notion d'appropriation linguistique.

Les 22 femmes retenues pour participer à la formation avaient l'idée de travailler auprès de jeunes enfants. Certaines d'entre elles avaient d'ailleurs quelques expériences antérieures. Elles sont arrivées en France, âgées de moins de 30 ans, entre 1975 et 2009, essentiellement par le regroupement familial, et se sont installées en région parisienne. La plupart sont originaires du Maghreb, d'Afrique francophone, d'Asie et d'Europe. Une seule est signataire du CAI, quand certaines relatent leur période de clandestinité ou encore d'acquisition de la nationalité française. La plupart sont déjà mères d'enfants nés pour la plupart peu de temps après leur arrivée en France. Leur profil linguistique est aussi très divers ; seules 4 d'entre elles précisent qu'elles ont appris le français avant leur arrivée en France et qu'elles en avaient un certain usage, essentiellement scolaire.

## 2.1 Des parcours d'apprentissage « chaotiques »

De manière générale, les femmes tendent à se définir comme « ne sachant pas ». Elles mettent en avant une incompétence voire une incapacité à communiquer, traduisant selon elles une forme d'incapacité à agir (du moins dans leurs représentations). Or cette incapacité d'action est plus profonde et se révèle toucher à des phénomènes d'ordre identitaire, si l'on sait entendre la part sensible exprimée par les femmes lorsqu'elles évoquent leur sentiment vis-à-vis de leur usage de la langue, leur illégitimité et insécurité linguistique. Lorsqu'elles explicitent leurs parcours, elles ont beaucoup de mal à reconstituer les étapes et à donner sens aux contenus. Une explication serait que d'un point de vue institutionnel (organismes de formation, associations), cela marque la difficulté d'articuler des offres pédagogiques et de rendre lisible leur activité afin d'identifier ce processus de formation, et d'expliciter le sens donné au projet d'apprentissage.

À partir des éléments partagés avec ces femmes, je retiendrai quatre parcours types d'apprentissage linguistique :
- participation aux cours de proximité animés par des bénévoles (quelques centaines d'heures décousues depuis leur arrivée) ;
- de l'atelier de proximité à la formation intensive en centre de formation (sans articulation) ;
- des passages en centres de formation (cumuls de milliers d'heures) ;
- de la formation intensive à la découverte de cours de proximité.

Ces schémas reconstitués mettent en évidence, d'une part, la disparité des parcours et le fait d'une appropriation individuelle toute relative. D'autre part, ces parcours sont faits de ruptures, d'incohérences entre les propositions et les attentes des personnes. Enfin, les projets de formation, d'apprentissage et de vie ne semblent pas être mis en lien, interrogés ni par les participantes elles-mêmes, ni par les acteurs les entourant. À cela s'ajoute le fait que plusieurs femmes présentent leurs activités de socialisation (autour de l'enfant, de la maternité) ou professionnelle avant même d'apprendre cette langue. Ce dernier point met donc en évidence des enjeux d'appropriation langagière en situation d'immersion quotidienne.

## 2.2 Des phénomènes d'appropriation sociolinguistiques trans-formatifs

La part d'apprentissage informel (présence de tierces personnes, ressources linguistico-culturelles, etc.) est souvent peu explicitée, ce qui renforce l'absence de réflexion sur le processus d'appropriation, ramenant systématiquement le propos à un état de fait linguistique. Les témoins parlent généralement d'un état de leur pratique de la langue relativement décontextualisée de leurs usages. Peu portent un regard réflexif sur leur capacité (partielle) à interagir à l'oral et à l'écrit. Elles s'évaluent essentiellement en regard de sentiments (illégitimité d'être locutrice), de représentations scolaires d'une langue enseignée à travers la norme, de représentations de ce que doit être « le bon niveau » en regard de figures légitimes (qui sont très rarement celles de leur entourage), de représentations véhiculées par les discours des professionnels les entourant, évaluant leurs capacités sur un mode négatif.

Aujourd'hui, les courants méthodologiques sont traversés par des visées dominantes pragmatistes de « la langue » occultant la part relationnelle et identitaire du rapport aux pratiques langagières pour les personnes. Ils laissent peu de place à ce que les personnes sont, pensent être, veulent être notamment en ce qui concerne la question du locuteur qu'elles sont et souhaitent devenir. La conception à la fois techniciste (apprentissage d'un code de communication) et pragmatiste (apprendre en fonction de besoins prédéterminés par la société d'accueil) de la formation linguistique ne laisse pas l'opportunité de concevoir une approche ontologique, favorisant la rencontre et la relation *à* et *avec* l'autre. Les projets d'appropriation langagière ne sont pas questionnés dans le temps « immédiat » de la formation. Ainsi, comment inscrire une dimension historicisante portée fondamentalement dans une démarche d'appropriation *en* et *de* langues ? On en revient alors à rendre compte de la question des processus migratoires, car ces derniers interrogent autrement les processus d'appropriation des langues en questionnant inévitablement les histoires et les projets individuels et/ou collectifs mais toujours singuliers. Castellotti (2014) invite alors à « *diversaliser* les orientations en didactique des langues ».

De fait, les situations et les pratiques langagières sont diversement appréciées car chacun d'entre nous est porteur et vecteur d'expériences *de* et *en* langues, d'expériences liées au savoir et à l'éducation et de projets de vie ensemble et avec les autres à l'extérieur de cette sphère *trans*-formative. Dès lors, chaque participant doit s'interroger sur le sens de ce maillon formatif dans un projet de vie teinté d'expériences migratoires. Tant que le projet d'apprentissage n'est pas discuté, explicité avec les participants en lien avec leur projet de vie, l'accumulation d'heures de français, prescrites comme remèdes au mal d'intégration, restera en partie vaine.

Le processus d'appropriation contribue à la transformation des êtres humains à travers une mobilisation réflexive notamment de leur expérience linguistico-culturelle. Il ne s'agit pas d'un simple développement de connaissances, voire d'une compétence en français, comme ce qui peut être visé par l'acquisition. L'appropriation se réalise dans une transformation, car le changement se passe dans la relation *à* et *avec* l'autre et pas seulement aux autres langues, ni avec d'autres qui pourraient être perçus comme identiques à soi. Il s'agit d'un processus instable, contingent où le partiel est de mise. La relation est alors prise dans une acception large qui ne se limite pas aux interactions verbales ou sociales, ni aux échanges mais elle englobe tout ce qui fait cette relation. Le fait que ces femmes aient accepté l'idée de réfléchir à leur parcours, avant d'accéder à leur projet de métier, est un point positif. Cela met en lumière le travail d'historicisation de leur parcours. En arrivant, elles voulaient travailler, dans ce moment d'immédiateté, aux accents d'urgence et de principe d'irréalité. Or, elles ont pris la mesure de ce qu'elles savent (expériences sociolinguistiques, professionnelles antérieures), des contraintes ou au contraire, de leur point d'appui (la famille, les enfants, certains lieux ressources) et de ce qu'elles sont.

Ces éléments de compréhension de parcours d'appropriation langagière invitent dès lors à réfléchir autrement sur la notion même de langue, en tant que phénomènes langagiers souples, instables et hétérogènes. C'est une ouverture sur une perspective relationnelle, invitant à la prise en considération des héritages et expériences linguistiques. En ce sens, il s'agit de développer une démarche réflexive quant aux manières d'*être* aux autres, à ses pratiques et usages linguistiques ; d'accepter et de gérer l'imprévisible, l'instable, l'inattendu propre à chaque relation. La déconstruction de la notion de langue permet ainsi de sortir des logiques de « niveaux », de « compétences », comme morceaux de choix d'un objet désincarné et d'envisager (aussi) la dimension ontologique de la relation langagière.

Dès lors, il s'agit de travailler et réfléchir *avec des personnes*, historicisées. Ceci a pour conséquence des implications fortes sur les formes et les manières d'enseigner, de mener des recherches, de guider et d'accompagner la personne.

# Références

Bruneau, Aurélie. 2015. *Apprendre le français, s'approprier, s'intégrer au féminin dans le Val-de-Marne : enjeux éthiques, politiques et institutionnels.* Tours : UFR Tours, thèse de doctorat.

Castellotti, Véronique. 2014. Quelle(s) didactique(s) pour quel(s) plurilinguisme(s) ? In Christel Troncy (dir.), *Didactique du plurilinguisme. Approches plurielles des langues et des cultures*, 435–441. Rennes : Presses Universitaires de Rennes.

Debono, Marc 2013. Enjeux de la contractualisation des rapports sociaux : le cas de la politique d'accueil et d'intégration linguistico-culturelle des migrants. *Écarts d'identité* 122. 27–36.

Van der Meulen, Katia. 2012. *Analyse des parcours linguistiques des migrants signataires du contrat d'accueil et d'intégration*. Grenoble : Université Stendhal – Grenoble 3, thèse de doctorat.

Michele Gazzola
# Language skills and employment status of adult migrants in Europe

**Abstract:** Using official data from Eurostat, this article examines the relationship between adult migrants' language skills and their integration in the European labour market. We use migrants' employment status as an indicator for integration. Results reveal that migrants who have good or very good skills in the official language of the host country are more likely to have better employment status than those with limited or no language skills. EU migrants tend to be better integrated than non-EU migrants.

**Résumé :** L'article s'appuie sur les données officielles d'Eurostat pour examiner la corrélation entre les compétences langagières des migrants adultes et leur intégration dans le marché européen de l'emploi. La situation des migrants en termes d'emploi sert d'indicateur de l'intégration. Les résultats montrent que les migrants qui ont de bonnes ou de très bonnes connaissances de la langue officielle du pays d'accueil ont des chances de décrocher un meilleur emploi que ceux qui ont des compétences langagières limitées ou nulles. Les migrants issus de l'Union européenne ont tendance à mieux s'intégrer que ceux de pays tiers.

# 1 Introduction[1]

In recent years, the question of migrants' language skills has become a topical issue in Europe. Language skills are viewed as a condition for migrants to be socially and economically integrated in the host country, and as a factor contributing to the international mobility of EU citizens. For example, in many countries, non-EU citizens are required to show adequate language skills in the official lan-

---

[1] The financial support of the EU 7th Framework Programme (MIME project – grant agreement 613344) is gratefully acknowledged. The goal of the MIME project ("Mobility and Inclusion in a Multilingual Europe", 2014–2018) is to discuss the relationships between international mobility, inclusion and language skills in Europe (http://www.mime-project.org); see Grin et al. (2014).

**Michele Gazzola,** Research Group Economics and Language (REAL), Department of Education Studies, Humboldt-Universität zu Berlin, Germany/Institute for Ethnic Studies, Ljubljana, Slovenia, E-mail: michele@michelegazzola.com

DOI 10.1515/9783110477498-040, © 2017 Michele Gazzola, published by De Gruyter.
This work is licensed under the Creative Commons Attribution-NonCommercial-NoDerivs 3.0 License.

guage of the host country in order to obtain a residence permit or citizenship (see Pulinx, Van Avermaet, and Extramiana 2014). In the communication *A New Strategic Framework for Multilingualism* the European Commission (2005) presents skills in foreign languages as a pre-condition for the achievement of the common market. Empirical evidence tends to support this view. People who learn and speak the official language of a country as a foreign language are five times more likely to move to that country (Aparicio-Fenoll and Kuehn 2016). In addition, proficiency in the official language of the host country has a positive effect on migrants' labour income in a range of 5% to 35% (for an overview, see Adserà and Pytliková 2016; Gazzola, Grin, and Wickström 2016; Chiswick and Miller 2014). Drawing on official data published by Eurostat, this article addresses the question of the relationship between adult migrants' language skills and their social and economic integration in the host country. We use migrants' employment status as a proxy indicator for integration.

## 2 The language skills of adult migrants

We use data from the Adult Education Survey (AES) published by Eurostat in 2013. Our initial sample consists of 179,617 statistical observations (corresponding to 240.8 million people), of whom 8,431 are migrants (corresponding to 15.7 million people). We examine 26 European states, that is, the 28 Member States of the EU, excluding Croatia and the UK because of a lack of data. All definitions apply to residents of the EU aged 25–64 (base year 2011). The sample is divided into three groups: EU citizens living in their home country or "nationals" (93%); EU citizens living in another member state or "EU migrants" (3%); and non-EU migrants (4%). Migrants tend to be long-term residents in the host country: 45% of EU migrants and non-EU migrants alike have been living in the host country for more than 10 years; 23% of EU migrants and 26% of non-EU migrants for six to ten years. Only 5% of EU migrants and 2% of non-EU migrants have been living for only one year or less in the host country at the time of the survey.

Non-EU migrants are more likely to belong to the first deciles of the income distribution than nationals. This means that, in general, their income is lower than nationals'. On the other hand, differences between EU migrants and nationals in this respect tend to be small. Similarly, differences between nationals and EU migrants as regards the level of education they have successfully completed are not large, whereas non-EU migrants, on average, are less educated than nationals and EU migrants.

Table 1 presents the percentage of EU and non-EU migrants who declare that they do not know the official language of the host country (or any official language in multilingual countries) either as mother tongue or as a foreign language (the AES provides data on respondents' language skills in up to seven foreign languages). We report results only if the sample at the level of the individual country contains at least 100 statistical observations, excluding nationals. Table 1 reveals that 5% of migrants living in the 17 countries examined do not know the official language of the host country.[2] On average, lack of language skills is more likely among non-EU migrants (6%) than among EU migrants (4%). Large differences exist among countries in this respect. Table 1 presents results also for Switzerland. Although it is not an EU member state, it may be useful to consider it.

The AES contains data on the level of language proficiency in the first and second foreign languages spoken by respondents. Three proficiency levels are defined using "can do" descriptors. A *fair* level is defined as "I can understand and use the most common everyday expressions. I use the language in relation to familiar things and situations"; a *good* level is defined as "I can understand the essentials of clear language and produce simple text. I can describe experiences and events"; and a *proficient* level corresponds to "I can understand a wide range of demanding texts and use the language flexibly. I master the language almost completely". In Austria, Germany, Greece, Italy, Luxemburg, Portugal and Switzerland at least two thirds (66%) of migrants declare that they know at least one official language of the host country at a good or proficient level. In Belgium, Denmark, France, and Spain this percentage is at least 50%, whereas in Cyprus, Estonia, Ireland, Latvia, Slovenia, and Sweden it lies below 50%. EU migrants have better language skills in the official language of the host country than non-EU migrants, except for the Czech Republic and Switzerland.

## 3 Language skills and employment status

Good and very good language skills are associated with a better occupational status, both for EU and for non-EU migrants. We focus on respondents who participate in the labour market, that is, people with a job (either full-time or part-time) and the unemployed. In the 17 EU Member States examined, 87% of EU-migrants declaring a good or proficient level of competence in the official lan-

---

[2] Respondents declaring no knowledge of the local language were probably assisted during the interview.

**Table 1:** Percentage of migrants who cannot use (at least one of) the official language(s) of the host country (17 EU member states and Switzerland)

| Country | Official/dominant language(s) | EU migrants | Non-EU migrants | Tot migrants | Corresponding population | N |
|---|---|---|---|---|---|---|
| Austria | German | 1% | 3% | 2% | 11,132 | (549) |
| Belgium | Dutch, French, German | 7% | 16% | 10% | 64,458 | (432) |
| Cyprus | Greek, Turkish | 19% | 26% | 22% | 20,811 | (516) |
| Czech Rep. | Czech | 39% | 12% | 28% | 25,837 | (104) |
| Denmark | Danish | 7% | 21% | 15% | 27,696 | (220) |
| Estonia | Estonian | 48% | 60% | 60% | 68,892 | (544) |
| France | French | 8% | 14% | 12% | 271,813 | (739) |
| Germany | German | 2% | 2% | 2% | 98,565 | (316) |
| Greece | Greek | 0% | 1% | 1% | 2,643 | (257) |
| Ireland | Irish/English | 7% | 6% | 7% | 19,674 | (1,329) |
| Italy | Italian | 7% | 7% | 7% | 111,402 | (412) |
| Latvia | Latvian | 22% | 21% | 22% | 6,352 | (119) |
| Luxemburg | Luxembourgish, French, German | 1% | / | 1% | 354 | (441) |
| Portugal | Portuguese | 2% | 2% | 2% | 4,597 | (376) |
| Slovenia | Slovene | 17% | 14% | 14% | 6,658 | (126) |
| Spain | Spanish | 0% | 0% | 0% | 8,847 | (1,385) |
| Sweden | Swedish | 13% | 30% | 22% | 75,425 | (249) |
| **Total population** | | 262,347 | 562,809 | | **825,156** | *(8,114)* |
| **% migrants** | | 4% | 6% | 5% | | |
| Switzerland | French, German, Italian | 1% | 6% | 2% | 36,833 | (3,478) |

Source: Eurostat, AES (2013)

guage of the host country (or in at least one of its official languages) are employed; 13% are unemployed. By contrast, 78% of EU-migrants declaring no knowledge or only a fair level of knowledge of the official language have a job; 22% are unemployed.

Turning to non-EU migrants, 77% of respondents declaring good or very good skills in the official language of the host country are employed, whereas 23% are unemployed. These percentages are, respectively, 68% and 32%, in the group of non-EU migrants declaring no knowledge of the local language or only a fair level of competence in it. Results do not change if we focus only on men.

These figures support the results of the studies quoted in the introduction: generally speaking, good and very good skills in the official language(s) of the host country are more frequent among those who have a better employment status, both for EU and non-EU migrants.[3] Clearly, this link does not mean causal relationship because other variables play a role in explaining the employment status of migrants, for example education (which in turn is usually correlated to foreign language skills). In order to confirm these results, multivariate analysis is needed, but unfortunately the AES does not always contain enough observations at the individual country level to carry out such an analysis.

Let us note, in concluding, that 88% of EU citizens who live in their home country and who are active in the labour market are employed and 12% are unemployed. Therefore, the percentage of employed EU migrants with good or very good skills in the official language of the host country (87%) is very close to the percentage of nationals who have a job in their home country. This can be viewed as one sign of the effective functioning of the European Single Market and further evidence of the positive effect of good language skills on migrants' economic integration.

# References

Adserà, Alícia & Mariola Pytliková. 2016. Language and migration. In Victor Ginsburgh & Shlomo Weber (eds.), *The Palgrave handbook of economics and language*, 342–72. Basingstoke: Palgrave.
Aparicio-Fenoll, Ainhoa & Zoë Kuehn. 2016. Does foreign language proficiency foster migration of young individuals within the European Union? In Michele Gazzola & Bengt-Arne Wickström (eds.), *The economics of language policy*, 331–56. Cambridge, MA: MIT Press.
Chiswick, Barry R. & Paul W. Miller. 2014. International migration and the economics of language. In Barry R. Chiswick & Paul W. Miller (eds.), *Handbook of the economics of international migration*. Amsterdam: North Holland.
European Commission. 2005. *A New Framework Strategy for Multilingualism*. Brussels: European Commission.
Gazzola, Michele, François Grin & Bengt-Arne Wickström. 2016. A concise bibliography of language economics. In Michele Gazzola & Bengt-Arne Wickström (eds.), *The economics of language policy*, 53–92. Cambridge, MA: MIT Press.
Grin, François, László Marác, Nike K. Pokorn & Peter A Kraus. 2014. Mobility and inclusion in multilingual Europe: A position paper on the MIME project.

---

[3] Some exceptions exist nevertheless, notably in Cyprus, Luxemburg, and in the Czech Republic for EU migrants, and in Austria, Denmark, France, and Portugal for non-EU migrants. In Switzerland, we do not observe significant differences in employment status between migrants who speak at least one of the official Swiss languages at a good or proficient level and migrants with limited or no linguistic competences.

http://www.mime-project.org/resources/MIME-POSITION-PAPER-V4.pdf (accessed 14 July 2016).

Pulinx, Reinhilde, Piet Van Avermaet & Claire Extramiana. 2014. *Linguistic integration of adult migrants: Policy and practice*. Strasburg: Council of Europe.
https://rm.coe.int/CoERMPublicCommonSearchServices/DisplayDCTMContent?documentId=09000016802fc1ce (accessed 14 July 2016).

Matilde Grünhage-Monetti, Alexander Braddell
# "Integration ... needs language, the language of the workplace": The contribution of work-related second language learning to the integration of adult migrants

**Abstract:** Labour market inclusion is a primary goal of integration policy. For millions of adult migrants in Europe, learning the language of the country of residence (L2) is a key enabler of access to and progression within the labour market. The Language for Work Network (LfW) brings together professionals working in this area to share and improve work-related language learning for migrants and ethnic minorities. It was created through a project funded by the Council of Europe's European Centre for Modern Languages.

**Résumé :** L'intégration sur le marché du travail est un objectif prioritaire de la politique d'intégration. Pour des millions de migrants adultes en Europe, l'apprentissage de la langue du pays de résidence (L2) est un facilitateur essentiel de l'accès au marché du travail et de l'évolution professionnelle. Le Réseau La langue par et pour le travail permet aux professionnels de ce domaine de partager et d'améliorer l'apprentissage de la langue en lien avec le travail par les adultes migrants ou des minorités ethniques. Il a été créé par un projet financé par le Centre européen pour les langues vivantes du Conseil de l'Europe.

## 1 A European challenge

The integration of millions of adult migrants is a challenge for Europe and more so now following the recent influx of refugees. Integration courses are standard in many European countries. They aim to equip migrants with the necessary language skills to cope with everyday life in the new country. Typically, though they

---

**Matilde Grünhage-Monetti** (corresponding author), Deutsches Institut für Erwachsenenbildung – Leibniz-Zentrum für Lebenslanges Lernen, Germany, E-mail: matilde.monetti@unitybox.de
**Alexander Braddell**, OSEC CIC Ltd, Oxford, United Kingdom, E-mail: abraddell@gmail.com

DOI 10.1515/9783110477498-041, [CC BY-NC-ND] © 2017 Matilde Grünhage-Monetti, Alexander Braddell, published by De Gruyter.
This work is licensed under the Creative Commons Attribution-NonCommercial-NoDerivs 3.0 License.

may touch on e.g. job-search, they do not claim to prepare learners for the labour market, let alone for a specific occupation.

In some European countries, labour force shortages and population ageing is leading to a growing concern for sustainable labour market integration of adult migrants. Communications skills in the majority language of the country of residence (L2) are widely recognized as a key enabler in the fight against exclusion from *and* within employment.

In response to this challenge, a range of approaches to work-related L2 learning for adult migrants is emerging across Europe, including
- pre-employment L2 learning for immigrants and in some countries for emigrants;
- L2 learning in vocational schools;
- L2 learning for specific occupational areas, and qualifications; and
- workplace L2 learning.

Work-related L2 learning is a complex, boundary crossing field. In addition to language learning, it encompasses work, migration, intercultural communication, social policy, didactics, literacy, linguistics, vocational education and training (VET), workforce development, management ... and more. It is shaped by policies regulating these diverse fields and is informed by a range of disciplines, from linguistics and educational sciences to the sociology of work.

## 2 Why work-related L2 learning?

The logic chain underlying this multi-dimensional field recognizes integration of migrants as essential for social inclusion. Work is central to migrant integration and communication is central to modern work practices. In today's workplaces employees need to understand safety and quality issues and workplace rights and responsibilities. They need to participate in relevant social networks, access training to cope with change and to improve career prospects. The ability to communicate effectively at work is crucial for migrants, employers, colleagues, customers, etc. The words of a Swedish care sector employer, "Better language skills, better care!" (SGRC 2011), encapsulate how improving the language skills of both migrant and native-speaker employees benefits the wider society too.

A group of researchers and practitioners, committed to the principles of inclusion and social justice and aware of how central work is to adult life and of the importance of communication in modern work practices, had the idea of networking professionals in Europe engaged in work-related L2 learning. With support between 2012 and 2015 from the Council of Europe's European Centre for

Modern Languages (ECML), the group created the Language for Work Network (LfW), an international network of researchers, practitioners, policy makers and others involved in the field. Now the group has won further support from the ECML for a follow-up project (2016–2018).

The aim of LfW is to promote and develop this area of linguistic integration, which is expected only to grow in importance during the years to come. Through its website (http://languageforwork.ecml.at) and programme of activities, LfW shares research, policy and practice across Europe, supporting the full range of practitioners engaged in this field.

## 3 Work as a vehicle for language learning

From both research and practice we know that, with the right support, work can provide an effective environment for language learning (Grünhage-Monetti, Halewijn, and Holland 2003; Arakelian and Braddell 2005; Extramiana 2012). It offers both the exposure to authentic language and opportunities for interaction that learners need, and the support, through management systems and team working, they require. For adult migrants, L2 development for, at and, particularly, through work has proved an efficient and sustainable instrument towards integration.

## 4 One issue, three projects

### 4.1 Odysseus and LfW 1

The earliest iteration of LfW came as long ago as 2000, with the ECML-sponsored Odysseus project, which brought together professionals who recognised the value of work-related language learning for migrants and ethnic minorities (Grünhage-Monetti 2003). This led to the first Language for Work project (2012–2015), "Developing migrants' language competences at work" (LfW 1), coordinated by a team of researchers and practitioners from Germany, France, Spain and the UK.

The project set out to create a European learning network for professionals interested in work-related L2, on the basis that we can all benefit from Europe's rich diversity of approaches to linguistic integration of adult migrants, as well as the diversity of its labour market structures and policies. A website was planned to operationalise the network, and three consultative meetings were organised to establish the network and develop the website.

The first consultative meeting, in 2012, attracted 20 specialists from 12 European countries. Specialists included civil servants, researchers, learning providers, trade unionists, and educational publishers. Knud Illeris, the Danish learning psychologist, introduced his research findings on workplace learning from the learners' perspective (Illeris 2011).

A year later, 26 specialists from 14 European countries attended the second consultative meeting. The workplace learning researcher Lorna Unwin (University of London) shared the "learning as work" model she and colleagues have developed (Felstead et al. 2011).

The final meeting, in 2015, at the close of the project, was attended by 46 specialists from 32 European countries. Guest speaker was Laurent Filliettaz (University of Geneva), who presented his findings on L2 learning in vocational apprenticeships together with insights from Australian researchers, such as Stephen Billet.

The consultative focus of these meetings was the purpose of a network and the functioning of the proposed network: Would a network be helpful? How should it function? What contribution should it aim to make? (Figure 1)

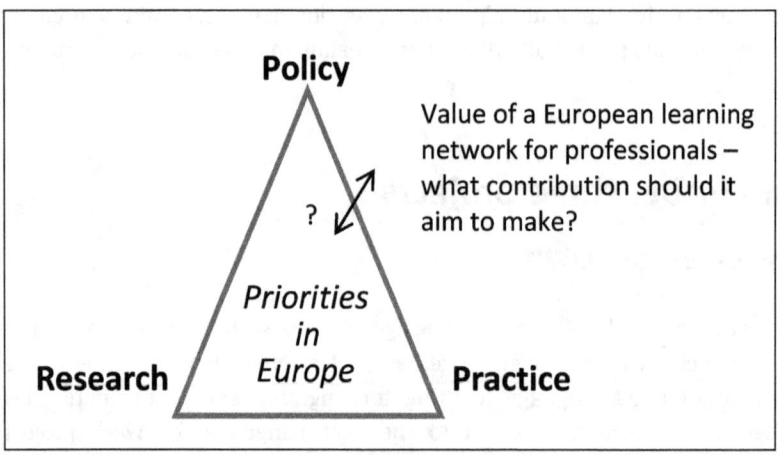

**Figure 1:** Consultative focus of Language for Work project meetings

Outcomes confirmed the demand for a network in Europe to raise awareness of the importance of work-related L2 learning for integration; to enable sharing of experience and resources; and to develop expertise. Objectives identified for the network included advocacy to promote awareness of work-related L2 learning at national and European levels; development of theoretical/conceptual models, of practice models and of quality frameworks; and provision of expertise, resources and professional development opportunities.

In addition, these meetings also tested iterations of the website developed by the project team (with technical support from the ECML). This website now comprises a resource centre with scientific, practical and policy-related resources, as well as a community section to support active networking. The network and the website were the major products of LfW 1.

At the time of writing, the LfW network consists of 75 members from 23 countries.

## 4.2 Language for Work 2 – Tools for professional development (2016 – 2018)

Now a follow-up project, titled "Language for Work – Tools for professional development" (2016 – 18) and again supported by the ECML, aims to build on this success. It is prompted by the new approaches to work-related L2 learning that are starting to emerge across Europe. These approaches, many of which are not widely known, have the potential to significantly widen the participation of adult migrants in L2 learning. Some of the approaches take established methodologies and adapt them. Others are wholly innovative, focusing on non-formal and informal learning. All make new professional demands on practitioners.

The new LfW project (LfW 2) aims to help equip practitioners to access these new approaches and so benefit both adult migrants and the wider societies where they live. Coordinated by LfW network members from Germany, France, Sweden and the UK, the project will create tools and resources to support the professional development of teachers, teacher educators and other practitioners in the field of work-related L2. It will use the learning network created by LfW 1 to make its outputs (which will include a professional development framework) accessible to practitioners.

To support refugee integration, the project will also develop a "quick guide" with key underlying principles and a selection of effective approaches (including non-formal and informal approaches) to support work-related L2 learning. All products will be made available online via the LfW Network's website (http://languageforwork.ecml.at/).

We end this paper with a quote from a participant at the closing meeting of LfW 1 in 2015: "What is particularly useful for me is the possibility to have access to an international network of professionals teaching a second language for work-related purposes" (Gorza Maisy, National Institute for Languages, Luxembourg) – and with an invitation to colleagues across Europe to join the network to share and develop practice in an area of considerable importance and rich potential for the linguistic integration of adult migrants.

## References

Arakelian, Catharine & Alexander Braddell. 2005. Bite-size adventures in the workplace. *Basic Skills Bulletin* 37. 6–8. http://languageforwork.ecml.at/Portals/48/HtmlTagFiles/7cb07e08–8393–4fc6–8394–2c8b3813ad55.pdf (accessed 20 June 2016).

Extramiana, Claire. 2012. *Learning the language of the host country for professional purposes: Outline of issues and educational approaches.* Strasbourg: Council of Europe. https://rm.coe.int/CoERMPublicCommonSearchServices/DisplayDCTMContent?documentId=09000016802faa70 (accessed 28 July 2016).

Felstead, Allan, Alison Fuller, Nick Jewson & Lorna Unwin. 2011. *Praxis 7: Working to learn, learning to work.* London: UK Commission for Employment and Skills.

Grünhage-Monetti, Matilde, Elwine Halewijn & Chris Holland. 2003. *Odysseus – Second language at the workplace; Language needs of migrant workers: organising language learning for the vocational/workplace context.* Strabourg: Council of Europe Publishing. http://archive.ecml.at/documents/pub125E2003GruenhageMonetti.pdf (accessed 20 June 2016).

Illeris, Knud. 2011. *The fundamentals of workplace learning: Understanding how people learn in working life.* Abingdon: Routledge.

LfW Network's website: http://languageforwork.ecml.at/ (accessed 20 June 2016).

SGRC (Stockholm Gerontology Research Center). 2011. *Better language skills, better care – SpråkSam is leading the way.* Stockholm: SGRC.

Alexander Braddell, Linda Miller

# Supporting migrants in low-paid, low-skilled employment in London to improve their English

**Abstract:** This paper describes research carried out in 2013 to identify the barriers to and enablers of English language development for migrants in low-paid, low-skilled employment in London, with a view to making practical recommendations on how to help this group improve their English. Sixty migrants were interviewed about their experiences of and preferences for English language learning. Work emerged as a key location for learning, along with a clear set of requirements to support language development in the workplace.

**Résumé :** Nous présentons les recherches faites en 2013 pour identifier les barrières et facilitateurs pour le développement de l'anglais pour les migrants ayant des emplois peu rémunérés et peu qualifiés à Londres, l'objectif étant de formuler des recommandations pratiques sur la manière d'aider ce groupe à consolider ses compétences en anglais. Soixante migrants ont été interrogés sur leur expérience de l'apprentissage de l'anglais et leurs préférences en la matière. L'emploi s'est avéré un lieu d'apprentissage essentiel, avec un ensemble clair de besoins pour soutenir le développement de la langue au travail.

## 1 Introduction

In 2009 the Greater London Authority (GLA), the administrative body for Greater London, published an integration strategy for refugees, migrants and asylum seekers. This strategy made access to "appropriate" English language tuition its primary objective (GLA 2009). Updated in 2013, the strategy reaffirmed that "increasing access to learning English has been, and remains, the key priority" (GLA 2013a: 7). In particular, the strategy prioritised support for "low paid workers to improve their English language skills and move into higher level jobs" and

---

**Alexander Braddell,** OSEC CIC Ltd, Oxford, United Kingdom (corresponding author),
E-mail: abraddell@gmail.com
**Linda Miller,** Institute for Employment Studies, London, United Kingdom,
E-mail: drlindamiller@outlook.com

DOI 10.1515/9783110477498-042, [CC BY-NC-ND] © 2017 Alexander Braddell, Linda Miller, published by De Gruyter.
This work is licensed under the Creative Commons Attribution-NonCommercial-NoDerivs 3.0 License.

advocacy for "innovative English language learning across London to support local integration" (GLA 2013a: 14).

Initial research commissioned to support the strategy noted "huge unmet demand" for English language learning (Gidley and Jayaweera 2010: 6), despite significant government investment from 2001 on (Gidley and Jayaweera 2010: 44); it also noted that low-paid workers were among the groups "disproportionately" affected by subsequent cuts to funding for English language provision (Gidley and Jayaweera 2010: 45) and identified a need "to more closely engage business and employers in the [English language learning] field, both in terms of investment and in terms of creating opportunities for learners" (Gidley and Jayaweera 2010: 47).

The GLA commissioned two further studies on English language learning by migrants. The first (NIACE 2012) investigated ways to support learners unable to access free provision, including migrants in low-paid work, who were often unable to attend college classes due to long work hours or high course fees and who rarely had access to workplace provision (NIACE 2012: 7–8). The study proposed three additional models of provision: family learning, on-line learning and volunteer befriending (NIACE 2012: 10–18).

The second study focused specifically on the needs of migrants in low-paid, low-skilled work. Prompted by the GLA's concern that this group be able to access and progress within the labour market, it aimed to identify enablers and barriers to English language learning and suggest what approaches might help these migrants improve their English. This paper is based on research undertaken for that second study (GLA 2013b).

## 2 Research

The research remit was to identify a sample of migrants with no or low levels of English, in low-paid, low-skilled work, where the migrant's level of English was a barrier to increasing hours/pay, vocational training or applying for higher skilled or preferred jobs. The sample was to include both migrants who were not managing to learn or improve their English and those who had found ways to do so. Low-paid work was defined as work paid at or below the London Living Wage (then £8.55 per hour). Low-skilled work was defined as work requiring educational attainment at no more than level 2 of the UK national credit and qualification framework (European Qualification Framework level 3) (GLA 2013b).

Between March and May 2013, the research team conducted one-to-one, face-to-face interviews with 60 migrants, recruited via employers, trade unions and migrant support organisations. A semi-structured discussion guide was used to elicit information about informants' work arrangements, their experiences of and preferences for English language learning. Following each interview the researchers assigned an estimate of the informant's spoken English ability, using the *Common European Framework of Reference for Languages* (CEFR; Council of Europe 2001). These ranged from A1 to C2, but the majority fell between A1 and B1. Fifteen individuals required full interpretation, two required part interpretation.

Fifty informants (31 females, 19 males) were in low-paid, low-skilled jobs (cleaners, care workers, kitchen assistants, admin assistants, bar tenders, builders, nannies, nursery nurse assistants, sales assistants and shop assistants). Just over half worked full time. Average hourly pay was £6.89. The other ten informants (7 females, 3 males), having found ways to improve their English, had progressed to jobs requiring intermediate level skills (HR assistants, business administrators, community workers). Female informants were aged between 17 and 65; males between 25 and 40. Some had left school without qualifications; others had post-graduate and professional qualifications. Many informants reported speaking two or more languages other than English. Only one reported using English at home with their family. Individuals had been resident in England for between three months and 40 years and collectively originated from 30 countries. Just over two-thirds hoped to live permanently in the UK with the remainder either unsure or planning to move to another country one day.

# 3 Findings

All informants reported that their level of English was a significantly limiting factor in their lives, particularly in relation to work. This included the ten informants in jobs requiring intermediate-level skills, several of whom had a high level of spoken English.

Likewise, informants uniformly reported that they saw value in improving their level of English, particularly in relation to work, both to help them better cope and/or progress in their current employment and to secure preferred jobs (e. g. via vocational education and training).

Most informants had attended at least one English course, often on arrival in the UK. Few, however, had persisted with such courses after finding work and only a small minority of the 60 informants were attending formal English classes at the time of interview. These classes were outside of colleges, e. g. a volunteer-run Saturday class for trade union members.

Informants identified ten barriers to English language learning: difficulty finding suitable courses; cost of courses; inconvenient location/timing of courses; lack of time/energy (i.e. for courses/self-directed learning); lack of childcare; lack of support at work; lack of communicative opportunity at work; lack of support at home; lack of effective personal learning strategies; lack of confidence (to interact in English).

Collectively, these factors undermined informants' motivation to persist with formal English courses and, though the majority said that they intended to resume English classes at some future point, they could give no indication of how they might address the barriers they identified.

While most informants reported some informal self-directed learning, e.g. reading free newspapers, or watching English-language programmes with the English subtitles switched on, some reported little or none. Informants who had managed to improve their English sufficiently to escape low-paid employment typically reported the more active and varied personal learning strategies to support informal self-directed learning, together with a determination to interact in English in daily life.

Nine out of ten informants made frequent (in many cases daily) use of the internet, including using e-mail, Skype, Facebook, shopping online, reading the news. Most had a personal computer and those who did not, typically said they used a friend's laptop. Over two-thirds had a smartphone and many reported habitually using Google Translate and online dictionaries in daily activity. Most had access to the internet at work, including via personal smartphone, although some (e.g. residential care workers) were not meant to use personal devices on duty.

A number reported valuable ad hoc support for their learning from colleagues/managers at work and, outside work, family and friends. Those who felt they did not receive such support identified this as a barrier to their learning.

The majority of informants reported that work was where they used English the most. This was the case even for those in jobs that reportedly involved minimal communication (e.g. restaurant dishwashing).

Regarding learning priorities, informants with lower levels of English identified spoken communication, including pronunciation. Informants with higher levels of English prioritised written communication and pronunciation.

Regarding learning support, informants wanted more opportunities for interaction that would extend their English (spoken and written). They wanted personalised guidance and feedback, both to help them learn effectively and also to motivate them to persist with their learning. They wanted this support to be easily accessible, i.e. affordable and available to them at a convenient location and time (i.e. when they were "mentally fresh").

Just as informants identified work as the location where they used English the most, so they identified their workplace as the most convenient location for support.

Informants tended to conceptualise this support in ways consistent with their previous experience of studying English. For most this equated to tutor-led classroom instruction, though many expressed a strong preference for one-to-one tuition and commented on how group learning had often failed to address their needs (hence the emphasis on personalised guidance and feedback).

# 4 Conclusions

A number of points emerge from these findings, including what one might call the low-pay, limited-English trap. Arriving with limited financial resources, the migrant needs to find work and build a support network quickly. Their lack of English limits them to low-paid, low-skilled jobs and to friends who share a language. They might, while seeking work, invest in an English course. Once employed, however, they drop out. Working long hours for low pay, they lack the time, money and energy for study. Moreover, they can survive without it. The problem, of course, is that with only limited exposure to English at work and at home, a migrant caught in this trap is left reliant on self-directed learning. Without unusual determination, confidence and effective strategies, they are unlikely to progress.

What, then, can be done to help them?

It is clear that this group of learners needs what any language learner needs: encouragement to engage in and persist with learning English; help to develop effective personal learning strategies; exposure to authentic English; opportunity to interact in English; help to understand the form of the language; and corrective feedback.

It is also clear that work is a key arena. This is where these migrants most use English; it is their preferred location for learning support. It is also an environment that provides structured opportunities to communicate and, in the shape of management systems, structured support.

Management systems already aim to ensure effective workplace communication and employers have a vested interest in making those systems work for migrant employees. Might it be possible to enlist employer support for self-directed learning at work, structured via management systems and peer support? If so, what would such an approach look like in practice?

It might, overall, be conceived of as a digitally-enabled scaffolding programme. In addition to incentives, e.g. reward schemes, for learners and employers to engage and persist in learning, it would help
- employers to support language development with guided learning materials, coaching and mentoring, work organisation, supervisory feedback, peer learning groups etc.;
- staff to form self-directed study groups with curricula and resources for self-directed learning programmes; and
- individuals to develop effective learning strategies with, e.g., apps to help personalise and support learning.

Such a programme would certainly require facilitation – perhaps a new role for learning providers?

# References

Gidley, Ben & Hiranthi Jayaweera. 2010. *An evidence base on migration and integration in London*. London: Greater London Authority.
https://www.compas.ox.ac.uk/media/PR-2010-Evidence_Migration_London.pdf (accessed 28 July 2016).
GLA (Greater London Authority). 2009. *London enriched*. London: GLA.
GLA (Greater London Authority). 2013a. *London enriched, update*. London: GLA.
GLA (Greater London Authority). 2013b. *Migrants in low-paid, low-skilled jobs: Barriers and solutions to learning English in London*. London: GLA.
NIACE (National Institute of Adult Continuing Education). 2012. *English language for all*. London: GLA.

Matilde Grünhage-Monetti, Anna Svet
# "The fight against exclusion from the labour market begins ... in the workplace": Work-related second language development towards inclusion and participation

**Abstract:** Communicative competence in the language of the workplace is a key enabler for sustainable inclusion in the labour market and society for migrant workers. The research project "German at the workplace" delivers empirical results to inform work-related second language (L2) development. The company ethnography gives evidence of the role of language as a key vocational competence in modern work practices. Together with the linguistic analysis of authentic oral exchanges and documents it gives suggestions to language professionals and policy-makers for improving L2 development at and for work.

**Résumé :** Pour les travailleurs migrants, la capacité à communiquer dans la langue parlée sur le lieu de travail est un facilitateur clé pour une intégration durable au marché du travail et à la société. Le projet de recherche « Deutsch am Arbeitsplatz » (« l'allemand au travail ») rend compte des résultats empiriques pour soutenir le développement d'une langue seconde liée à l'emploi. L'ethnographie de l'entreprise atteste que la langue comme compétence professionnelle essentielle joue un rôle dans les pratiques actuelles. Linguistes et décideurs empruntent à ces résultats et à l'analyse linguistique des échanges oraux et des documents pour soutenir le développement de la L2 au travail et pour le travail.

## 1 Second language matters

In Germany, where the research was carried out, migrants have been contributing substantially to the economic and social development of the country over the last half century. While overrepresented in low-paid, dangerous and vulnerable jobs, and over-proportionally threatened by long-term unemployment, they are still underrepresented in education. Yet their L2 development is particularly

---

**Matilde Grünhage-Monetti** (corresponding author), Deutsches Institut für Erwachsenenbildung — Leibniz-Zentrum für Lebenslanges Lernen, Germany, E-mail: matilde.monetti@unitybox.de
**Anna Svet,** Friedrich-Schiller-Universität Jena, Germany, E-mail: anna.svet@uni-jena.de

DOI 10.1515/9783110477498-043, © 2017 Matilde Grünhage-Monetti, Anna Svet, published by De Gruyter.
This work is licensed under the Creative Commons Attribution-NonCommercial-NoDerivs 3.0 License.

fundamental for sustainable inclusion and participation in work and social life. In tune with the focus of social learning theories on the learning potential of work, interest for work-related L2 development is increasing.

Funded by the VolkswagenStiftung, the study group *Deutsch am Arbeitsplatz* ('German at the workplace') carried out the research project "Deutsch am Arbeitsplatz (DaA) – Research on workplace communication as a basis for organizational second language development", 2007–2009. The study groups consisted of researchers and practitioners of renowned institutions of adult education in Germany and Austria.[1] The project investigated workplace communication in different sectors in order to get empirically sound insights on language requirements and to improve work-related L2 provision. The focus was on little-investigated fields such as communication on the shop floor of small and medium-sized enterprises (SME) in food processing, electrical appliances, metal, and plastics as well as a logistics enterprise. SMEs are a constituent part of the German economy and offer employment to large numbers of migrants. One large industrial goods manufacturer was included because of its experience in work-related language development. Care of the elderly was also included because it employs an extremely high percentage of migrants and reports a constant growing need for workers.

Thanks to the good contacts of the providers represented in the study group, it was not difficult to find 15 companies willing to release a few employees for an interview with researchers who wanted to find out about language requirements, and were ready to report on their findings. Awareness of the role of communication in work practices among staff and managers had grown in the last decade in comparison to the attitude revealed in a survey conducted by the Deutsches Institut für Erwachsenenbildung in the EU Project "Setting up Partnerships against Social Exclusion at the Workplace", 2000–2002. The opinion of most employers and providers then can be epitomised by the surprised comment of a supervisor in a phone interview: "Why communicating at the workplace? They are there to work!"

Some 15 years later both staff and management agree that language skills are necessary "to understand the work and to produce quality, to communicate goals, to ensure procedures" (works manager); to create a feeling of belonging: "Integration means fun, esprit, irony, a language, the language of the company"

---

[1] Deutsches Institut für Erwachsenenbildung – Leibniz-Zentrum für Lebenslanges Lernen (coordinator), ERFA Wirtschaft Sprache, Friedrich-Schiller-Universität Jena, Institut für Gesprächsforschung, Verband Wiener Volksbildung, VHS Arbeit und Beruf GmbH Braunschweig.

(manager) – "You must talk about all sort of things every day, 'cause there is always something new" (metal worker).

When it came to recording authentic oral interactions at work and in the breaks for linguistic analysis, the DaA study group was confronted with great reservations. It took a year to build trust. Only then was it possible to record some 70 oral interactions at work for further analysis.

The project results were articulated in two parts: company ethnography and linguistic analysis of a corpus of authentic oral interactions and written texts.

## 2 Company ethnography

### 2.1 Methodology and research questions

For the company ethnography 33 semi-guided qualitative interviews were carried out with different stakeholders in companies: migrant and non-migrant employees, supervisors, heads of personnel and human resources, managers, members of the workers' councils, and in one case the owner himself. A content-analytical evaluation of the interviews was integrated with the findings of the participant observations. The results were presented in various articles and informed company profiles, which are used in training for providers and teachers to raise awareness of the challenges and specific features of workplace L2 development.

The leading questions of the research focused on the communicative requirements linked to tasks and roles, on the factors impacting on communication, and the consequences of L2 development for practice and research.

### 2.2 Key findings

The research verified our key hypothesis of the central role of communication in modern work practices based on international literature (e. g. Boutet 2001) and VET (vocational education and training) didactics (e. g. Dehnbostel 2008). Communicative competences are vital for employability and vocational competences independently of economic sector, trade, qualification profile, position. We were and are of course aware of the differences in requirements according to the sectors: in order to promote L2 development in less obvious sectors than care, such as food, metal or plastic processing industries, it was necessary to show that skilled and semi-skilled workers in all sectors need communicative competences to access the labour market, to secure their jobs, to participate in vocational education and training, to progress in their career and escape the low-pay trap.

We took care to bring evidence of the impact of structural changes on communication practices and their implications for new or more complex language skill requirements for shop floor staff. Table 1 shows a few tendencies.

**Table 1:** The language of change

| Structural changes | Language requirements | Quotes from the DaA interviews |
| --- | --- | --- |
| Decentralised work organisation | Communicate and explain decisions/solutions to colleagues and management | "The employee has to make independent decisions at night. He also needs to justify his decisions" (operation manager) |
| Quality assurance | Communicate work processes | "We have so-called 5 minute talks every morning to discuss quality assurance" (operation manager) |
| Automation, robotisation, new technologies | Communicate changes | "You cannot rely on work routines. Sometimes there are small changes – you have to read it thoroughly every time" (worker) |
| Certification/ auditing | Describe and explain own error management | "The auditor … asks the workers on the shop floor, points to the defect-catalogue and asks: 'What do you do in case of such an error?" (head of personnel) |

Health and safety legislation, client orientation, personnel appraisal, innovation and the consequent need for training, and a multilingual workforce are further examples of structural change impacting on communication: communicative competence has become a key vocational competence for all employees in all sectors and positions. It is a central factor of inclusion and participation in working life, in order to perform tasks, exercise rights and duties as an employee, improve career prospects, participate in relevant social networks, and strengthen ones' professional identity.

# 3 Linguistic analysis

The linguistic analysis examined 56 conversations, 100 e-mails, and various notices and bulletins of the collected corpus in terms of grammatical structures, vocabulary, and functions, laying the foundation for a description of work-related German based on authentic data.

## 3.1 Methodology and research questions

The recorded oral exchanges were transcribed and analyzed according to the main categories and levels of *Profile deutsch 2.0* (Glabionat et al. 2005), the German implementation of the CEFR. The analysis aimed at finding out which communicative functions occur in the investigated work contexts, on which linguistic levels they are realised (in terms of grammar and vocabulary), and whether there are sector-specific communicative functions and realisations.

## 3.2 Key findings

Our findings suggest that communicative functions (not only) in the workplace are not scalable, but range across all A and B levels as regards grammatical complexity. The consequences are twofold. First, "strictly following *Profile deutsch* progression ... does not prepare for the actual communicative practices ... in their workplaces", unless they wait years before joining the labour market (Knötig 2010: 16). Secondly, "communicative functions in the workplace ... can be consciously formulated within the constraints of a specific grammatical level, even the lowest (A1) level, making them much more accessible ..." (Knötig 2010: 16). Recommended are: focusing course design on a progression according to functions rather than grammar, and awareness-raising activities for German-speaking colleagues and managers. At present, alternative teaching approaches like the scenario technique and language awareness training for different workplace actors have been developed. Innovative arrangements like *Sprachpaten* ('language champions') for nursery school assistants, who support migrant employees in coping with the complexity of language in real working life.

Among other insights, the DaA study group stresses the prominent role of prosody in spoken interaction. By changing intonation, a question can become an ironical remark or a command, as in the DaA data. Politeness is conveyed through intonation. Stronger attention to prosody is vital for L2 development in the context of work, where power relations shape interactions.

Of consequence for L2 didactics is another insight: the "transgressive" cases of oral communication following the written 'monologue' model – e.g. health and safety instructions– and of written communication following the oral 'dialogue' model – e.g. birthday invitation to colleagues via e-mail. The growing use of communication technology is expected to enhance this tendency, which L2 didactics has to take into account.

As to the importance of vocabulary for specific purposes, the DaA corpus shows a differentiated role for technical terms: a minor role in informal workplace oral exchanges and a great(er) role in formal communication (reading and writing of documents/manuals, health and safety instructions, etc.). Recommended is the development of learning strategies at word, sentence and text level, and of communicative strategies for cultural appropriateness.

Finally, only one example of sector-specific communicative functions could be found: describing a procedure while undertaking it, which seems to be typical of person-related care.

# 4 Conclusions

The lessons to be learnt from the DaA research address policy-makers as well as educationalists. Sustainable integration of migrant workers is an economic and democratic issue. Work-related L2 development is an instrument towards that end and needs policies which
- recognize the joint responsibility of all parties involved (employers, the state, migrants, providers);
- regulate the financial responsibility of employers (as in France and Switzerland);
- recognize communicative skills as vocational skills (not only for migrants), as in France;
- give incentives for supporting work-related L2 development;
- trigger cooperation among relevant parties such as ministries, social partners, migrants' organizations, researchers, practitioners;
- turn time-limited projects into regular provision.

# References

Boutet, Josiane. 2001. La part langagière du travail: bilan et évolution. *Langage et societé* 98. 17–42.

Dehnbostel, Peter. 2008. *Berufliche Weiterbildung. Grundlagen aus arbeitnehmerorientierter Sicht*. Berlin: sigma.

Glaboniat, Manuela, Martin Müller, Paul Rusch, Helen Schmitz & Lukas Wertenschlag. 2005. *Profile deutsch: Gemeinsamer europäischer Referenzrahmen*. Berlin & Munich: Langenscheidt.

Knötig, Manuela. 2010. Analysing workplace language in Germany. *Workplace Learning and Skills Bulletin* 8. 16–17.

Kerstin Sjösvärd, Alexander Braddell
# Using workplace learning to support the linguistic integration of adult migrants – lessons from a decade of work in Sweden

**Abstract:** This paper reviews learning from a decade-long series of large-scale projects to support the linguistic integration of adult migrants employed in adult social care in the Stockholm region. Despite the assumption that employment was in itself a guarantee of language learning, at the outset it was found that for many migrants, secure long-term employment in the sector had led to very limited progress learning Swedish. The projects set out to remedy this, developing a holistic approach that enabled the sharing of responsibility for language development.

**Résumé :** L'article revient sur les leçons de plusieurs projets d'envergure menés pendant une décennie pour soutenir l'intégration linguistique des migrants adultes employés dans les services de protection sociale des adultes dans la région de Stockholm. Alors qu'on supposait que l'emploi constitue en soi une garantie de l'apprentissage de la langue, il s'est avéré que les progrès en suédois de beaucoup de migrants ayant un emploi durable dans ce secteur ont été très limités. Les projets mis en œuvre pour remédier à cet état de fait ont adopté une approche globale et une vision partagée des responsabilités pour le développement de la langue.

## 1 Background to the work

### 1.1 Migration in Sweden

Sweden's population today is about 10 million, of which around 1.5 million (15%) are migrants (i.e. residents born in other countries), 65% of whom come from non-EU countries. Migration has been a source of population increase in Sweden only since the 1940s, when importation of labour, primarily from other Nordic countries and in particular Finland, started to reverse many deca-

---

**Kerstin Sjösvärd** (corresponding author), Stockholm Gerontology Research Center, Sweden, E-mail: Kerstin.Sjosvard@aldrecentrum.se
**Alexander Braddell,** OSEC CIC Ltd, Oxford, United Kingdom, E-mail: abraddell@gmail.com

DOI 10.1515/9783110477498-044, © 2017 Kerstin Sjösvärd, Alexander Braddell, published by De Gruyter.
This work is licensed under the Creative Commons Attribution-NonCommercial-NoDerivs 3.0 License.

des of net emigration. This managed labour importation continued until the late 1960s, alongside the arrival of political refugees from Eastern Europe, until 1967 when immigration controls were introduced due to labour market saturation. From then on, most arriving migrants have been refugees and their relatives from non-EU countries, e.g. former Yugoslavia, the Middle East, Africa and Latin America (Swedish Institute 2015).

## 1.2 The linguistic integration of adult migrants in Sweden

The main vehicle for the linguistic integration of adult migrants is *Svenskundervisning för invandrare* (SFI, 'Swedish for immigrants'), created in 1965. Its aim is to ensure that immigrants have the Swedish they need to function at a basic level. The programme is free for migrants registered with their local authority and participation is voluntary, though welfare benefits may sometimes be made conditional on participation. It aims to take learners aged 16 and over from complete beginner to CEFR level B1. Some of the SFI programmes may include work placements. For adults wishing to study beyond level B1, courses (not necessarily free) are available through adult education centres.

In practice, migrants themselves tend to prioritise paid work over formal study of Swedish. A recent survey (Örstadius 2016) found that only a minority of SFI learners complete their programme, some not attending at all, and many of those who started, leaving as soon as they secure employment. The survey also found that those who did complete the programme were more likely to be in work eight years later.

Historically, policy makers had not been greatly concerned by migrants leaving SFI prematurely to start work, due to an assumption that employment itself was a direct route to linguistic integration, i.e. once employed, the migrant was sure to acquire Swedish. More recently, however, doubts have emerged regarding just how much language development unsupported employment offers to migrants (Sandwall 2010, 2013).

## 1.3 Workforce development in Stockholm

That approach had its origins in a large skills development programme for public sector workers launched in the early 2000s by the City of Stockholm. Over a four-year period, some 45,000 workers received vocational education and training (VET) through this voluntary programme, including some 1,400 care workers (Johnsson, Högberg and Wallenberg 2007). It became evident to employers, however, that the programme was not reaching a cohort of staff who were clearly reluctant to participate. Even when managers succeeded in pressuring these individuals to enrol, results remained poor.

Investigation by the project leaders suggested that this resistance was linked to lack of confidence. It was also realised that a large of proportion of these reluctant learners – particularly in adult social care – were migrant staff, many of whom had only limited Swedish. These low language levels among experienced workers (Table 1) came as a shock to the system, directly contradicting the assumption that employment guaranteed acquisition of language skills.

**Table 1:** Staff profiles from SpråkSam project (2009–2011), based on self-reporting by 253 migrants employed in adult social care and participating in the project's workplace learning programme.

| Years employed in elderly care | | Years in school* | |
|---|---|---|---|
| 0–6 years | 21% | 0–6 years | 20% |
| 7–9 years | 31% | 7–9 years | 18% |
| Over 10 years | 48% | 10–12 years | 38% |
| | | Over 12 years | 24% |

* May mean "a few days a week, when there was no war"

This led to consultation between the City of Stockholm's competence development project and the National Centre for Swedish as a Second Language. Two questions arose. The first was a workforce development question: how to help staff with limited Swedish improve both their Swedish and their vocational skills? The second question focused on linguistic integration: How to realise the potential of work for language learning?

Between 2007 and 2013, an extended series of projects investigated these two questions in the context of adult social care workforce development in the Stockholm region. These projects began with the state-funded APU project (2007–2008), then continued with the SpråkSam (2009–2011) and ArbetSam (2011–2013) projects funded through the European Social Fund (SGRC 2009, 2011, 2013). These projects were followed by a European transfer-of-innovation project, TDAR (2013–2015), which explored the results of the Stockholm projects in Belgium, Germany, Spain and the UK (SGRC 2015).

Alongside those projects, the Swedish Research Council for Health, Working Life and Welfare funded a three-year research project to deepen understanding of written and oral interaction in the working life of carers and to investigate what strategies and techniques the carers develop that help them complete their work effectively and overcome possible language and literacy-related problems (Jansson, Karlsson and Nikolaidou 2014). Findings from this research informed work in the SpråkSam and ArbetSam projects.

## 2 The work

### 2.1 Skills development in adult social care

The overall workforce development objective was to help adult social care providers to modernize their services to cope with growing demand for increasingly complex services. High on this agenda was the professionalization of care workers, i.e. developing the enhanced knowledge, skills and understanding staff require to deliver, e.g., person-centred dementia care.

The existing workforce development model for the sector was straightforward: recruit new entrants to the labour market, pre-qualified via relevant upper-secondary school vocational courses. From the 1990s onward, however, this system had struggled to supply sufficient staff to the sector, obliging employers to recruit unqualified adults, often migrants with limited Swedish.

Once in employment, moreover, access for these staff to formal learning of Swedish was very limited, due to the structure of both SFI and VET and also to the acute operational and funding constraints on employers. The nub of the matter, then, was that staff could not be released for formal learning (of either Swedish or care skills) and that learning was only available in education centres.

The challenge therefore was to create a new workforce development model consistent with the needs and constraints of both staff and employers.

### 2.2 Development of the ArbetSam model

Over the course of the three projects (APU, SpråkSam and ArbetSam), a comprehensive system of workplace learning, incorporating formal, informal and non-formal learning, was developed (SGRC 2013). The formal learning (delivered in the workplace by care trainers team-teaching with SFI teachers) gave staff opportunities to achieve national vocational qualifications while improving their Swedish language skills. The approach created two new roles to harness the non-formal learning opportunities of management systems (i.e. supervision, team meetings etc.), including a workplace language advocate and a reflective discussion leader. Both were voluntary roles designed for care staff (with the approval and support of their manager), who received training in the roles from project staff. These roles, together with the incorporation into formal learning of constant reference to daily work activity, also aimed to support as much informal learning as possible through everyday work activity and interactions with colleagues.

The approach was inclusive, addressing needs of all staff, migrant as well as non-migrant, and partnership-based, connecting employers, VET and SFI learning providers. It focused on reflective learning, with language development for all staff (SGRC 2013).

## 2.3 Large scale projects

The projects themselves, particularly SpråkSam and ArbetSam, were large scale, providing formal learning in care and Swedish language skills to more than 1000 staff in the Stockholm region. Programmes included three hours of formal workplace study per week over terms of 40 weeks, typically for one to two years. In addition, the projects delivered significant amounts of training for managers, key personnel in more than 100 workplaces, employing 10,000 staff.

The projects involved extensive partnership working between the Stockholm Gerontology Research Centre, local authorities, care providers, VET providers, SFI, and researchers from the universities of Stockholm and Södertörn, in addition to co-operation with the Swedish Municipal Workers' Union, Stockholm County Board and, finally, partners in other European countries.

# 3 Outcomes and conclusions

## 3.1 Key elements of the approach for the linguistic integration of adult migrants at work

In relation to the two questions this work addressed ("How to help staff with limited Swedish improve both their Swedish and their vocational skills?" and "How to realise potential of work for language learning?"), the following points can be made:
- This was a sector-based approach that promoted workforce development linked to quality improvement.
- It treated language as a core vocational competence, something all staff needed to do their jobs properly.
- Managers were engaged as full partners in all aspects of the learning process (planning, delivery, evaluation).

- The two new roles created for staff, i.e. the reflective discussion leader and language advocate (champion), were key to sustaining the workplace focus on language and offering individual colleagues ad hoc support.
- Sustainable language development was achieved through via non-formal and informal learning, embedded into workplace routines and requiring no external funding.
- The approach demonstrated the potential of cooperation between education systems and working life.

### 3.2 Lessons for LIAM

Finally, then, what are the lessons for the linguistic integration of adult migrants?
- Clearly, work itself offers no guarantee of language learning – it may even be negative. With support, however, that same work can provide real opportunities for language development – and significantly, learning at work may be the only way to support certain groups of migrants.
- Responsibility for language development must be shared between worker, employer, colleagues and state.
- Linking language learning to job learning is motivational for individuals, but engagement from managers is key to individual progress. The learner needs to see that their manager cares about their learning.
- Cooperation between education and workplace on structural, organisational and individual levels is essential and building structures for this to happen is necessary.

# References

Jansson, Gunilla, Anna-Malin Karlsson & Zoe Nikolaidou. 2014. *Skrift- och samtalspraktiker i äldreomsorgen* [Care as language work]. Stockholm: SGRC.
Johnsson, Ernst, Olle Högberg & Jan Wallenberg. 2007. *Utvärdering av Stockholms stads kompetensfond* [Evaluation of Stockholm Competence Fund]. Stockholm: Stockholm University.
Örstadius, Kristoffer. 2016. Lättare få arbete för den som klarat SFI [Easier to get work if you've done SFI]. *Dagens Nyheter*, 15 May.
Sandwall, Karin. 2010. "I learn more at school": A critical perspective on workplace-related second language learning in and out of school. *TESOL Quarterly* 44(3). 542–574.
Sandwall, Karin. 2013. *Handling practice – second language students' opportunities for interaction and language learning at work placements*. Gothenburg: University of Gothenburg.

SGRC (Stockholm Gerontology Research Center). 2009. *APU project*. Stockholm: SGRC.
SGRC. 2011. *SpråkSam project*. Stockholm: SGRC. http://www.aldrecentrum.se/spraksam (accessed 27 May 2016).
SGRC. 2013. *ArbetSam project*. http://www.aldrecentrum.se/arbetsam (accessed 27 May 2016).
SGRC. 2015. *TDAR project*. http://www.aldrecentrum.se/tdar (accessed 27 May 2016).
Swedish Institute. 2015. *Sweden and migration*. Stockholm: Swedish Institute. https://sweden.se/migration/ (accessed 27 May 2016).

Sonya Sahradyan
# Learning and maintaining languages in the workplace: migrant NGO practitioners in Finland

**Abstract:** This article reports on a linguistic ethnographic study exploring migrant NGO practitioners' language learning and maintenance at work. The findings suggest that the migrants learnt not only the language of the receiving society, in this case Finnish, but also English as an additional language through work. The narratives also show that the workplace supported migrants in maintaining both their home language and additional languages. Overall, the study highlights the importance of language learning and maintenance, which promote the linguistic integration and social inclusion of migrant NGO practitioners in the workplace.

**Résumé :** L'article rend compte d'une étude ethnographique sur l'apprentissage et la consolidation de la langue des praticiens qui travaillent dans des ONG de migrants. Elle conclut que les migrants ont appris non seulement la langue du pays d'accueil – dans ce cas, le finnois – mais aussi l'anglais comme langue supplémentaire, par le biais du travail. Les auteurs montrent également que le travail aide les migrants à consolider la fois leur langue maternelle et des langues étrangères. De façon générale, l'étude souligne l'importance de l'apprentissage et de la consolidation de la langue pour favoriser l'intégration linguistique et sociale des praticiens migrants dans les ONG sur le lieu de travail.

## 1 Introduction

In Finland, language has increasingly become a policy priority, and linguistic research has recently focused on various migrant groups working in different sectors. The Finnish integration policy supports migrants in learning national languages, Finnish and Swedish, and in maintaining their mother tongue, regardless of their legal status (Act on the Promotion of Immigrant Integration 1386/2010). In addition, scientific studies have revealed that migrants have an opportunity to develop their Finnish language skills in the workplace (e.g.

---

**Sonya Sahradyan**, Centre for Applied Language Studies, University of Jyväskylä, Finland,
E-mail: sonya.s.sahradyan@jyu.fi

Suni 2010; Tarnanen, Rynkänen, and Pöyhönen 2015). Several studies have also indicated that the workplace enables migrants to maintain their home language within the Finnish context (e.g. Rynkänen et al. 2014). Even though language learning and maintenance have been studied among migrants working in the Finnish public and private sectors, relatively little research has been conducted on migrants working in the third sector, namely a non-governmental organization (NGO), or their language learning and maintenance at work.

This article, therefore, attempts to fill the above-mentioned gap by providing answers to the following question: "How do migrant NGO practitioners learn and maintain languages in the workplace?" The linguistic ethnographic study presented in this paper is conducted in a superdiverse NGO based in Finland. The key participants in the study are migrant NGO practitioners, that is, employees, apprentices, trainees, interns, and volunteers.

## 2 A sociocultural approach

In my research, I draw upon the sociocultural perspective on language learning. From this perspective, language is situated in a context co-created in social interaction and is learned from others within this interaction (Vygotsky 1978). In addition, I build on workplace learning research, which emphasises that learning is a product of involvement in social practices, for example, happening in workplaces (Billett 2002). The study conducted by Billett also highlights that learning is formed by "workplace participatory practices" and can be "co-participative" (2002: 1). Moreover, Malloch and her colleagues shed light on the fact that learning and performance are "embodied phenomena" (Malloch et al. 2011: 24). By combining these two strands of research, I consider language learning to be situated in different settings and to take place through social interaction and participation at work (see Tarnanen, Rynkänen, and Pöyhönen 2015), which concerns language maintenance in the workplace as well (see Rynkänen, Sahradyan, and Tarnanen 2014).

## 3 Informants, data, and methods

The study focuses on migrant NGO practitioners (n = 22) who were first-generation adult migrants. They were working as part- or full-time employees, apprentices, trainees, interns, or volunteers in the superdiverse organisation located in Jyväskylä, Finland. The informants had various cultural and socio-economic backgrounds, and they all spoke more than two languages. At the time of the interviews, the informants were between 23 and 61 years old, and they had resided in Finland for between three and 29 years. The level of education the informants had received before moving to Finland ranged from primary to university, whereas their level of education obtained in Finland ranged from integration training to university education.

Within the framework of linguistic ethnography, I collected different types of data through multi-site ethnographic fieldwork for a one-year period in the NGO. In addition, I conducted interviews with the informants. In this paper, only the interview and observational data are reported. Narrative analysis is applied to the multilingual data accumulated in four different languages: Finnish, English, Russian, and Armenian.

## 4 Language learning and maintenance in the workplace

All the migrants participating in this study were multilingual, and they had different proficiency levels in different languages. In the case of Finnish, the informants' proficiency levels ranged from basic to advanced, and they learnt Finnish both within and outside formal educational settings. Based on the data analysis, the NGO as a workplace provided the informants with opportunities to develop their Finnish language skills. In their narratives, the informants repeatedly talked about Finnish language learning at work, which is illustrated in the following quote: "I was learning Finnish every single day from colleagues and visitors, from job-related activities, tasks and paperwork" (Hudi, trainee). Like Hudi, most of the other informants also recognised the importance of the workplace for learning Finnish. However, whether they could improve their written or oral skills or both in Finnish depended on their type of employment.

In general, the informants learnt Finnish by participating in various activities and events organised in the workplace. One of them is ABC-Basic Finnish language learning, provided to migrant learners, especially to newly arrived, elderly, and illiterate migrants as well as to stay-at-home mothers. The informants were involved in this activity as mediators and had an opportunity to enhance their Finnish skills while helping with the interpretation or elaboration of what is said by migrant learners and Finnish volunteers acting as teachers. The homework club is another important activity in which the informants' Finnish language learning took place during the completion of young migrants' homework for different school subjects. However, during cultural evenings, the informants developed not only Finnish but also English skills by presenting and discussing the history, culture, language, and religion of their home countries. Similarly, ethno-cafés supported the informants in learning both Finnish and English while cooking traditional food together with Finns and migrants from different parts of the world.

Almost all the informants also found staff meetings very useful for developing their language skills in Finnish, and some informants mentioned that the meetings could help them to overcome challenges related to understanding and communicating in spoken Finnish. One of the informants said: "We usually had staff meetings every week in order to plan and organise activities with colleagues ... It was good to be there, 'cause I had difficulties in *suomen puhekieli* [spoken Finnish], but in meetings I could learn *puhekieli* [spoken language] and even could use it outside of work" (Sara, intern). Such a narrative is common in the stories of migrants and, in particular, interns' and trainees' stories. Additionally, another informant gave the following description: "Meetings that we had with authorities were only in Finnish, but meetings with partner projects or organisations were sometimes in Finnish and sometimes in English or both in Finnish and English ... In those meetings I practised Finnish as well as English" (Fabian, employee). As seen from the last two excerpts, the meetings with insiders supported the informants in improving mainly Finnish skills, whereas the meetings with outsiders enabled them to enhance both Finnish and English skills.

In addition to language learning, the workplace considerably influenced the maintenance of informants' languages, especially their home language. For example, it is illustrated in Bela's narrative: "At work I use also my mother tongue, Russian ... At the beginning of my work, it was a bit difficult to remember *русские слова* ['Russian words'] as after moving to Finland I used English and then Finnish *дома или с друзьями* ['at home or with friends'] ... I think I was gradually losing my mother tongue before getting this job" (Bela, employee). Apart from the informants' stories, my observational field notes reveal that the workplace also supported informants in maintaining their additional languages. One of the participant's observational field notes are presented here:

> One afternoon we were discussing different countries' holidays in our Russian discussion group. The group leader, *Лаура* ['Laura'], was Russian and we, the participants, were both Finns and migrants. Laura was helping us to use a correct *թերականական խոնարհում* ['grammatical conjugation' (Armenian)] and was giving a short explanation in Russian and/or Finnish. During the conversation, Klara who had a migrant background asked Laura to explain in English as well, if possible, because, she told, that she had only basic level in Finnish. Laura smiled and replied "Well, it's better for me to say also in English, I can refresh my English and can keep it alive" (Laura, volunteer).

## 5 Conclusions

In this article, I have addressed one main question related to the language learning and maintenance of migrant NGO practitioners in the workplace. The analysis reported above suggests that the workplace supported the informants in developing additional languages, such as Finnish, the language of the host society, and English. Also, it was found that the informants had an opportunity to preserve their home and additional languages with the help of their work. Furthermore, the narratives show that language learning (see also Tarnanen, Rynkänen, and Pöyhönen 2015) as well as language maintenance (see also Rynkänen, Sahradyan, and Tarnanen 2014) are situated, and they take place through social interaction and participation in different workplace settings. The study thus illustrates that language learning and maintenance foster the informants' linguistic integration and social inclusion at work. In the light of these findings, the paper gives new insights into migrants' workplace language learning and their language maintenance through work.

## Acknowledgements

The study is part of bigger research projects "Transforming Professional Integration" (principal investigator, Professor Sari Pöyhönen) (2011–2014 / http://integration.jyu.fi) and "Language and Superdiversity: (Dis)identification in Social Media" (principal investigator Professor Sirpa Leppänen) (2012–2016; https://www.jyu.fi/hum/laitokset/kielet/tutkimus/hankkeet/lgsd), funded by the Academy of Finland and implemented at the University of Jyväskylä.

The paper draws on the empirical data collected by the author for her doctoral dissertation, which is funded by the Kone Foundation and the Centre for Applied Language Studies, University of Jyväskylä.

## References

Billett, Stephen. 2002. Workplace pedagogic practices: Participation and learning. *Australian Vocational Education Review* 9(1). 28–38.

Integration Act. 2010. *Act on the Promotion of Immigrant Integration 1386/2010*. Ministry of Interior, Finland. Unofficial translation.

Malloch, Margaret, Len Cairns, Karen Evans & Bridget N. O'Connor (eds.). 2011. *The SAGE handbook of workplace learning*. London: Sage.

Rynkänen, Tatjana, Sonya Sahradyan, Mirja Tarnanen, David Hoffman & Sari Pöyhönen. 2014. *The coffee room as threshold – social dynamics in workplaces in Finland*. Paper presented at the International Conference on Sociolinguistics Symposium 20: Language, Time, Space, University of Jyväskylä, 15–18 June 2014.

Suni, Minna. 2010. Työssä opittua: työntekijän näkökulma ammatilliseen kieli- ja viestintätaitoonsa. ['Learned at work: An employee's perspective on their professional language and communicative skills']. In Mikel Garant & Mirja Kinnunen (eds.), *AFinLA-e: Soveltavan kielitieteen tutkimuksia 2*. 45–58. Jyväskylä: Finnish Association for Applied Linguistics.

Tarnanen, Mirja, Tatjana Rynkänen & Sari Pöyhönen. 2015. Kielen käyttö ja oppiminen aikuisten maahanmuuttajien integroitumisen ja identiteettien rakennusaineena ['Language use and learning in integration and construction of identities among adult migrants']. In Teppo Jakonen, Juha Jalkanen, Terhi Paakkinen & Minna Suni (eds.), *AFinLA vuosikirja 73: Kielenoppimisen virtauksia – Flows of language learning*. 56–72. Jyväskylä: Finnish Association for Applied Linguistics.

Vygotsky, Lev. 1978. *Mind in society: The development of higher psychological processes*. Cambridge, MA: Harvard University Press.

7 **Towards linguistic integration: specific learner groups**
Les groupes d'apprenants spécifiques : vers une intégration linguistique

Samira Moukrim
# Barrières linguistiques et problèmes de communication dans les milieux de la santé

**Résumé :** L'auteur aborde le problème des barrières linguistiques en explorant, à partir d'un corpus authentique, le ressenti de femmes immigrées non-francophones dans des situations de soins de la santé et en mettant en évidence la réalité particulière de cette catégorie de femmes issues de l'immigration.

**Abstract:** The author discusses the problem of language barriers by exploring, based on an authentic corpus of material, the feelings of non-French-speaking immigrant women in healthcare-related situations and highlighting the particular circumstances of this category of women of immigrant origin.

## Introduction

La France, comme toute l'Europe, est de plus en plus diverse et poursuit son évolution vers une société multiculturelle. Selon les statistiques de l'INSEE, au 1$^{er}$ janvier 2014, 11,6 % des personnes qui vivent en France sont nées à l'étranger[1]. Souvent arrivés à l'âge adulte ou plus jeunes avec leurs parents, nombre de ces immigrés éprouvent des difficultés à parler le français et sont confrontés à des problèmes de communication dans tous les champs de la vie sociale.

La barrière de la langue peut poser de réels problèmes notamment en milieu de soins. Lorsque la santé est en jeu, il est indispensable que les interlocuteurs (patient et intervenant) se comprennent bien. La communication et la compréhension mutuelles constituent le fondement d'un traitement médical réussi. Or, bien des patients issus de l'immigration ne disposent souvent pas des connaissances linguistiques nécessaires.

Dans cette analyse, il sera question des barrières de la langue dans les milieux de la santé, dans le cas des femmes immigrées non-francophones. Les études qui portent sur la communication *patient-praticien* ne présentent généralement que la perspective des praticiens. C'est la perspective des patients qui

---

[1] http://www.insee.fr/fr/themes/document.asp?reg_id=0&ref_id=T16F037 (consulté le 10 mai 2016)

**Samira Moukrim**, Université Sidi Mohammed Ben Abdellah, FLSH-Fès, LLL (UMR 7270 – Université d'Orléans – Université de Tours – BnF – CNRS), E-mail : samiramoukrim@yahoo.fr

DOI 10.1515/9783110477498-046, © 2017 Samira Moukrim, published by De Gruyter.
This work is licensed under the Creative Commons Attribution-NonCommercial-NoDerivs 3.0 License.

sera mise en exergue à travers l'exploration du ressenti des femmes immigrées non-francophones dans des situations de soins de la santé.

## 1 Le corpus

Le corpus a été constitué dans le cadre du programme *Langues en Contact à Orléans* (LCO), module du Projet *Enquêtes sociolinguistiques à Orléans 2* (ESLO2)[2], piloté par le Laboratoire Ligérien de Linguistique de l'Université d'Orléans (LLL). LCO a pour objectif de dresser un portrait du multilinguisme dans la ville d'Orléans. Il se propose :
- de répertorier les pratiques linguistiques et culturelles des immigrés au moyen d'enquêtes sur le terrain ;
- d'analyser la vie de ces langues. Quels sont leurs modes de transmission ? Où sont-elles parlées, par qui, dans quelles circonstances ?
- de réaliser des enregistrements des différentes langues telles que parlées à Orléans pour les mettre à la disposition de la communauté scientifique, voire d'un public plus large.

Un sous-corpus a été constitué auprès de locuteurs arabophones et amazighophones (berbérophones) résidant à Orléans. Pour améliorer la représentativité du corpus, nous avons essayé de diversifier les situations enregistrées ainsi que les catégories de locuteurs en différenciant sociologiquement les témoins selon l'âge, le sexe le niveau scolaire, la profession et les langues parlées.

Nous avons constitué un corpus de « données situées » : il contient, en plus des données primaires (les enregistrements de la parole), une riche documentation sur ces données et sur leur contexte de production. Nous avons tenu également à expliciter notre démarche, à documenter les conditions de constitution du corpus ainsi que nos choix théoriques et techniques. Toutes ces informations sont d'une grande importance pour rendre le corpus disponible.

Pour réunir le plus de données possible, nous avons eu recours à l'entretien semi-directif (face à face). Un guide d'entretien a été réalisé afin de faire parler les témoins. Les questions que nous avons choisies portent d'une part sur les langues utilisées par nos informateurs à Orléans, sur leur importance et sur ce qu'elles représentent pour eux ; d'autre part, sur la culture et les traditions transplantées du pays d'origine au pays d'accueil.

---

[2] Pour plus de détails sur le programme ESLO voir : http://www.lll.cnrs.fr/eslo-1

Lors des entretiens, certaines femmes non-francophones déclarent éprouver le besoin de parler français dans certaines situations, notamment dans les milieux de la santé. Ce qui a attiré notre attention sur le problème des barrières linguistiques et leurs effets à la fois sur les patients et sur le personnel médical.

Pour étudier la question des barrières linguistiques dans les milieux de la santé, nous nous sommes appuyée sur l'étude d'un groupe de huit femmes non-francophones, âgées de 25 à 65 ans, d'origine maghrébine (marocaine). Ces femmes déclarent parler l'arabe et/ou le berbère et éprouver des difficultés à comprendre ou à parler le français.

## 2 L'enquête

La qualité de la constitution du corpus est un facteur de la relation de confiance établie entre nous, en tant que personne (de la même communauté linguistique) et aussi en tant que chercheur (qui peut, du point de vue des témoins, contribuer à la promotion de la diversité linguistique et culturelle), et les enquêtés.

Avant de commencer l'enregistrement, nous essayons de nous familiariser avec le témoin pour qu'il se sente parfaitement à l'aise et que la conversation enregistrée soit aussi naturelle que possible. En effet, nous avons pris systématiquement le temps de discuter avec le témoin pour gagner sa confiance. Tout cela a l'avantage d'atténuer « le paradoxe de l'observateur » (Labov 1976 : 116–117 & 289–290) et d'accéder au vernaculaire du locuteur. Comme le précise Bourdieu (1993 : 1395) : « La proximité sociale et la familiarité assurent en effet deux des conditions principales d'une communication »non violente« ».

Notre relation privilégiée avec les témoins vient du fait que nous partageons avec eux un certain nombre de traits : même origine (pays d'origine), même(s) langue(s), même situation en France (appartenance à la population immigrée), etc. Nous sommes membre à part entière de la culture vernaculaire. Nous la connaissons de l'intérieur et nous la comprenons profondément. Cela permet, selon Labov (1978 : 10) de « réussir une percée plus profonde ».

## 3 Les barrières linguistiques et culturelles

Au cours des entretiens, les femmes en question déclarent éprouver des difficultés à parler (et à comprendre) le français, ce qui leur pose problème dans tous les champs de la vie sociale. Les deux premiers témoins ont précisé spontanément que « c'est dans les milieux de la santé qu'[elles] sent[ent] le plus le besoin de parler français ». Ce qui nous a poussée, par la suite, à poser la question à toutes les enquêtées et aussi à leur demander la raison de cette gêne dans les milieux de la santé. Leurs réponses peuvent être résumées par les points suivants :

Dans les milieux de la santé,
- elles ont besoin d'expliquer de quoi elles se plaignent et de comprendre le personnel médical sans être obligées de dévoiler leur intimité devant un accompagnateur (y compris les membres de leur famille...) ;
- elles se sentent frustrées de ne pas se faire comprendre, impuissantes, complètement démunies, étrangères...

Leur ressenti peut être traduit par la citation de Tania de Montaigne (2006) : « Être étranger, c'est être sous l'eau quand d'autres vous parlent à la surface, les sons pénètrent, mais pas le sens[3] ».

Les barrières linguistiques sont souvent accompagnées de barrières culturelles, notamment la différence dans la perception et l'expression de la maladie, la douleur, le traitement, etc., et aussi le manque de familiarité avec le système de la santé dans le pays d'accueil.

S'ajoute à cela la réalité particulière de cette catégorie de femmes issues de l'immigration :
- la pudeur embarrassante de ces femmes (peur de se dénuder devant le personnel de sexe différent, peur de livrer une part de leur intimité...) ;
- les interdits religieux ou liés à la tradition qui musellent ces femmes (la peur de recevoir des soins par un intervenant de sexe différent, tabous culturels, etc.) ;
- le rôle effacé de la femme dans la société d'origine (domination du mari, du père ou du frère, statut d'infériorité, etc.), statut qu'elles continuent à préserver dans le pays d'accueil ;
- l'isolement lié au contexte de l'immigration ;
- l'invisibilité sociale due au statut de la femme immigrée dans la société d'accueil : femme « accompagnante » (Conseil de l'Europe 1995), presque jamais considérée comme une personne « individualisée », « autonome ».

Il y a une sorte d'intersection des dimensions du genre et des barrières linguistiques (et culturelles).

La diversité culturelle est à percevoir, selon le Comité européen de la Santé[4], comme une caractéristique de la population de l'Europe actuelle dans son en-

---

3 http://evene.lefigaro.fr/citation/etre-etranger-etre-eau-autres-parlent-surface-sons-penetrent-se-77397.php (consulté le 10 février 2016).
4 Comité d'experts sur les services de santé dans une société multiculturelle, Exposé des motifs : « Adaptation des services de santé à la diversité culturelle dans une Europe multiculturelle » : https://wcd.coe.int/com.instranet.InstraServlet?command=com (consulté le 12 février 2016).

semble. Il est mis en avant que les notions de santé, de maladie et de mort sont profondément ancrées dans la culture de chaque groupe humain ou pays et que cette culture conditionne le mode de traitement des malades, ainsi que les rituels qui entourent les mourants. Or, ce fait n'est pas toujours assez reconnu par les services et institutions de santé des États membres. Le mandat du Comité d'experts souligne que le respect des droits et de la dignité de la personne impose de prendre en compte cette diversité culturelle dans le cadre des services de santé.

Le Comité souligne que l'intérêt de la communauté internationale pour des « soins culturellement différenciés » va de pair avec de récentes innovations médicales telles que la notion de soins centrés sur le patient, l'adoption de chartes des droits des patients, ainsi que l'importance croissante attachée au résultat des interventions médicales et à la satisfaction des patients.

## 4 Des patients exclus de la recherche

Dans les recherches sur la communication patient-praticien, les patients qui ne maîtrisent pas la langue officielle sont souvent exclus des enquêtes (Bowen 2001). Différentes études montrent que les minorités ethniques[5] ne sont pas correctement représentées dans ce type d'enquêtes et qu'elles ne bénéficient pas des améliorations basées sur la gestion de la qualité (alors qu'elles sont peut-être celles qui en ont le plus besoin).

Ces patients sont souvent systématiquement exclus et ainsi sous-représentés dans les échantillons utilisés en recherche clinique et dans les recherches sur les services de santé et ce, pour diverses raisons :
- leur maîtrise insuffisante de la langue officielle ou leur analphabétisme ;
- le manque de compétences permettant de concevoir des outils de recherche transculturels valables, qui pousse souvent les chercheurs à les exclure de leurs études cliniques ;
- l'hésitation fréquente des personnes appartenant à une minorité ethnique à participer aux projets de recherches biomédicales, par crainte de subir des discriminations ou d'être utilisés comme cobayes pour tester des substances ou traitements expérimentaux, ce qui pose des difficultés de recrutement.

---

5 Le terme « minorité ethnique » désigne un groupe de personnes qui se sentent proches les unes des autres, parce qu'elles estiment (subjectivement) avoir une origine commune, parfois une même langue, une culture partagée et une forme de conscience collective en laquelle chacun se reconnaît quelle que soit sa position sociale dans le groupe.

Les effets des barrières linguistiques sur la relation patient-intervenant ne sont donc pas bien explorés. En outre, l'exclusion de ces patients de la recherche signifie que les études ne décrivent pas l'expérience de tous les patients dans la société. Ce qui aurait un impact sur la conception d'une politique de santé valable pour toute la société.

## 5 La barrière de la langue : quelques effets

Les barrières linguistiques perturbent tout le processus de la consultation du début à la fin. Selon Cosnier *et al.* (1993), les différentes séquences de la consultation se présentent comme suit : l'ouverture, la définition du problème, l'examen clinique, le diagnostic (ou résultats de l'examen), la discussion du diagnostic, la prescription, la clôture.
- Comment aborder ces étapes de la consultation quand on ne parle pas la même langue ?
- Comment établir un diagnostic fiable quand le patient ne comprend pas les questions posées ?

La barrière de la langue peut avoir des effets aussi bien sur le patient que sur l'intervenant, comme il apparaît dans le tableau suivant :

*Quelques effets de la barrière de la langue*

| Patient | Personnel médical |
|---|---|
| – Impossibilité de fournir une information utile ou compréhensible pour sa prise en charge | – Difficulté/impossibilité de comprendre de quoi se plaint le patient |
| – Incompréhension des questions posées | – Incapacité d'établir un diagnostic |
| – Détresse psychologique | – Multiplication des examens et tests supplémentaires afin d'identifier le problème |
| – Manque de confiance | |
| – Mauvais usages des traitements, erreurs de médication | – Problème d'accès aux antécédents médicaux du patient (vaccination, allergies, antécédents familiaux, etc.) |
| – Insatisfaction | |
| – Manque d'informations sur la promotion de la santé ou sur la prévention des maladies | – Insatisfaction |
| – Non recours ou recours tardif aux soins[6] | |

---

[6] Le non recours ou le recours tardif aux soins de la santé pourrait avoir des implications catastrophiques pour la santé tant individuelle que publique. Par ailleurs, les barrières linguistiques peuvent constituer un vrai problème de santé publique dans le cas des maladies transmissibles.

Pour Margot Phaneuf (2009 : 7), travailler auprès des immigrés appartenant à diverses cultures et religions suppose une certaine ouverture d'esprit, une compréhension minimale de leur réalité et de leurs besoins particuliers : « si c'est la compréhension de la langue qui pose problème, il nous faudra alors trouver des moyens alternatifs pour les aider à s'exprimer afin de mieux les comprendre ». L'auteur considère que le fait d'imposer quelque chose à quelqu'un qui ne comprend pas est une forme de *violence.*

Les barrières linguistiques influencent le taux d'utilisation des services en le diminuant ou en l'augmentant (Bowen 2000), elles influencent aussi l'accès initial et affectent le diagnostic et le traitement car elles peuvent gêner ou empêcher une personne de demander une évaluation initiale et des soins, comme elles peuvent affecter la qualité des soins reçus, ce qui augmente la fréquence de l'utilisation des services des urgences. Les barrières linguistiques peuvent donc entraver l'obtention de la qualité et de l'équité en ce qui concerne les soins de santé.

Dans Muela Ribera *et al.* (2008), il a été souligné que les barrières linguistiques peuvent augmenter les coûts médicaux par deux moyens principaux : en augmentant le risque d'erreurs médicales et de complications de la maladie, et en produisant des coûts inutiles.

Pour la France, les données manquent pour élaborer une politique de santé appropriée à la diversité culturelle en milieu de soins, notamment sur les barrières de la langue et leurs effets. C'est la raison pour laquelle il est important de procéder à la collecte des données sur les situations où les obstacles linguistiques pourraient avoir des répercussions sur la qualité des soins.

En somme, on sait relativement peu de choses concernant les effets des barrières linguistiques sur le résultat du traitement. C'est la raison pour laquelle, aux États-Unis et en Europe occidentale, la résorption de la barrière linguistique est considérée comme le domaine où des interventions s'imposent de la manière la plus urgente et la plus évidente.

# 6 Limites et perspectives

Cette étude présente certaines limites dans la mesure où elle porte sur un nombre restreint de témoins et aussi du fait que l'objectif initial de l'enquête n'était pas les barrières linguistiques mais l'étude du plurilinguisme à Orléans. D'où la nécessité d'une recherche accrue sur cette question des barrières linguistiques dans les milieux de soins afin d'élaborer des politiques basées sur des éléments concrets et surtout pour sensibiliser.

## Références

Bourdieu, Pierre (dir.). 1993. *La misère du monde*. Paris : Seuil, collection « Points ».
Bowen, Sarah. 2000. *Introduction to Cultural Competence in Pediatric Health Care*. Préparé pour Santé Canada, Services gouvernementaux Canada.
Bowen, Sarah. 2001. *Barrières linguistiques dans l'accès aux soins de santé*. http://www.hc-sc.gc.ca/hcs-sss/alt_formats/hpb-dgps/pdf/pubs/2001-lang-acces/2001-lang-acces-fra.pdf. (consulté le 14 juin 2016).
Conseil de l'Europe. 1995. *Les femmes immigrées et l'intégration*. Strasbourg : Conseil de l'Europe.
http://www.coe.int/t/dg3/migration/archives/Documentation/Series_Community_Relations/Immigrant_women_and_integration_fr.pdf (consulté le 15 février 2016).
Cosnier, Jacques, Michèle Grosjean & Michèle Lacoste. 1993. *Soins et communications. Approches interactionnistes des relations de soins*. Lyon : Presses Universitaires de Lyon.
De Montaigne, Tania. 2006. *Tokyo c'est loin*. Roman. Paris : Flammarion.
Labov, William. 1976. *Sociolinguistique*. Paris : Les Éditions de Minuit.
Labov, William. 1978. *Le parler ordinaire*. Paris : Les Éditions de Minuit, collection « Le sens commun ».
Phaneuf, Margot. 2009, révision février 2013. *L'approche interculturelle, communication et soins dans un contexte d'ouverture*. http://www.prendresoin.org/wp-content/uploads/2013/02/pproche5Finterculturelle-communi-cation_et_soins_dans_un_contexte_da%CC%82%E2%82%AC%E2%84%A2ouver....pdf (consulté le 14 juin 2016).

Marcello Amoruso, Mari D'Agostino
# Teenage and adult migrants with low to very low education levels: learner profiles and proficiency assessment tools

**Abstract:** This article presents data and student experiences acquired within the frame of the inclusion project of the Italian Language School for Foreigners at the University of Palermo. The programme, established five years ago, has created and provided educational courses for adults and unaccompanied minors of low to very low schooling level, most of them between 16 and 18 years old.

**Résumé :** Le rapport présente les profils d'étudiants et les expériences acquises dans le cadre du " Projet d'inclusion dans l'Ecole de langue pour l'italien Langue étrangère " de l'université de Palerme. Le programme, créé il y a cinq ans, dispense des cours à des adultes et à des mineurs non accompagnés ayant un niveau d'instruction faible à très faible, la majorité ayant entre 16 et 18 ans.

## 1 New arrivals and old faces welcomed

Our project began in early July 2012 in Palermo, a multilingual city (D'Agostino 2012, 2015b, 2015c). While schools and youth centres close for the yearly summer break, the ex Convento di Sant'Antonino, home of the University of Palermo's Italian Language School for Foreigners, buzzes with life. For many years now, young people from all over the world have been attending intensive summer courses at the school, where they study Italian language and culture, but also learn about different lifestyles, fall in love and make lifelong friendships. As well as lots of students from international communities, an increasing number of adult migrants (often refugees or asylum seekers) have been attending the courses, most of them highly educated people who need to learn their host country's language as soon as possible.

During summer 2012, the school began to receive more and more requests for incoming students. At our office door, for the first time ever there were also young people looking lost and bewildered, accompanied by their child care in-

---

**Marcello Amoruso,** University of Palermo, Italy, E-mail: marcello.amoruso@gmail.com
**Mari D'Agostino** (corresponding author), University of Palermo, Italy,
E-mail: mari.dagostino@unipa.it

DOI 10.1515/9783110477498-047, [cc BY-NC-ND] © 2017 Marcello Amoruso, Mari D'Agostino, published by De Gruyter.
This work is licensed under the Creative Commons Attribution-NonCommercial-NoDerivs 3.0 License.

stitution tutor. The official name for these new students is "unaccompanied foreign minors". From the start of the project until now almost 1000 minors have taken part in our courses. Many of them come from Bangladesh, though the vast majority come from Western African countries such as Gambia, Senegal, Mali, Ghana, Nigeria, Ivory Coast, Guinea, Guinea-Bissau and Sierra Leone. Many are of Arab origin, coming from North Africa, mainly from Egypt and Tunisia. In terms of their level of education, only a few students have had more than five years of schooling, very few of them have had eight, and 30–40% are completely illiterate (Amoruso et al. 2015; D'Agostino 2015a; Amoruso and D'Agostino 2016a, 2016b). We did not know how challenging this was going to be as we knew very little about the learner profile of an unaccompanied foreign minor. We also did not know how much the presence of these new students would change the normal teaching structure and layout of our school. For these "boat kids", what would be appropriate teaching material? What outdoor activity might be of interest to them? And above all, how would we integrate new and old students? After a couple of weeks we knew that adding one more chair in the classroom wasn't sufficient, we needed to make bigger changes.

## 2 The language course: a meeting place

From the beginning we realized that in our classrooms there was an unusual mix of people from very different backgrounds. But they were sharing time and space, exercise sheets, scissors, and songs just like in any other class at the start of any Italian language course in any part of the world. Where and how could we imagine such different worlds – in terms of experience, everyday life and future expectations – would meet? The setting of this unlikely meeting was the University of Palermo.

It was there that young people met educated people, and their worlds suddenly became full of books and hopes for the future, along with the desire to go and see the world. These young people were often without parents, fleeing from tragic events involving their families or countries, living in a state of uncertainty, often in hostile environments over which they had little control. Nonetheless, they were full of hope for the future, having had to adapt to such horrible circumstances. Teaching and educational changes were more important than our own failures and frustrations. In the class, the minors could integrate with different cultures and different ways of living and behaving, something very different from what they were used to. The mixed nature of the group also allowed the other students to get to know cultures and lifestyles that they had only ever seen on TV. They also learnt to give faces and names to the empty labels that the media regularly shows us. They learnt to see the human behind the label, their history, their love for their family, friends, homeland, from whom they were so far that their only connection was through the screen of their mobile phone. All students also took part, without even realizing it, in an integration project which belongs to Palermo and all of Italy. After all, are integration policies not an important part of culture? The meeting of the two groups of students was enriching for both parties: between the walls of a language classroom the minors discovered new opportunities that were previously unheard of and the others opened their eyes to other cultures by learning about different personal experiences and lifestyles.

# 3 Project overview: the stages

The situation outlined in the previous section was the general background against which our project took place. However, the internal structure of the project itself has been changing over time in response to the progressive definition of the linguistic and human profile of the minors and an ongoing analysis of the teaching experience day by day. It is possible to identify five different stages, each of which is the result of the specific choices made about the general structure of the project and its consequent repercussions at the educational level.

## 3.1 Stage 1

Integration may be identified as the first stage of our project. As seen before, it has been an *a priori* choice or even a "non-choice". The interaction between the minors and the highly educated students that usually attend our courses became a priority above all others. This can be considered as both a daring and a safe approach. During a later stage of the course we were forced to reconsider this choice as the progression of the course and the analysis of the results made us consider more structured and flexible educational models. Integration, however, remains the core choice for our work.

## 3.2 Stage 2

We analysed results to find out what had succeeded and what had not, what was worth keeping and what was not. The resulting actions were not conclusive but, as mentioned before, this process allowed us to gather more data in order to build a definitive educational model specifically aware of the new learner profile, which was considered to be "illiterate". At this stage two new types of course were introduced: literacy teaching and verbal skills-based courses. Literacy courses were focused on the skills that the students lacked: reading and writing. The target audience for this course was minors only. In the second type of course, which focused on verbal skills, the group was made up of different learner profiles that were kept together and the course content focused only on the abilities they all had in common: speaking and listening.

## 3.3 Stage 3

It was at this stage that the literacy course for minors was included in the educational offer of the School and a specific module was inserted in the program of our master's course, *Teoria, progettazione e didattica dell'italiano come lingua seconda e straniera* ('Italian as a second and foreign language: theory, project-based course design and teaching'), to analyse the profile of this new learner, the illiterate or low-literate learner (Arcuri and Mocciaro 2014).

Beyond the complexity of the linguistic profile of the minors that we were dealing with, we now had to define the overall profile of those students that we had come to meet regularly and with whom we shared experiences outside of the school. What life experience, hopes or wishes were hiding behind uncertain words, laughs and shyness? What people were hidden behind those Facebook profiles who shyly became "friends"?

At this stage, two important activities that were organised within the project allowed an increasing mutual trust and facilitated a stronger, though still uncertain, relationship between the school and the minors: a workshop about *Drama and Storytelling* (Amoruso et al. 2015) and a series of interviews with some of the students (De Fina et al. 2016).

## 3.4 Stage 4

It was at this stage that we were able to collaborate on a theoretical and didactic level with other research centres, drawing on national and international studies on the specificity of second language learning for poorly educated learners. We did not take any further steps in our educational choices at this stage, but we elaborated on the previous ones. For the minors, this was also a very important stage where they acquired a prominent role in telling their own stories (De Fina et al. 2016). As a follow-up of the storytelling workshop, they then moved from oral to visual work. This consisted of three projects which allowed them to show their stories and the image they wanted to give of themselves to the public. The three projects were: the video *The Butterfly Trip* by Yousif Latif Jaralla, the photography exhibition *A-tratti* by Antonio Gervasi, and the performance *Echi della lunga distanza* directed by Yousif Latif Yaralla (Amoruso et al. 2015; Amoruso and D'Agostino 2016a, 2016b).

## 3.5 Stage 5

The ongoing analysis we did of the educational project was based on a strong irrefutable fact: the particularly slow learning process of these students often signified a higher risk of fossilization or actual interruption of the learning process. That fact and other more strictly linguistic features, led us all to search for alternative answers, but more importantly to better formulate questions that addressed the issue at hand. This led to our need to broaden our research boundaries by getting in touch with other research groups that were facing the same issues: the multi-country and multi-target-language research group named LESLLA (Low Educated Second Language and Literacy Acquisition).

The results obtained by our research into cognitive processes connected with the acquisition of language by LESLLA subjects, the production of educational materials designed for literacy classes, and the trialling of new teaching models. These results have been successfully distributed around public schools, particularly in those schools with a high percentage of low-educated migrant students. In the first weeks of 2016, the Italian Language School for Foreigners and the public institution responsible for adult education (known as CPIA) launched a joint project with two lines of intervention: in-service teacher training and lessons in the CPIA courses taught by teachers from the School.

In the last two years many photos and stories told in the many native languages of unaccompanied minors have been shared with scholars, researchers and educators around the world in our various conferences and symposiums.

# References

Amoruso, Marcello, Mari D'Agostino & Yousif Jaralla (eds.). 2015. *Dai barconi all'università. Percorsi di inclusione linguistica per minori stranieri non accompagnati.* Palermo: Scuola di lingua italiana per Stranieri.
Amoruso, Marcello & Mari D'Agostino. 2016a. Migrant adolescents and adults with low and very low education level: Experiences and challenges for Sicilian educators. Paper

presented at the conference *Migrants & refugees seeking a new life*, Georgetown University, Washington DC, 7 April.

Amoruso, Marcello & Mari D'Agostino. 2016b. Analfabeti plurilingui: Prospettive della ricerca e modelli di didattica. Paper presented at the *International conference on acquisition and didactics of Italian,* SILFI Conference, Madrid, 5–6 April.

Arcuri, Adriana & Egle Mocciaro. 2014. *Verso una didattica linguistica riflessiva*. Palermo: Scuola di lingua italiana per Stranieri.

D'Agostino, Mari. 2012. *Sociolinguistica dell'Italia contemporanea*. Bologna: Il Mulino.

D'Agostino, Mari. 2015a. Chiamo uomo chi è padrone della sue lingue. Modelli di plurilinguismo da Lampedusa in su. Paper presented at the *International Conference of SLI*, Malta, 24–26 settember.

D'Agostino, Mari. 2015b. L'Italia delle Italie ieri e oggi. Paper presented at the ACIS conference *Fertile spaces, dynamic places: Mapping the cultures of Italy*, Sydney, 1–4 July.

D'Agostino, Mari. 2015c. L'Italia linguistica plurale di ieri e di oggi. Qualche storia e alcuni dati. Paper presented at the *Symposium on language in Italy in the 21st century*, The British Academy, London, 19 November.

D'Agostino, Mari & Giuseppina Sorce (eds.). 2016a. *Nuovi migranti e nuova didattica*. Palermo: Scuola di lingua italiana per Stranieri.

De Fina, Anna, Marcello Amoruso & Giuseppe Paternostro. 2016b. Learning about the other: Unaccompanied minors asylum seekers in Sicily. Paper presented at Research Working Group Language – Culture – Identity on Mediterranean Basin, Paris, 25 June.

Stefano Kluzer, Rocco De Paolis
# Using tablets for L2 learning with illiterate adult migrants: results from experiments in Piedmont and Emilia Romagna

**Abstract:** In this article, we describe the origin of the Tabula initiative concerning the use of tablets with illiterate and low-educated Italian L2 adult learners, and the collaboration that grew out of this innovative experience among teachers in two Italian regions. Then we summarize the Tabula approach's main features with respect to didactics and the use of digital technology. Finally, we briefly discuss the main impacts observed on the learners and make some suggestions about future steps.

**Résumé :** Nous revenons sur la genèse de l'initiative Tabula, dans le cadre de laquelle des tablettes ont été utilisées dans les cours d'italien L2 destinés aux apprenants adultes illettrés ou ayant un faible niveau d'instruction, et sur la collaboration instaurée par les enseignants de deux régions italiennes à partir de cette expérience innovante. Nous proposons ensuite une synthèse des principaux éléments de l'approche Tabula du point de vue de la didactique et de l'utilisation des technologies numériques. Enfin, nous examinons brièvement les principaux effets observés sur les apprenants et formulons quelques suggestions pour les étapes suivantes.

## 1 A short history of the Tabula experience

The Tabula experience started in 2012 when a teacher in the adult education centre CTP Parini in Turin[1] decided to explore the use of his iPad with illiterate foreign students who had repeatedly shown an interest in the device. He spent the first months searching for and testing different applications (henceforth apps) among those designed to teach children to read and write, and identifying useful functions in them. A few school colleagues joined these early informal trials,

---

[1] Adult education centres/schools in Italy used to be called CTP and have recently been reorganised and are now called CPIA (*Centri provinciali per l'istruzione degli adulti*).

**Stefano Kluzer,** Ervet S.p.A., Italy, E-mail: s.kluzer@gmail.com
**Rocco De Paolis,** Gruppo Ricerca Azione Tabula Torino, Italy, E-mail: rdepaolis@hotmail.com

DOI 10.1515/9783110477498-048, © 2017 Stefano Kluzer, Rocco De Paolis, published by De Gruyter.
This work is licensed under the Creative Commons Attribution-NonCommercial-NoDerivs 3.0 License.

which raised much enthusiasm among both students and teachers. Formazione 80, an adult education specialist association in Turin, was asked to prepare a project to explore systematically on a larger scale the use of tablets with Italian L2 adult learners and to submit the project to a national call of the European Integration Fund.

The Tabula project was approved with a budget of €130,000 for the school year 2013–2014. Besides Formazione 80, the coordinator, the partners involved were five CTPs in Turin and nearby Moncalieri and the ASAI–Terremondo associations, working with migrant families, refugees and disadvantaged youth. Videocommunity, a team of activist video-makers, also joined to produce visual documentation of the project's development and contribute to some of its activities.

Pre-A1/A1 Italian L2 courses run by CPIAs usually last about 200 hours. In the Tabula project, these were split into two modules: October–January and February–May. Tablets were used during 20 sessions lasting 2.5 hours each in one of the two modules of each course run by the partner schools. The 50 hours of tablet use thus correspond to about half of the classroom time of one module and a quarter of the duration of the full course.

In total, 138 students registered for the Tabula courses and 133 completed them; such very high attendance confirmed the validity of the Tabula approach. Participants' features: 68% were women (mostly 30–50 years old) from Northern Africa (51% from Morocco) and other regions; 22 were young men aged 16–19; 68% had never been to school (the majority) or had up to five years of school experience. About one third were newcomers who had been in Italy for less than one year. Almost 40% had been living in Italy longer than three years and were often quite fluent in oral Italian.

The project staff was composed of 12 experienced Italian L2 teachers, four tablet facilitators (who helped teachers design tablet-based learning activities, engaged in classroom work, and took care of the ten iPads available in each school), and five multimedia experts, who video-documented the project and ran specific Tabula labs, especially with young people.

While the Tabula project was running in spring 2014 staff from Ervet, the Emilia Romagna regional development agency, undertook a study visit to Turin. This resulted in a case study report[2] and two dissemination workshops organised for teachers in Bologna and Modena (June 2014) to illustrate the Tabula

---

2 *Tablets and video-conferencing in L2 Italian courses: two case studies from Turin and Fornovo Taro.* http://www.ervet.it/wp-content/uploads/downloads/2015/04/Pig3_ICT_Case-studies_ENG.pdf (accessed 4 May 2016)

project's method and results. Building on this input, CPIA Modena I designed its own *E tablet sia!* ('Let there be tablets') project to adapt and replicate the Tabula approach.³ Staff from Torino held a two-day teacher training session in Modena in January 2015 and collaboration between the two groups then continued through online exchanges and occasional visits.

After the end of the Tabula project, a composite action-research group named *Ricerca Azione Tabula Torino* gradually took shape. It is now made up of teachers from CPIAs, educators from NGOs, trainees, university students and researchers, volunteers, video-makers and other artists, evaluators and software developers. With support from the Piedmont regional government and the European Integration Fund during the 2014–2015 school year, this group continued the experimentation with tablets and extended the Tabula activities to other CPIAs in Cuneo, Biella, Alessandria – Novi. A total of 22 courses and 260 adult learners had experienced the Tabula approach by mid-2015.

These experiences showed the need for an entry-level app to learn simple words through syllables in the Italian language. Available apps are mostly in English or other foreign languages, and have features designed for young children that are often not appropriate for adults. To address these shortcomings, in spring 2015, Ervet funded and coordinated a joint effort with the *Tabula Torino* group and the Modena teachers, which developed the app *Fare Parole* ('Making words'). This web app is available free at http://www.fareparole.it and it can be used online (with the Chrome browser) or downloaded to a tablet, PC or smartphone. It contains 150 pages of learn-and-play exercises, with 140 words (selected according to CEFR pre-A1 and A1 levels) and related images and 700 recorded sounds.

At the time of writing, a pre-A1/A1 course curriculum had been developed for use with tablets, with eight didactic units addressing: personal identity; origin and nationality; body and appearance; health; the five senses; clothes; the house; work. The Tabula approach had become a regular feature in courses for illiterate and low-educated adult learners in some CPIAs in Piedmont and continued in Modena with the *E tablet sia!* project. The *Tabula Torino* group was exploring the use of tablets in new directions, e. g. active citizenship education. Other teachers around Italy were testing *Fareparole* and Ervet was exploring how to develop it further.

---

3 We want to thank Rosalia Italia of CPIA Modena I for her contribution to this article.

## 2 Didactics in the Tabula approach

Tabula envisages an accurate integration of tablets' use in the curriculum. This is done by detailed planning of teaching goals (in terms of communication functions, lexicon, grammar and instrumental skills to be developed) and related learning activities, and by identifying which apps can best enable and support them, and when and how the apps should be used. A specific planning grid was designed and tested to support this process.

Tabula considers it essential to undertake initial teacher training and follow-up activities, along with continuous didactic coordination through monthly meetings. These are needed to motivate and support teachers in their innovation effort: learning to use the planning grid, tablets and apps; discussing problems and solutions; sharing information about teaching methods and apps usage; suggesting new apps and functions to use. Tabula's mantra is "Never leave the teacher alone!"

Especially at the beginning, most teachers also need the support of a multimedia/tablet facilitator in planning and running classroom activities. At first, facilitators help to improve the students' digital skills, which tend to be low among illiterate adult users. As students' digital proficiency grows over time, the pace and diversity of individual activities in the classroom increase and facilitators help the teacher to respond to the challenge of effectively orchestrating group learning.

Finally, the Tabula approach encourages teachers to systematically document classroom activities and students' products with photos and videos, to keep a diary with descriptions and reflections, and to share these items within the didactic coordination process, by using free, easy-to-use online services such as Dropbox.

## 3 Technology in the Tabula approach

From a technological point of view, the Tabula approach envisages the flexible and complementary use of tablets – possibly one per student, although some activities may involve two students using the same tablet – and traditional tools and materials such as blackboard, exercise book, pen, pencil, eraser and paper clips. Each tool performs different practical and often symbolic functions. For instance, students like tablets because it is easy to correct or delete mistakes, and this makes them braver at trying things out. On the other hand, when a word or a sentence is eventually written correctly, it is usually copied into the exercise book. This is perceived as a more reliable back-up support and it can be taken home, whereas tablets must be left at school. Symbolically, paper is where "real writing" occurs. Interestingly, students also started using smartphones to take photos of their activities' output or to install apps that they enjoyed using on the tablets for re-use elsewhere.

Tabula adopted different types of apps, usually free and used selectively depending on planned activities. Some are apps already installed on the iPad (Pages and Fotocamera); others are from well-known internet services (Google Search, Google maps and YouTube); some provide tools for creative tasks (Little Story Creator, Pic Collage, Sand Artist and Strip Design); only a few are specifically designed for literacy purposes (Abc Easy Writer, Alphabet Tablet, Blackboard). Over time, additional useful apps were added to this list and the *Fare Parole* app was even developed specifically for illiterate Italian L2 adult learners.

Finally, the Tabula approach identified three roles for video projectors, Apple TV and interactive whiteboards. Teachers and facilitators relied on them to visualize explanations about how to use new devices, apps and functions, to facilitate collective reading with dynamic visualization (e. g. highlighting, isolating or magnifying letters and syllables) and to show and share the results of individual and group learning activities.

## 4 Impact and final considerations

The main visible impacts of using tablets following the Tabula approach have been a much higher than usual course attendance, stronger student engagement in learning, and greater social interaction in the classroom. Tabula teachers and evaluators have also identified a range of enhanced cognitive abilities, language/ communication and alphabetical skills, along with improved learner self-esteem and motivation. These effects have not yet been measured and analysed in detail, but they seem to stem from a number of factors. For instance, students enjoy very much the opportunities for personalized learning and creative expression (through free drawing, easy choice and change of colours, fonts, patterns etc.), and the playful but also authentic aspects of shooting photos and videos, during simulations, dialogues and other activities at school and out of school (e. g. a visit to an open-air market). Mothers also seem to gain an enhanced status in their family and beyond, from being seen to be capable of using a symbol of modern technology such as the iPad and other tablets. More generally, there seems to be a strong empowerment effect on illiterate or low-educated adults as they become literate, learn a second language and gain digital competence, all at the same time. Learning to use new digital devices and online services is increasingly perceived as a key to full citizenship in our society.

Given these first positive results, more effort should go into scaling up the current small-scale and often isolated experiences and establishing networks at national and European levels of researchers, teachers and other practitioners. Promising new research and trials could focus on how to exploit mobile devices (tablets and smart phones) to support adult literacy and L2 learning as a continuous process inside and outside of school.

Fernanda Minuz, Alessandro Borri
# Literacy and language teaching: tools, implementation and impact

**Abstract:** Course planning and language assessment tools for Italian L2 have recently been developed. *Italiano L2 in contesti migratori: Sillabo e descrittori* (IL2S) is based on the *Common European Framework of Reference for Languages* (CEFR; Council of Europe 2001). Focusing on illiterate and semi-literate adults, IL2 sets standards and recommends criteria for teaching both literacy and L2. This paper discusses the results of the validation procedure of IL2S, which aimed to verify its accuracy in terms of descriptive power, its validity for course design and language assessment, and its impact on teaching.

**Résumé :** Des outils ont récemment été développés pour planifier les cours d'italien en L2 et évaluer le niveau de langue. « Italiano L2 in contesti migratori. Sillabo e descrittori » s'appuie sur le *Cadre européen commun de référence pour les langues* (CECR, Conseil de l'Europe 2001). Destiné aux adultes illettrés et « semi-alphabétisés », IL2 définit des normes et recommande des critères pour les cours de littératie et de L2. L'article passe en revue les résultats de la procédure de validation IL2S, en vue de contrôler son adéquation en termes de capacité à décrire, sa validité pour la conception des cours et l'évaluation du niveau de langue, et son impact sur l'enseignement.

## 1 Syllabus and descriptors for illiterate, semi-literate and literate users: from illiteracy to A1 level

The need to identify descriptors of language proficiency for first levels in migration contexts – specifically, for levels that are lower than those of the CEFR, has become more and more apparent in many member states of the Council of Europe. As a side effect of the legal requirements established in many European countries, the significant presence of illiterates, semi-literates and persons with

---

**Fernanda Minuz** (corresponding author), Johns Hopkins University – SAIS Europe, Italy, E-mail: ferminuz@tin.it
**Alessandro Borri,** CPIA Montagna, Castel di Casio (Bologna), Italy, E-mail: alexandros@cpia montagna.it

learning difficulties has become visible to both the public and to educational authorities.

To address this group of language learners, specific language and literacy programmes have been set up and CEFR integration for some national languages have been issued, such as Beacco et al. (2005) for French.

*Italiano Lingua Seconda in contesti migratori* (IL2S; Borri et al. 2014) is a tool to plan courses, create teaching materials and prepare tests at levels preceding the level A1 of the CEFR, to which it is explicitly related. It consists of two parts. The syllabus defines the domains – private, public, professional, educational – and six thematic areas; and the descriptors present the levels of language competence and literacy in terms of "can do" – that is, the actions that learners should be able to perform in each domain and the language content they should know in order to carry out those actions (Spinelli and Parizzi 2010). The third section presents the literacy objectives, divided into technical skills (the ability to draw letters and combine graphics and phonetics) and study skills. As we consider literacy a part of communicative language competence, the literacy objectives are strongly linked to the preceding sections. A word list defines the lexical objectives. IL2S sets out four stages, in relation to different learning profiles:

- Pre-Alpha A1, for pre-literates: non-educated adults, whose mother tongue is not written or is not the medium of schooling in the country of origin.
- Alpha A1, for illiterates: adults who cannot read and write in their mother tongue and have never been educated.
- Pre-A1, for semi-literates: adults who received a low level of education in their mother tongue or partially lost their literacy skills because they do not read and write.
- A1, corresponding to the CEFR level, for literates.

# 2 Assessment of IL2S

## 2.1 Scope and objectives

A validation procedure was set up for IL2S to assess its *accuracy* (descriptive power), its *validity* (its appropriateness in determining teaching objectives and testing criteria), and its *impact* on the quality of language teaching and testing. The trial focused on the development of writing ability, starting from instrumental and functional literacy.

## 2.2 Steps and methodology

- *Sampling of the participants.* We selected the educational agencies participating in the assessment taking into account their diversity (five state adult education centres, four voluntary associations, one private vocational training centre) and regional distribution (ten towns, across Italy). 19 teachers participated on a voluntary basis, after a brief period of training.
- *Overview of the teaching situations.* Using two questionnaires, we established the research participants' profiles (educational background and teaching experience), the composition of the classes (students' countries of origin, L1s, L2s, levels of literacy), and the learners' profiles (linguistic repertoires, literacy and schooling, contacts with Italian speakers).
- *Collection and analysis of samples of learners' written productions.* In order to assess the accuracy and validity of the tool, we tested the descriptors on 800 samples of writing produced by students at different stages of the Pre-Alpha, Alpha A1, Pre-A1 courses.
- *Feedback from the research participants.* The research participants piloted IL2S by integrating it into their everyday practice. At the end of the trial, we asked for feedback through structured interviews to assess the impact of IL2S.

## 2.3 Results

### 2.3.1 Teaching setting, classes, and teachers

The research participants used IL2S to plan and implement 14 courses, lasting 60 hours on average (ranging from 30 to 100 hours). 167 students attended the courses, from 18 countries, and with 19 mother tongues. 48 of them spoke at least one L2 (11 L2s other than Italian).

The research confirmed well-known problems. All classes were highly diverse in terms of the language competence, literacy, and linguistic backgrounds of the students, in some cases ranging from illiterates without any knowledge of Italian to A2 educated students. Moreover, individual students rarely presented homogeneous profiles: some students who were pre-A1 in writing skills could speak Italian up to B1. Thus, teachers – all of them with relevant experience or education – claimed to use differentiated teaching techniques, mostly based on cooperative learning approaches.

Course attendance was irregular, even when learners were motivated to learn. Most teachers commented that the class ambiance was pleasant, cooperative and motivating. However, illiterates could show "distress", "discouragement", "confusion".

The need for a quick response to the sudden and irregular presence of refugees and asylum seekers in a given area has affected the size of classes (up to 40 students), the duration of courses (30 hours in some cases), and teaching activities.

### 2.3.2 Accuracy and validity of IL2S

The research results broadly confirmed the accuracy of IL2S as a descriptive and assessment tool and its validity in representing the development of communicative language skills and literacy.

We tested the descriptors on samples of writing produced by the students, as in the following example (Figure 1). It was produced as a response to the task "Write a shopping list", which the class had practised several times; the student wrote the words without assistance.

```
3. SCRIVI LA LISTA DELLA SPESA   __/5

1. ......LATTE...................................
2. ......PA.ME...................................
3. ......SOLE...................................
4. ......VOSAVASO..............................
5. ......ROSA...................................
```

**Figure 1:** Sample of writing

The sample corresponds to Alpha A1 descriptors such as: *He/she understands the relation between the spoken and written language; He/she can write single words, which are of personal interest or familiar (capital script).* The student has understood the alphabetic principle (*correspondence between phonemes and graphemes*), although with some uncertainty in combining sounds and letters (*vosavaso – vaso*). However, she produces a list made up of individual words (*milk, bread, sun, vase, rose*), confirming that the ability to write a simple text as a shopping list pertains to the level Pre-A1.

The student appears to focus on showing her ability to write the words that she has practised in the literacy exercises (bi-syllables, paroxytone words). However, the ability to implement reality-oriented tasks requires that learners understand the aims, formats, and conventions of the learning activities. This understanding is a result of schooling and is stated as a literacy objective in IL2S at the level Alpha A1: *He/she starts to recognize the types of exercises and teaching activities.*

All research participants remarked that IL2S was valuable in outlining the profiles of students, thus in better designing tailor-made courses. They appreciated the stress on different forms of illiteracy, expressed in the continuum from illiterates to strong literates, and heterogeneous individual profiles, which led them to question the notion of levels *per se*.

The relation between the development of oral ability and literacy has emerged as a critical issue. The classroom experience that illiterates most likely need more time to learn oral language than semi-literate or literate learners seems to be confirmed by research, although still at an early stage (Tarone and Bigelow 2005). According to this assumption, IL2S defines sequences of language content that proceed in parallel for written and oral skills. This has prompted some participants to balance the teaching of literacy and oral skills.

## 2.4 Impact

All research participants reported a positive impact of IL2S on their teaching, with obvious differences due to experience and competence. They said one positive feature was its coherence with the CEFR, which all of them used, and the relation between literacy programmes and CEFR. More specifically, they appreciated the articulation between primary literacy and language teaching in the communicative perspective. This approach, already adopted by some of them, encourages the view that literacy acquisition involves more than mastery of technical skills.

Other positive impacts of the tool were that it helped teachers create a more systematic organization of learning objectives, more accurately plan courses, and more realistically pace the presentation of content.

One issue with the tool that the experimentation has brought to light is the twofold function of the stages identified before A1. On the one hand, they are designed in relation to specific groups of learners: Alpha A1 descriptors refer to the probable performance of illiterates after 150 hours of instruction. In this sense, the stages do not prefigure a progression for all students, who enter the stage appropriate to their profile. However, the two literacy stages Pre-Alpha and Alpha A1 (and to a lesser extent Pre-A1), can represent levels, in the sense of steps toward the acquisition of literacy. Further classroom research is needed.

# 3 Conclusions

The results of the validation procedure show that IL2S has a positive impact on the quality of teaching. It helps the teachers better understand the educational needs of learners. It provides them with practical suggestions about the content of teaching and its progression according to the learners' needs, the aim of the course, and the teaching setting.

Although IL2S focuses on the Italian language, we propose it as a contribution to a European L2 and literacy syllabus. Migration has both local and international dimensions, as the constantly changing routes and forms of people's movements show. We are convinced that ongoing revision of the CEFR to make it more suitable to language learning and teaching in migration contexts is a European endeavour, to which experiences from each country can contribute.

This syllabus must be able to give an account of the diversity of learning profiles, and of the specificity of literacy in L2. The language and literacy learning paths are strongly connected and interlinked, but they do not overlap. Instead of "progression", "progressions" are to be described. The syllabus must also consider the vast array of communicative situations and language needs that migrants meet across a multilingual Europe, including individual as well as social and educational conditions.

# References

Beacco, Jean Claude, Mariela De Ferrari, Gilbert Lhote & Christine Tagliante. 2005. *Niveau A1.1 pour le français: Référentiel et certification (DILF) pour les premiers acquis en français*. Paris: Didier.

Borri, Alessandro, Fernanda Minuz, Lorenzo Rocca & Chiara Sola. 2014. *Italiano L2 in contesti migratori. Sillabo e descrittori dall'alfabetizzazione all'A1*. Torino: Loescher.

Council of Europe. 2001. *Common European Framework of Reference for Languages: Learning, teaching, assessment*. Cambridge: Cambridge University Press. http://www.coe.int/t/dg4/linguistic/Source/Framework_EN.pdf (accessed 10 August 2016).

Spinelli, Barbara & Francesca Parizzi. 2010. *Profilo della lingua italiana. Livelli di riferimento del QCER A1, A2, B1, B2*. Firenze: La Nuova Italia.

Tarone, Elaine & Martha Bigelow. 2005. Impact of literacy on oral language processing: Implications for second language acquisition research. *Annual Review of Applied Linguistics* 25. 77–97.

Marie Hélène Lachaud

# La « raison orale », un levier pour la formation linguistique des migrants et l'intégration dans le pays d'accueil

**Résumé :** Cette recherche se déroule en France. Elle concerne les formations linguistiques à visée d'insertion professionnelle d'adultes peu qualifiés, francophones ou non. L'étude porte sur les processus d'acquisition des savoirs scripturaux. Nous interrogeons la relation entre les savoirs et savoir-faire mobilisés à l'oral et l'apprentissage de l'écrit. Les résultats identifient les compétences de ces adultes dont certaines sont proches de l'écrit. Verbalisées, elles mettent au jour la « raison orale » et constituent un levier pour la formation et l'insertion socio-professionnelle.

**Abstract:** This research is being carried out in France. It relates to language education aimed at integrating both French and non-French speaking low-skilled adults into the employment market. The study covers the processes involved in acquiring written knowledge. The author examines the relationship between the knowledge and skills used for speaking a language and for learning to write it. The results show the skills these adults possess, some of which are more inclined towards writing. When applied orally, they bring to the fore an "oral logic" and can serve as a lever for training and socio-professional integration.

## 1 Étude du langage et de l'écrit au travail : cadre conceptuel

Cette étude est menée dans le cadre de notre thèse de doctorat en Sciences du langage et du Groupe de recherche action formation en français, intégration et compétences (GRAFFIC) du Laboratoire de Linguistique et Didactique des Langues Étrangères et Maternelles (LIDILEM). Elle concerne la formation d'adultes peu lecteurs-scripteurs, francophones ou non, inscrits dans des parcours d'insertion professionnelle. Notre pratique de formation nous conduit à constater de nombreuses compétences techniques mobilisées par les adultes sur les postes de

---

**Marie Hélène Lachaud**, LIDILEM – Université Grenoble Alpes, France, E-mail : lachaud.marie-helene@free.fr

travail. Nous interrogeons la nature de ces compétences ainsi que leur mise en relation avec les savoirs à acquérir pour le développement des compétences scripturales.

## 1.1 Compétence langagière et représentations sociales

La compétence langagière se compose de la compétence orale et scripturale. Peytard (1970 : 37) distingue ce qui relève de l'oral par des éléments audibles « réalisés par articulation » de ceux qui se rapportent à l'écrit par ce qui peut être lu et produit par la graphie. Les notions de représentations sociales et de « rapport à » sont des éléments constitutifs de la compétence scripturale (Dabène 1992). Les actes d'écriture et de lecture sont imprégnés des représentations sociales construites au fil du temps par la personne, en relation avec son environnement social, professionnel et personnel. Selon la norme sociale, certains écrits sont plus valorisés que d'autres. Toutefois, Dabène souligne le continuum qui existe entre les différents types d'écrits. Ils sont reliés par un élément commun : le geste d'écriture. La compétence scripturale est donc composée d'un ensemble de savoirs et savoir-faire d'ordre « linguistique [...], sémiotique, sociologique, pragmatique, textuel » (Dabène 1992 : 104) qui se construisent progressivement dans et par l'acculturation à l'écrit.

## 1.2 Littératie : point de vue pluridimensionnel de l'écrit

De même que la compétence scripturale définie par Dabène met en relief d'autres éléments que la maîtrise du code, celle de la littératie considère l'écrit sous l'angle de la complexité. « La *littératie* c'est à la fois un ensemble d'habiletés comportementales et intellectuelles incorporées (par le scripteur et le lecteur), un système d'objets et de dispositifs (crayon ou ordinateur, bureau ou bibliothèque), un régime de certification sociale (les « papiers », les dossiers) et d'affiliation symbolique (les savoirs fondamentaux, les savants) » (Privat 2015 : 116). Depuis les années 1980, les travaux sur la littératie et les apports pluridisciplinaires des *New Literacy Studies* soulignent la pluralité « des formes sociales d'usage de l'écriture » ainsi que la variation de sa mise en œuvre d'un contexte à un autre (Fraenkel & Mobj 2010 : 12–13). La complexité concerne la variété des supports et des écrits. Ce sont également les activités mentales générées par la lecture et l'écriture, dont la compréhension, le raisonnement et les représentations sociales. Ces opérations mentales se trouvent reliées au contexte dans lequel elles sont mises en œuvre ainsi qu'à sa variation culturelle et temporelle (Jaffré 2004). Dans cette étude, nous nous intéressons au développement de la compétence scripturale. En conséquence, nous envisageons l'écrit dans son contexte d'utilisation à partir de la variété des supports, des formes et des pratiques mais aussi des savoir-faire mis en œuvre dans la lecture et l'écriture.

### 1.3 Rationalité dans l'oralité et raison graphique

Des actions relatives à la gestion du temps et l'espace sont réalisées sans avoir recours à l'écrit. Ces actes offrent la possibilité d'avoir une emprise sur l'environnement, ce sont les « manières de faire » et les « astuces » décrites par de Certeau (1990). Nous verrons dans le paragraphe suivant que dans le travail de nettoyage, les employés développent des savoir-faire en matière de structuration des tâches dans le temps et dans l'espace. Ils planifient, délimitent l'espace, font face à des imprévus et réorganisent le travail pour être efficaces. Ce sont des savoir-faire rationnels qui témoignent d'une emprise sur le temps et l'espace (Lahire 1995). Ces savoir-faire issus de l'oralité peuvent être rapprochés de la raison graphique, car ils s'apparentent à l'écrit et à la rationalité propre à l'écriture qui consiste notamment à classer, ordonner et mettre en relation des informations (Goody 1979). Ainsi, oralité et scripturalité peuvent être envisagées en continuité à partir d'un élément commun : la rationalité.

## 2 Enquête sur la littératie au travail

Notre objectif est d'étudier l'écrit et sa maîtrise dans le contexte de son utilisation. Dans la continuité des travaux menés sur le langage au travail, nous distinguons les écrits du travail réel de ceux du travail prescrit (Borzeix & Fraenkel 2001). L'enquête se déroule auprès de dix-sept agents d'entretien dans cinq entreprises françaises. Nous procédons à des observations de postes de travail et à des entretiens semi-directifs menés auprès des employés, de leur responsable et des formateurs. Enfin, des données ethnographiques collectées dans le cadre du GRAFFIC complètent ce recueil.

### 2.1 Écrits et pratiques de littératie invisibles

Malgré les déclarations des responsables et d'autres professionnels recueillies lors des entretiens, nous relevons un grand nombre d'écrits sur les lieux de travail des employés du nettoyage. Ces écrits se répartissent en quatre catégories.

Ce sont les écrits règlementaires transmis par les entreprises pour organiser l'activité comme les consignes de sécurité et les fiches de poste. Une seconde catégorie comprend les écrits du travail réel. Empruntée aux travaux des ergonomes, la notion de travail réel et prescrit distingue les écrits émis par l'entreprise de ceux que les employés produisent spontanément pendant l'activité. Il s'agit des aide-mémoire et des messages adressés aux usagers. La troisième catégorie est celle des écrits de l'environnement de travail. Elle rassemble les écrits destinés aux usagers des lieux entretenus par les employés. Ce sont par exemple, la désignation des services et des bâtiments, les revues déposées dans un hall d'entrée et des éléments de numératie comme la numérotation des bureaux et des bâtiments. Enfin, la quatrième catégorie comprend d'autres marques de l'univers sémiotique de l'entreprise telles que les logogrammes, les pictogrammes les schémas et les couleurs qui codifient le matériel.

## 2.2 Traces de littératie dans l'oral

La parole des employés occupe également une place de choix dans le recueil de données. Il s'agit d'une part des interactions entre pairs, avec la hiérarchie et avec les usagers des lieux entretenus. D'autre part, les employés s'expriment sur leur travail et d'autres thèmes sans être sollicités, tout en travaillant.

## 2.3 Rationalité des gestes professionnels

Les observations confrontent la parole avec les gestes, au regard de la gestion de l'espace et du temps. Par gestes, nous entendons les mouvements corporels, les déplacements et les postures adoptées par les employés lorsqu'ils réalisent le travail.
- l'autonomie dans l'organisation du travail,
- la planification des actions,
- l'observation fine des lieux et l'analyse des informations pour adapter le travail aux différentes contraintes,
- l'analyse des situations imprévues,
- l'adaptation aux différentes situations de communication,
- la mémorisation des lieux, des habitudes, des tâches et de leur succession.

Verbalisées pendant l'activité, ces capacités, dont les tours de main et manières de faire, constituent des savoir-faire qui relèvent de l'oralité.

## 3 Pistes didactiques

Cette étude met l'accent sur l'identification des compétences ignorées des adultes. Verbalisées, ces compétences mettent au jour la raison orale. Il s'agit de capacités mises en œuvre dans les actes du quotidien. Ces savoir-faire sont rationnels et ne sont pas spontanément évoqués au moment des entretiens. La verbalisation et l'explicitation sont des moyens d'accéder à ces savoir-faire et donc aux acquis en particulier pour les moins scolarisés. Interroger le curriculum linguistique et le parcours professionnel à partir des manières de faire pour développer de nouveaux savoirs permet d'établir un inventaire des acquis. Dans les formations, prendre appui sur ces acquis revient à adapter les contenus aux savoirs et savoir-faire déjà construits. Cela favorise leur circulation d'un contexte à un autre et permet ainsi d'adapter la formation aux besoins de chacun.

## Références

Borzeix, Anni & Béatrice Fraenkel, 2001. *Langage et travail. Communication, cognition, action.* Paris : CNRS Editions.
Dabène, Michel. 1992. Compétences scripturales et pratiques d'écriture. In Jean-Marie Besse, Marie-Madeleine de Gaulmyn, Dominique Ginet & Bernard Lahire (dir.), *L'illettrisme en questions*, 101–107. Lyon : Presses universitaires de Lyon.
De Certeau, Michel. 1990. *L'invention du quotidien. Vol. 1, Arts de faire.* Paris : Gallimard.
Fraenkel, Béatrice. 1993. Enquête sur les pratiques d'écriture en usine. In Béatrice Fraenkel (dir.), *Illettrisme. Variations historiques et anthropologiques*, 267–283. Paris : Centre Georges Pompidou. Bibliothèque publique d'information.
Fraenkel, Béatrice & Aïssatou Mbodj, 2010. Introduction. Les New Literacy studies, jalons historiques et perspectives actuelles. *Langage et société, 133*, 7–24.
Goody, Jack. 1979. *La raison graphique.* Paris : Les Éditions de Minuit.
Jaffré, Jean-Pierre. 2004. La litéracie : histoire d'un mot, effets d'un concept. In Christine Barré-De Miniac, Catherine Brissaud, & Marielle Rispail (dir.), *La littéracie. Conceptions théoriques et pratiques d'enseignement de la lecture-écriture*, 21–41. Paris : L'Harmattan.
Lahire, Bernard. 1995. *Tableaux de familles. Heurs et malheurs scolaires en milieux populaires.* Paris : Seuil/Gallimard.
Peytard, Jean. 1970. Oral et scriptural : deux ordres de situations et de descriptions linguistiques. *Langue Française, 6*, 35–47.
Privat, Jean-Marie. 2015. Pr. Jack Goody (1919–2015), *Revue française de pédagogie.* http://rfp.revues.org/4714 (consulté le 11 janvier 2016).

Antonella Benucci, Marilisa Birello
# Immigrants and prison: good practices in Europe[1]

**Abstract:** Within the RiUscire project an important section was devoted to the collection and analysis of good practices that may support the linguistic and social integration of a particular group of adult migrants: those in the prison systems of Spain, Italy, France, Germany, and Portugal. The collection of these practices is necessary and pivotal to start a shared action at a European level. Best practices were surveyed through analysis grids that ensure respect for diversity and the right to rehabilitative actions thanks to linguistic and communicative competences as well as professional development.

**Résumé :** Un volet important du projet RiUscire a été consacré à la collecte et à l'analyse des bonnes pratiques susceptibles de soutenir l'intégration linguistique et sociale d'un groupe particulier de migrants adultes, incarcérés en Espagne, en Italie, en France, en Allemagne et au Portugal. Le recueil de ces pratiques est nécessaire et essentiel pour lancer une action commune au niveau européen. Les bonnes pratiques ont été examinées à l'aide de grilles d'analyse qui garantissent le respect de la diversité et le droit à des mesures de réinsertion grâce à des compétences linguistiques et de communication, ainsi qu'au développement professionnel.

## 1 Introduction

RiUscire[2] intends to take advantage of the multi/plurilingual and intercultural dimension of the prison context to turn it into a place of resources, empowerment

---

[1] This article is the result of a collaborative effort: Antonella Benucci wrote sections 1 and 4, and Marilisa Birello wrote sections 2 and 3.
[2] RiUscire (Rete Universitaria SocioCulturale per l'Istruzione e il Recupero in Carcere) 2014-1-IT02-KA204-003517. Partners: Università per Stranieri di Siena (coordinator); Université Paris VII Diderot; Otto-Friedrich Universität-Bamberg; Fundação Fernando Pessoa–Universidade Fernando Pessoa; Universitat Autònoma de Barcelona; Istituto Superiore di Studi Penitenziari (ISSP), Rome.

**Antonella Benucci,** Università per Stranieri di Siena, Italy, E-mail: benucci@unistrasi.it
**Marilisa Birello** (corresponding author), Universitat Autònoma de Barcelona, Spain,
E-mail: marilisa.birello@uab.cat

DOI 10.1515/9783110477498-051, © 2017 Antonella Benucci, Marilisa Birello, published by De Gruyter.
This work is licensed under the Creative Commons Attribution-NonCommercial-NoDerivs 3.0 License.

and rehabilitation through integrated training courses addressed to foreign prisoners, prison staff and teachers working in prison. The goals of the project are:
- to promote and utilize the plurilingualism and cultural diversity inherent in prison contexts;
- to promote the education of inmates through intercultural communication and the improvement of linguistic-cultural competencies and linguistic-professional abilities;
- to motivate educational action and personal development/improvement;
- to provide operators and teachers with tools for better understanding the processes of communication with foreign inmates.

The recognition of what is being done in European prisons aims to identify good practices and their typology and to propose a model for better promoting adult education in the prison context through intercultural communication, developing the linguistic-cultural and linguistic-professional skills of detainees for social and occupational reintegration. Finally, we ask ourselves whether and how a practice can be considered a model if it is reused in other socio-linguistic and socio-cultural contexts.

## 2 Good practices: a definition

The terminology referring to good examples is varied and controversial: sometimes *best practice* is used, other times *good practice,* or also *learning practice.* We prefer to use *good practice* because we do not want to consider only those areas of *learning* and we believe that *best* is limiting in that it does not leave room for improvement, which instead is our ultimate goal.

By "good practices" we mean the best examples of practice in the fields of personal and professional development, education and instruction, approaches, instruments, and use of technology, etc., used to advance the conditions and re-insertion of inmates. These practices must also be easily transferable to other similar situations with similar goals.

In the penitentiary context, a broad variety of courses are organized, but not all of them can be considered as good practices. Good practices are educational, pedagogical and treatment actions or activities that, in the socio-educational penitentiary context, allow the actors to achieve the expected results.[3] According

---

[3] Regarding European prisons, see among others Hawley, Murphy & Souto-Otero (2013), Puy Roca and Aliaga (2007), Benucci (2015).

to Banelytė, Sternadel and Brožaitis, they constitute desirable models for all European countries and a starting point for the development of new shared good practice:

> The aim of the identification and sharing of good practices is to capture evidence on the effectiveness of a practice, to improve its visibility and dissemination so that it becomes easily accessible and reusable by all informed stakeholders: decision-makers, socioeconomic partners, NGOs, academia, media, and civil society at large, and facilitates learning from others. It is expected that the sharing of good practices will inspire further change and "better practice". (Banelytė, Sternadel, and Brožaitis 2015: 5)

In RiUscire good practice is defined by educational as well as pedagogical activity, action or treatments (projects, guidelines, educational material, internships or work experience etc.) that allow the agents to set actions to reach the planned results in the specific socio-educational context of a prison.

This paper provides some general reflections of the most common prison practices in the five European Countries of the project (Italy, Germany, France, Portugal and Spain); the context of the study is limited to a sample from the data collected in different prisons.

## 3 Methodology and instruments

The analysis of good practices in RiUscire was based on 10 general criteria selected according to the most frequent research in this field (Benucci and Cortés 2014; Benucci 2015):
1. effectiveness (results on target with the objectives of the project and suitable concerning the direct and indirect effects on the final recipients in relation to professional reintegration);
2. efficiency (positive balance between the resources used for the realization and the results obtained);
3. coherence (inner and outer coherence, that is adult education and EU recommendations);
4. reproducibility (in new, similar or different contexts from the situation in which it was originally realized);
5. level of involvement and satisfaction (supports the technical, cultural and human resources of the reference target, evokes positive attitudes among the participants);
6. innovation (new and creative solutions for the project/process; it encourages the active participation of the beneficiaries and other subjects; it involves social agents, from without the penitentiary context);

7. accessibility (practicality in the organization and participation);
8. added value (produces changes in the penitentiary and social context, e.g. reducing the rate of second offenses committed, improving the competences of teachers and penitentiary staff);
9. institutional recognition (if the practice is recognized, respected or promoted at institutional level);
10. sustainability (founded on existing resources or able to create new ones, ability to carry on producing effects well over the duration of the project).

We are aware that the parameters used for measuring the results of a practice are often subjective and not standardized.

Obviously this initial analysis is inherently superficial, and can only give an orientation and overview of our work. Instead, the criterion of innovation offers sufficient proof of reliability because it allows us to highlight those practices and countries which stand out among the others for their originality.

Keeping in mind the above-mentioned elements, we created a form containing the best combination of the elements observed during our investigations. In particular, the form includes a series of sections with different levels of both descriptive and analytic data. For each practice identified by the internal and external collaborators of the project, a form is completed, following these sections: country and practice number; concise description of the project (title, programmatic context, sector, contact person, budget); description of the material/specifications of the projects (aims, description, contextualization, innovative aspects); informative data about the project (practice) participants; contact information; availability of good practices material; description of the RiUscire data base.

The completed forms were then sent to 16 referees from different countries, external to the project but with solid competences in the following fields: communication, language didactics, evaluation of project and didactic/operational/scientific material. The referees were asked to evaluate each practice based on the description given on each form (and when possible, examining the practice itself) and invited to award a score from 1 to 5 (low to high) for each of the 10 criteria. To be considered "good", a practice needed to have a minimum score of 3.

## 4 Data and conclusions

As we are writing this paper 120 good practices have been collected (still in progress), of which ten were considered not good. In total we have 108 good practices: 61 had a score between 3 and 3.9 and 47 had a score between 4 and 5.

Regarding the scores from 1 to 5 (1 = unsatisfactory, 5 = very good) on each criterion, we can affirm that the average never goes below *satisfactory* (3). The two highest-scoring criteria in the corpus are *reproducibility in other contexts* (4.16) and the degree of *involvement and satisfaction* (4.12), while the lowest are *institutional recognition* (3.46) and degree of *innovation* (3.58). Innovation is quite strongly present in Italy and Spain, with a variety of practices and encouragement of such diversity. By contrast, Portugal is among the least innovative, with fewer genuinely re-educational interventions.

Here, in order, are the most common activities within the typologies considered:
- Job training (35%), with consistent collaboration between prisons and companies to facilitate reinsertion of inmates in the world of work, with the presence of specific courses (i.e. online cookery class; sound technician; green spaces maintenance): most common in Italy, least common in Germany.
- Languages/forms of expression (19.2%.), i.e. theatre, dance, photography, radio broadcasting: most common in Germany, absent in Spain.
- Social reconstruction (11.7%), to prepare inmates for reinsertion in society after prison; activities to improve the psychological and physical health of inmates: most common in France, absent in Portugal and Spain.
- Training for prison personnel and teachers (10.8%), deconstruction of prejudices and intercultural sensitivity training and analysis and suitability of lesson plans: most common in Italy, present in France and Spain.
- Teaching L2 or L1 with a particular focus on reading skills (6.7%): present in Germany and France.
- Writing courses (5.8%), especially workshops on journalistic language: present in Germany and Italy, less so in Spain.
- Communication techniques (4.2%), general and intercultural, with particular focus on artistic practices: most common in France.

The least common typologies of activities include *transversality of learning* (interdisciplinarity and study of various subjects), *secondary and post-secondary education* (usually via e-learning), *computer courses, reading courses*.

In order to be able to use these criteria in the evaluation of good practices, one should focus on the intrinsic as well as the extrinsic problems of the concept itself. When it comes to intrinsic difficulty it is already very clear that the ten criteria mentioned are not sufficient to define the concept of good practices and cannot guarantee correct categorization. Extrinsic difficulties especially concern the differing didactic traditions in the way linguistic and glottodidactic theories are spread in the different countries, and the different value attributed to performance arts as re-education in the countries considered.

Activities in prison are heterogeneous, hardly ever coordinated between institutions, and do not sufficiently allow for positive results in other countries/local contexts. Once a level of first alphabetization or A1 (sometimes A2) has been reached, cultural/linguistic education is no longer of much or widespread interest.

# References

Banelytė, Viltė, Dalibor Sternadel & Haroldas Brožaitis. 2015. *Monitoring good practices in the areas of employement, social affairs and inclusion*. Brussels: European Commission.

Benucci, Antonella. 2015. Oltre i confini del carcere: buone pratiche per l'italiano L2. Introduzione. In Giulia Bertolotto, Serena Carmignani & Giovanna Sciuti Russi (eds.), *Percorsi di ricerca e formazione linguistico-professionale: DEPORT "Oltre i confini del carcere"*, I–III. Siena: Tipografia Senese Editrice.

Benucci, Antonella & Diego Cortés Velásquez. 2014. Buone pratiche in intercomprensione: una visione d'insieme. *SeLM* 1–3. 10–17.

Hammerschick, Walter. 2010. Report on e-Learning in European prisons: Concepts, organisation, pedagogical approaches in prison education. LICOS (Learning Infrastructure for Correctional Services). https://ec.europa.eu/epale/sites/epale/files/report_on_e-learning_in_european_prisons.pdf (accessed 17 August 2016).

Hawley, Jo, Ilona Murphy & Manuel Souto-Otero. 2013. *Prison education and training in Europe*. http://ec.europa.eu/education/library/study/2013/prison_en.pdf. (accessed 25 May 2016).

Puy Roca, Òscar & José Miguel Aliaga. 2007. *White Paper – Prison Work in Europe*. Barcelona: CIRE. http://archivio.transnazionalita.isfol.it/file/White%20Paper%20-%20Prison%20work%20in%20Europe%20-%20CIRE%20-%20EQUAL%20AD%20644.pdf (accessed 17 August 2016).

## 8 Linguistic integration: teachers and researchers
Intégration linguistique : enseignants et chercheurs

Massimiliano Spotti
# "Crawlers, footers and runners": language ideological attributions to adult language learners in a Dutch as L2 classroom

**Abstract:** This paper deals with a volunteer teacher teaching Dutch as an L2 to asylum seekers at a Red Cross asylum seeker centre in West Flanders, Belgium. More precisely, it investigates the practical professional knowledge of this volunteer teacher, taking a peek into her meta-pragmatic judgements about language and her views on her students' literacy skills (or lack thereof). It further shows how her students manage to challenge her authority through jocular moves which reveal the value of their multilingual repertoires and the literacy skills they already own through their previous experiences with various literacy systems.

**Résumé :** Dans cet article consacré à une enseignante bénévole qui enseigne le néerlandais en L2 aux nouveaux arrivants dans un centre de demandeurs d'asile de la Croix-Rouge, dans la province belge de Flandre-Occidentale, nous nous intéressons plus particulièrement aux compétences de l'enseignante en situation, à ses jugements méta-pragmatiques sur la langue et à ses opinions sur les compétences (ou le manque de compétences) des apprenants. Nous expliquons également comment les apprenants se servent de l'humour pour contester son autorité, valorisant ainsi leur répertoire multilinguistique et les compétences déjà acquises grâce à leur expérience antérieure de différents systèmes.

## 1 Introduction

Wherever and whenever it occurs that newcomers enter a country and seek refugee status, we see a storm of institutional demands confronting them. One of these, and most likely the most compelling one, is the learning of the host country's official language. Language and literacy skills therefore become an important currency in the heavily institutionalized and languagised world they enter. This is so because the host country language counts even more than any other language the newly arrived migrant may already master. In fact, it counts during

---

**Massimiliano Spotti,** Babylon Centre/Department of Cultural Studies, Tilburg University, The Netherlands, E-mail: m.spotti@tilburguniversity.edu

DOI 10.1515/9783110477498-052, © 2017 Massimiliano Spotti, published by De Gruyter.
This work is licensed under the Creative Commons Attribution-NonCommercial-NoDerivs 3.0 License.

the process that leads to the granting of refugee status but it also counts – and even more so – once somebody enters the civic integration pathway (see Spotti 2011 for the case of The Netherlands). It is the mastering of the official language that functions as key in many gate-keeping institutions, e.g., those granting access to integration trajectories into (low) paid jobs and to social security. It is again the mastering of the official language that shows the loyalty of the newcomer – contrary to what the host countries' public and political discourses flag out – so that s/he can function in mainstream society. The situation described above is rather naive and it makes sociolinguists turn pale. This is so not only because it poses as central the term "integration" (*inburgering*), a term that is extremely hard to define, but in particular because it relies on a legacy of language, understood as a transparent, stable denotational code, accompanied by a clearly defined syntax and clearly definable ways in which phonemes should be mapped onto graphemes in order to gain the right, and by this I mean standard, pronunciation. Language and language learning *stricto sensu* result that are anchored in a regimented and strongly normative field often linked to – as outlined above – ideological arguments of integration, participation (*meedoen*) and of who can be considered to be a full loyal citizen of country X (see Pulinx, Avermaet, and Extramiana 2014), often neglecting the equality of languages and of language varieties as well as the validity of the sociolinguistic resources newly arrived migrants already own.

Against this background, the present paper explores the attribution of linguistic resources (or lack thereof) to multilingual students in a Dutch as L2 classroom run by a volunteer teacher at an asylum seeker centre in West Flanders, Belgium. After being introduced to the context of the study, the reader gains access to a glimpse of the language-ideological apparatus that informs the teacher's view on her students' languages and it zooms in on a classroom episode that highlights how the patterns of interaction in this class point toward a monolingual management of a multilingual classroom reality. Here we see a case of what Bourdieu has termed (mis)recognition (Bourdieu 1990) where the language knowledge held by these students is deemed inappropriate. The paper concludes by offering some reflections on the issue of language learning for adult migrants.

## 2 Research context

The setting in which Dutch as L2 is taught here is not that of a regular school classroom. Rather, we find ourselves at a Red Cross asylum seeker centre (henceforth AZC) in West Flanders, the Dutch-speaking part of Belgium, right on the border with France. At the time of data collection, October 2013, the centre was running at full pace with a total of 67 asylum seekers out of a maximum capacity of 69, plus myself, Max the ethnographer, interested in these people's lives and in understanding the meaning of doing and being a migrant seeking asylum at a time of globalisation, that is at a time in which asylum seekers are strongly networked through the web in transnational ties that range from the country of origin to both the host continent and host country of residence. Being run by the Red Cross, the centre's sole obligation is to give a roof, a bed and food to its guests. Activities like those aimed at introducing these guests to the norms and values of mainstream Belgian society do not fall under the basic provision system, and although hosted by the centre and welcomed by its personnel, they all happen as the result of a bottom-up community effort.

Among these activities we find the teaching of Dutch as L2 carried out by Miss Frida, an elderly lady on a pension with a background in teaching. Her commitment to the centre has been in place for a number of years and she claims to enjoy what she does, given that at her age "there are people who like to drink coffee while I like people, so that's why I do it" (Interview Frida 10102013:1). That is why, once a week, Miss Frida teaches Dutch as L2 for one hour using the didactic resources that she sees most fitting to the needs of her students, who are all literate and have a basic knowledge of Dutch. Given that the centre does not have a proper classroom, lessons generally take place in the activities' room, i.e., a large room with desks and a whiteboard where I have observed activities that range from knitting – mainly for women – to integration talks dealing with gender equality in Europe. The students in Miss Frida's class are not – as in a regular L2 classroom – compelled to attend an integration programme. Students can walk in freely at any time during class, making sure though that they are no bother to those who have been attending class from the start.

## 3 Findings and discussion

In what follows, although space is limited, we focus on a classroom episode that deals with Frida's way of teaching Dutch as L2; we then move on to Frida's metapragmatic judgments about her students and their literacy skills. It is October 10, 2013 and class should start at 13:00 sharp. At 13:03, the lesson opens as follows:
01. Armenian guy {reading from the board}: if you find yourself [...] from my room an'
02. Frida: Niet, vandaag geen Engelse les he', vandag nederlandse les hey? Oke', dus we starten op bladzijde zes. Iedereen heeft een copie?

[*No, today no English lesson, right? Today is Dutch lesson, right? Okay so we start on page six, has everyone got a copy?*]

After preparing her worksheets for the day and handing them out, at 13:06 Miss Frida starts reading each word from the worksheet that she is holding while standing on the right hand side of the whiteboard facing the whole class. The lesson, which in a retrospective interview Miss Frida says was designed to increase her students' vocabulary in Dutch, unfolds as follows:

03. Frida: Haan [...] Jan [...] lam [...] tak [...] een boom [...] —— [with a descending intonation on the double vowel b{oo}m]

[*hen, Jan, lamb, branch, a tr[e]e*]

04. Frida: Oke' [...] hier is Nel, hier [pointing to the ground in front of her] hier, hier, hi[ii]er, hier is Nel. Nel is naam, naam voor vrow, Fatima, Nel, Leen, naam voor vrouw.

[*Okay, here we have Nel, here, here, here, here is Nel. Nel is a name, a name for a woman, like Fatima, Nel, Leen, a name for a woman*]

05. Armenian guy: Waarom naam voor vrouw mitz zu [uh] klein leter?

[*Why then is the name for a woman with a small cap?*]

06. Frida: Dat is basis nederlands, BASIS [Frida onderstreep dit:MS]. Eerst starten wij met de basis, wij lopen niet! wij stappen [...] na stappen, wij stappen vlucht, daarna gaan wij lopen, dus nu stappen wij. Maar dat is juist.

[*That is basic Dutch, BASIC [Frida stresses this:MS]. First we start with the basics, we don't walk, we make steps, after making steps, we step faster, and then we get walking, so now we make steps. Though, that is right.*]

## 3.1 Meta-pragmatic judgements

In the episode above, we find a catechistic approach to L2 language teaching. Miss Frida, whose aim is to increase the vocabulary breadth and – later on – the vocabulary depth of her students, is reading aloud clusters of monosyllabic words, which her students will then be invited to repeat out loud. Interesting is the way in which Frida clearly defines that in this class at that very moment there is no English lesson going on, de-legitimising the use of English and stressing this boundary through the use of the tag "hey" (01). In line (04), Frida further stimulates other learning channels to make her students understand what the locative pronoun "here" (*hier*) means. She repeats the word, stressing the [r] at the end. She also points her finger to the ground where she is standing. In the retrospective interview, Miss Frida pointed out that she has developed a knowledge of English by working as a volunteer at the centre and that she has some knowledge of Africa because of the holidays she has spent there. Although only one third of her classroom on that day came from the African continent, this consideration is reminiscent of a construction of "the other" that comes from far. In the retrospective interview, she asserts: "yes, once you go to those places it is all hands and feet in order to understand each other and here is the same", adding: "look these people have languages, beautiful languages, but they are not really languages, if you know what I mean, aren't they?" Here several issues emerge from her discourse practices. First, there is a conceptualization of the students in front of her through the lens of Africa: in Africa there are foreigners who don't speak Dutch and thus everything has to go through gestures, and the same holds for her class. Second, there is disqualification of the languages of foreigners in general. To her these languages, although "beautiful", are "not really languages", which possibly reflects the fact that they are not European languages and do not have a subject–verb–object structure. Interestingly enough, though, the lesson snapshot above sees one of her students (who is not from Africa) asking a question that, although posed with the clear intent to challenge the teacher's authority, is also meant to show that he holds basic literacy skills and that although Frida is addressing the class as an assemblage of blank slates, there is valid literacy present there. Frida's reply is very telling for two reasons. She first reiterates firmly how she sees the learning of L2, through the metaphor of "*we don't walk, we make steps, after making steps, we step faster, and then we get walking, so now we make steps*". Yet again through the adversative clause that closes her sentence in line (06) – "*but that is correct*" – she has to give up her authority, admitting that there is indeed a mistake on the worksheet and that the student's observation is actually a valid one.

# 4 Final considerations

The switch from a language teaching approach that sees language as countable reality to a vision where speakers use language to engage in language learning and bring in their previously encountered literacy skills, does not mean that languages and their normativities no longer exist. This becomes especially clear in education, where the official language of a country in its standard variety is at the same time the medium of instruction and the target language (see Kurvers & Spotti, 2015). A main characteristic of the teaching episode in Miss Frida's class is a "one way" normativity. This includes the existence of clear and respected (grammatical and pronunciation) rules that – although influenced by the strongly local variety of Dutch used by Miss Frida – are invested with the authority of what language should be taught, and in particular how it should be taught to students like hers, newly arrived adult migrants. In urging students to follow what she thinks they need, e.g. words, this class turns them into members of an ideological linguistic community – that of foreign speaker of Dutch – which overshadows these students' previously acquired literacy skills in that they are seen as blank slates to be filled by the repository of knowledge held by the teacher. In response to this, Blommaert and Backus (2013) provide a programmatic perspective on language education which addresses many of the questions that we are confronted with in the episode and in Frida's reasoning. They consider learning languages as a matter of developing repertoires that consist of asymmetrical contextual competences. This language learning takes place in a context of power relationships, i.e., formal education, in which, as a consequence of educational normativity, some varieties are credited and others are discredited. It takes place, moreover, in different ways – i.e., specific language resources become part of a learner's repertoire through "a broad range of tactics, technologies and mechanisms" as well as of their previous – albeit informal – language learning trajectories (see Spotti & Blommaert forthcoming). This implies that there are quite a few different ways of learning languages (or acquiring linguistic resources) that lead to different levels and forms of "knowing" a language. Following this, Blommaert and Backus (2013) distinguish: (1) highly formal and patterned *comprehensive language learning* in schools, (2) *specialized language learning* related to specific and specialized skills and resources, e.g., learning academic English, (3) highly informal and ephemeral out-of-school *encounters with language* (e.g., age group slang learning, temporary language learning, single word learning, recognizing language), and (4) *embedded language learning*, i.e., learning a language that can only be used if another language is used as well (e.g., computer technology-related English used while speaking Dutch). For each of these types of competence, they then distinguish: (1) maximum competence, (2) partial competence, (3) minimal competence, and (4) recognizing competence (2013: 22). Such a revised understanding of language learning also asks for a new mindset in teachers – whether regular or voluntary. It makes modes of in- and out-of-school language learning acceptable and valid resources for institutionalized environments. Needless to say, as shown here, there is still quite some work to be done, but in a contemporary globalized reality like that of an asylum seeker centre, these changes are nonetheless crucial.

# References

Blommaert, Jan & Ad Backus. 2013. Superdiverse repertoires and the individual. In Ingrid De Saint-George & Jean-Jacques Weber (eds.), *Multilingualism and multimodality: Current challenges for educational studies*, 11–32. Dordrecht: Sense Publishers.

Bourdieu, Pierre. 1990. *The logic of practice*. Stanford: Stanford University Press.

Kurvers, Jeanne & Massimiliano Spotti. 2015. The shifting landscape of Dutch integration policy: From L1 literacy teaching to literacy in Dutch as entrance criterion to the Netherlands. In James Simpson & Anna Whiteside (eds.), *Adult learning, education and migration: Challenging agendas in policy and practice*, 173–186. Abingdon: Routledge.

Pulinx, Reinhilde, Piet Van Avermaet & Claire Extramiana. 2014. *Linguistic integration of adult migrants: Policy and practice. Final report on the 3rd Council of Europe survey.* Strasbourg: Council of Europe. https://rm.coe.int/CoERMPublicCommonSearchServices/DisplayDCTMContent?documentId=09000016802fc1ce (accessed 2 July 2016).

Spotti, Massimiliano. 2011. Ideologies of success for superdiverse citizens: The Dutch testing regime for integration and the online private sector. *Diversities Journal* 13(2), special issue: *Language and superdiversity*. 39–52.

Spotti, Massimiliano & Jan Blommaert. 2017. Bilingualism, multiligualism, globalisation and superdiversity – toward language repertoires. In Ofelia García, Nelson Flores & Massimiliano Spotti (eds.), *Handbook of language and society*, 161–178. Oxford: Oxford UniversityPress.

Maude Vadot
# Qu'est-ce que l'intégration ?

Analyse de discours de formateurs et formatrices linguistiques intervenant auprès de migrants adultes en France

**Résumé :** L'institutionnalisation de la formation linguistique des migrants adultes en France s'est accompagnée du choix du terme *intégration*, consacré par la parution du *Référentiel Français Langue d'Intégration* fin 2011. On analyse ici comment des formateurs spécialistes du domaine actualisent et commentent les lexèmes *intégration, intégrer, s'intégrer* et *être intégré*. On montre ainsi que si une partie d'entre eux est consciente de la mémoire discursive charriée par le terme, le concept reste pour eux difficilement saisissable. Ces résultats permettent d'envisager quelques orientations pour la formation initiale et continue des formateurs linguistiques.

**Abstract:** The institutionalisation of language education for adult migrants in France has gone hand in hand with the choice of the term *intégration*, as laid down in the *Référentiel Français Langue d'Intégration* [French as a Language of Integration – Reference guide] published at the end of 2011. This article analyses how specialist trainers in this field are actualizing and reacting to the lexemes *intégration, intégrer, s'intégrer* and *être intégré*. It shows that, while some of them are aware of the term's discursive load, the concept remains difficult for them to grasp. These results could give rise to guidelines on the initial and further training of language trainers.

## Introduction

La parution du *Référentiel Français Langue d'Intégration (FLI)* (Vicher *et al.* 2011), sur commande de la Direction de l'Accueil, de l'Intégration et de la Citoyenneté, a été suivie de vives réactions – circonscrites au domaine de formation et de recherche concerné – portant, entre autres, sur le recours au terme *intégration*. Cette publication réactivait en effet la polémique touchant à l'emploi et la prescription des termes constituant le paradigme *insertion, intégration, assimilation* – et plus récemment *inclusion* et *acculturation* (Vadot 2016). Ces termes,

---

**Maude Vadot,** Laboratoire Dipralang EA739, Université Paul-Valéry Montpellier 3,
E-mail : maude_vadot@yahoo.fr

qui ont circulé d'un camp politique à un autre dans les dernières décennies, sont souvent critiqués comme manquant de contenu sémantique : il est de fait assez rare d'en trouver des définitions qui permettent de les mettre en contraste. Pour autant, les changements de mots accompagnent parfois des changements idéologiques qui ont, pour leur part, des conséquences en matière d'action publique et de travail social (Lemière 2006).

Je m'intéresse ici aux actualisations réalisées par des formateurs et formatrices intervenant auprès de migrants adultes en France, pour dégager au moins partiellement la mise en discours et en sens de la dénomination *intégration* ainsi effectuée. L'enjeu consiste à approcher la façon dont ils se saisissent des enjeux des formations linguistiques à visée d'insertion ou d'intégration. Comment conçoivent-ils l'intégration des personnes migrantes ? Sont-ils conscients des querelles de mots et si oui, quel sens prennent-elles pour eux ? Comment se situent-ils dans ces débats ?

# 1 Méthodologie de recueil et d'analyse

Le corpus est composé d'entretiens semi-directifs menés auprès de trois formateurs et quatorze formatrices âgés de 25 à 45 ans, en poste ou en recherche d'emploi au moment de l'entretien. Tous ont entre un et dix ans d'expérience auprès de migrants, principalement en organisme de formation. Le protocole suivi consistait à aborder les thèmes d'entretien sans prononcer aucun des termes du paradigme, afin de ne pas imposer l'emploi de l'un ou de l'autre. Ce n'est que lorsqu'aucun terme n'avait été prononcé lors des premiers échanges qu'on confrontait l'interlocuteur au lexème *intégration*, le plus souvent en l'interrogeant sur sa connaissance et sa réception du *Référentiel FLI*, et ce pour observer sa réaction sans pour autant initier la constitution du terme en objet de discours.

Afin de mettre au jour les éléments du programme de sens actualisés par les formateurs et formatrices employant les unités lexicales *intégration, intégrer, s'intégrer* et *être intégré*, je me suis inspirée des propositions de l'Analyse de Discours à Entrée Lexicale (Née & Veniard 2012), et notamment d'une sémantique des constructions. Il s'agit de relever toutes les occurrences des unités étudiées et d'observer non seulement la fréquence à laquelle les locuteurs y ont recours, mais également leur mise en syntagme au sein des constructions nominales et des constructions verbales dans lesquelles elles apparaissent, puis d'en dégager les effets. J'ai exclu du relevé les occurrences incluses dans les expressions « contrat d'accueil et d'intégration », « français langue d'intégration » et « ouvrir l'école aux parents pour réussir l'intégration », syntagmes quasi-lexicalisés appartenant au discours institutionnel et repris dialogiquement par les formateurs.

## 2 Posture critique *vs.* acceptation du lexème

Le premier résultat observable consiste en ce qu'on peut diviser les formateurs en deux groupes. Neuf d'entre eux ne se positionnent pas face au terme et, pour la plupart, l'emploient sans difficulté. Incarnant une posture différente, les huit autres commentent le lexème de façon critique, voire affirment refuser d'y avoir recours au quotidien :
(1) parler des valeurs enfin ou même dire **le mot intégration**[1] ça me donne de l'urticaire c'est <((en riant légèrement)) pas possible> (Alice[2])

Faisant du mot l'objet du discours, les formateurs du second groupe ont tous recours à des actualisations autonymiques du lexème nominal ou verbal, dans lesquelles le signe renvoie à lui-même en tant que signe. Les commentaires énoncés relèvent témoignent de la réflexivité des locuteurs sur la langue et les discours, qui est mise au service de l'argumentation (Micheli 2011 ; Sitri 2003) : les locuteurs visent alors à problématiser l'emploi du terme.

Pour leur part, les formateurs qui ne critiquent pas le terme ne réalisent pas, à une exception près, d'emplois autonymiques des lexèmes. La seule qui le fait vise, à l'inverse des formateurs critiques, à valider le recours au terme :
(2) intégration oui il faut que: enfin ça par contre euh / je le: / je lui mets pas de connotation derrière (Aurélie)

Ces emplois autonymiques ne seront pas pris en compte dans les analyses qui vont suivre dans la mesure où ils constituent des mises à distance du terme par les formateurs concernés. Il en va de même pour les énoncés appartenant au discours rapporté, ainsi que pour les actualisations faisant l'objet d'une modalisation autonymique, qui témoignent également d'un refus au moins partiel de la responsabilité énonciative par le locuteur.

Cependant, malgré les critiques qu'ils formulent et le rejet parfois virulent qu'ils expriment, six des huit formateurs critiques ont recours au terme en emploi standard sans qu'il leur soit imposé.

---

[1] C'est moi qui souligne.
[2] Tous les prénoms ont été modifiés pour garantir l'anonymat des participants.

## 3 Se saisir du concept. Caractéristiques syntagmatiques des actualisations de la dénomination *intégration* et de ses variantes lexématiques

### 3.1 Recours au nom vs. recours aux verbes

Les caractéristiques des actualisations réalisées par les deux groupes de formateurs, au total 144 occurrences, sont assez proches. Un élément distingue toutefois les deux profils : les formateurs critiques ont plus fréquemment recours aux formes verbales (69 %) qu'à la forme nominale du lemme (31 %), là où la tendance est inverse pour les formateurs non critiques (40 % *vs.* 60 %). On peut faire l'hypothèse que critiquant le nom et faute d'avoir recours à une autre dénomination, les formateurs critiques sont obligés d'actualiser les formes verbales du lemme.

Or le recours au nom *intégration* permet une abstraction plus grande. Là où il est en effet possible de dire :
(3) des contenus qui sont tournés vers l'intégration (Étienne)
sans préciser d'arguments (actants et actés), l'emploi d'une forme verbale du lemme oblige le locuteur à préciser au moins un argument dans le cas de la construction passive ou réfléchie, voire deux en construction transitive active :
(4) elles sont pas du tout intégrées (Étienne)
(5) on va essayer de t'intégrer (Lydie)

Par ailleurs, le nom permet de ne pas se prononcer quant à l'agentivité ou à l'inscription du procès dans le temps. Le syntagme « l'intégration des migrants dans la société » pourrait ainsi être reformulé en :
– les migrants s'intègrent dans la société
– on a intégré les migrants dans la société
– les migrants seront intégrés dans la société
– etc.

Le choix énonciatif effectué de façon préférentielle par les formateurs non critiques est donc générateur d'énoncés dont le degré d'abstraction est plus élevé.

## 3.2 Actualisations nominales

La majorité des occurrences (65 %) se présente sous la forme « article défini + nom ». Les occurrences faisant intervenir d'autres déterminants sont très rares (3 au total) ; elles produisent un effet de sens bien différent qui laisse envisager la possibilité d'intégrations différenciées selon les personnes, ou d'une intégration par pallier, comme le laissent entendre les exemples suivants :
(6) **une** intégration de base (Laura)
(7) **mon** intégration à moi (Sylvie)

Par ailleurs, le syntagme nominal est très souvent réduit à sa structure minimale : seuls 20 % des syntagmes nominaux comportent une épithète ou un complément du nom. Il en résulte une très faible restriction du sens du lexème. De plus, ces restrictions du sens sont peu spécifiques : deux des trois arguments relevés réfèrent à l'énonciateur, qui parle alors de son expérience en tant qu'enseignant de français à l'étranger. Le dernier désigne une catégorie générique (« des personnes »). Pour leur part, les circonstants actualisés, indiquant des lieux, sont situés à une échelle très large, celle du pays ou de la société. À une exception près, aucun locuteur ne qualifie de domaine dans ou par lequel le processus d'intégration se réalise.

## 3.3 Actualisations verbales

Un premier constat concerne la répartition des occurrences entre les trois formes verbales du lemme : sur la totalité des emplois, la préférence est largement donnée aux constructions en *être intégré* (51 %) et en *s'intégrer* (43 %). De plus, les constructions au passif ne reçoivent jamais de complément d'agent qui viendrait préciser l'actant du procès mis en scène : pour *être intégré* comme pour *s'intégrer*, le seul argument exprimé est le sujet de la forme verbale. Il en résulte que dans l'ordre du discours des formateurs, la responsabilité de l'intégration est placée entre les mains de ceux qui en sont l'objet – ici les adultes migrants.

L'observation des arguments des formes verbales conjuguées permet de constater que dans les deux tiers des cas, les formateurs mettent en scène des catégories génériques (« la personne », « les migrants »), évoquant ainsi des cas virtuels. Seuls un tiers des énoncés réfèrent à des situations vécues – la leur ou celle d'un tiers.

Enfin, un tiers des occurrences sont dotées de compléments entrant dans la construction des syntagmes verbaux relevés, qui se répartissent entre spécification d'un lieu ou d'un espace social dans lequel l'intégration a lieu, des moyens par lesquels elle est réalisée, ou encore d'un degré d'intensité. Les dénominations employées, qu'il s'agisse de lieux ou de moyens envisagés, restent là aussi très générales. Enfin, il est intéressant de constater que la moitié de ces compléments a trait à l'intensité du procès *s'intégrer* ou de l'état *être intégré*.

## Conclusion

A l'issue de ces analyses, on peut avancer que la notion d'intégration est, dans les discours, appréhendée de façon très globalisante et vague par les formateurs et formatrices. Les formateurs parlent rarement de situations particulières qu'ils seraient en mesure de comparer les unes aux autres pour illustrer ou étayer leur propos ; les lieux ou les groupes humains mobilisés restent très vastes et généraux. Les processus sont donc appréhendés d'une façon tellement globale qu'il n'est pas possible d'en saisir les tenants et les aboutissants, les modalités, les spécificités, les variables, etc. De plus le rôle de la société d'accueil, de ses institutions, de ses membres, de son histoire, etc. est totalement « invisibilisé ». Cela revient alors à désigner les migrants comme seuls acteurs du processus, ce qui ouvre ensuite la possibilité de les renvoyer à leurs prétendues seules responsabilités.

Bien sûr, l'étude des constructions syntaxiques ne dit pas tout, et une analyse thématique des entretiens permet de faire apparaître des voies et des domaines que les formateurs identifient comme vecteurs d'intégration. Il reste qu'en discours, et ce malgré la formulation d'éventuelles critiques, l'intégration constitue une réalité dont les modalités et les enjeux restent à travailler.

Dans un moment où, en France, la formation linguistique des migrants est de plus en plus liée à des orientations idéologiques, et où le rapport entre langue et intégration semble aller de soi, la construction de la professionnalité des formateurs passe également par la construction de connaissances sociologiques sur les processus d'intégration et la manière dont ils ont été travaillés par le politique au cours des dernières décennies. Ces éléments font partie intégrante de la « contextualisation du terrain », comme l'a souligné Bretegnier en s'attachant à décrire les compétences et les ressources nécessaires à la construction d'une posture de réflexivité éthique (Bretegnier 2011). Il semble donc nécessaire de réfléchir aux manières dont on peut améliorer dans ce sens les formations de formateurs, tant initiales que continues.

# Références

Authier-Revuz, Jacqueline. 1995. *Ces mots qui ne vont pas de soi. Boucles réflexives et non coïncidences du dire*. Paris : Larousse.

Bretegnier, Aude. 2011. Formation linguistique en contextes d'insertion : vers un cadre de référence(s) en matière de professionnalité de formateurs. In Aude Bretegnier (dir.), *Formation linguistique en contextes d'insertion : compétences, posture, professionnalité, concevoir un cadre de référence(s)*, 213–242. Berne, Berlin & Bruxelles : Peter Lang.

Lemière, Jacques. 2006. De l'importance et de l'urgence d'étendre dans le travail social, la critique des catégories d'intégration et d'immigré. In Élisabeth Prieur, Emmanuel Jovelin & Martine Blanc (dir.). *Travail social et immigration*, 91–103. Paris : L'Harmattan.

Micheli, Raphaël. 2011. Quand l'affrontement porte sur les mots en tant que mots : polémique et réflexivité langagière. *Semen. Revue de sémio-linguistique des textes et discours* 31. 97–112.

Née, Émilie & Marie Veniard. 2012. Analyse du Discours à Entrée Lexicale (A.D.E.L.) : le renouveau par la sémantique ?. *Langage et société* 140. 15–28.

Sitri, Frédérique. 2003. L'autonymie dans la construction des objets de discours. In Jacqueline Authier-Revuz, Marianne Doury & Sandrine Reboul-Touré (dir.). *Parler des mots. Le fait autonymique en discours*, 205–216. Paris : Presses Sorbonne Nouvelle.

Vadot, Maude. 2016. De quoi INTÉGRATION est-il le nom ? L'importation d'une querelle de mots dans le champ de la formation linguistique des migrants. *Argumentation et Analyse du Discours* 17. http://aad.revues.org/2228 (consulté le 14 juillet 2015).

Vicher, Anne, Hervé Adami, Amandine Bergère, Sophie Étienne, Pascal Lambert, Gaëlle Poirrier & Claire Verdier. 2011. *Référentiel FLI – Français Langue d'Intégration*. Direction de l'Accueil, de l'Intégration et de la Citoyenneté. http://www.immigration.interieur.gouv.fr/content/download/38544/292981/file/FLI-Referentiel.pdf. (consulté le 02/12/2016).

Eric Mercier
# Langues et insertions : pluralité des parcours et des perceptions

Quelle pertinence à l'obligation de formation et d'examen linguistique ?

**Résumé :** En Europe, les différentes politiques linguistiques s'accordent sur une représentation selon laquelle l'apprentissage de la langue nationale serait une condition préalable à l'intégration des adultes migrants. La conséquence « logique » de cette représentation est de conférer un caractère obligatoire à l'enseignement de la langue nationale (cf. en France, le Contrat d'Accueil et d'Intégration). À travers l'exemple du DILF, on réfléchira sur les façons dont ce cadre d'obligations législatives influence l'évolution de dispositifs formatifs et l'action des formateurs.

**Abstract:** In Europe a common feature of language policies is the idea that learning the host country's language constitutes a precondition for the integration of adult migrants. The "logical" consequence thereof is obligatory language education (as under France's Reception and Integration Contract scheme). The example of the DILF (Initial French Language Diploma) serves as a basis for consideration of the ways in which this legal framework laying down obligations is influencing the development of training schemes and trainers' activities.

La création du Contrat d'Accueil et d'Intégration (CAI) en 2006 marque un tournant dans les politiques d'intégration françaises, d'une part en rendant les formations linguistiques obligatoires, d'autre part en créant un niveau de certification unique en Europe (le niveau A1.1), assorti du Diplôme Initial en Langue Française (DILF).

Parmi les obligations qui découlent du CAI pour les acteurs, je m'intéresserai à cet examen DILF (dont la passation est obligatoire jusqu'en 2016), en interrogeant quelques contradictions entre les objectifs de l'examen et leur mise en œuvre, dans le cadre d'obligations dans lequel celles-ci doivent s'intégrer. Sans intention d'intenter un « procès » au DILF, il s'agit de problématiser la manière dont l'ingénierie sociale peut se faire « rattraper » par une idéologie qui lui est opposée. Les observations ont été réalisées dans une structure de formation

**Eric Mercier,** EA 42 46 PREFics-Dynadiv, Université François Rabelais, Tours,
E-mail: eric.mercier@etu.univ-tours.fr

agréée pour la préparation à l'examen et notamment dans une classe « Alpha », qui regroupe les stagiaires les plus à même d'éprouver des difficultés pour le DILF. Dans cette structure[1], le DILF se préparait jusqu'en 2016 en 250 h de formation maximum, à raison d'environ 12 h de formation par semaine. Malgré la fin programmée du DILF, la certification linguistique à des fins d'évaluation de l'intégration reste, dans les politiques publiques, l'objectif à long terme de ces formations (le DELF B1 étant exigé pour la demande de naturalisation).

# 1 Les objectifs du DILF

## 1.1 Une reconnaissance symbolique

Le niveau A1.1 vise un niveau facilement atteignable pour être accessible à tous, afin d'encourager la formation : « Certains pays ont choisi de fixer ces seuils à des niveaux très élevés. (...) [I]l est préférable de retenir un niveau minimal requis accessible à tous pour encourager l'amorce de parcours de formation. » (Beacco et al. 2005 : 9). Il a également pour but « (...) de reconnaître et d'encourager l'engagement volontaire des personnes dans leur premiers pas vers une meilleure intégration linguistique. » (Beacco et al. 2005 : 15). Le DILF symbolise alors cette reconnaissance, puisqu'il permet de « (...) valorise[r] les efforts qui ont été accomplis lors de l'apprentissage » (Beacco et al. 2005 : 189) : les taux de réussite au DILF sont effectivement élevés, presque 92 % des signataires du CAI l'ont obtenu en 2010 (CIEP 2011 : 20).

## 1.2 Prise en compte de la pluralité des parcours et du plurilinguisme

Le niveau A1.1, en tant que repère pour les acteurs des formations, vise à mieux considérer la diversité des stagiaires (pluralité de statuts, de langues d'origines et de degrés de maîtrise de ces langues, de niveaux de scolarisation, de rapports au français). Dans le cadre de ces considérations, le plurilinguisme en présence ne doit pas être ignoré : « Il importera de ne pas perdre de vue que ces formations en français sont aussi l'occasion d'identifier et de valoriser le répertoire

---

[1] Mais cela peut différer d'une structure à l'autre et d'une classe à l'autre, selon les contraintes des stagiaires, ou selon les directives de l'OFII (formations intensives de 18 h par semaine recommandées en 2015).

linguistique des participants, en particulier au moyen du *Portfolio européen des langues.* » (Beacco *et al.* 2005 : 23)

## 1.3 Mise en œuvre d'une didactique adaptée

Ce niveau vise aussi à « (...) aménager les propositions de formation pour qu'un public de très faible niveau, n'ayant souvent pas pu bénéficier d'une véritable scolarisation puisse trouver des démarches formatives adaptées à ses besoins » (Beacco *et al.* 2005 : 23).

Mariela de Ferrari, qui a participé à la création du référentiel, s'est exprimée en 2008 sur l'arrivée du DILF et espérait qu'il favorise « des évolutions significatives sur les plans didactiques et pédagogique ainsi que sur la construction et le suivi de parcours pertinents et individualisés » (De Ferrari 2008 : 25).

## 1.4 Privilégier l'oral

La préparation au DILF dont les formateurs ont la charge doit plutôt prioriser l'oral, comme l'attestent les quelques citations suivantes : « Cette formation vise l'acquisition de compétences linguistiques orales de base correspondant aujourd'hui au niveau A1.1 oral du *Cadre européen commun de références pour les langues* » (Beacco *et al.* 2005 : 3) Ainsi, « (...) le niveau A1.1 oral peut devenir le premier objectif réaliste d'un primo-arrivant. » (Beacco *et al.* 2005 : 10).

# 2 Quelques observations de terrain et leur interprétation

Je m'arrêterai sur quelques effets de cette centration sur l'examen, en tant qu'elle peut venir freiner l'apprentissage de certains stagiaires. Les quelques exemples de situations/parcours qui suivent relèvent de cas de figures de stagiaires qui n'apprennent pas de la façon prescrite par le cadre de formation, les impératifs de formation et la préparation au DILF venant *conforter* cette non-conformité.

## 2.1 Le *Dilfotage*, frein à la diversification ?

Le néologisme *dilfotage*, construit sur le terme *bachotage*[2], est employé pour désigner une formation dont l'objectif principal devient la préparation à l'examen, avec des modalités de formation calquées sur les épreuves.

Différents aspects du contexte de formation freinent la diversification des contenus :
- Le peu de ressources didactiques existant pour le niveau infra A1.1 autres que les manuels de préparation au DILF[3].
- La réussite des apprenants qui est un enjeu important pour les structures, ces formations étant en soi une « préparation au DILF ». Or, le temps de formation obligatoire est toujours plus court pour atteindre les mêmes objectifs de cet examen (400 h maximum en 2006, 250 h depuis 2013). De même, les formations complémentaires de l'Office français de l'immigration et de l'intégration (OFII) ont disparu : désormais les « parcours » sont réduits à cette seule formation. Une certaine pression s'exerce sur les formateurs pour assurer la réussite à l'examen en ces temps impartis.
- Des situations de vie qui rendent parfois l'apprentissage difficile voire impossible dans l'immédiat (précarité, traumatismes liés à la guerre, problèmes psychologiques, de scolarisation, difficultés liées à l'âge, peu d'échanges sociaux, etc.). Certains stagiaires stagnent dans cette classe sans pouvoir suivre la progression plus rapide de la majorité.

L'idée régulièrement répétée par certains formateurs de « marteler » sur les thèmes et contenus de l'examen pour les classes alpha semble significative de cette tendance au dilfotage. Une formatrice revendiqua lors d'une réunion de travailler plusieurs semaines sur la même compétence tant que celle-ci n'est pas *acquise*. Bien qu'une progression logique ou spiralaire puisse être mise en place, la formation tend à se techniciser à travers la priorité donnée aux thématiques et formats de l'examen. Le dilfotage prime alors sur l'appropriation des savoir-faire (selon différents parcours, besoins, usages et pratique hors formation).

---

2 Préparation intensive au baccalauréat (dit communément *bachot* ou *bac*).
3 Soulignons que ces manuels ont le mérite de proposer des contenus didactiques qui tendent à s'adapter à de petits niveaux à travers des thématiques de la vie courante.

## 2.2 Focalisation exclusive sur le français *vs.* prise en compte de la pluralité

Le nouveau cahier de charges de l'OFII précise que le formateur doit s'exprimer « exclusivement en langue française[4] » (OFII 2015 : 13) et ce, bien que certaines indications du référentiel semblent contraster avec une telle intransigeance (cf. *supra*). De même dans la structure où je travaille, il est indiqué que le formateur explicite dès le test de positionnement qu'il ne parle que français, considérant que c'est la meilleure manière d'amener à faire parler français. Cette posture fortement monolingue est justifiée par différentes raisons :

– Par les objectifs du dispositif CAI et l'importance attribuée à la langue pour l'intégration. Bien que cette posture exclusivement monolingue soit fréquente ailleurs, certains arguments sont spécifiques à l'intégration : le temps de plus en plus court des formations obligatoires par exemple, qui exigerait d'autant plus que seul le français se fasse entendre. La formation est alors considérée garante de faire parler français en un temps imparti.
– Par l'examen qui exige du migrant une production orale en français. L'usage exclusif du français peut donc se justifier en tant que mise en situation de l'examen oral. Le DILF vient appuyer l'idée que le formateur aurait un devoir de ne « faire parler » que français. Les stagiaires qui ne passent pas suffisamment à la production en français posent alors problème, comme par exemple H., stagiaire venu apprendre avec assiduité, tout en refusant de s'exprimer en français. Il est resté dans une optique de compréhension pendant ses 250 h de formation, par exemple en répétant en anglais pour avoir confirmation de sa compréhension. Malgré ses difficultés, ce stagiaire veut apprendre, mais cet apprentissage qui passe par la traduction se voit rejeté. Ce rejet amène le formateur à occulter sa compétence plurilingue, à répondre exclusivement en français, voire à faire semblant de ne pas comprendre. Ce comportement reproduit la « situation d'examen » : lors de la partie orale du DILF, aucune autre langue ne trouvera d'interlocuteur.

Au-delà de l'indulgence vis-à-vis de l'utilisation d'autres langues entre les stagiaires, cette exclusivité du français disqualifie toute possibilité pour le formateur de s'appuyer sur ces langues, en tant qu'elles pourraient jouer un rôle important dans l'apprentissage et favoriser la production en français. Une plus

---

[4] Précisons que les formateurs peuvent être inspectés par des auditeurs de l'OFII, inspection durant laquelle le français est de mise.

grande tolérance vis-à-vis de la communication plurilingue ne pourrait-elle pas être tout autant mise à profit pour le même objectif ?

### 2.3 Focalisation sur l'écrit

Le critère principal de positionnement en classe « Alpha » est le niveau d'alphabétisation en français du stagiaire, lorsque lecture et écriture sont insuffisantes pour le DILF. La classe « Alpha » mélange par conséquent des stagiaires aux profils d'apprentissage très divers : des débutants complets, des stagiaires peu ou pas scolarisés, allophones ou non, des stagiaires non alphabétisés en français – malgré un niveau d'oral qui peut être bon, si bien que parfois, certains stagiaires de ce niveau parlent déjà bien français.

Ce critère contrevient ainsi à l'objectif de centration sur l'oral, objectif initial du DILF, mais aussi objectif de certains stagiaires, comme par exemple M. lorsqu'il me confie son avis sur ce critère de l'écrit :

> Alors, M. ça va les cours de français ?
> Ça va. Mais... Parler oui. Moi, parler ! La Caf, la préfecture, parler !
> Pas écrire ! (...) Moi écrire non ! Après !
> (M., réfugié irakien, 27 ans, plus de 120 heures de formation, le 02/02/2016)

Forme et contenu du message semblent ici se faire écho : la forte volonté de communiquer de M. compense son manque de vocabulaire, illustrant le décalage entre l'importance donnée à l'écrit en formation et son projet d'apprentissage axé sur la communication orale. Du fait de la nécessité de se préparer à la partie écrite du DILF, M. s'est vu ainsi refuser de passer au niveau supérieur à plusieurs reprises : l'écrit devient là un impératif immédiat. Les obligations de préparation au DILF ont ici été privilégiées, au détriment de la posture d'appropriation du stagiaire.

## Conclusions

La possibilité de « résistance » des structures face à cette idéologie est difficile, tant sur le plan éthique que didactique – mais les acteurs sont-ils toujours conscients de la façon dont se traduit cette idéologie dans leurs propres pratiques ? À travers les exemples évoqués, un certain dévoiement des objectifs initiaux du DILF se dessine : évaluationnisme, monolinguisme strict, écrit limitant. L'apprentissage doit se plier à ces contraintes, ce qui compte est que ces stagiaires jouent le jeu – qu'ils soient ou non dans une posture d'appropriation. L'ouverture qui était espérée vers une diversification des formations me semble rattrapée, in fine, par l'idéologie linguistique qui est au fondement des politiques d'intégration française, marquant le passage d'une logique de reconnaissance à une logique d'imposition de l'apprentissage – d'ailleurs parallèle à l'évolution qui s'est faite du droit vers le devoir de la langue.

Outre la forme à y mettre, je pense qu'il est primordial d'interroger les fondements de ces politiques linguistiques, ainsi que les obligations qui en découlent pour leurs acteurs. Au vu des durcissements généralisés de ces mesures en Europe (Pochon-Berger & Lenz 2014 : 9–10 ; Huver 2016 : 193–196), les différents examens en langue des pays d'accueil en faveur de l'intégration des migrants devraient plus que jamais interroger les chercheurs et praticiens sur ce que ces examens prétendront mesurer, mais aussi sur les logiques idéologiques dans lesquelles ils s'insèrent et leurs effets sur l'ensemble des acteurs.

# Références

Beacco, Jean-Claude, Mariela de Ferrari, Gilbert Lhote & Christine Tagliante. 2005. *Référentiel A1.1 pour le français, référentiel et certification pour les premiers acquis en français.* Paris : Didier.

Centre International d'Études Pédagogiques. 2011. *Les diplômes nationaux de français langue étrangère DILF et DELF : innovations et perspectives pour les publics migrants.* 2011. Paris : CIEP, http://www.ciep.fr/sites/default/files/migration/dilf/docs/presentation-expolangues-2011.pdf (consulté le 7 mai 2016).

De Ferrari, Mariela. 2008. Penser la formation linguistique des adultes migrants en France – Nommer autrement pour faire différemment. *Le français dans le monde* 44. 20–28.

Huver, Emmanuelle. 2016. L'évaluation linguistique des adultes migrants : contrôle, preuve, technicisation. In Fabienne Leconte (dir.). *Adultes Migrants, langues et insertions sociales*, 191–224. Paris : Riveneuve.

OFII. 2015. Marché n° 15 24007. *Cahier des clauses particulières. Formation linguistique.*

Pochon-Berger, Évelyne & Peter Lenz. 2014. *Les prérequis linguistiques et l'usage de tests de langue à des fins d'immigration et d'intégration – une synthèse de la littérature académique.* Rapports du Centre scientifique de compétence sur le plurilinguisme. Fribourg : Institut de Plurilinguisme.

Marie-Cécile Guernier, Marie-Hélène Lachaud
et Jean-Pierre Sautot

# Conceptions linguistiques et méthodes pédagogiques : quelle efficience pour l'intégration des adultes migrants ?

**Résumé :** La perspective est didactique et s'intéresse aux processus d'enseignement apprentissage de la langue française chez des migrants adultes faiblement scolarisés. Les analyses portent sur les pratiques de formation linguistique dans les dispositifs spécifiques au regard des performances langagières et des habiletés littératiques des apprenants dans leurs langues première, secondes et étrangères (plurilinguisme), selon deux modalités. Ces pratiques privilégient une conception linguistique de la compétence langagière qui fonde une pédagogie compartimentée au détriment d'une conception intégrant les compétences discursives et pragmatiques. Cette seconde option permet de prendre appui sur les acquis des apprenants et facilite l'intégration sociale et professionnelle des personnes migrantes.

**Abstract:** This article looks at teaching, with a particular focus on the processes involved in teaching and learning French in the case of adult migrants with little school education. The analyses relate to the language education practices followed in the specific courses studied, which are examined from the standpoint of the learners' language competence and literacy skills in their first, second and foreign languages (plurilingualism) using two methods. These practices focus on a linguistic conception of language competence, forming a basis for compartmentalised teaching, to the detriment of a conception embracing discursive and pragmatic skills. The second option makes it possible to build on the skills the learners already possess and facilitates migrants' social and professional integration.

---

**Marie-Cécile Guernier,** LIDILEM, Université Grenoble Alpes, France,
E-mail : marie-cecile.guernier@univ-lyon1.fr
**Marie-Hélène Lachaud,** LIDILEM, Université Grenoble Alpes, France,
E-mail : lachaud.mariehelene@free.fr
**Jean-Pierre Sautot,** ICAR, Université Claude Bernard Lyon, France,
E-mail : jean-pierre.sautot@univ-lyon1.fr

DOI 10.1515/9783110477498-055, © 2017 Marie-Cécile Guernier, Marie-Hélène Lachaud et Jean-Pierre Sautot, published by De Gruyter.
This work is licensed under the Creative Commons Attribution-NonCommercial-NoDerivs 3.0 License.

## 1 Analyser les pratiques de formation auprès des adultes faiblement qualifiés

Les éléments d'études présentés dans cette communication sont issus des travaux du Groupe Recherche Action Formation Français Insertion Compétence (GRAFFIC) qui analysent les pratiques de formation mises en œuvre dans les actions dédiées aux adultes faiblement qualifiés en vue de leur insertion sociale et professionnelle. Le GRAFFIC adopte les principes méthodologiques de la recherche action formation (RAF) et réunit des chercheurs et différents acteurs (formateurs, responsables pédagogiques) de la formation d'adultes inscrits dans des parcours d'insertion et/ou professionnelle. Une des visées est la professionnalisation des formateurs de ce secteur, que conformément aux principes de la RAF, le GRAFFIC cherche à construire par le moyen de la recherche et de la réflexivité sur les pratiques pédagogiques, dans l'esprit de la démarche du « praticien réflexif » (Schön 1993). Dans cette perspective, le GRAFFIC a réalisé plusieurs enquêtes dans différents organismes de formation de la région Rhône-Alpes (France), sous la forme : d'observations directes de séances de formation, dont certaines ont été filmées, d'entretiens auprès des formateurs dans l'objectif d'identifier leurs conceptions pédagogiques et linguistiques, d'enquêtes auprès des adultes en formation pour recueillir leurs avis sur les formations en fonction de leurs besoins et demandes, d'enquêtes sur les postes de travail afin d'identifier les compétences linguistiques et discursives au travail. L'approche du GRAFFIC est didactique, c'est-à-dire qu'il s'intéresse aux processus de transpositions des savoirs linguistiques par les formateurs et aux processus d'appropriation de ces savoirs linguistiques par les apprenants adultes, dans des situations didactiques.

## 2 Un public hétérogène

Les personnes inscrites dans ces formations constituent un public hétérogène aux compétences linguistiques et aux besoins très divers, voire contradictoires (Leclercq 2008). Il peut s'agir de personnes étrangères récemment arrivées en France et qui ne maîtrisent pas le français, et dont certaines n'ont pas été scolarisées dans leur pays d'origine ; de personnes étrangères installées en France depuis de nombreuses années et qui ne maîtrisent pas bien le français ni à l'oral ni à l'écrit ; de personnes françaises et non francophones qui n'ont pas appris le français depuis leur arrivée en France et qui sont souvent issues des anciennes colonies françaises ; de personnes françaises et francophones en situation d'illettrisme.

Rares parmi ces personnes en formation sont celles qui viennent de leur plein gré. La plupart vient par obligation. Elles ont divers statuts :
- salarié d'une entreprise et envoyé en formation dans le cadre de la formation professionnelle continue, afin d'améliorer leur maîtrise des discours écrits et oraux professionnels et de pouvoir satisfaire à la « part langagière du travail » (Boutet 2004) ;
- demandeur d'emploi envoyé en formation par Pôle emploi (agence française publique et nationale de prise en charge des demandeurs d'emploi) ;
- personne repérée comme illettrée soit dans son entreprise soit à Pôle emploi ;
- étranger envoyé par l'Organisme français d'immigration et d'intégration (OFII) afin d'apprendre le français.

Les besoins de formation de ces différents publics sont extrêmement variés. Or ils se retrouvent fréquemment ensemble dans des formations dont les objectifs ne répondent pas nécessairement à leurs besoins spécifiques. Cela constitue un problème didactique qui devrait être résolu.

# 3 Fondements théoriques

Notre conception des apprentissages linguistiques et discursifs s'inscrit dans un double ancrage didactique et anthropologique. Cette conception s'appuie sur l'idée que la langue se réalise dans deux ordres : l'ordre oral « dans lequel est situé tout message réalisé par articulation et susceptible d'audition » (Peytard 1970 : 37) et l'ordre scriptural « dans lequel est situé tout message réalisé par la graphie et susceptible de lecture » (*ibid.*). Ainsi, les compétences orales et scripturales se construisent dans une interaction forte. De plus, la compétence langagière ne se réduit pas à la maîtrise des savoirs linguistiques et des opérations de communication, mais intègre des habiletés littératiques constituées d'une part par les représentations sociales et le rapport au langage oral et écrit du sujet (Barré-De Miniac 2000 : 73, 2002 : 33), d'autre part par les usages et les pratiques orales et scripturales (Goody 1979, 1994 ; Jaffré 2004).

## 4 Problématique

Les enquêtes que nous avons menées dans le cadre du GRAFFIC nous ont permis de mettre en évidence que les actions de formation « savoirs de base », « compétences clés », « écrits pros », dans lesquelles sont inscrits les apprenants migrants développent une approche majoritairement linguistique de l'apprentissage du français au détriment d'une approche davantage littératique et de ce fait ne prennent pas en compte les habiletés déjà là des apprenants. Cette communication veut montrer, premièrement, que les apprenants migrants inscrits dans les formations savoirs de base ont construit des habiletés littératiques développées qui se manifestent dans leurs pratiques langagières ordinaires et professionnelles, et, deuxièmement, que les actions de formation destinées à ces personnes ne prennent pas en compte ces habiletés, donc les besoins réels des apprenants.

## 5 Étude de la littératie au travail

Lorsque l'on observe les postes de travail d'employés peu qualifiés comme ceux des agents de nettoyage (Lachaud 2011), on recueille de nombreux écrits. Dans le cadre de travail construit par l'employeur, ces écrits donnent lieu à des pratiques complexes de réception, alors que les tâches de production écrite sont réduites au minimum. Il s'agit de tableaux à double entrée comme les plannings ou des documents sur lesquels les agents doivent inscrire des horaires et apposer une signature. En revanche, dans le travail réel, les employés produisent des écrits élaborés tels que des aide-mémoire ou des messages adressés aux usagers.

Nous avons aussi procédé à des enregistrements audio des interactions pendant l'activité. L'analyse des discours des employés met au jour de nombreuses compétences qui se caractérisent par des indicateurs de réflexivité. Parmi ces indicateurs, nous relevons des formes discursives « méta » qui sont des marques de distanciation vis-à-vis de la situation concrète. Elles apparaissent lorsque les employés parlent spontanément de leur travail, de la manière dont ils l'organisent dans le temps et dans l'espace, des lieux qu'ils entretiennent ou encore des habitudes des usagers. Certains évoquent les tâches immédiates, tandis que d'autres parlent de leur activité dans son ensemble, font référence à leur expérience, et, voire, font des propositions pour améliorer le travail. Ces marques de distanciation sont repérées dans l'oralité et sont proches de la littératie. Un autre indicateur de réflexivité est celui de l'usage distancié du vocabulaire technique. Lorsqu'ils parlent des produits d'entretien, certains employés citent la destination finale (« du produit pour le sol »), d'autres, sa fonction (« du produit détergent ») et d'autres un élément de la composition chimique (« du produit alcalin »).

L'étude de la littératie au travail permet ainsi de mettre au jour des écrits, mais aussi des pratiques langagières, et donc des compétences utiles pour l'acquisition de la lecture et de l'écriture.

## 6 Analyse des situations de formation(s)

Une part de nos enquêtes consiste à observer les situations de formation. Ces formations situées dans un cadre professionnel mettent en œuvre des référentiels de formation qui visent une meilleure insertion sociale et professionnelle. Une des questions auxquelles doivent répondre ces observations est celle de l'adéquation des pratiques des formateurs aux besoins des formés. Nous relevons plusieurs difficultés et ambiguïtés qui apparaissent fréquemment dans le travail de formateurs.

Une première difficulté apparait dans un rapport concomitant aux apprentissages linguistiques et à l'acte graphique. Sans qu'aucune pertinence n'en soit démontrée, les formations organisent fréquemment un enseignement graphique (maitrise de l'alphabet, orthographe ...) au moyen de l'ordinateur. L'apprentissage se fait alors au détriment d'un apprentissage manuscrit. La motivation de cet enseignement par le numérique est double : effacer l'obstacle de l'apprentissage de la graphie et réduire les erreurs, d'orthographe notamment. Il se construit là une double ambiguïté dans le rapport à l'erreur, où le formateur semble vouloir que l'apprentissage se réalise sans que l'apprenant se trompe, et dans le rapport à la norme, où le formateur semble refuser d'être le véhicule de normes qu'il est pourtant chargé de transmettre.

Une seconde difficulté se révèle dans un positionnement des formateurs qui se situent le plus souvent dans une altérité aux pratiques scolaires. La réalité des pratiques observées montrent au contraire une grande proximité de ces pratiques avec les pratiques scolaires françaises. Il y a donc un hiatus entre les déclarations et les pratiques. Un des points sur lesquels cette volonté d'altérité devrait être marquée porte sur les apprentissages linguistiques de bas niveau. Or nous constatons une fréquence élevée des enseignements linguistiques de bas niveau (morphologie, vocabulaire...). De plus la pédagogie de la langue est calquée sur des pratiques scolaires (table de conjugaison, exercices lacunaires...) qui ont montré leurs limites.

Concernant des approches de plus haut niveau linguistique (sens du texte, production de discours), les référentiels de formation incitent à un travail sur des écrits professionnels. Ces écrits sont essentiellement fonctionnels et s'ancrent fortement dans les situations de travail. Les types de discours représentés sont variés (Guernier et al. 2015). Les situations de formation exploitent cependant assez peu ces potentialités discursives. Ici encore, on retrouve des pratiques scolaires comme le questionnement du texte. On observe peu d'enseignement de la construction du sens d'un document, de grammaire de texte ou de productions discursives dérivées (transposition de la situation de l'oral vers l'écrit, variations de la situation...). Alors que les apprenants doivent apprendre à maitriser des discours professionnels écrits et oraux, les enseignements discursifs se révèlent faibles, et la communication orale est essentiellement utilisée par les formateurs comme un vecteur de convivialité dans le groupe et pas comme un objet d'apprentissage. Il y a donc une ambiguïté de positionnement de la formation au regard des apprentissages discursifs.

## Conclusion

Les référentiels tentent de répondre au besoin d'un milieu professionnel ou social sans que l'adéquation avec le besoin de l'apprenant soit toujours prise en compte. Il conviendrait donc de définir les besoins respectifs du milieu et de l'apprenant et de mesurer leur possible congruence. Mais les difficultés pédagogiques fréquentes que nous observons apparaissent indépendantes du référentiel de formation qui préside à la formation observée. Ce sont donc les pratiques de formation qu'il convient de questionner. Or, on ne peut douter a priori de l'engagement des formateurs dans leur travail. Le problème à résoudre se situe donc en amont de la mise en œuvre pédagogique. Le recours aux démarches scolaires pourtant rejetées montrent un fort déficit de la transposition didactique en direction de ces formations d'adultes. C'est donc cette didactique du français qu'il faut conforter par la construction de propositions alternatives. Dans le même temps, il semble nécessaire d'interroger le processus de formation initiale et continuée des formateurs. Il serait illusoire d'imaginer des solutions didactiques sans questionner la possibilité de leur diffusion.

## Références

Barré-De Miniac, Christine. 2000. *Le rapport à l'écriture. Aspects théoriques et didactiques.* Lille : Presses Universitaires du Septentrion.
Barré-De Miniac, Christine. 2002. Le rapport à l'écriture. Une notion à plusieurs dimensions. *Pratiques* 113/114. 29–39.

Boutet, Josyane. 2004. La part langagière du travail : bilan et évolution. *Langage et société* 98. 17–42.

Goody, Jack. 1979. *La Raison graphique. La domestication de la pensée sauvage.* Paris : Éditions de Minuit.

Goody, Jack. 1994. *Entre l'oralité et l'écriture.* Paris : PUF.

Guernier, Marie-Cécile, Marie-Hélène Lachaud, Jean-Pierre Sautot & Luciane Boganika. 2015. *Les écrits professionnels dans la formation des adultes faiblement qualifiés : quelle didactique du français ? Communication au colloque international Pratiques et l'enseignement du français : bilan et perspectives.* Metz : Université de Lorraine, 8, 9, 10 avril 2015.

Jaffré, Jean-Pierre. 2004. La litéracie : histoire d'un mot, effets d'un concept. In Christine Barré-de Miniac, Marielle Rispail & Catherine Brissaud (dir.), *La littéracie. Conceptions théoriques et pratiques d'enseignement de la lecture-écriture.* 21–42. Paris : L'Harmattan.

Lachaud, Marie-Hélène. 2011. *Contribution à la formation à l'écrit en milieu professionnel : le cas des métiers de la propreté.* Université de Grenoble, thèse de doctorat.

Leclercq, Véronique (dir.). 2008. *Mieux connaître les adultes peu qualifiés et peu scolarisés. Transformations Recherches en éducation des adultes.* Lille : USTL – CUEEP – Trigone.

Peytard, Jean. 1970. Oral et scriptural : deux ordres de situations et de descriptions linguistiques. *Langue Française* 6. 35–48.

Schön, Donald. 1993. *Le praticien réflexif. À la recherche du savoir caché dans l'agir professionnel.* Montréal : Éditions Logiques.

Carla Bagna, Luana Cosenza and Luisa Salvati
# New challenges for learning, teaching and assessment with low-educated and illiterate immigrants: the case of L2 Italian[1]

**Abstract:** Through the project "Rete e Cittadinanza 2014–2015" ("Network and Citizenship 2014–2015"), supported by the European Integration Fund of Third-Country Nationals (EIF), the University for Foreigners of Siena has been engaged in the implementation of continuing training courses addressed to Italian language teachers who work with illiterate or semiliterate migrant learners. This paper reports the results of a survey of teachers' needs.

**Résumé :** Le projet « Rete e Cittadinanza 2014–2015 » (Réseau et citoyenneté 2014–2015) est financé par le Fonds européen d'intégration des ressortissants de pays tiers. Il a permis à l'université pour étrangers de Sienne de mettre en place des cours de formation continue pour les professeurs d'italien qui enseignent à des apprenants migrants illettrés ou « semi-alphabétisés ». L'article présente les résultats d'une enquête sur les besoins des enseignants.

## 1 Introduction

One of the main missions of the University for Foreigners of Siena is teaching Italian as a second language, especially through innovative methodologies and in sensitive contexts. Through the project "Rete e Cittadinanza 2014–2015" ("Network and Citizenship 2014–2015"), supported by the European Integration Fund of Third-Country Nationals (EIF), the university has been engaged in the implementation of continuing training courses addressed to Italian language teachers who work with illiterate or semiliterate migrant learners, and that is the principal focus of this paper.

---

1 Carla Bagna is the author of sections 1 and 4; Luisa Salvati is the author of section 2; and Luana Cosenza is the author of section 3.

---

**Carla Bagna** (corresponding author), **Luana Cosenza** and **Luisa Salvati**, University for Foreigners of Siena, Italy, E-mail: bagna@unistrasi.it, cosenza@unistrasi.it, salvati@unistrasi.it

DOI 10.1515/9783110477498-056, © 2017 Carla Bagna, Luana Cosenza and Luisa Salvati, published by De Gruyter.
This work is licensed under the Creative Commons Attribution-NonCommercial-NoDerivs 3.0 License.

## 2 The teachers' training needs: a survey in Tuscany

### 2.1 Objectives

The research reported here set out to investigate the training needs of those who teach L2 Italian to learners who are illiterate or low-educated in L1 and/or L2. The main objectives were: to investigate the perceptions and experiences of teachers in respect of such learners; to understand the issues related to this context of teaching/learning; and to identify strategies and best practices to respond to the particular communication and training needs of learners.

The decision to focus the research objectives on the teachers' training needs was dictated by a growing demand from teachers for specific training on these issues. During the different projects carried out by the University for Foreigners of Siena in the field of teaching Italian to adult immigrants teachers have frequently referred to the difficulty of managing a growing number of illiterate or semi-literate learners, for whom, unlike what happens in other countries of the European Union such as Germany (Feldmeier 2008) or Austria (Plutzar and Ritter 2008), there is no *ad hoc* course of study. As a result, they are often mistakenly put in A1 level classes, which causes a series of didactic problems. It is often difficult for teachers to manage learners with different levels of prior schooling within the same class, even when – as occasionally happens – there is the possibility of establishing a pre-A1 level class *ad hoc*.

The lack of official information about the management of learners with a level below A1, a dearth of published materials in L2 Italian for illiterate learners, and a steady increase in the number of such learners, mainly in the Centres for Adult Education (as noted in the previous paragraph), prompts teachers to develop new skills in this direction. In this sense, the present survey, carried out with a sample of teachers working in Tuscany, is offered as a case study that is representative of the Italian situation.

### 2.2 The structure of the questionnaire and the profile of the informants

The survey was conducted by administering a questionnaire which is divided into two main sections.

The first part of the questionnaire aimed at eliciting the following information: the type of institutions where the teachers/informants work and L2 Italian courses they provide (from pre-A1 to C1 level); the level of demand for courses below A1; the sociolinguistic characteristics of those who request such courses (gender, origin, age); how the institutions surveyed respond to such demand; and the types of illiterate learners the teachers teach or who attend courses. The second part of the questionnaire, whose results will be given in detail in the next section, focuses on identifying the areas in which the teachers/informants are experiencing or have experienced major problems.

Before presenting a quantitative analysis of the results from the questionnaires, it seems appropriate to focus on the types of illiteracy which, starting from the studies of Minuz (2012) and Borri et al. (2014), have been considered, with some modifications, in our research:
- pre-literate learners whose L1 has no writing system;
- totally illiterate learners whose L1 has a writing system that they have not acquired for lack of schooling or some other reason;
- weakly literate learners in L1, with up to three years of schooling;
- literate learners, but in a non-alphabetic writing system so they are unfamiliar with alphabetic writing;
- literate in a non-Latin alphabet;
- weakly literate in L2, independently of the L1 writing system or the first language in which they acquired literacy.

The questionnaire was administered in 2015 to 36 teachers from Centres for Adult Education (33), where there is more demand for courses with a level below A1; voluntary organizations (7) and universities (1). The training offer of the institutions where the informants teach involves, to varying degrees, all language levels (Table 1).

**Table 1:** Number of L2 Italian courses required for illiterate and low-educated learners

| | |
|---|---|
| A1 | 33 |
| A1 | 34 |
| A2 | 35 |
| B1 | 22 |
| B2 | 17 |
| C1 | 14 |
| C2 | 14 |

Of the 36 interviewed teachers, 35 stated that there is a demand for courses below A1 at their schools. The extent of this demand is medium (15) and high (5) and the institutions respond by organizing classes *ad hoc* for illiterate or low-educated learners (17), or inserts such learners at A1 level classes trying, however, to create differentiated learning paths, or by adopting different solutions based on the available resources (4). Finally, the types of illiterate learners are quite varied (Table 2):

**Table 2:** Types of illiterate learner in L2 Italian classes

| | |
|---|---|
| weakly literate in L1 | 23% |
| totally illiterate | 19% |
| literate in a non-Latin alphabet | 19% |
| pre-literate | 15% |
| weakly literate in L2 | 14% |
| literate in non-alphabetic writing | 14% |

From a first analysis, therefore, the informants' profile corresponds to what teachers say who have experience in teaching different types of illiterate learners. The demand for language courses is increasing in an education system that does not always succeed in responding to the real needs of these learners by creating classes designed especially for them.

# 3 Analysis and discussion of results

As mentioned before, the survey aimed to elicit teachers' perceptions and experiences in teaching illiterate or low-educated learners. Specifically, we paid attention to educational issues encountered in this teaching/learning context. In addition to quantitative data, we collected qualitative data in order to identify teachers' impressions regarding the difficulties found in teaching illiterate and low-educated learners. We asked the teachers the following question:

*When do you face major problems in teaching illiterate and low-educated learners?*

Informants responded to this question by selecting from a number of options; they were also able to add comments and suggestions (Table 3).

The first choice of informants was: *designing diversified didactic paths according to different illiteracy typologies.* Without a syllabus for L2 Italian specifically designed for illiterate learners, it is difficult to implement diversified didac-

**Table 3:** Some examples of problems found by teachers for each activity and strategies proposed to resolve them

| | | |
|---|---|---|
| 1 Designing diversified didactic paths according to different illiteracy types | More homogeneous groups of learners (3)* | Flexible didactic paths. Focused learning units respecting learning time of illiterate students (3) |
| 2 Identifying different illiteracy types | Improving teacher training (5) | Administering specific tests (5) |
| 3 Sourcing *ad hoc* didactic materials | It is often necessary to create *ad hoc* tools or to adapt what is already shared on the web (but not enough time to do it) | Schools should make sure appropriate didactic materials are available (2) |
| 4 Time management in respect of short-term goals (learning unit) and long-term goals (didactic planning) | Different learner profiles in the same classroom do not make it possible to meet their communicative needs (5) | Need for more teaching hours (2) |
| 5 Carrying out didactic activities in classroom | It is difficult to promote interaction among illiterate learners and to keep their motivation constantly high | Teaching based on ludic activities (2) |
| 6 Induction (registration, collecting personal and sociolinguistic data) | The registration form usually used for foreign students is not sufficient for illiterate learners because it is necessary to collect more data in order to identify their illiteracy profile (16) | Providing for a simplified registration form (personal data), translating it into immigrant languages Providing for a registration form (home country, L1, years of education, etc.) with short writing/reading tasks (2) |
| 7 Identifying proficiency levels (placement and achievement tests) | Training opportunities for teachers | Designing and using reliable and valid tests capable of verifying levels <A1 (6) |

\* Figures in brackets indicate the number of teachers who identified the problem or strategy

tic paths in the same classroom according to different illiteracy profiles. In response to the issues raised, informants proposed more homogeneous groups of learners, flexible didactic paths, and focused learning units respecting learning time of illiterate learners.

The second choice concerned the *identification of different types of illiteracy*: institutions do not share information, so it is difficult to recognize the type of illiteracy and, in some cases, illiterate learners as well. For these reasons, teachers proposed: administering specific tests and expanding the induction phase for learners. Everything must be integrated with more teacher training opportunities on issues related to language assessment and illiteracy.

The third answer highlights the difficulty in *sourcing ad hoc didactic materials:* it is difficult to find adequate books and to create *ad hoc* tools or to adapt what is already shared on the web. Moreover, according to the informants, schools should ensure the availability of teaching materials and should encourage greater collaboration among teachers in order to share tools and experiences.

The last choice concerns the *identification of proficiency levels (placement and achievement tests):* levels below A1 are not institutionally acknowledged and there is a lack of tools available to teachers for the management of this particular type of learner, so informants were aware that they need training in the design and administration of reliable and valid tests to verify proficiency levels below A1.

In order to sum up, the presence of illiterate or low-educated learners within the Italian L2 classes suggests the need for:
- a framework with descriptors that capture illiterate learner profiles (totally illiterate, weakly literate etc.);
- tests to assess levels below A1 in order to create homogenous classes;
- a reference syllabus to support the development of adequate didactic materials and activities;
- more teaching hours to reach level A2 starting from levels below A1 according to learning goals;
- teacher training and research about the learning paths followed by illiterate and low-educated learners and the learning time they require.

# 4 Conclusion

To conclude, the promotion, dissemination and implementation of projects like those described here can constitute an example of fruitful cooperation between university, research and society in order to support concrete actions for social inclusion.

It should also be emphasized that social inclusion and language acquisition have to be understood as two dimensions of a bi-directional process: language learning and teaching (and the teachers are important in this regard) should not be treated as the pre-requisite for social inclusion: social inclusion is reinforced and facilitated through language learning. This is the main reason why, in this case, we are talking about language as a key factor in fighting against and reducing inequality.

# References

Borri, Alessandro, Fernanda Minuz, Lorenzo Rocca & Chiara Sola. 2014. *Italiano L2 in contesti migratori. Sillabo e descrittori dall'alfabetizzazione all'A1*. Torino: Loescher Editore.
Feldmeier, Alexis. 2008. The case of Germany: Literacy instruction for adult immigrants. In Martha Young-Shoulten (ed.), *Low educated second language and literacy acquisition*, Proceedings of the Third Annual Forum, Newcastle University, 7–16. Durham: Roundtuit Publishing.
Minuz, Fernanda. 2012. *Italiano L2 e alfabetizzazione in età adulta*. Roma: Carocci.
Plutzar, Verena & Monika Ritter. 2008. Language learning in the context of migration and integration – challenges and options for adult learners. Strasbourg: Council of Europe. https://rm.coe.int/CoERMPublicCommonSearchServices/DisplayDCTMContent?documentId=09000016802fc1d6 (accessed 29.08.16).

Rola Naeb, Martha Young-Scholten
# International training of teachers of low-educated adult migrants

**Abstract:** The project "European Speakers of Other Languages: Teaching Adult Immigrants and Training their Teachers" has from 2010 to now been tackling, at an international level, the improvement of the educational outcomes for non-/low-educated migrants.[1] The current project ("EU-Speak 3") is the culmination of efforts to test the effectiveness of on-line teacher training and development.

**Résumé :** Depuis 2010, le projet « Locuteurs européens de langues étrangères : enseigner aux migrants adultes et former les enseignants » observe l'évolution au niveau international des résultats d'apprentissage des migrants illettrés ou ayant un faible niveau d'éducation. Le projet actuel (EU-Speak 3) marque l'aboutissement des mesures prises pour tester l'efficacité de la formation et du développement de la formation en ligne des enseignants.

## 1 Introduction

Since 2010, the training and development of the teachers of Low-Educated Second Language and Literacy Acquisition (LESLLA) learners has been addressed by a three-phase project, "European Speakers of Other Languages: Teaching Adult Immigrants and Training their Teachers (EU-Speak)". From 2010 to 2012, the eight project partners shared ideas about a range of topics relating to the educational support of adults with little or no literacy in any language upon immigration. At the final workshop, a subset of the larger group agreed to take teacher training and development forward for the next phase. Below we discuss the evo-

---

[1] We gratefully acknowledge Grundtvig and Erasmus funding: 2010-1-GB2-GRU06-03528; 539478-LLP- 1-2013-1-UK-GRUNDTVIG-GMP; 2015-1-UKo1-KA204-013485
Nous remercions Grundtvig et Erasmus+ pour leur aide financière : 2010-1-GB2-GRU06-03528; 539478-LLP-1-2013-1-UK-GRUNDTVIG-GMP; 2015-1-UKo1-KA204-013485

---

**Rola Naeb** (corresponding author), Northumbria University, United Kingdom,
E-mail: rola.naeb@northumbria.ac.uk
**Martha Young-Scholten**, Newcastle University, United Kingdom,
E-mail: martha.young-scholten@newcastle.ac.uk

DOI 10.1515/9783110477498-057, © 2017 Rola Naeb, Martha Young-Scholten, published by De Gruyter.
This work is licensed under the Creative Commons Attribution-NonCommercial-NoDerivs 3.0 License.

lution of the project from its inception through EU-Speak 2 during which the set of knowledge and skills needed by teachers was agreed to EU-Speak 3 which involves design and delivery of six on-line modules.

## 2 Assumptions about LESLLA learners

We know from research over the last decade that adult immigrants with little or no formal education or home language literacy take up to eight times longer than educated adults to reach A1 of the *Common European Framework of Reference for Languages* (CEFR; Council of Europe 2001) in second language (L2) reading (e. g. Schellekens 2011). Studies since the 1970s on adult immigrants indicate that neither age nor lack of schooling are barriers in acquisition of morphosyntactic competence in an L2 (Hawkins 2001), nor is age a barrier to learning to read for the first time in an L2 (Kurvers, Stockmann, and van de Craats 2010; Young-Scholten and Strom 2006). Given their potential, LESLLA learners' slow progress is likely due to external factors. This prompted EU-Speak to consider how best to address LESLLA learners' slow progress. Well-qualified teachers are key (Condelli, Cronen, and Bos 2010), yet there are reports of teaching which fails to meet quality standards (Paget and Stevenson 2014; Schellekens 2011). This is a sector which includes not only full-time but also part-time and unpaid volunteer teachers. Sub-standard teaching is also connected to pervasive lack of specific training or continued professional development available – particularly striking when one considers how much those who teach young children reading or a L2 to educated learners receive. In all countries, the economic downturn has impacted funding and in turn retention of skilled, knowledgeable full-time teachers. In some countries this has led to a major shift to provision of basic skills teaching for LESLLA learners by unpaid volunteers (e. g. England) where this was not already the case (e. g. Spain).

The EU-Speak project's starting assumption was that training/development should ideally be offered internationally given the similarities of LESLLA learners and poor educational provision for them in most of the countries in which they resettle. This also meant offering training/development not only in English but also in learners' target languages since those who teach their native language might not need and might not therefore have sufficient academic English to participate in training/development in English.

## 3 EU-Speak 2010 – 2012

Project partners at the Workers' Education Association (UK), Funen Further Education (Denmark) and the Universities of Amsterdam, Cologne, Granada, Leipzig, Newcastle and Stockholm held intensive workshops in each country to discuss similarities and language, culture and political differences in all aspects of basic language and literacy provision for LESLLA learners, from initial resettlement and placement to innovative materials, classroom techniques, teacher training and citizenship. These seven workshops confirmed that while there are differences among European countries ranging from highly commendable and innovative practice to unfortunate policy (under-funding in the UK; unrealistic expectations in the Netherlands), there are fundamental commonalities across countries, the most prominent of which is little or no specialist training/development in teaching LESLLA learners.

## 4 EU-Speak 2013 – 2015

A subset of the partners (Universities of Amsterdam, Cologne, Granada, Jyväskylä and Newcastle along with US partners Virginia Commonwealth University, American Institutes for Research, and the Center for Applied Linguistics) set out to agree a set of knowledge and skills LESLLA teachers need.

### 4.1 Survey on knowledge and skills

The first of two surveys was disseminated to teachers, trainers and programme managers and several hundred responses were received from partner countries as well as beyond. Respondents were asked to report on the knowledge and skills they felt were important to help them support their LESLLA learners. The results fed into a lengthy list of skills and knowledge/understanding and were then whittled down to a top ten:

*Skills: Ability to use ...*
(1) teaching methods that facilitate learners' active participation in a classroom environment and that allow them to contribute their own knowledge and experience;
(2) authentic conversational situations in teaching that reflect learners' daily experiences;

(3) materials that low-educated immigrant adults encounter in their daily lives;
(4) methods to teach oral language skills (pronunciation, grammar, pragmatics and vocabulary) to non-/low-literate migrant adults;
(5) multimodal materials for literacy and modify them to meet learners' needs in their daily lives and work-related situations;
(6) and the ability to guide learners in the process of developing reading and writing strategies that they can apply independently outside the classroom and in situations involving written language;

*Knowledge*
(7) understanding of learners' backgrounds, current situations and learning potentials and consideration of these when planning and teaching LESLLA learners;
(8) awareness of current teaching materials suitable for developing LESLLA learners' oral language and literacy skills;
(9) awareness, when planning and teaching, that learners' competence and skills in their mother-tongue/first language affects literacy development in the L2;
(10) awareness of the kinds of written information that learners encounter and use in their daily lives.

## 4.2 Survey on opportunities for training/development and to corroborate the top ten

LESLLA experts in the partner countries and beyond were consulted, they agreed with the top ten, and made additional suggestions. The first survey did not include attitudes but, based on the experts' suggestions, the second survey did. Again several hundred responded to the second survey (some the same as the first survey) about their views on the top ten and about their opportunities for training/development in relation to their LESLLA teaching. The results indicated that the majority of respondents had fewer than 75 hours of specialist training or development and also showed that the content was not always relevant to their teaching.

The project team then designed and piloted a five-week module on vocabulary learning motivated by the Jyväskylä team's research pointing to vocabulary as a serious bottleneck in LESLLA learners' reading development (Tammelin-Laine and Martin 2015) and supported by the Cologne team's expertise on an aspect of incidental vocabulary learning by beginners (fast mapping; Rohde and Tiefenthal 2000). The module was translated from English into the additional project languages – Dutch, Finnish, German and Spanish – and made available via Moodle to LESLLA teachers around the world. Teachers were recruited from Belgium, Canada, Finland, Germany, the Netherlands, New Zealand, Spain, the UK and the USA. The module included ideas and activities for teachers to try out with their learners and a discussion forum in each language. Participant evaluation suggested that the module contributed to their knowledge and skills, irrespective of their amount of teaching experience. The evaluations also confirmed the expectation that international on-line provision would succeed. One participant from Spain commented that she "had taken courses online before, but never on this scale. [She] could interact with people from other European countries and even other continents, which I find absolutely rewarding. This is what really characterizes distance learning: people who are many kilometres apart and are interested by a common theme and share their knowledge."

The project team then met to design a curriculum for LESLLA teacher training and professional development based on the set of agreed knowledge/understanding and skills along with attitudes and on the success of the pilot of the vocabulary module.

## 5 EU-Speak 2015 – 2018

The final phase of EU-Speak, EU-Speak 3, is rolling out the curriculum in the form of six on-line modules. Although the modules comprise a curriculum, they are self-standing. Each module is designed by a project partner and these now include the Universities of Cologne, Granada, Jyväskylä, Newcastle and Virginia Commonwealth University, with the Universities of Northumbria and Boğaziçi as new partners. Northumbria is responsible for social media, module evaluation and human-technology interface/computer-assisted learning. The University of Amsterdam, American Institutes for Research and Center for Applied Linguistics partners are now members of an advisory board whose key function is, along with an independent evaluator, to check module content before it goes live. Module participants are mentored through the discussion forum in each partner language. Modules are:
– Working with LESLLA Learners, February–March 2016
– Bilingualism and Multilingualism, May–June 2016
– Language and Literacy in their Social Contexts, October–November 2016
– Reading from a Psycholinguistic Perspective, February–March 2017
– Vocabulary Acquisition, May–June 2017
– Acquisition and Assessment of Morphosyntax, October–November 2017

The project team is evaluating the success of each module through a combination of pre- and post-module tests (of the knowledge participants are expected to gain), of uptake of module activities as shown in the discussion forums, of participant evaluations of the module, and of mentor self-evaluation. The project is currently investigating ways to encourage participants to share evidence of their learners' language and literacy progress in response to participants' new knowledge and skills.

These modules will each be delivered a second time in 2017 and 2018. The project welcomes offers to translate (at their own expense) modules into languages in addition to English, Finnish, German, Spanish and Turkish, and has the capacity to include more languages on its Moodle site. Contact the authors for further information.

# References

Condelli, Larry, Stephanie Cronen & Johannes Bos. 2010. *The impact of a reading intervention for low-literate adult ESL learners*. National Center for Education Evaluation and Regional Assistance, Institute of Education Sciences. Alexandria, VA: US Department of Education. http://ies.ed.gov/ncee/pubs/20114003/pdf/20114003.pdf (access 22 June 2016).

Council of Europe. 2001. *Common European Framework of Reference for Languages: Learning, teaching, assessment*. Cambridge: Cambridge University Press.

Hawkins, Roger. 2001. *Second language syntax: A generative introduction*. Oxford: Blackwell.

Kurvers, Jeanne, Willemijn Stockmann & Ineke van de Craats. 2010. Predictors of success in adult L2 literacy acquisition. In Theresa Wall and Monica Leong (eds.), *Low educated second language and literacy acquisition*, 47–62. Calgary: Bow Valley College.

Paget, Ally & Neil Stevenson. 2014. *Making ESOL policy work better for migrants and wider society: On speaking terms*. London: Demos.

Rohde, Andreas & Christine Tiefenthal. 2000. Fast mapping in early L2 lexical acquisition. *Studia Linguistica* 54. 167–174.

Schellekens, Philida. 2011. *Teaching and testing the language skills of first and second language speakers*. Cambridge: Cambridge ESOL.

Tammelin-Laine, Taina & Maisa Martin. 2015. The simultaneous development of receptive skills in an orthographically transparent second language. In Martha Young-Scholten (ed.), *Writing Systems Research* 7(1), special issue: *Adolescents and adults who develop literacy for the first time in an L2*. 39–57.

Young-Scholten, Martha & N. Strom. 2006. First-time L2 readers: Is there a critical period? In Jeanne Kurvers, Ineke van de Craats & Martha Young-Scholten (eds.), *Low educated adult second language and literacy acquisition: Proceedings of the Inaugural Conference*, 45–68. Utrecht: LOT.

Véronique Castellotti, Emmanuelle Huver et Fabienne Leconte
# Demande institutionnelle et responsabilité des chercheurs : langues, insertions, pluralité des parcours et des perceptions

**Résumé :** Cet article vise à questionner la place, le rôle et la responsabilité des chercheurs en sociolinguistique et en didactique des langues dans le domaine de l'intégration linguistique des migrants, domaine de recherche-intervention particulièrement à l'interface de la demande politique et sociale. Pour ce faire, nous interrogerons quelques évidences sur lesquelles se fondent les politiques linguistiques d'intégration et les formations linguistiques qui en résultent. Nous évoquerons notamment la corrélation usuellement établie entre langue et intégration ainsi que les modalités de prise en compte de la diversité linguistique, culturelle, mais aussi biographique dont les migrants sont porteurs.

**Abstract:** This article sets out to examine the place, role and responsibility of researchers in sociolinguistics and language education with regard to the linguistic integration of migrants, an area of interventional research that is very much at the confluence of political and social demands. To this end the authors will analyse a number of obvious facts on which linguistic policies for integration and the resulting language courses are based. In particular, this article will address the correlation usually established between language and integration, and also ways of taking into account migrants' linguistic, cultural and biographical diversity.

## Introduction

La question des rapports entre recherche, politique et intervention est désormais ancienne et classique (Beacco 2013). Les sociolinguistes et les didacticiens des langues sont actuellement particulièrement concernés, du fait de la place croissante (et renouvelée) accordée aux dimensions linguistiques et culturelles

---

**Véronique Castellotti,** Université F. Rabelais, Tours, France,
E-Mail : veronique.castellotti@univ-tours.fr
**Emmanuelle Huver,** Université F. Rabelais, Tours, France, E-Mail : huver@univ-tours.fr
**Fabienne Leconte,** Université de Rouen, France, E-Mail : fabienne.leconte@univ.rouen.fr

dans les politiques d'accueil et d'insertion des migrants, en Europe plus particulièrement (Bretegnier 2011).

Dans ce domaine, la demande actuellement adressée à la recherche par les instances politiques relève essentiellement de l'application : il s'agit de « tirer profit des enseignements de la recherche » pour « éclairer les décisions » et « aider à élaborer des mesures cohérentes et efficaces » (appel à communication de ce symposium).

Différents éléments poussent les chercheurs à s'aligner (plus ou moins volontairement) sur cette visée pragmatique. On peut (rapidement) relever les éléments suivants :
1. la position d'expertise dans laquelle est ainsi placé le chercheur lui procure un certain nombre d'avantages (financement de ses recherches, visibilité, prestige, etc.)[1] ;
2. « l'interaction avec l'environnement social » constitue désormais un important critère d'évaluation des chercheurs eux-mêmes ;
3. un positionnement critique sur la demande est rapidement interprété (y compris par les chercheurs) comme un désengagement politique (voire moral) des chercheurs de la vie de la cité (cf. la métaphore fréquemment convoquée de la tour d'ivoire), a fortiori lorsque les enjeux sont présentés sous l'angle de l'urgence, de l'humanitaire ou du sécuritaire.

Or, cette conception utilitariste de la recherche cantonne le chercheur, au pire à un rôle de caution scientifique, au mieux à un rôle de prestataire au service de l'ingénierie sociale (i.e. de « bonnes pratiques » directement utilisables et reproductibles), contribuant au maintien et – donc – à la diffusion des implicites sur lesquels la demande se fonde.

Il n'est pas question de défendre ici l'idée que la recherche devrait nécessairement se concevoir hors de toute préoccupation ou visée sociopolitique et/ou interventionniste ou d'adopter une attitude moralisante en émettant des jugements a priori sur l'éthique des chercheurs dans des situations de collaboration avec des institutions. Nous considérons au contraire que la sociolinguistique et la didactologie/didactique des langues constituent, justement, des disciplines d'intervention, dans lesquelles les relations entre recherche et intervention sont à envisager comme des relations en tension, la tension elle-même constituant un ferment de la réflexion, *à condition qu'elle soit problématisée comme telle*.

---

[1] La polémique autour du Français Langue d'Intégration en France illustre en partie cela, même si elle ne se résume pas à des enjeux de pouvoir, un certain nombre d'enjeux sociopolitiques étant également très fortement présents.

Nous avons choisi d'exemplifier cette réflexion en mobilisant deux problématiques qui sont souvent traitées sur le mode de l'évidence dans les discours et les représentations circulants (y compris au sein de la communauté scientifique elle-même parfois) et qu'il revient donc aux chercheurs de questionner, nuancer, remettre en question : le lien langue(s)/intégration d'une part et la place et le statut de diverses formes de diversité dans les situations de migration d'autre part. Pour ce faire, nous nous focaliserons plus spécifiquement sur le cas de la France, dans la mesure où le lien entre langue, intégration et cohésion nationale y est particulièrement prégnant[2].

# 1 Langue(s) et intégration

La corrélation entre langue et intégration est souvent pensée comme une « évidence », la maitrise de la langue constituant un « gage » d'intégration réussie (Hambye & Romainville 2014). Or, si les dimensions linguistiques constituent un atout, ce n'est pas nécessairement ni toujours le plus important, ni un facteur suffisant pour assurer la socialisation (que nous emploierons ici de préférence à intégration), pas plus que des compétences partielles dans la langue du pays d'accueil seraient source principale de difficultés. La langue intervient alors comme un prétexte pour masquer une conception à sens unique de l'intégration, dont une langue et une seule serait le vecteur principal. Pourtant, d'autres facteurs sont souvent largement aussi influents.

## 1.1 La socialisation socio-professionnelle

Dans certains secteurs, l'expérience antérieure du métier et des missions exercées et sa confrontation avec celle d'autres professionnels est primordiale, à la fois dans la socialisation et l'appropriation langagière progressive. En témoignent les propos de médecins étrangers travaillant en France, qui expliquent que leur connaissance de la pathologie s'applique aussi bien ici qu'ailleurs et que le discours n'est pas toujours déterminant dans l'accomplissement du métier. Ils décrivent aussi des formes d'intercompréhension, avec notamment l'anglais ou le latin comme « passerelles » (Levacic 2016). Ce n'est donc pas ici la compétence

---

[2] Cet article est complémentaire de ceux d'E. Lebreton, E. Mercier et A. Bruneau, également publiés dans ce volume et qui illustrent et approfondissent les orientations esquissées dans ce texte.

langagière qui précède ou conditionne l'insertion professionnelle et la socialisation, mais parfois l'inverse, et la communication professionnelle s'avère alors souvent plus aisée que la communication « familière ». On peut donc, dans de telles situations, imaginer des formations linguistiques qui s'appuient sur la communication professionnelle pour favoriser le développement de compétences plus générales.

## 1.2 Pluralité linguistique, réception, appropriation

En France, les formations sont organisées autour de l'apprentissage exclusif du français, sans mobiliser, voire en interdisant, la présence d'autres expériences langagières. Cette conception, s'appliquant aux migrants comme aux formateurs, est souvent néfaste aux tentatives de socialisation (Mercier ici-même). Il importe donc de réorienter les formations linguistiques vers la pluralité des compétences, y compris en tenant compte du rôle que peuvent jouer des variétés régionales ou dialectales (Eloy 2003).

La dimension prioritairement productive des formations renforce en outre la dimension négative de cet exclusivisme linguistique. En effet, les capacités en réception sont souvent plus élevées que celles en production, qui pourraient alors – partiellement et selon les cas – s'exprimer de façon plurielle. Cela invite à rééquilibrer les formations vers le pôle réceptif de l'apprentissage en valorisant la compréhension et en sensibilisant les accueillants et les formateurs à une tolérance à l'erreur et à l'approximation.

Cela conduit aussi à interroger la notion de « maitrise », qui entraîne l'idée de perfection, de centration sur le code et les structures, et appelle le contrôle pour vérifier l'exactitude, a-situationnelle. La maitrise, supposée la même pour tous, oriente les formations de façon instrumentale, avec un idéal d'exhaustivité, où le résultat détermine le contenu et l'évaluation pilote l'ensemble du dispositif (Mercier, ici-même). Nous proposons à l'inverse une politique formative reposant sur une exigence d'appropriation, liée à des histoires singulières, qui fasse sens dans des parcours d'expérience diversifiés et qui permette aux personnes migrantes de devenir non seulement acteurs de leur socialisation, mais auteurs de celle-ci.[3]

---

[3] Ce qui, en retour, met à mal la visée de contrôlabilité dont les formations linguistiques actuelles relèvent massivement.

## 2 L'occultation de la diversité langagière et sociale

Depuis une vingtaine d'années, les migrations se diversifient socialement et géographiquement. Les répertoires langagiers des migrants sont ainsi souvent plus complexes, davantage littéraciés. Aux langues premières et de scolarisation, il faut ajouter des langues de socialisation ou véhiculaires.

La diversité concerne aussi les ressortissants de l'UE : la chute du rideau de fer a encouragé les migrations Est-Ouest. Pourtant, les politiques linguistiques des États ont tendance à occulter les langues parlées avant/pendant la migration et à réduire les politiques publiques à la seule langue du pays d'accueil. Le fait de lier droit au séjour et performance linguistique conduit à différentes catégorisations qui ont peu à voir avec les répertoires langagiers, les qualifications, les projets des personnes. Nous en retiendrons trois : l'appartenance à l'UE, la durée du séjour et la scolarisation.

### 2.1 Appartenance à l'Union Européenne

En France, seuls les non-Européens sont concernés par le Contrat d'Intégration Républicaine, et donc, les formations linguistiques qui en relèvent. L'effet peut être paradoxal : par exemple, dans le cadre d'un Programme Régional d'Intégration des Populations Immigrées, seules les femmes en situation régulière originaires d'un pays tiers ont été retenues pour le programme *Accompagnement des femmes migrantes*. Les Roumaines ainsi que beaucoup de femmes d'origine maghrébine ayant obtenu la nationalité espagnole ou italienne dans ces pays ont été exclues du dispositif. Elles ressemblaient pourtant au public ciblé.

Se dessine en creux la figure d'un Européen mobile d'un pays à l'autre, qui n'aurait ni de besoins langagiers lors de ses déplacements (il parle « l'européen » ou toutes les langues de l'Union), ni de besoins d'informations spécifiques sur les institutions du pays où il réside désormais. La diversité linguistique, culturelle et biographique, y compris européenne, se trouve ainsi réduite et occultée.

### 2.2 Durée du séjour

Ce même dispositif était réservé aux femmes en France depuis moins de cinq ans. L'État français considère qu'au-delà de 5 ans de présence, les besoins langagiers des migrants ne concernent plus que l'analphabétisme ou l'illettrisme (cf. circulaire Valls de mars 2015). Le critère de la durée du séjour est en outre corrélé à l'obtention des cartes de séjour.

Le droit au séjour et à la nationalité française est de plus en plus conditionné par un niveau de langue attesté. La carte de séjour délivrée est d'abord d'un an, à l'issue duquel le niveau Diplôme initial de langue française (DILF) est censé être obtenu. Puis une carte pluriannuelle jusqu'à 4 ans peut être obtenue, un niveau A2 est censé être alors acquis, lequel permettra l'obtention d'une carte de résident. C'est le sens de la loi du 7 mars 2016 qui modifie l'article 2 : « la connaissance suffisante de la langue française » requise pour un titre de séjour devient « connaissance de la langue française qui doit être au moins égale à un niveau défini ». Le dossier de presse accompagnant la loi stipule qu'il s'agit du niveau A2, mais le danger de cette formulation est que le niveau de langue, non inscrit dans la loi, peut augmenter sur simple décret.

## 2.3 Scolarisation

L'organisation des formations linguistiques se fonde sur le critère de la scolarisation : sont identifiées comme relevant du « FLE » les personnes scolarisées. Elles sont alors différenciées des « personnes peu ou pas scolarisées », dénommées « alpha » ou « post-alpha ». Plus récemment, ont été organisées des formations FLI qui préparent les personnes au test linguistique (B1 oral) pour accéder à la nationalité. Comme la passation des tests tend à déterminer le droit au séjour, le risque est grand que cette instrumentalisation des formations se généralise. Dans tous les cas, la complexité et la richesse des répertoires des migrants se trouvent réduites à des manques de compétences, à l'écrit ou en français. Les langues d'appui (anglais, arabe, russe, etc.) sont rarement prises en compte dans les démarches formatives et uniquement là où les formateurs ont été initiés aux démarches plurilingues.

# Conclusion

Lorsque les chercheurs répondent à une demande institutionnelle sans l'interroger, ils contribuent à donner aux préconisations effectuées des allures de pratiques inattaquables, puisqu'elles apparaissent alors comme des dispositifs techniques scientifiquement légitimés. Cependant, toute politique se fonde sur des présupposés qui restent bien souvent implicites, comme l'illustrent les quelques exemples présentés ici. Or, le fait que ces présupposés restent implicites tend à occulter la part de choix (la part de politique, donc) dont ils éma-

nent. Interroger (publiquement) la demande institutionnelle (et non la critiquer
« gratuitement ») constitue ainsi une condition (éthique) de l'intervention de
recherche, *y compris si la demande se fonde sur des valeurs et des idéaux qui
correspondent aux valeurs et idéaux personnels du chercheur.*

Il ne suffit pas, pour venir à bout de la problématique, d'ajouter des considérations éthiques aux préconisations techniques effectuées. Il s'agit au contraire d'historiciser et d'épistémologiser la réflexion (et notamment les notions mobilisées), pour que les choix qui fondent la demande puissent être mis en évidence et, ainsi, mis en discussion, la discussion constituant le socle de tout débat démocratique.

# Références

Beacco, Jean-Claude (dir.). 2013. *Éthique et politique en didactique des langues.* Paris : Didier.

Bretegnier, Aude (dir.). 2011. *Formation linguistique en contextes d'insertion. Compétences professionnelles, posture, professionnalité : concevoir un cadre de référence(s).* Berne : Peter Lang.

Eloy, Jean-Michel. 2003. Langues d'origine, langues régionales, français. Intégration et plurilinguisme, *Ville-École-Intégration Enjeux.* 133. 134–146.

Hambye, Philippe & Anne-Sophie Romainville. 2014. Apprentissage du français et intégration. Des évidences à interroger. *Français & Société.* 26–27.

Leconte, Fabienne (dir.). 2016. *Adultes migrants, langues et insertions sociales. Dynamiques d'apprentissage et de formation.* Paris : Riveneuve.

Levacic, Michelle. 2016. *Mobilisation et transformation de compétences professionnelles et langagières dans des parcours de mobilité géographique et culturelle de médecins allophones.* Tours : Université F. Rabelais (Tours), thèse de doctorat.

www.ingramcontent.com/pod-product-compliance
Lightning Source LLC
Chambersburg PA
CBHW061341300426
44116CB00011B/1940